T0315504

HATRED

HATRED

Understanding Our Most Dangerous Emotion

Berit Brogaard

OXFORD
UNIVERSITY PRESS

Oxford University Press is a department of the University of Oxford. It furthers
the University's objective of excellence in research, scholarship, and education
by publishing worldwide. Oxford is a registered trade mark of Oxford University
Press in the UK and certain other countries.

Published in the United States of America by Oxford University Press
198 Madison Avenue, New York, NY 10016, United States of America.

Library of Congress Cataloging-in-Publication Data
Names: Brogaard, Berit, author.
Title: Hatred : understanding our most dangerous emotion / Berit Brogaard.
Description: New York : Oxford University Press, 2020. |
Includes bibliographical references and index.
Identifiers: LCCN 2020006630 (print) | LCCN 2020006631 (ebook) |
ISBN 9780190084448 (hardback) | ISBN 9780190084462 (epub)
Subjects: LCSH: Hate.
Classification: LCC BF575.H3 B76 2020 (print) | LCC BF575.H3 (ebook) |
DDC 152.4—dc23
LC record available at https://lccn.loc.gov/2020006630
LC ebook record available at https://lccn.loc.gov/2020006631

9 8 7 6 5 4 3 2 1

Printed by Sheridan Books, Inc., United States of America

For my sweet daughter Rebecca. You are the bravest and most compassionate girl I have ever known. Each day I become increasingly more humbled by your intelligence, your sense of justice and the sheer goodness of your heart. My greatest wish is that the rest of the world one day will become as wise, caring and forgiving as you.

CONTENTS

ACKNOWLEDGMENTS

Over the years many people have contributed in one way or another to the life of this book. For personal enrichment, I am grateful to my lovely and beautiful daughter Rebecca, the rest of my Danish family, and close friends. For emotional support, I am also indebted to my two cats Bertrand Russell and Roderick Chisholm, as well as my dog William James (a.k.a. Nemo). For theoretical input, I am grateful to three anonymous reviewers for Oxford University Press and to Brendan Balcerak Jackson, Magdalena Balcerak Jackson, Sarah Beach, Aaron Ben-Ze'ev, Hanne Brogaard, Niels Brogaard, Rebecca Britney Brogaard Salerno, John Broome, Otávio Bueno, Alex Byrne, Charles Carver, Nick Cherup, Elijah Chudnoff, Nick Cisneros, Andy Cui, Casey Landers, Ingelise Dalberg-Larsen, John Doris, Eduardo Elena, Ed Erwin, Simon Evnine, Daniel Garber, Dimitria E. Gatzia, David Miguel Gray, Danny Guo, Jared Hanson-Park, Kari Hanson-Park, Aleks Hernandez, Risto Hilpinen, Vicky Hu, Brian Leiter, Azenet Lopez, Peter Ludlow, Zoe Ma, Ruth Barcan Marcus, Mike Martin, Curtis Miller, Nick Nicola, Arina Pismenny, Jesse Prinz, Mark Rowlands, Michael Slote, Ken Taylor, Hugh Thomas, Amie Thomasson, Somogy Varga, Melisa Vivanco, and Jack Weinstein; and audiences at Aarhus, British Columbia, Brown, Colorado-Boulder, Copenhagen, Duke, Memphis, Miami, Missouri–Columbia, Missouri–St. Louis, Oslo, Southern California, Stanford, Syracuse, Texas–Austin, Vermont, and WashU. Special thanks go to my wonderful editor Peter Ohlin for his patience, super-helpful feedback, and critical comments on the manuscript, and copyeditor Wendy Keebler, proof-reader Sylvia Cannizzaro, and senior project manager Rajakumari Ganessin, who all did a fantastic job copyediting, fact-checking, and proof-reading. Finally, I am forever grateful and indebted to my uncle Jørgen Dalberg-Larsen, my Ph.D. supervisor Barry Smith, and my postdoc supervisor David Chalmers for inspiring me to follow in their footsteps as philosophers and for the many hours we have spent talking about philosophical issues. I am a better person and thinker because of them.

My work on this book was made possible by a Center for Humanities Fellowship at the University of Miami, a Cooper Fellowship at the University of Miami, and an Engaged Faculty Fellowship at the University of Miami.

PROLOGUE

(OR, WISHING YOUR SON WERE NEVER BORN)

In today's hate-infused society, hate has garnered a bad reputation. The mere mention of this complex emotion often triggers grisly images of psychopathic serial killers, torch-bearing neo-Nazis, mass shooters, or hijacking terrorists. The virulent hatred sown by cable news and social media has caused massive political polarization. But is hatred purely a bad thing, or is it more complex than that—even, sometimes, a good thing? My hope is that this book will help provide a more nuanced picture of this complicated emotion. I argue that it isn't hatred that's the enemy but its lack of justification.

In a 2014 *New Yorker* interview, Peter Lanza, the father of Adam Lanza, the Newtown, Connecticut, school shooter, said that he wished his son had never been born.[1] He added that he could no longer look at photos of Adam, once it dawned on him that one could not be more evil than his boy. For a father to find the courage to openly express this level of animosity toward a killer, when said killer is his own son, is not only rare but also admirable. Peter Lanza's words are an expression, if not of hate, then at least of an attitude reminiscent of hate.

But if we applaud Peter Lanza for taking this attitude toward his own offspring and expressing sympathy for his son's victims, then hate cannot always be the deeply destructive emotional state that it is often made out to be. This is one of the sentiments I hope to be able to bring to the fore with this book.

Usually, hate isn't a laudable emotional state. Hate that spurs atrocities like genocide, mass shootings, and other violent attacks on innocent minorities is never justified. It rides roughshod over details;

99.99 percent of group hate is based on sweeping generalizations, the kinds that reek of logical fallacy. The persistent hatred toward Native Americans today, for example, is rooted in myths, stereotypes, and "palpable truths," like the falsehoods that indigenous people hunt for food with bow and arrow, that there are no longer any sovereign Native Nations in the United States, that Native American aren't U.S. citizens, that indigenous identities are made up, that people can discover their tribal affiliation through a DNA test, that Native Americans receive financial support from the government and don't need to pay for college, that Native reservations are tax-exempt, or that Natives have a federal clearance for the use of illicit drugs.[2]

Although group hate could perhaps be justified in theory, in practice it never is. Personal hate, on the other hand, has the precision that group hate lacks. But personal hate that is dehumanizing, coupled with retaliatory wishes, or not serving any worthwhile ends is nonetheless still indefensible. But I argue that no such ugly facet is essential to hate. When kept apart from its mean-spirited siblings, hate can be a gateway to moral vision.

The term "hate" has a multiplicity of meanings. When asked informally what we mean by hate, we often cite extreme versions of other emotions, such as strong dislike, stomach-churning disgust, dehumanizing contempt, or all-consuming resentment.[3] While our everyday characterizations of hate for the most part lack exactitude, it is true that "hate," in one of its senses, is synonymous with "strong dislike." I hate fried liver. It has a mushy texture and a bitter iron taste. It's repulsive. Nauseating. Vile. When I say I hate fried liver, I obviously don't intend to convey that I think of fried liver as a malevolent wrongdoer. All I mean is that I have a strong dislike for this old Scandinavian favorite. This is also the sense most of us have in mind when we say that we hate being put on hold, waiting in doctors' offices, getting a flat tire, reading work emails, getting by on too little sleep, watching commercials (except during the Super Bowl), coming down with the flu, getting stuck in airports for hours, getting caught in the rain without an umbrella, or being woken up in the middle of the night by a false fire alarm.

This book does not explore hate in the "strong dislike" sense. Rather, its focus is on anger- and disgust-based hate directed toward individuals or groups. Thus restricted, "hate" has a wide and a narrow sense. In its narrow sense, it attributes malevolence or evilness to a person for her perceived wrong- or evildoing. When not otherwise specified, I will use "hate" in this sense.

In its wide sense, hate encompasses both narrow hate and contempt. This is the sense of the term most salient in expressions such as "hate group," "group hate," "hatemonger," "hate rally," "collective hate," "racial hate," "hate crime," "hate speech," "hate campaign," and "hate mail."

Although contempt is not simply the result of filtering out narrow hate's raw anger, it can be seen as a kind of distilled hatred. Contemners—those who have contempt—are typically colder, calmer, and more callous in their attitude toward their target than haters. While the primary subject of this book is narrow hate, we will also explore the philosophy and psychology of contempt and look at how it stands apart from hate.

There is one type of hate that I wish that I could have dealt with more extensively in this book, namely self-hate. I touch on self-hate in Chapter 4 in the context of the cluster B personality disorders and in Chapter 6 in the context of female misogyny, but there is much more to be said about this self-directed emotion than I am able to say here. I hope to explore its intricacies in future works.

The chapters to follow are divided into two parts. The first explores hate in social and intimate relationships, looking for an answer to the question of why our intimate relationships can survive hate and resentment but not disrespect or contempt. I argue that where contempt creates an irreparable power imbalance, hate is tied to fear or reprehension, which the brain is capable of reinterpreting as thrill, attraction, or arousal. But this facet of hate can also make it a dangerous emotion that brainwashes us into hanging on to abusive relationships. When tied to vengeance or dark personality types, such as narcissism, sadism, or psychopathy, hate is not only hazardous but also dehumanizing. Neither acts of vengeance nor dark personality traits are essential to hate, however. Without them, hate can have more commendable ends.

The book's second part explores the inner workings of group hate. Why is group hate so prominent today? The answer is not clear-cut. In fact, the list of reasons for hate's montane heights is long and grim. Among them are the tendency for historical hatred to linger in societies for centuries, the spontaneous polarizing forces that can bias cohesive groups of like-minded individuals, and the rising popularity of corrupt politicians who distort historical records and exploit people's anxiety and despair in a time of crisis or social inequity. But even that is only the tip of the iceberg.[4]

Ever since the political philosopher Hannah Arendt achieved international fame with her theory of the banality of evil, most intellectuals have jumped on that banality bandwagon, arguing that haters, even when active participants in incomprehensible atrocities, are just ordinary people, like you and me, caught up in extraordinary circumstances.[5] David Cesarani, a historian, has taken issue with Arendt's theory, suggesting that haters aren't simply average individuals trapped in a bad situation.[6] Rather, they are plain people who *become* evil when thrown into highly unusual and macabre circumstances.

I find it hard to believe that heinous group crimes like slavery, large-scale torture, or genocide are primarily executed by ordinary people who are propelled along by dire circumstances and a handful of psychopathic commanders. The uncanny truth, I argue, is that in every society, a considerable percentage of the citizenry have malevolent or evil traits that need no more than a little extra nurturing and caressing to burst open and cause seemingly ordinary people to morph into heinous monsters. To put the point differently: I am highly skeptical that we would all have become murderous killers in kindred circumstances, which is the eerie implication of both Arendt's and Cesarani's philosophies. But we only reach this startling conclusion (admittedly in good company) if we ignore the fact that in a large population there are bound to be enormous differences among people's personality and character traits, and this population-wide heterogeneity predicts that people will behave in radically different ways even in situations that strong determine behavior.

Deranged authority figures and hatemongers do have the power to unleash the dark traits that many of us harbor. But sinister character traits may only lead to evildoing once various enabling conditions are in place, such as an economic crisis or widespread social inequity, limited possibilities for upward mobility, political corruption, lingering ethnic biases, and spontaneous group forces, like group polarization.

But if today's hate crisis is the result of a wide assortment of factors, then there should be countless ways to intervene and prevent it from escalating. Politicians and policymakers, I argue, have it in their power to address group hate in Europe and the United States. One way is by regulating expressions of hate, not in the way it's currently done in Europe but in a novel way that preserves the original incentive behind the First Amendment right to free speech. I'm not calling for radical restrictions on freedom of expression. In fact, I am an avid fan of free speech, free press, and academic freedom, and I am one with those of you who argue that merely giving every citizen a vote doesn't satisfy the demands of democracy. Democracy, by its very nature, requires that everyone has a vote as well as a voice. If we focus on regulating the purpose of speech rather than its content, and use novel strategies to ensure that more people have the opportunity to be heard, then we can preserve the democratic ideal envisioned by the framers of the U.S. Constitution and help prevent today's hate crisis from spiraling out of control, or so I will argue.

Needless to say, limited restrictions on free speech are not a stop-all-hate tool, not even if we start listening to our fellow citizens. The million-dollar question is what else Western societies can do to conquer hate. Simply preaching that we need to become more tolerant is not the answer. A promising strategy for pushing back against the growing far-right movement and its hateful narratives is to educate the young before it's too late. But that's a futile tactic for squelching hatred in the not-so-young and the youngsters raised by hatemongers. Luckily, there are other promising strategies for combating hate, some more long-term than others, for instance, electing representatives dedicated to putting an end to political corruption and mitigating the massive social inequality between rich and poor, making upward mobility feasible for more people, giving everyone a political voice, and adopting fair voting systems.

HIT ME WITH YOUR BEST SHOT
AN ANATOMY OF THE ANTAGONISTIC EMOTIONS

Personal hatred can overtake us so completely that it crowds out reason, drains our deepest reservoirs of self-control, and morphs us into murderous marionettes moved by invisible strings. This is the grisly lesson of the ancient Greek playwright Euripides' *Medea*. Medea is a former princess of the kingdom of Colchis who plots revenge on her husband, Jason, after her painful realization that he is making arrangements to marry Glauce, the daughter of King Creon of Corinth. Overtaken by hatred, she sends her children off to Glauce, her husband's wife-to-be, with some poisoned robes. Vain as she is, Glauce immediately puts them on. The fast-acting poison consumes the legs of the princess, and she falls to the floor and soon dies in excruciating pain. Trying to save her, her father gets poisoned and died as well. In the play's most chilling scene, Medea wrestles with herself over whether she can bring herself to kill her own children. Convinced that depriving Jason of his progeny will cause him unbearable suffering and propelled by her obsessive thirst for revenge, she resolves to stab her own children to death.

There could hardly be a better illustration of hatred run amok. Medea's rancor is so ravenous that not even her own kin gets spared. She is the very personification of all-consuming devilish hatred.

Personal hate is not always so theatrical in its manifestations. Many of us hate in silence. Either way, however, most of us are intimately familiar with personal hate. It's built into our cultural heritage, the theme of immortal plays, poems, novels, speeches, songs, and sayings. But what exactly is it?

Historically, many scholars have emphasized hate's elusive nature, its resistance to analysis or definition. In *A Treatise of Human Nature* (1739–1740), the eighteenth-century Scottish Enlightenment philosopher David Hume argued that hatred is "altogether impossible to define."[1] Similar sentiments were voiced by the eighteenth-century German philosopher Immanuel Kant and the British evolutionary biologist Charles Darwin.[2]

I am more optimistic about the possibility of a definition of hate. In this chapter, I argue that hate is a complex emotion, built out of the negative emotions: resentment, condemnation, and reprehension. I further argue that disrespect is the component that unites antagonistic emotions such as anger, resentment, indignation, envy, blame, contempt, and hate. But first let's have a closer look at the nature of the human emotions.

The Human Emotions

Our emotions are among the most culturally celebrated aspects of our mental lives. Countless movies, songs, books, and plays have been named after them, for instance, Gregory Hoblit's 1996 movie *Primal Fear* starring Richard Gere; Aretha Franklin's 1967 signature song "Respect"; Jane Austen's 1813 romantic novel *Pride and Prejudice*; and Edward Albee's 1962 play *Who's Afraid of Virginia Woolf?*—to mention just a few.

Judging by the number of results yielded in a Google search I ran in August 2018, sadness, pride, trust, hate, and love are the most discussed among the human emotions.[3] Runners-up include anger, fear, jealousy, grief, regret, and envy. Yet the human emotions encompass such incredibly diverse mental phenomena as enthusiasm, nostalgia, tenderness, homesickness, despair, frustration, heartbreak, boredom, relief, and sympathy.

There are also quite mundane emotions that don't have a name in English. To be able to talk about them, we need to borrow words from other languages, such as "Schadenfreude," the German word for the feeling of pleasure directed at someone else's misfortune; "malu," the Indonesian word for the feeling of awkwardness around people of higher status; "kaukokaipuu," the Finnish word for the feeling of longing for a place you have never been to; and "hygge," the Danish word for the self-reflective feeling of mindfully enjoying yourself in a relaxing moment.[4] But even with the help of loan words, countless emotions remain nameless in English and some in all known languages. As the product-scientist character Chase (played by Alan Aisenberg) puts it in the 2018 movie *Second Act* when asked about his rival: "Look, there are millions of words in the English language but there is no combination that accurately describes the feeling I have of wanting to beat his ass with a chair."

It's not just the language of emotions that's specific to specific cultures, the emotions themselves are also partially constrained and defined by culture. Just as your great-great-great-grandmother wouldn't be able to recognize a computational device left behind by a time traveler *as* a MacBook Pro, so you would not be able to experience jealousy, say, if we humans weren't in the habit of entering into relationships in which we feel entitled to other people's love, time, and attention. Without that feeling of entitlement, we wouldn't experience the threat of loss that defines jealousy.

Our emotions, while often despised, are our most efficient free tool for monitoring and safeguarding our personal or social concerns.[5] Although they can, and often do, misfire, they can also guide us in the right direction; they can help us avoid real danger, stand up to bullies, finish an education, restore social imbalance, cut ties with toxic people, make up for past wrongs, heal broken relationships, and recover from the losses of loved ones.

Emotions are not simply bodily feelings, like headaches and back itches. They are special ways of mentally relating to people, events, and objects in the external world. In trade parlance, our mental relations to things outside the mind are also known as "attitudes." Perceptions, thoughts, beliefs, desires, and emotions are prime examples of attitudes. But only desires and emotional attitudes, or emotions for short, have a significant tie to bodily feelings. We sometimes refer collectively to our emotions as "our feelings," and when aiming for precision in our portrayal of them, we instinctively enlist the language of touch and bodily sensations, as in this powerful quote from Sarah Addison Allen's novel *The Sugar Queen*: "Like magic, she felt him getting nearer, felt it like a pull in the pit of her stomach. It felt like hunger but deeper, heavier. Like the best kind of expectation. Ice cream expectation. Chocolate expectation."[6]

Emotions do indeed routinely surface as feelings. But the word "feeling" has a plethora of meanings. A friend of mine once related this anecdote to me. During his philosophy of art class, philosophy professor Robert Kraut had asked the class what art is, to which a student responded: "Art is when you feel something." Kraut instinctively replied, "I feel something when my double chin gets caught in a waffle iron. That doesn't make it art!"

The pain in your double chin, the feeling of your heart banging against your ribcage, and the sensation of a lump in your throat are bodily feelings, not emotions. You can feel your heart banging against your ribcage if you run really fast, and you can feel a lump in the throat when you have a sore throat.

Attributing your bodily feelings to an external happenstance does not magically transform them into emotions, either. Suppose your throat feels thick, your nose stuffy, and your eyes teary. You initially attribute these bodily feelings to the fact that your kid just spilled bleach on your leather couch, completely ruining it. But you soon realize that you are not upset. You always hated that couch, and now you have an excuse to get rid of it. The bodily feelings—the irritated throat, the stuffy nose, and the tears—are not *emotional* reactions to your couch being ruined. Rather, they are physical reactions to the strong fumes from the bleach.

For your bodily sensations—the irritated throat, the stuffy nose, and the tears—to have been the embodied aspect of sadness, your brain would have had to interpret the ruined couch as a loss that impacted you negatively, even if only in a small way. Sadness's tight inverse connection to well-being, or flourishing, is one of its hallmarks. It is this inverse relationship that explains why sadness, as we typically experience it, is an unpleasant emotion. Owing to its ordinary unpleasant character, it's also said to have a "negative valence." We can think of an emotion's negative valence as an embodied protest of what the emotion is about; for example, the negative valence of grief can be seen as an embodied protest of a traumatic loss.

But sadness and grief are not unique in this regard. Other negative emotions work the same way. So do positive emotions, such as joy, excitement, or enthusiasm. Because joy ordinarily is a pleasurable emotion, it is also said to have a "positive valence," which we can think of as an embodied celebration of the enrichment that brings it about, say the birth of your niece or granddaughter.

How an emotion feels is partially shaped by whether it's pleasant or unpleasant and partially by its accompanying bodily feelings (if any). Which bodily feelings come to be associated with the different kinds of emotions varies considerably across people, times, and cultures. Sadness, for instance, can feel like a fist reaching inside your torso and brutally ripping out your heart, or it can feel like a tiny sting, as if you had been bitten by a gnat, or it can feel like nothing at all.

When you experience an emotion viscerally, bodily feelings alert you to its presence. For example, if you feel your muscles tense up, your knees become wobbly, and your heart drum against your chest, your brain may interpret this as fear.

Although emotions are closely associated in our minds with bodily feelings, emotions are *about* what goes on in our body. If you are afraid of contracting Covid-19, this may cause your knees to become wobbly, but surely your fear isn't *about* your wobbly knees; it's about a possible future event, namely that of contracting the novel coronavirus. All our emotions are about things or events that appear to be external to us or separate from us. Even when our emotions are about the mind or body (e.g., anxiety about a growth in your armpit, frustration about your recurrent headache, or happiness about your infant meeting the expected milestones, the things or events these emotions are about are typically experienced as separate from us.

The aboutness, or intentionality, of emotions plays a key role in their classification. Indeed, the different types of emotions are about different types of things or events. Anger is about an apparent wrongdoing or injustice, say, being a victim of identity theft or being paid less than your coworkers merely because of your gender or ethnicity. The thing or event that appears to have triggered the emotion is also known as the *focus of concern*, or *focus* for short.

There is a growing consensus among emotion researchers that while paradigm cases of emotions are couples with bodily feeling, emotions often occur in the absence of bodily feelings, especially purely intellectual emotions such as intellectual doubt sympathy (e.g., being sympathetic to a certain political theory), (e.g., doubt about the truth of a premise), endorsement (e.g., endorsing a particular philosophical view.)

But it's not just intellectual emotions that may lack a bodily component. Your frustration when you realize you forgot your laptop as you are backing out of your driveway need not bring about any noticeable physiological response. Emotions that lack a bodily component are akin to evaluative perception, for instance, a diamond watch looking expensive, a rollercoaster ride sounding scary, or a soccer player's stunt to secure a penalty kick seeming unfair.[7]

Emotions can also hide in the unconscious corners of the mind. This is another way in which emotions differ from bodily feelings: you can be angry yet not be consciously aware of it. But you cannot have a tummy ache, sore muscles, or an itchy mosquito bite without being consciously aware of it. If you are not aware that you are sore or itchy, then you are not sore or itchy. End of story.

Imagine otherwise:

"You're in pain," your doc says after examining the images from your brain scan.

"But I don't feel any pain," you reply, perplexed.

Your doc writes some mysterious symbols on a piece of paper and hands it to you. "Here is a script for morphine. Take two capsules twice a day until our next appointment."

Bewildered, you grab the prescription but stealthily drop it in the trash can on your way out.

Although the brain can process information about physical and emotional damage in the absence of consciousness, the notion of unconscious pain is a contradiction in terms. The notion of an unconscious emotion is not. When we hold on to, say, sadness or anger for a long time, we are consciously aware of it only intermittently. For example, if you are angry at someone for a long time, your anger may be lurking mostly below the level of conscious awareness, and when it finally makes itself fully consciously present, it may no longer seize you with the visceral fervor it once did.

All emotions can go under the radar in this way, even those most closely associated in our minds with conscious feelings, such as love and grief. Even when an emotion operates mostly below the radar of consciousness, it can nonetheless pop up and say hello when you least expect it. Trauma, for example, remains mostly hidden below the surface until a trigger yanks it out of hiding. Even when old scars are hermetically sealed off from conscious awareness, they tend to leave a stain on how we behave. For example, trauma is often an automatic trigger of avoidance behavior.

Target versus Focus

As we have seen, emotions are directed at things or events we perceive to be external to us. This outward directedness of a mental state is also known as "intentionality." It is their intentionality that sets emotions apart from moods. Unlike emotions, moods are not about a particular thing or event. If you are in a depressed mood, it may feel like the whole world is against you, but moods and mood disorders are not about anything in particular. This distinction between moods and emotions is not always reflected in the language we use to talk about them. If you say that you are depressed, you could mean that you have a depressed mood or that you are depressed about an unpleasable situation or event, for instance, graduating without a traditional graduation ceremony. When "depressed" is used in this latter sense, your depressed state is not a mood or mood disorder but an emotion.

An emotion's *focus*—a notion we encountered earlier—should be kept distinct from its *target*.[8] If you are angry at your neighbor for not trimming her side of the hedge, then the *target* of your anger is your neighbor. She is the one you are angry at. She is the one you hold responsible for the hedge being untrimmed to the point of tipping over.

But your anger is not *about* your neighbor; it's about her failure to trim the hedge, which is your shared responsibility. It's what the target has done, or rather hasn't done, that's the *focus of concern* of your anger. Your neighbor's failure to trim the hedge is the focus of concern of your anger. It's what concerns (or bothers) you. If we want to inform others that we are angry, several options are available to us: we can simply say that we are angry without revealing whom we are angry with or why we are angry. But we also have the option of explicitly mentioning the target of our anger but not the focus of concern, or vice versa. "I am so mad at you," for example, explicitly names the target of the anger but not its focus of concern, and "Americans are angry about facemasks" explicitly mentions the focus of concern but not the target.

All instances of a given emotion type, be it anger, fear, or sadness, have the same type of focus of concern. This is what makes it an emotion of that particular type. For an emotion to be anger, its focus must be a perceived injustice or wrongdoing though not necessarily a *moral* wrongdoing, like cheating, lying, or stealing. Sometimes we get angry with people who transgress epistemic norms, aesthetic norms, or cultural norms like the norms governing professional soccer. If, for example, Cristiano Ronaldo deliberately threw himself to the ground to secure a penalty kick, this is almost guaranteed to anger members of the competing team.

All emotions have a focus. Some have two. For example, one focus of hate is the targeted person's alleged misdeed; a second is their sinister, or evil, character. We return to hate later in this chapter.

While all emotions have a focus, not all have a target. The focus of sadness is a perceived loss. If you are sad because your best friend, Morgan, no longer lives close to you, the focus of your sadness is the loss of Morgan's proximity to you. But your sadness doesn't have a target who can (reasonably) be held accountable for your sadness. Even if you were to hold Morgan's boyfriend Jake accountable for her move, he is not the target of your sadness.[9]

Complex Emotions

Emotion researchers commonly distinguish between basic and non-basic emotions. The distinction was coined by evolutionary psychologist Paul Ekman, who achieved international recognition for his "atlas of emotions," a compendium of more than ten thousand emotion-induced facial expressions. Ekman's basic emotions, which he took to be biologically "hard-wired," encompass joy, surprise, anger, sadness, fear, disgust, and contempt.[10] Ekman labeled these seven emotions as basic because they are marked by unique facial expressions that can be found across almost all cultures. For example, when your eyes are wide open, causing wrinkles on the forehead, and your lips are stretched horizontally, people across different cultures will be able to recognize this as an expression of fear. Similarly, when one lip corner is curled upward, producing a distinctly derisive or sardonic smile or sneer, people across different cultures will be able to recognize this as an expression of contempt.

While the basic emotions have unique facial expressions that can be recognized by people pan-culturally, there are many other ways basic emotions can be expressed. The expressions of two distinct basic emotions can even be almost indistinguishable. For example, we sometimes cry when we are happy, smile when we are angry, and laugh when we are nervous. Psychologist Oriana Aragón and her colleagues found that when we are in the grip of an overwhelming emotion, dissonance in how it's expressed can lower its intensity and help us regain control.[11] Dissonant emotional expressions are not ubiquitous, however, but vary substantially cross-culturally, which lends support to the thesis that the culture we live in shape both our emotions and their expressions.[12]

Unlike basic emotions, non-basic emotions such as hate, envy, jealousy, grief, trust, nostalgia, and loneliness are not expressed in a unique or ubiquitous way. Grief is a paradigm example of a non-basic emotion that is conceptualized and expressed differently cross-culturally. As emotions are categorized on the basis of their focus, they have the same focus across all cultures, which in the case of grief is traumatic loss. In spite of the fact that traumatic loss is the focus of grief across all cultures, grief isn't the same everywhere. Culture shapes what types of loss are perceived as traumatic, how people interpret the concept of a traumatic loss, and how they react to it. For example, in orthodox Islamic cultures, it is permissible for a man to request a divorce but according to orthodox teachings, divorce is the "most despised of permissible acts by God" and can therefore be more traumatic than death.[13] Grief is also displayed differently cross-culturally.[14] Grand emotional displays of grief, for example, are frowned upon in some cultures but encouraged in others. In European Catholic and Protestant traditions, it's customary for people to grieve quietly and stoically, whereas African, Caribbean, and Islamic cultures encourage showing grief openly, for example, by crying loudly.[15] Finally, the norms for the proper conduct of funerals and burials as well as for proper mourning and memorialization varies considerably cross different cultures.

Even within a single culture, grief is not associated with a unique facial or other bodily expression. According to the Kübler-Ross model of grief, also known as the "five stages of grief," first introduced by Elisabeth Kübler-Ross in her 1969 book, *On Death and Dying*, grief involves five stages: denial, anger, bargaining, sadness, and acceptance.[16] After the loss of a loved one, for example, you may first deny that the person is gone, simply refuse to believe it. Once the truth dawns on you, you may feel outraged and attempt to convince your beloved to come back or beg God or the universe's spirits to reverse their decision. Once you realize things are not going to change, sadness may set in. You may experience an unbearable visceral yearning for the absent person or the irretrievable relationship. Over time, you may finally accept the loss. These stages need not occur in this order, and each stage may occur several times or not at all. The different emotional stages can also overlap. After an unwanted breakup, you may both be angry at your ex and try to bargain with them, or you may both ferociously deny the loss of the relationship and still cry all day long. Because of the complexity and its cultural and individual variability, grief is not associated with a unique, let alone ubiquitous, facial or other bodily expression.

The basic emotions, in Ekman's sense, should not be confused with what we can call the "simple emotions." Simple emotions are not composed of other emotions. Complex emotions, by contrast, have other emotions and attitudes as parts. Resentment, disappointment, regret, jealousy, and grief are examples of complex emotions. Resentment, for example, is composed of blame and anger, and disappointment is thwarted expectations coupled with low levels of sadness.

Which emotions are simple is still up for debate. One suggestion is that all and only the basic emotions are simple. However, there is evidence to suggest otherwise. As philosopher Jesse Prinz has argued, at least some of Ekman's basic, or "universally recognizable," emotions are complex. Surprise, for example, can be divided into a positive sense of interest or wonder and a low level of panic, and anger can be analyzed as aggression combined with goal frustration.[17]

Contempt, which Ekman classified as a basic emotion some years after he created his original list, also fails to qualify as simple.[18] Psychologists have argued that contempt is anger coupled with disgust, citing the evidence that contempt's characteristic facial expression partially overlaps with the characteristic facial expressions of anger and disgust. [19] However, the cited evidence is lending equal support for contempt as a blend of disgust and condemnation. I develop this idea later in this chapter.

The Antagonistic Emotions

Let's now turn to what I call the "antagonistic emotions." They include emotions like blame, anger, resentment, indignation, envy, disrespect, disgust, contempt, and hatred. This list is not exhaustive. Emotions such as annoyance, vengefulness, and schadenfreude are also antagonistic. But the emotions on the former list are the ones that are most relevant to the analysis of hate.

The antagonistic emotions target people or groups. Not all forms of anger and disgust are antagonistic, but garden-variety anger and disgust are directed at people or groups. Most antagonistic emotions have a negative valence, which means that we associate them with displeasure. [20] Anger, disgust, hate, and contempt are examples of unpleasant antagonistic emotions. But there are also pleasant ones, emotions with a positive valence. Schadenfreude, which is pleasure in response to another person's misfortune, is a prime example.

Three key features set the unpleasant antagonistic emotions apart from other emotions (with one exception). One is that they are reactions to the target's perceived offensive behavior or practices. For example, if you despise Gwyneth Paltrow for her pretentious health advice, you regard her advice as offensive, and your emotional state is a reaction to that. [21]

A second hallmark of the unpleasant antagonistic emotions is that, with the exception of disgust, they present their target as blameworthy, where blameworthiness requires accountability and the absence of a legitimate excuse. As we will see below, if we find person's behavior or appearance appalling, this need not involve an attribution of blame. In fact, it need not even involve an attribution of accountability. But the other unpleasant antagonistic emotions attribute blame to the target. If, for example, you resent a school bully who calls you ugly names, your resentment involves an attribution of blame.

The third hallmark of the antagonistic emotions is that they all have disrespect as a component, which is tied to their inherently socially comparative nature. Contempt and hate stand out from anger and resentment by involving disrespect for the target for her character traits and not just her actions. For example, if you disrespect Bruce Willis for demanding over-the-top remuneration for a particular film role, then the focus of your disrespect is his action. If, on the other hand, you disrespect him for demanding over-the-top remuneration for all his film roles, then the focus of your disrespect may be his character traits rather than just his action.

Let's now have a closer look at the subset of the antagonistic emotions that lie at the heart of the analysis of hate: anger, resentment, indignation, envy, blame, disrespect, and contempt.

Frustration versus Antagonistic Anger

While anger is perhaps the best example of an antagonistic emotion, anger need not be antagonistic. For example, you may feel angry about how things have turned out for you, yet not hold anyone responsible for your misfortune. Imagine you are incredibly busy at work when your child's teacher calls you to request that you pick up your son who has come down with a fever. As you get off the call, you seethe with anger, yet you are not angry at the teacher. Nor are you angry at your son. You just feel angry. This is an example of targetless anger, or what we call "frustration." It's this kind of anger that causes children to throw temper tantrums in grocery stores and adults to kick vending machines that won't deliver. ("Venting machine" may be a more fitting term.)

We also sometimes experience targetless anger when grieving a traumatic loss. For example, you may feel angry about the traumatic loss of your spouse without being angry at him or at anyone else. In the envisaged case, your anger is a kind of protest against the unfair turn of events.

Unlike targetless anger, antagonistic anger is tied to accountability and blame. If you are angry at someone for something they did, you hold them accountable for what they did and blame them accordingly. Imagine again that your son's teacher calls you to tell you to pick up your feverish kid on an insanely busy day. You know rationally that it's not the teacher's fault. But you nonetheless lay it on her. In this case, your anger is antagonistic. By directing your anger at the teacher, you thereby hold her responsible and blame her for you falling even further behind.[22] In its more sinister form, antagonistic anger is also known as "rage" or "wrath."

Resentment, Indignation, and Envy

Resentment and indignation are species of simple anger. Like anger, they involve a presumed injustice. Resentment and indignation tend to last much longer than a brief fit of anger. They can linger for weeks or months on end, perhaps even years—staying mostly hidden under the flimsy veil of consciousness, but occasionally checking in with you.

In resentment and indignation, we react to a perceived injustice.[23] In resentment, we perceive the injustice as *personal*, that is, it's an injustice done to us. Indignation, or what is sometimes called "outrage," is the vicarious analogue of resentment. When you are indignant, what concerns you is an injustice done to someone else—perhaps a social injustice. For example, you may feel indignation upon learning that the board of trustees of a company approved a fifty-percent raise for its CEO—despite recently letting two hundred of its workers go.

Resentment is closely related to envy. Envy is a reaction to feeling shortchanged. In envy, we resent the envied for a possession or advantage we wish we had. Suppose you envy your coworker for getting a promotion you hoped to get. Here, you resent your coworker for being promoted instead of you.

Philosophers sometimes distinguish between benign and malicious envy. Benign envy is said to be focused on *the envier's* perceived disadvantage, whereas malicious envy is focused on *the envied's* seeming advantage.[24] Unlike malicious envy, benign envy is supposed to be morally praiseworthy, because it motivates the envier to take steps to get to where the envied is. However, I don't think the comparative emotion that can motivate us to work harder is envy in its distilled form. Rather, it seems to be competitiveness or zeal. In any event, I will set aside the use of "envy" as a term denoting a positive emotion.

Envy implies that the envier perceives herself as at least as deserving of the advantage or possession as the envied. For example, if you envy your coworker for getting the promotion you were hoping to get, then you think you deserve it at least as much as he does. This aspect of envy is sometimes said to be based on the envier's perception of similarity between the envier and the envied.[25] There is a sense in which that is true. You are probably more inclined to envy a coworker who works the same job as you than you are to envy the CEO of the company. But you might envy the CEO of the company simply because you resent her for being able to afford a Lamborghini and live in a big mansion when you barely can make ends meet. Likewise, we are prone to envy celebrities and extraordinarily successful, wealthy, beautiful, or smart people. You may be more keenly aware of feeling delight at their downfall than feeling envious of them. But being delighted by someone else's misfortune, or what is also known as schadenfreude, is an emotional reaction to the failings of someone we resent, envy, or hate. As philosopher Sara Protasi has pointed out, envy can occur even when it wouldn't be possible for the envier to obtain the envied possession or advantage.[26] For example, if you are infertile, you may well envy people who have their own biological children, even though you can't obtain the envied good.

In common parlance, "jealousy" is often used synonymously with "envy." But they are in fact distinct emotions.[27] Whereas envy is a reaction to someone else's perceived unfair advantage or possession, jealousy is a reaction to the perceived threat of losing someone you already "possess" in some sense—usually a person with whom you have a special relationship—to a third party. The two emotions are core themes in William Shakespeare's play *Othello*. Envious of Othello's possessions and success, Iago manipulates Othello into believing that his wife, Desdemona, is having an affair with his friend Cassio. When Othello finds out, he becomes sick with jealousy and murders Desdemona, and then kills himself.

Envy as portrayed in *Othello* is closely related to what philosophers call "ressentiment." The term originates with the Danish existentialist Søren Kierkegaard, but it was made famous by the nineteenth-century literary philosopher Friedrich Nietzsche.[28] Sometimes translated as "resentment," the term's original French spelling is usually left intact to mark its distinctive meaning. As Nietzsche was using the term, ressentiment is an unpleasant reaction to a perceived lowly or declining social status that prompts a retaliatory attitude toward those perceived as more powerful. As we will see, resentment, ressentiment, envy, and hate are closely related. Resentment is a component of both envy and hate (although hate can also have indignation as a component). Retaliatory hatred is furthermore often fueled by envy, typically envy that motivates the envier to lash out at the envied by harming them in some way, for instance, by destroying the good that is "unfairly" in their possession. This is what Protasi calls "spiteful envy." Philosopher Robert Solomon sums up the thoughts of the spiteful envier as: "If I can't have it, no one will."[29] Spiteful envy is the kind of envy that most closely resembles ressentiment, and it's envy of this kind that is thematized in Shakespeare's *Othello*.

Envy is rarely a rational emotion. This is because envy's target is not typically at fault for having what the envier wants. Envy is a kind of misplaced resentment. But it can be rational on the rare occasions where the envied is responsible for having the possession or advantage you wish you had. If you envy your coworker for getting the promotion you had hoped for, and you happen to know he was promoted because he slept with the boss, your envy is rational, as long as it's not spiteful.[30] We will revisit the question of the rationality of the antagonistic emotions in Chapter 3.

Emotional Blame

The word "blame" is commonly used to refer to the speech act of criticizing someone else, whether it's done calmly or by screaming or shouting. But verbal criticism is merely a vehicle for expressing blame. When we verbally criticize others, we verbally express a negative emotional reaction to them. But we can blame a person without expressing it, as can be seen from the coherence of saying things like "I still blame my wife for her betrayal, even though I never told her that."

Private, or unexpressed, blame can be directed toward people we are not in a position to verbally criticize because they are dead or too far away for us to do so, or because we don't know them, such as when we blame Hitler or Stalin or point the finger of blame at the parents of obese children.

While we blame people who are incapable of feeling remorse, such as psychopaths. We sometimes use verbal criticism, or scolding, to correct the behavior of children, but this is a far cry from actually blaming them. The same goes for mentally disabled people who lack the concept of moral wrongdoing and people in the grip of a hallucination or delusion that causes them to regard their misconduct as an act of goodwill or self-defense.

When you blame someone, you hold them responsible, or accountable, for their actions or the foreseeable consequences of those actions. But blame is not merely an attribution of responsibility. You can hold people responsible for their actions or the foreseeable consequences of those actions and yet not blame them. If your child commits a crime, you may take her to be responsible for that crime, yet not have it in you to blame her.

But what is blame over and above a perception of someone's guilt? Philosopher Thomas Scanlon has argued that to blame someone is to take her to manifest a relationship-impairing attitude and to acknowledge that this gives you reasons to adjust your attitudes toward the relationship in light of this impairment, above all your intentions and expectations. Scanlon recognizes that when we blame people, we might also feel resentment or indignation. But, he says, "this is not required for blame, in my view—I might just feel sad."[31]

A commonly voiced objection to Scanlon's account is that it doesn't seem to apply to our fleeting relationships with strangers.[32] If a stranger steals your purse while you are sightseeing in a foreign city, and you never see them again, no past, present, or future relationship is impaired. Yet you may still blame them for stealing your purse. Similarly, if your sister is murdered by a stranger who is never caught, the killer didn't impair your relationship, as you never did and never will have any kind of relationship with the murderer. Yet you still blame them.

This is not a knock-down objection to Scanlon's view, however. Although you don't have a personal relationship with the thief or the killer, the two of you do have a social relationship. You are part of the same moral community, and therefore reasonably hold each other to certain expectations. For example, you can hold others to the expectation that we don't steal from each other or kill each other. Because the thief and the killer violated those expectations, it is reasonable for you to take them to manifest a relationship-impairing attitude and to acknowledge that this gives you reasons to adjust your attitudes toward your relationship in light of this impairment. This is so regardless of your level of acquaintance with them. So, I don't think this objection presents a real challenge for Scanlon's account.

My concern with his account is that it doesn't generalize to all forms of blame. For example, we routinely blame people for possessing attributes we happen to disfavor—attributes such as excessive pride, greed, lust, envy, gluttony, wrath, sloth, jealousy, cowardice, emotional instability, grumpiness, pessimism, obesity, poverty, unemployment, drug addiction, procrastination, impatience, incompetence, impulsivity, gullibility, ignorance, and so on. The first seven of these even enjoy a special status as the seven deadly sins.

Despite blaming people for possessing features we disfavor, we far from always take them to manifest a relationship-impairing attitude by virtue of possessing these features. In many cases, it would be utterly absurd to do so. If, for example, you were to blame your friend for becoming obese, it is highly unlikely that you would take her obesity to reflect a friendship-impairing attitude. Even if you blame her for having gained weight, it would be ludicrous for you to take her to have done so out of a lack of concern for your friendship.

How then should we understand blame? An alternative to Scanlon's proposal is to understand the emotion as a kind of inner protest. An account along those lines has been developed at length by philosopher Angela Smith. Blame, she argues, is inner protest of a moral imbalance the wrongdoer has created.[33] If someone harms you intentionally or recklessly, they are acting arrogantly. Their act implicitly conveys that they think that they are morally superior to you, and that they therefore have the right to treat you as they wish without fear of repercussion or backlash. They are falsely claiming that you are "low" and therefore don't deserve to be treated with decency and respect. Philosopher Pamela Hieronymi puts this latter point as follows:

> I suggest that a past wrong against you, standing in your history without apology, atonement, retribution, punishment, restitution, condemnation, or anything else that might recognize it as a wrong, makes a claim. It says, in effect, that you can be treated in this way, and that such treatment is acceptable.[34]

The point is this. If someone harms you with specific intent or reckless disregard for your rights, then their action reflects that they falsely assume that your human rights don't really matter in the circumstances. This false assumption, Smith argues, calls for a response that can help set things right. You can set things rights by blaming the perpetrator and thereby protesting their false assumption. If your blame is not outwardly expressed, the inner feeling of protest can nonetheless help correct the offender's faulty assumption in your own mind. Even when there is no "true" justice to be had, at least there is the blame.

If you convey your blame to your assailant, this may inspire them to acknowledge that they made a false assumption about your rightful treatment. They can express their faux pas by apologizing. In less severe cases this may suffice to nullify the reason you initially had for blaming them. Even if they apologize, they are still responsible for what they did, but they may no longer be deserving of blame. In more serious cases, atonement or restitution may be needed to set things right. Perhaps there are also cases where nothing can make up for what has already gone down.

I am sympathetic to Smith's proposal that protesting the aggressor's false assumption about the victim's rights can help set things right. However, her proposal fails for much the same reason that Scanlon's does: it doesn't generalize to all instances of blame. If you blame your obese friend for her weight gain, it would be ludicrous for you to regard the actions that led to her weight gain as conveying false information about your rightful treatment.

To be fair, neither Scanlon nor Smith is in the business of providing a general account of blame. But it is highly unlikely that "blame" expresses one concept when used to refer to a negative attitude toward a person who has injured you and another concept when used to refer to a negative attitude toward someone who is, say, obese, poor, or addicted to drugs. Fortunately, we don't need to posit ambiguity. In the subsequent section I propose a unified account of blame based on the notion of disrespect, but first let's have a closer look at the different meanings of "respect" and "disrespect."

Blame as Disrespect

According to a poll conducted by Gallup in 1999, the three people who enjoyed the greatest respect in America in the twentieth century were Mother Teresa, Martin Luther King, Jr., and John F. Kennedy.[35]

What exactly do we mean by respect? In his 1977 seminal essay "Two Kinds of Respect" philosopher Stephen Darwall distinguishes between two kinds of respect: appraisal respect and recognition respect. Appraisal respect is so called because it involves a positive appraisal of a person for her moral excellence on the whole or her excellence as engaged in a specific pursuit (e.g., taking the SATs or serving as an eyewitness) or a type of pursuit (e.g., parenting, teaching, or cooking).[36]

The appraisal respect Americans had for Mother Teresa, Martin Luther King, Jr., and John F. Kennedy in 1999 is a positive appraisal of these public personas for their moral excellence overall. When appraisal respect is directed at someone for her overall moral excellence, our attitude can also be thought of as a kind of profound awe. Americans revere Mother Teresa, Martin Luther King, Jr., and John F. Kennedy.

While the appraisal respect we have for outstanding public personas tends to be based on their overall moral performance, whether we regard someone as worthy of appraisal respect typically depends on how they perform in a specific pursuit or type of pursuit, for example, as a commencement speaker at the University of Miami's fall 2017 commencement ceremonies, a tennis player at the 2018 Summer Youth Olympic Games, or a leading actress in the 2019 Broadway play *Moulin Rouge*. When appraisal respect is directed at someone for her performance in a specific pursuit or type of pursuit, our attitude is not one of profound awe but rather one of admiration, or holding in high esteem.

The focus of appraisal respect is the target's conduct on the whole or as engaged in a specific pursuit. What it takes to earn respect within a specific pursuit depends on whatever standards are held to be appropriate to that pursuit. Even in pursuits that depend heavily on the mastery of certain skills, the actions relevant to whether the person is deserving of respect often go beyond the mere display of mastery of the skill, as it does in the case of Darwall's boisterous tennis player. While the player is widely regarded as one of the best in the world, he is not widely respected by his fellows, as he "constantly heckles his opponent, disputes every close call to throw off his opponent's concentration, [and] laughs when his opponent misses a shot."[37]

Even when demonstrating mastery of a skill is necessary for earning people's respect, displays of bad character during the pursuit can thus cancels out even perfect mastery of the skill. But appraisal respect in a specific pursuit typically doesn't require excellence of character. A tennis player judged to one of the best players in the world can be a little bit out of line character-wise without thereby losing his fans' respect for him as a tennis player.

Darwall contrasts appraisal respect with a rather different kind of respect, which he calls "recognition respect." This is the kind of respect all people are owed, irrespective of their specific virtues, sentiments, attitudes, or choices. In other words, recognition respect does not involve an appraisal of a person on the basis of their achievements.[38] As the label suggests, to have recognition respect for another person is to recognize their inherent worth, where recognizing a person's inherent worth implies treating them with a minimum of decency. Because all people have inherent worth, all people are entitled to recognition respect, regardless of their normative standing.[39]

The idea that all people are entitled to be recognized as worthy of respect lies at the heart of Kant's moral philosophy.[40] According to Kant, it is morally wrong to treat people merely as a means to an end, because all people have dignity, where "dignity" is the word used as a translation of Kant's term "die Würde" (*the worth*). Morality demands that we respect all people as dignified individuals, which requires respecting their fundamental human rights, such as the rights to self-govern, make autonomous decisions, and keep sensitive personal information private.[41] It is respect in this sense that Darwall calls "recognition respect."

Where appraisal respect is a matter of degree—you may respect both Eddy Murphy and Jerry Seinfeld as comedians but have greater respect for Murphy than Seinfeld—recognition respect is an on-or-off matter. In this regard, respecting others is like passing a driving test. You cannot pass it a little or a lot. You either pass, or you don't. Similarly, you either treat a person with the respect owed to all people, or you don't. There is no middle ground. This is not to say that depravity is not a matter of degree, but only that a withdrawal of *some* but *not all* of your recognition respect in response to "middle of the road" depravity isn't an option.

There are other kinds of respect besides appraisal and recognition respect. In a short note of 1973, Joel Feinberg calls attention to a third kind of respect, which is the kind of respect we have in mind when we say things like "My fear of the sea turned into respect," "My sister's accident taught me to have respect for all guns, even BB guns," or "Your class has given me a renewed respect for the dangers of binge drinking."[42] When making such statements, we are not saying that we are holding the sea, guns, or binge drinking in high esteem, or that we recognize their inherent dignity. Rather, the respect we have for, say, the sea is a watchful or apprehensive appreciation of its perceived power or danger. To emphasize the fear component, I shall refer to it as "apprehensive respect," or just "apprehension."

Apprehensive respect isn't just directed at non-human entities, such as the sea, guns or viruses. We often have apprehensive respect for people we perceive to be powerful or dominant. In the words of Feinberg, we express our apprehensive respect for people "by trying to avoid arousing their enmity, or by attempting to placate them once they are aroused, or by arming ourselves and treading cautiously."[43] An illuminating example of how apprehensive respect comes apart from appraisal respect can be seen in Mark Twain's 1884 novel *Adventures of Huckleberry Finn*, where Huck Finn seems to respect his father out of fear but disrespect him for the drunken, weak man that he is.[44] As we will see, apprehensive respect is a central component of hatred.

Let's move on to disrespect, the component that unifies the antagonistic emotions. Disrespect is not simply an absence of respect. If you have never heard of a person, you don't respect her, because you can't. Nor do you disrespect her. But you may also lack both respect and disrespect for people you inadvertently take no notice of or don't presently interact with. This is what the eighteenth-century Scottish philosopher and economist Adam Smith was alluding to when he wrote, "To be overlooked, and to be disapproved, are things entirely different."[45] If you overlook or unintentionally ignore a person, then you have neither respect nor disrespect for them. Disrespect is therefore not the absence of respect but an emotional attitude in its own right.

The three kinds of respect identified above correspond to three kinds of disrespect, which I will call "critical disrespect," "dehumanizing disrespect," and "hubris." Critical disrespect is so called because it involves a negative appraisal of a person for their questionable conduct.

Consonant with the definition of appraisal respect, we can define "critical disrespect" as an emotional disapproval of people who have revealed themselves as profoundly morally despicable or as unskilled or detestable participants in a specific pursuit or type of pursuit. The critical disrespect we have for Harvey Weinstein, Bill Cosby, or Derek Chauvin, the police officer who killed George Floyd in May, 2020 is a negative appraisal of them for their profound moral despicability.

While the critical disrespect we have for despicable public personas can be based on their moral performance, whether we regard someone as deserving of critical disrespect is more likely to depend on how they perform in a specific pursuit or type of pursuit, for example, how they perform as a film producer, scientist, or participant in the 2019 Boston marathon. Marc Hauser, a former Harvard University psychologist who fabricated and falsified data and made false statements about experimental methods in six federally funded studies,[46] is deserving of critical disrespect as an evolutionary biologist, though not necessarily as a father or a tennis player.

As for the case of appraisal respect, what it takes for a person to be deserving of critical disrespect within a specific pursuit or kind of pursuit depends on what standards are held to be appropriate to that pursuit. Even in pursuits that depend greatly on the mastery of certain practical skills, people may be deserving of critical disrespect despite mastering all relevant practical skills to perfection, as in the case of Darwall's boisterous tennis player who falls short of meeting the standards of the profession. Poor mastery of a skill can, of course, also elicit critical disrespect, especially if the failing or mess up reflects partial responsibility for not mastering the skill on the part of the agent.

The second form of disrespect, dehumanizing disrespect, is an entirely different creature. To have dehumanizing disrespect for someone is to regard them as lacking the inherent worth that entitles them to be treated with respect. To disrespect a person in this sense is to treat them as subhuman, or a "nonentity," whose sole purpose is to serve "real" people.

A "nonentity." This is the term forty-four-year-old Sara Packer used to describe her fourteen-year-old daughter who became a pawn in Packer and her boyfriend's rape-murder fantasy.[47] In an emotionless tone of voice, Packer testified to the court in March 2019 that she had gazed into her daughter's eyes while the girl was being choked to death, telling her "it was okay to go." Packer didn't merely hold her daughter in disesteem, she regarded her as a mere tool for satisfying her and her boyfriend's sadistic sexual desires.

The third form of disrespect, hubris, is an act of fearless overconfidence that betrays a foolish lack of apprehensive respect, often found alongside contempt for the advice of others. If you hold professional fireworks in your hand and light them as a way of showing off to your buddies, then you are displaying a particularly foolish form of disrespect for the dangers of explosive objects, a paradigm example of hubris. In ancient Greek mythology, hubris was an act of arrogance before the Gods, which was avenged by Nemesis, the goddess of divine retribution.[48]

Let's turn now to the promised account of blame in terms of disrespect. To emotionally blame a person for an action is to hold her responsible for her conduct and convey (even if only to yourself) that you disrespect her for performing an action you disapprove of. If, for example, you blame your friend for becoming obese, you hold her responsible for the excessive weight gain *and* disrespect her for, say, eating too much and moving too little.

Although blame can involve dehumanizing disrespect, I suspect that when we blame people for what they have done rather than for who they are, the blame is more likely to be critical than dehumanizing. Conversely, when we blame people for who they are rather than for what they have done, the blame is more likely to be dehumanizing. I will refer to the blame we direct at people for their flawed character as "condemnation." To condemn a person for their flawed character is to disrespect them for cultivating or failing to unlearn the corresponding bad "habits," to borrow a term from Aristotle.

In his book *In Praise of Blame* philosopher George Sher argues that people don't deserve blame for their bad traits because it makes no sense to hold them responsible for being the kind of person they are.[49] Although this is probably true for some narrowly defined traits, I am doubtful that it is true in general. The reason that it makes sense to hold people responsible for their character traits is that character traits can be cultivated through practice, as Aristotle argued, that is, the degree to which we possess a particular virtue or vice depends on how we *choose* to act across a range of different circumstances. To illustrate, consider a trait like *being funny*, or what Aristotle called "wittiness" (*eutrapelia*). The sheer amount of on-line advice on how to be funny suggests that it is largely up to you whether or not you choose to cultivate wittiness, which is to say, it makes sense to hold you responsible for lacking wit. That said, we often blame people for traits or conditions that they are not respon-sible for. Fat shaming, which is fueled by blame and disgust, is a case in point. Obesity is probably rarely (if ever) the result of "deadly sins" like sloth and gluttony. Mounting evidence suggests that the culprit in obesity and comorbidities like insulin resistance and high blood glucose is chronic low-grade inflammation that has an envi-ronmental source.[50] But if obesity is due to factors beyond our con-trol, blame directed at obese people is misplaced, as it rests on a false assumption about the cause of obesity.

The proposed account of blame in terms of disrespect seems more readily applicable to both moral and non-moral blame than the theories advanced by Scanlon and Smith. Scanlon, recall, holds that to blame someone is to take them to manifest relationship-impairing attitudes and acknowledge that this gives you reasons to adjust your attitudes to-ward the relationship in light of this impairment. This account works well to explain what it means to blame, say, a friend for betraying you. By betraying you, your friend manifested friendship-impairing attitudes and this gives you reasons to adjust your attitudes toward the relation-ship, for example, by changing your willingness to trust your friend. But if you blame a friend for not being able to hold up a job due to her tendency to procrastinate, you are unlikely to take your friend's procrastination on the job to be impairing your friendship. After all, they may not have any bearing on your interests. Similar remarks apply to Smith's account of blame as a protest of the message conveyed by the target's actions to the effect that you are inferior to him, and that his actions therefore were justified. This proposal works well for the case of moral blame. If a friend betrays you, her act of betrayal does indeed seem to convey that you mean "nothing" to her. But it would be ludicrous for you to take your friend's inclination to procrastinate on the job to imply that you don't mean much to her. So, Scanlon's and Smith's proposals both appear to be limited in their scope.

The proposed account of blame as disrespect seems better suited as a unified treatment of all the different varieties of blame. If your friend can't hold down a job, you may blame her for underperforming on the job, even if her failures have no effect on your friendship. If, however, your friend's poor job performance doesn't change your friendship, then it would be ludicrous for you to take it to convey false information about your worth or to constitute evidence that your friend's attitude toward your friendship is a destructive one. It is far more plausible that your blame of your friend for habitually procrastinating on the job is a form of disrespect. Disrespecting her in this regard is consistent with simultaneously respecting her for, say, her dependability and kindness as your friend.

This approach to blame has the advantage that it yields the same predictions as Scanlon and Smith's accounts in the relevant scenarios. It implies that when you blame a friend for, say, betraying you, then you also have reasons to change your attitudes toward your relationship. In this sort of scenario, disrespecting your friend for betraying you is a way of objecting to her treatment of you. So, the blame helps to repudiate a false assumption about your relative status, as suggested by Smith.

As we will see, disrespect is not merely a central component of blame. It's an integral part of antagonistic emotions like anger, resentment, indignation, contempt, and hate.

Primitive Disgust

Most of us naturally react with disgust to bodily excretions and skin growths, such as warts, cold sores, abscesses, urine, feces, saliva, pus, mucus, dandruff, phlegm, ear wax, vomit, snot, sweat, semen, and menstruation. Tears, a bodily excretion, are a peculiar exception. Tears can be delightful in a way that snot cannot. Seeing, smelling, hearing, touching, or tasting what we believe are bodily excretions typically triggers a distinctive visceral response that can be followed by vomiting, regurgitation, dry heaves, nausea, or a wrinkled nose.

Other common triggers of disgust include smelly, decaying, sticky, or slimy-looking entities such as cockroaches, slugs, maggots, lice, fungus, toxic green algae, open wounds, rotten meat, and corpses.

Our natural disgust reaction to bodily excretions and smelly, decaying, sticky, or slimy-looking entities is an involuntary reflex akin to a knee-jerk reaction in response to a doctor's hammer. Call disgust that elicits a "yuck" reflex of this kind "primitive disgust."

Primitive disgust is likely to have evolved as a biological mechanism that once assisted in keeping our ancestors away from pathogens and infections. But this picture is not an accurate description of primitive disgust in humans today.

Disgust in response to open wounds, warts, snot, vomit, and blood can be found across most cultures in the world. But the ubiquity of disgust is the exception, not the rule. In his classic book *The Expression of Emotions in Man and Animals*, Darwin noted that what people find disgusting varies substantially from culture to culture. Recalling an incident on his expedition to South America, Darwin observed:

> In Tierra del Fuego a native touched with his finger some cold preserved meat which I was eating at our bivouac, and plainly showed utter disgust at its softness; whilst I felt utter disgust at my food being touched by a naked savage, though his hands did not appear dirty.[51]

What we find disgusting can vary tremendously from culture to culture, even when the cultures are not light years apart. I grew up in Denmark, a short boat ride away from Sweden. Yet I continue to be baffled by the Swedes' love of decaying herring, or what they call *surströmming*. It smells like a cocktail of rotten eggs, sour milk, open sewer, and fish that has gone bad (with a twist of skunk). In other words, it stinks! Its stench, should you happen to get any of the brine on you, will linger for days, making you feel like your nose hairs are being pulled out with tweezers. Even dogs have been seen projectile-vomiting when exposed to its smell.[52] There is a reason *surströmming* is banned in most apartment complexes and almost never is served at restaurants. Yet the Swedes consider it a delicacy.

The cultural variation in what we find disgusting suggests that disgust, even in its primitive form, need not be (or have been) evolutionarily advantageous. Rather, it's probably to a large extent the result of cultural influence. This point lies at the center of political philosopher Martha Nussbaum's writings.[53] Fear and disgust, she argues, are both instinctual responses to things we take to carry a risk of harming us. They are not directly correlated with known risk, however.[54] For example, most people will refuse to ingest a cockroach, even if it has been sterilized. This is the finding of psychological studies carried out by psychologist Paul Rozin and his collaborators.[55]

In one of their studies, the researchers asked the study participants to watch them sterilize a cockroach. The subjects denied seeing any danger in eating it. Yet they refused to consume it. The experimenters then sealed a sterilized cockroach inside a digestible plastic capsule guaranteed to come out intact in the feces. But to no avail. The volunteers refused to swallow the capsule.

In another study, also conducted by Rozin and collaborators, research participants were asked to sniff a box and then relate whether they found the smell disgusting. The researchers found that whether participants exposed to the same odor perceived it as disgusting depended on what they were told was in the box prior to smelling it. When told the box contained feces, the participants reported being utterly disgusted, but when told that it contained barrel-aged Italian cheese, they savored their sniff. As the odor was exactly the same in the two cases, the participants' beliefs about the contents of the box thus altered their perception of the odor, which suggests that what we find disgusting is theory-laden.

As Nussbaum points out, in Western cultures, disgust is tied to fear of death and our own bodily decay as we get older. We associate things that remind us of our animal nature with contamination or impurity, such as corpses, rotting meat, and bodily fluids, because we fear and despise our mortal bodily humanity.

The idea of the body as contaminated or impure predates modern religion. The ancient Greek philosopher Plato thought of the body and the material world as imperfect transient existences compared to the soul. When we die, Plato argued, our body decays, and eventually none of our material existence is left. But the soul is immortal. After death, it enters the true realm of Platonic forms. It is eventually reborn, thus becoming trapped in a decaying material body, longing for the perfection of the Platonic heaven, until it once again escapes the imperfections of the material world.

What we find disgusting today is a reflection of Plato's own aversion toward the decaying body and his worship of the eternal soul. Many of the things that elicit disgust in us today are those that remind of our imperfect material existence, our entrapment in our decadent and deteriorating bodies. As Nussbaum puts it, disgust is an escape mechanism, a way of turning "our aversion to death into a strange symbolic project of transcendence."[56]

Social Disgust

Although our culture's negative portrait of the body emerged as a way of regulating behavior, our primitive disgust reactions—such as our instinctive recoil at the sight or smell of cockroaches, vomit, or rotten meat—are not inherently regulatory or disciplinary; rather, they are a basic survival response that informs us that we are in too close proximity to material that could potentially kill us or make us sick.

At some point in the history of civilization, however, our primitive disgust system was co-opted by our value system as a tool for regulating the behavior of other people in our community or social group.[57] For example, most Westerners regard culturally disvalued practices, such as cannibalism, incest, self-amputation, and body snatching, as repugnant. Cultivating disgust in each other in response to culturally disvalued practices is a convenient tool for discouraging each other from engaging in them.

Let's refer to primitive disgust repurposed as a tool for regulating culturally disvalued practices as "social disgust." The regulatory and disciplinary role of social disgust is so ingrained in us that we are prone to jump to the conclusion that the practices we abhor are morally wrong. Yet disgust is a notoriously unreliable guide to morality. Many of the practices we perceive as repulsive are just life as usual in other cultures. For example, the Ptolemaic people in ancient Egypt, the most famous of whom is Cleopatra, often married their brothers or sisters, or nieces or nephews. Melanesians of Papua New Guinea and the Wari people of Brazil used to honor their dead by eating them. The Dani people of West Papua used to expect the women and children of deceased family members to cut off chunks of their own fingers as a sacrifice to the spirits, and the Malagasy people of Madagascar are still regularly digging up the remains of their deceased relatives, so they can clean them, dress them in their favorite clothes, and take them on a walk around town.

Because we find such practices repulsive, we mistakenly leap to the conclusion that they are morally wrong.[58] But when asked to provide a reason for their alleged wrongfulness, we are hard pressed to come up with one. A common reason against incest is it increases the risk of birth defects. However, this isn't a good reason to think incest is morally wrong, as having intercourse with a sibling or parent doesn't increase the risk of birth defects. The risk emerges only if you have children with them.

Not all practices that diverge from our own elicit social disgust. For example, we don't find it repugnant that Greek kids don't hide their baby teeth under their pillows and wait for them to be swapped for cash by a fairy but instead toss them onto the roof and make a wish for strong and healthy grown-up teeth. Strange, yes, but not disgusting. So, what's special about the practices we find disgusting? The short answer is that we tend to feel repulsed by social practices we associate with our greatest fears: our own animal nature, our sexuality, our bodily excretions, our decadent and imperfect body, and its gradual decay and eventual demise.[59] So the ancient image of the body as impure, unrefined, and transient and the soul as pure, noble and true also lies at the root of social disgust.

These fears continue to be exploited by conservative and religious groups around the globe to stigmatize and outlaw practices such as homosexuality, miscegenation, masturbation, and premarital sex—practices most people don't naturally frown upon.

Interestingly, even though intellectual and artistic practices tend to be seen as finer and purer than bodily activities, they too can elicit social disgust. In the early twentieth century, the Danish physician and art critic Carl Julius Salomonsen started a critical movement against modern art. This was in the early days of modernism. Salomonsen found modern art repugnant. He was so appalled by it that he became convinced that the artists had contracted a contagious mental illness, which had caused them to become obsessed with "distorted" and "hideous" forms.[60]

Although repulsive practices are the primary focus of social disgust, people and groups can also become the focus when we associate them with practices that we find repulsive. The stronger our association between a given practice and sexual perversion, animal decay, or bodily destruction, the more likely we are to project our disgust toward the practice onto people we associate with that practice. This is the reason we commonly refer to perverts as "creepy."

The 2009 BBC documentary "My Car Is My Lover," which is part of the documentary series *Strange Love*, features so-called mechaphiles, men who have romantic or sexual relationships with their cars.[61] One of the mechaphiles, Edward Smith, who lives in Yelm in Washington State, has never had a lasting relationship with another human. His only human sexual experience was a one-night stand with a woman in San Francisco. But he is sexually attracted to cars and regularly has sex with them. It's the forms and curves of cars that turn him on, though he is also attracted to the orifices of cars. "The tailpipe represents the car's anus in more ways than one. And it's just like having anal sex with the car," Smith tells the incredulous BBC reporter. "The final ecstasy is when you are about to explode in love, you just place it in there, maybe grease it up a little, with some lubricant, it's fantastic, the sensation is unbelievable." But it's not just about the sex. Smith alleges that he has been in love with his 1974 VW Beetle named "Vanilla" since 1982.

The repulsive nature of Smith's interactions with his car makes most of us view Smith as a creep. Regarding a person as creepy does not entail blaming him. Disgust is not essentially bound up with blame or condemnation. If we feel anything other than disgust for mechaphiles like Smith, it's more likely to be pity, which the eighteenth-century Swiss philosopher Jean-Jacques Rousseau argued was the basis of our compassion for others.[62] But as philosopher Richard Boyd has pointed out, pity isn't a purely positive emotion.[63] To pity someone is to be aware of their unfortunate condition while at the same time deeming yourself lucky that their burden is not your own.

Contempt

In ordinary language, contempt is often subsumed under hate. When we speak of hate speech, group hate, hate groups, hate crimes, hate campaigns, and hate mail, this is the sense of "hate" we have in mind. This may also be the sense of "hate" that is most salient in the evergreen "I hate your face" memes.[64] Call this the "wide sense of 'hate.'" When not otherwise specified, I will use "hate" in its narrow sense.

It's sometimes said that where hate (in its narrow sense) presents its target as powerful, contempt presents its target as "low," or unworthy of respect. Disrespect, on this view, is a component of contempt but not hate. But that's not right. We take the judgmental high road in both hate and contempt. To see this, consider this scenario: Beatrice contemns her next-door neighbor for his greed, but she hates Jason, the youth soccer coach who raped her 12-year old daughter.[65] If disrespect were only a component of contempt but not of hate, then we should expect Beatrice to have more respect for the grown man who raped her child than for her greedy neighbor. But that's ludicrous. Clearly, Beatrice doesn't regard her child's rapist as worthy of more respect than her pitiful neighbor. She disrespects both of them, but her disrespect for the miscreant who assaulted her daughter is indefinitely greater than her disrespect for her measly neighbor.

When we hate someone or have contempt for them, we judge, or condemn, them for their flawed character. Judging a person on account of their flawed character is a form of disrespect.[66] If you hate your classmate Simone (in the narrow sense of "hate"), you condemn her for her perceived malevolent or evil character traits. If you have contempt for her, by contrast, then you condemn her for her perceived "lowly" character traits, for instance, her greed, cowardice, or lack of willpower.

Contempt is social disgust's judgmental cousin. In contempt, we look down on a person for vices they possess—vices tied to repugnant practices, such as gluttony, sloth, lust, pride, envy, greed, and wrath. It should not come as a surprise that many of the vices that elicit contempt are thought of as "deadly sins" in Christianity and other religions.[67] They are the motivating force behind practices that tends to elicit disgust in us, for example, binge eating, alcohol overconsumption, masturbation, promiscuity, prostitution, perversion, or whatever else reminds us of our own animal nature, sexuality, bodily excretions, or decadent body.

To condemn people for their vices is in part to disrespect them— we regard those we hold in contempt as inferior to ourselves.[68] When the disrespect component of contempt is dehumanizing, so is the contempt. Likewise, contempt that has critical disrespect as a component is itself critical. Whereas dehumanizing contempt fails to recognize the inherent dignity of its target, critical contempt is not in the business of questioning people's dignity.

Dehumanizing contempt is often the driving force behind rape, although—as we will see in Chapter 6—dehumanizing hatred is the basis of "corrective" rape. Because it robs the victim of her entitlement to the kind of respect owed to all people, dehumanizing contempt is never morally defensible.[69] It was contempt of this ilk that Kant had in mind when he maintained that contempt is incompatible with the principle of respect:

> The respect that I have for others or that another can require from me (*observantia aliis praestanda*) is therefore recognition of a dignity (*dignitas*) in other human beings, that is, of a worth that has no price, no equivalent for which the object evaluated (*aestimii*) could be exchanged—Judging someone to be worthless is contempt.[70]

But contempt need not deprive its target of the kind of respect owed to all people. Critical contempt, the less objectionable form, sees its target as "low" in a way that has no bearing on her entitlement to recognition respect. A literary critic, for example, might see you as inferior to other "finer" novelists on account of your perceived lack of sophistication and elite education and your breach of time-honored literary principles. Yet if she recognizes your inherent worth as a person, her contempt is critical, not dehumanizing. Elitism, however appalling, is therefore not inherently dehumanizing.

Critical contempt is often limited to only certain aspects of a person's character. This is what philosopher Aaron Ben-Ze'ev has in mind when he writes:

> The inferiority associated with contempt does not have to be global: it can merely refer to a few aspects of the other person's

characteristics. I can feel contempt for another person's accent or looks but still realize her general superior status.[71]

As we will see in Chapter 3, whereas dehumanizing contempt is never morally defensible, critical contempt can sometimes be morally appropriate.

Hate

Personal hate is bound up with actions that are seen as particularly wicked, as illustrated by this passage from Simon Hall's novel *Evil Valley*:

> Thank you so much for your email. It's good to know that I'm not alone in what I'm suffering. He beat me again tonight. My hands are shaking and I can feel the bruises spreading across my ribs. I'm just about holding back the tears but they keep leaking and dripping onto the keyboard. I don't know whether I want to cry, or scream and shout and hit out. I just don't know what I'm going to do.
>
> He has gone to sleep after another two bottles of red wine, and the kicking he's just given me. He sounds really peaceful and content.
>
> I hate him, I hate him, I hate him, I hate him, I hate him, I hate him, I HATE HIM!![72]

The main character's hatred for her partner is fueled by his physical abuse. She hates him; she doesn't merely resent him, because she realizes that his repeated abuse of her is rooted in his sinister character traits.[73]

Hate of this kind is backward-looking. One of its focal points is an assumed past evildoing. But hate can also be aimed at people who haven't yet acted on their dark traits. Envisioning that they might well do so in the future can elicit hatred toward them. Hatred of this kind is forward-looking.

Regardless of whether it's backward- or forward-looking, hate has a dual focus. One is the target's envisioned past or future evildoing.[74] The other is the target's assumed malevolent or evil character. When we hate someone, we resent them (or have indignation for them) for their envisioned past or future evildoing, and we judge, or condemn, them for their assumed malevolence.

As we have seen, to judge, or condemn, a person for her vices is to disrespect her for possessing those vices, where the disrespect can be either dehumanizing or critical. But if we disrespect both the people we hate and those we hold in contempt, why then does it often feel as if we look down on the people we contemn but not the ones we hate?

The different "feels" of hate and contempt stem from a difference in the kinds of vices the two attitudes bring into focus. Malevolence, the vice that is central to hatred, is associated in our minds with power and danger, capacities that call for apprehensive respect and sometimes even full-out admiration.

Although apprehensive respect is not conceptually linked to critical or dehumanizing disrespect, the former can mask the effects of the latter when both are mentally present. This is because the character traits that elicit apprehensive respect very often are associated with admirable traits like ingenuity, imagination, and dexterity. We will look closer at this aspect of hate in the next three chapters.

There is more to the feeling of hate (when felt at all) than the sensation rooted in the intricate interplay between apprehensive respect and disrespect. When asked to describe hate, people often use adjectives like "heated," "explosive," "extreme," "intense," "obsessive," and "all-consuming."[75]

We need to be careful about how we interpret these ordinary-language descriptions, however. Hate can indeed be all-consuming. This correlates with an increase in norepinephrine and dopamine signaling in the brain's prefrontal cortex. This is also what happens after a big hit of methamphetamine or cocaine. Like the stimulants, all-consuming love and hate can raise your self-confidence and motivate you to act impulsively, for instance, take drastic measures to alleviate the lingering pain of yearning or injustice. This rise in self-confidence and the drive toward action can, in turn, motivate you to overcome enormous obstacles to be near the other person, whether it's in order to kiss and hug them, tell them off, fight them, or kill them.

It is also true that hate can feel painfully intense, as suggested by its popular depictions, but bear in mind that the felt intensity of an emotion is an unreliable indicator of its magnitude. Emotions differ from pain and pleasure in this respect. If the pain you experience in response to a particular stimulus is felt as more intense than the pain I experience in response to the same stimulus, then you are in greater pain than I am. But if we both hate our classmate Simone, but you feel the hatred more intensely than I do, that doesn't entail that you hate Simone more than I do. My somewhat blunted hatred could present Simone as more malevolent, powerful and dangerous than your more intensely felt hatred.

Why is that? Well, we know that long-lasting emotions can go under the radar, especially when we have something more pressing on our mind. Say you just fell madly in love with Alice (while still hating Simone). You would likely be preoccupied with emotions and thoughts related to your infatuation, and this could well temporarily push your hatred of Simone down below the level of conscious awareness. But despite its lack of felt intensity, your hate hasn't vanished, as if by magic. So felt intensity is not always a good indicator of magnitude.

But there is another reason that we shouldn't treat felt intensity as a reliable guide to magnitude. Some people are naturally more prone to emotional arousal than others. One and the same emotional stimulus could induce the exact same physiological changes in you and me, and yet our brains could interpret the induced changes in radically different ways, perhaps owing to differences in our past experiences. As a result, you might go ballistic while I motionlessly watch you in utter bewilderment.

Emotions so intense that they nearly consume us are widely regarded as irrational, or pathological, because they are likely to interfere with our ability to function optimally.[76]

In my opinion, this common sentiment isn't exactly right. Intense grief following a traumatic loss can put you out of commission, but that doesn't make it irrational or pathological. In fact, allowing yourself to properly grieve a traumatic loss can spare you from a delayed, aggravated response down the road. Grief is not regarded as a clinical pathology unless it turns into complicated grief, which is grief that persists for years without appearing to wane in intensity over time.

While all-consuming emotions need not be irrational, emotions that continue to interfere with your ability to function optimally are irrational. But irrationality isn't reserved for the antagonistic emotions. In fact, even emotions with a positive valence, such as compassion, love, gratitude, self-confidence, enthusiasm, pride, optimism, and cheerfulness can be irrational or pathological. So, let's not leap to the conclusion that hate is inherently irrational because it *can* have corrosive effects on the hater's well-being or ability to function optimally. As we will see in Chapter 3, hate can sometimes be a rational and morally defensible emotion.

The idea that hatred is sometimes rational and morally defensible is highly controversial. Hate is one of the least celebrated emotions today, and in cultures built on Christianity or traditional Eastern religions, it's socially taboo. We see this in sayings like "Whatever the question, hate is never the answer," "Haters are on the fast train to hell," "Hate is the grisly mask of shame," "Hate is a projection of a feeble mind," "Holding on to hate is like grasping a hot coal with the intent of throwing it at someone else; you are the one who gets burned."

Hate is sometimes frowned upon because haters often become vengeful. Nussbaum has in several works argued that anger is never justified.[77] Anger, as she uses the term, encompasses all the anger-type emotions: simple anger, resentment, indignation, outrage, envy, and hate. What she says about anger thus applies with equal force to hate. Outrage in response to social injustice is the exception that proves the rule, according to Nussbaum. This is also what she calls "transition anger." She admits that the latter can be socially useful in mobilizing support for a worthwhile cause, and that it can be justified in ideal circumstances where we humans are much less prone to become vindictive. But circumstances are rarely, if ever, ideal, and she doubts that we can willfully prevent vengeance from impregnating our outrage when we are witnesses to social injustice in real life.

Nussbaum's argument for this view rests on the assumption that anger-type emotions such as anger, resentment, and hate are conceptually tied to retaliation, which she argues serves no purpose other than multiplying suffering.

I am sympathetic to Nussbaum's position that retaliatory responses to wrongdoing are pointless at best and deeply immoral at worst. I am also at one with Nussbaum in thinking that anger-type emotions often are tainted with retaliatory desires. But, as I will argue in Chapter 3, the anger-type emotions are not *conceptually* tied to retaliation. Contrary to conventional wisdom, when confined to the realm of intimate relationships, even hate can have worthwhile ends. But before drawing the contours of this argument, I will explore the norm-regulating function of hate in our personal relationships.

2 | IT'S A THIN LINE BETWEEN LOVE AND HATE

WHEN WE HATE THE PEOPLE WE LOVE

We expect a lot from strangers, for instance, that the valet guy doesn't steal our wheels, that the babysitter doesn't abduct our children, and that the barista at Starbucks doesn't pour poison in our white chocolate mocha. But romantic relationships, friendships, parent-child relationships, and other varieties of intimate relationships introduce a whole new dimension to what we expect and demand of each other.

It's against the backdrop of our intimate relationships that we sign prenups, make custody agreements, write wills, and open joint bank accounts. But most of our interactions in intimate settings are shaped not by contractual agreements but by our preferences, core values, and prior expectations about how other people should behave. No wonder people embark on relationships with clashing concepts of what count as oversights, slights, betrayals, or unforgivable sins. Our differing expectations, preferences, and core values in relationships, even when they fall into the realm of the reasonable, create ample opportunities for misunderstandings to arise and escalate into shouting matches and long-standing blistering hostility.

It is no surprise, then, that antagonistic emotions, such as disrespect, resentment, hate, and contempt, can cause long-term damage in intimate settings that far exceeds the immediate and short-term emotional impact.[1] But, as we will see, the antagonistic emotions are not equally detrimental. Our intimate relationships can survive the torrents of hate and resentment, but they crumple under the deluge of disrespect and contempt.

Up-Close and Personal

What makes a social relationship count as personal? Your fleeting social encounter with the driver who cuts you off on the highway or the stranger you happen to share the elevator with is clearly not personal. But even if we set aside our short-lived relationships with random strangers, most of our social relationships are impersonal. For example, most of us do not have personal relationships with our local barista, our hairstylist, our kid's babysitter, our teachers, or our cleaning lady.

Philosopher Hugh LaFollette has argued that a series of repeated interactions with another person counts as a personal relationship just when "each person [intentionally] relates to the other as a unique individual; the other does not merely fill a role or satisfy a need."[2]

The repeated interactions that transpire between you and your hairstylist do not constitute a personal relationship. Your hairstylist contentedly kills an hour washing, trimming, and styling your hair once a month, but he doesn't do it because he cares about you or is foolishly altruistic. He is in it for the money. By washing, trimming, and styling your hair, he satisfies one of your needs, and by paying him, you satisfy one of his. You and your stylist are in a transactional, or service, relationship, not a personal one.

Because of how we typically relate to one another as spouses, relatives, friends, coworkers, and neighbors, these kinds of relations are not typically a matter of merely filling a role or satisfying a need. They tend to be personal. But simply being related by blood, marriage, co-ownership, workplace, or address doesn't make the connection personal. Suppose you choose to enter into a transactional relationship with your estranged father because he is the only remaining hairstylist in town. He trims and styles your hair, and you hand over the cash, but shun all other intentional encounters. In the envisaged scenario, your parent-child relationship isn't personal.

Some social relationships are both service-oriented and personal. If, for example, you are a student in a large lecture course with only nominal professor-student face-to-face interaction, your relationship with the professor is bound to be impersonal and service-oriented. But if a teacher is able to relate to his students as unique individuals and not merely as students, these interactions may count as personal, while also being service-oriented.

Our social relationships can also be characterized in terms of how close they are. This feature of relationships is reflected in sundry English idioms. If you have quarreled with your family and are no longer in touch with them, we can say that you are "estranged." If you build a "wall" between you and your partner, we can say that you are emotionally "distant" or "detached." And we habitually divide our friends up into those who are "close" and those who are more "distant." Likewise, it makes good sense to ask others whether they are "close" with, say, their siblings or cousins.

Whereas *feeling* close to someone doesn't require reciprocity, actually *being* close to them does, at least as far as capable adults are concerned. When friends do their part to try to achieve closeness with us, we say that they are good or close friends. But what does it mean to be close?

A popular way of thinking of close relationships borrows inspiration from the theory of virtue and human flourishing developed by the Ancient Greek philosopher Aristotle. According to Aristotle, close relationships, for example, close friendships, require a strong mutual commitment to acting virtuously and a shared willingness to encourage one another to become virtuous agents.[3] If your friend tells you in confidence that he is having an extra-marital affair, which he is not prepared to end, although he doesn't want his marriage to suffer, it's your job to knock some moral sense into him and encourage him to promptly end the affair and stay faithful to his wife going forward. The value of close friendships, on this time-honored view, lies in the opportunities they bring for moral transformation and growth.

This makes good sense in theory. But the question is whether it is possible for all of us to undergo significant moral improvements, and whether a mutual pursuit of moral perfection is a necessary or even a desired mark of a close relationship.

It's doubtful that we all have the capacity for significant moral enhancement. But even if we do, striving for moral perfection need not be a desirable mark of a close relationship.

Aristotle defined moral perfection, or perfect virtue, rather broadly. To be morally perfect, he argued, is to optimize eudaimonia, or human flourishing.[4] Aristotle thus conceived of the virtues as those character traits that are necessary for us to flourish, such as honesty, courage, temperance, generosity, having a good temper, having a sense of justice, being a good friend, and having a sense of humor. For Aristotle, to act virtuously, or with moral perfection, is not simply a matter of doing something to an extreme degree. Rather, it's a matter of doing whatever optimizes your flourishing. For example, to act courageously is to act with exactly the amount of courage that is needed for you to flourish. Acting courageously even when doing so is foolish runs counter to moral perfection. Say you see someone jump out in front of a fast-approaching train. Aristotle would say that jumping onto the tracks in the hope of saving the other person would be foolish, as the chance of making it out alive is miniscule.

It's questionable, however, whether Aristotle is right that a close relationship requires a commitment to strive for moral perfection. Suppose you are standing on a platform, waiting for a train. The platform is empty except for a parent with a young child some hundred yards away. Suddenly the child falls down on the tracks just as a freight train is fast approaching. You are too far away to get to the child. The parent is close enough, but she doesn't do anything. She doesn't even move. She just watches as the child is killed by the train.

You initially assume that the parent must have been paralyzed by shock. But then you learn that she did nothing because she quickly judged that jumping onto the tracks most likely would get both of them killed. As a good Aristotelian, the parent is committed to acting virtuously, and in this case jumping onto the tracks to try to save the child would have been foolish, not virtuous.

But is the perfectly virtuous parent really a good parent? I have my doubts. On its modern conception, a good relationship is a close relationship, which means that there are circumstances in which you must be willing to put the other person's interests ahead of your own, even if it's risky or foolish to do so.

A good relationship, on its modern conception, furthermore demands being open to the possibility of accepting the other person the way they are without trying to correct their flaws. This is also true of friendships. An unwavering commitment to educating friends who fail on the moral scale makes you less of a friend. If, say, you encourage your philandering friend to stay faithful to his wife on purely moral grounds, that would seem to suggest that the pursuit of virtue is more important to you than doing what's in your friend's best interest.

But your uncompromising pursuit of virtue doesn't make you a good friend. By modern standards, good friendships are guided by a mutual desire to promote each other's interests, not unbending moral maxims.

There may even be cases in which acting immorally can make you a better friend than aiming at sainthood. Imagine: just short of eighteen, your best friend, Morgan, who has just been unceremoniously dumped by her boyfriend of three years, calls you crying, begging you to come over. The sticky issue is that your dad has absolutely forbidden you to hang out with her because of her drug problem, so you tell your dad that you are going to your mom's house. Your lack of honesty may count as a character flaw, but your imperfection doesn't make you a bad friend. Quite on the contrary. Perfection of character can compromise friendship and be a fast track to loneliness.

Aristotle's vision of friendship as involving a mutual pursuit of moral perfection is thus irreconcilable with our current understanding of what makes for a good friendship.

Parents too must relinquish moral high grounding. For example, being a good parent can require periodically lying to your children. I am not just talking about the Tooth Fairy and Santa Claus. When my daughter was a preschooler, tantrums and hissy fits were her most powerful nuclear weapons. To keep them from detonating, I'd lie with a straight face: "No, we can't go to the Magic House. It's only open when it's raining," "No, you can't have any chocolate, you ate the rest of it yesterday, and it's sold out at the store," "No, honey, the Starbursts and gummy bears have gone bad, and the chocolate chip cookies in the cupboard are the ones only grown-ups can eat," "Polly Bird isn't with us anymore, sweet pea, she wanted to go home to her mommy and daddy and little sister," "You silly you, I didn't throw out your drawings, that's not a trash can, it's called a recycling bin, Mommy's special saving cabinet," "Your old tool bench from when you were two? Yeah, hate to break it to you, baby girl, but the cats tore it to pieces. There was literally nothing left."

I'd steal as well. I remember sneak-donating stuffed animals to Goodwill because my preschooler was a hoarder, and convincing her to let go of worn-out fluffies like Giant Golden Retriever, Care Bear, Curious George, or Giant Shark would take a team of psychiatrists and a straitjacket.

Philosophers Dean Cocking and Jeanette Kennett make similar points about the incompatibility of close relationships and moral perfection. They write:

> It would be foolish to suggest of those cases where friendship moves us against competing moral reasons that we thereby exhibit a lesser friendship or realize less of the good of friendship. It might not be morally praiseworthy of me to spin a tale to my colleague and break my promise to her so that my friend and I can go off to the movies together. But it is hardly the case that I am not being a good friend here. I might be a perfectly good friend. I might just not be a perfectly moral one. And the nature of the interest I have in her as my friend, and the reasons I have to act as

her friend which I do not share with others, such as, for example, my colleague, is more naturally explained by my special receptivity to her direction than by any distinctively moral concern for her welfare.[5]

Our willingness to brush aside our moral scruples for the sake of helping our close friends, family members, or significant others lies at the heart of the old adage that a friend will help you move house, but a good friend will help you move a body. Needless to say, the encapsulated piece of wisdom is not to be taken literally. While being a good friend can require acting contrary to virtue's demands, it doesn't oblige you to help your friend get away with murder.[6]

In *Personal Relationships*, LaFollette develops an account of close relationships that weakens the concept's historical tie to the shackles of moral perfection without demanding lawlessness and preposterous self-sacrifice.[7] According to LaFollette, close relationships are marked by a "mutual [robust] desire to promote the other's interests."[8] A desire is robust if it has sufficient motivational strength and duration.

I'm going to tweak LaFollette's definition shortly. But first a word on the notion of an interest. In common parlance, our interests are those activities we take pleasure in performing. For example, if I say, "Sebastian's main interests are poetry and knitting," you will likely take me to mean that Sebastian enjoys reading poetry and knitting.

But this isn't the sense of "interest" that is relevant to our current pursuits. Rather, your interests are those states of affairs that further your overall flourishing, or well-being. Performing an unpleasant activity can be in your best interest by promoting your overall well-being. Colonoscopies are notoriously unpleasant, but people voluntarily submit to the invasive procedure because it may contribute to their overall well-being, which includes catching colon cancer early.

Your interests are not just about you. If you and your good friend have a mutual, robust desire to further each other's interests, your interests become intertwined. If you have an interest in getting help moving a body, but your friend would become deeply traumatized were she to come to your assistance, then it's not in *your* interest to solicit *her* help, though it could still be in your interest to solicit someone's help.

LaFollette's definition is a good first approximation, but it needs tweaking. If close relationships are marked by a *mutual* desire to promote the other person's interests, many relationships that are naturally thought of as close are not all that close after all.[9] Infants, for example, have a highly diminished capacity for forming desires to promote other people's interests. So, if we take LaFollette's definition at face value, parent-infant relationships would lack closeness. So would our relationships with severely demented relatives or gravely disabled friends or partners.

To avoid these undesirable outcomes, let's stipulate that we can have close relationships with people with a diminished capacity for forming robust desires to promote other people's interests, despite the lack of reciprocity. This tweak is in line with LaFollette's suggestion that a close relationship just is a loving relationship. In my view, this observation is spot on. Indeed, as I will argue below, love involves an attitude of closeness.

Another issue plagues LaFollette's definition of a close, or loving, relationship, however. Say Jordan and her new love interest, Kenny, have a mutual, robust desire to promote each other's interests but are unaware of the mutuality of that desire. By LaFollette's definition, they are in a close relationship. Intuitively, though, people have a close relationship only if the reciprocity is shared knowledge between them.[10] Further, as philosopher Mark Alfano has argued, the shared knowledge requirement is not satisfied by each person obtaining the information about the other person from a third party.[11] The shared knowledge must be based, at least in part, on first-person evidence.

LaFollette's account of close relationship faces a more serious issue. It entails that you and your enemy could harbor a mutual robust desire to promote each other's interests as a result of coercion by a third party. Say a psychopath is threatening to shoot both of you if you don't do your best to further each other's interests. As you don't want to die, you go out of your way to promote each other's interests. Yet this doesn't make you and your enemy close friends.

We can avoid this outcome by requiring that the desire to promote the other person's interests be grounded in a matching core value, for instance, the other person's flourishing. Your core values are the values that matter to who you are—your self or identity. I value spending time with my daughter, and I value having vanilla ice cream for dessert. Although I can clearly exercise agency around vanilla ice cream, for example, by freely choosing to have it for dessert, being able to make this choice is not important to who I am. So, unlike being able to spend time with my daughter, being able to have vanilla ice cream for dessert is not among my core values.

This requirement on closeness makes the notion closely bound up with a valuational account of the self (or a person's identity) along the lines of the account of agency advanced by philosopher John Doris in his 2015 monograph *Talking to Our Selves*.[12] Our core values, we can say, are (partly) constitutive of our "selves." You assert your "self" when you perform an action that is an expression of your core values.[13]

The objects of our core values range from what we already have or do, such as our ability to spend time with friends or exercise our rights to life, liberty, and the pursuit of happiness, to what we want to do or have in the future, such as getting a professional degree, having children, or traveling around the world. Although we are not always aware of what our core values are or what place they occupy in our hierarchy of values, they often reveal themselves in the stories we tell when asked to explain or defend ourselves.[14] For example, if asked why I quit smoking, I may refer to the evidential link between smoking and lung cancer, which reveals that staying healthy is among my core values.

The notion of a core value should be kept apart from that of a (mere) preference, which is also a kind of value. You might prefer wearing dress pants to jeans at work but prefer jeans to dress pants at home. In more technical parlance, we can say that your (mere) preferences are hierarchically ordered situation-dependent values. They are *not* part of what makes you you.

Although our core values can have the same content as our desires, intentions, preferences, and needs, they are distinct attitudes. A heroin addict trying to quit his addiction wants and intends to get more of the drug and prefers heroin to meth or coke, but getting more of the drug is not among his core values.

Doris suggests irreplaceability as a criterion for determining whether you truly value something, or whether it is merely hard to resist it or a convenient way of satisfying some general need.[15] As he puts it:

> If the object of desiring can be replaced without loss—if life can go on pretty much as it did—then that object is not an object of value. [. . .] Significant human relationships [. . .] aren't supposed to be so easily interchangeable: the jilted and bereaved may learn to love again, but some of what they lose may seem quite irreplaceable.
>
> The non-fungibility requirement could also be erected as a bulwark against the somewhat unattractive thought that "mere needs" are values. If alternate modes of nutrition were readily available to humans, it might be that people could forgo eating with no loss; eating is the object of desire, yet doesn't have the "specialness" associated with value. (That gourmets, gourmands, and other foodies could not switch without loss makes the point; they do value eating.) In the end, a mere needs exclusion might not be mandatory; in conditions of scarcity, the objects associated with mere needs can start to seem pretty special.[16]

Although Doris doesn't employ the notion of a core value, what he says here seems to be more pertinent to core values than "trivial" values. Suppose you are hungry and heat some instant Mac and Cheese in the microwave. Even though being able to satisfy your need for food is among your core values, eating Mac and Cheese is not, as some other food could easily have satisfied your need. Or suppose you have an overpowering desire for sex and have a one-night stand with someone you right-swiped on Tinder. Although being able to meet your desire for sex may be among your core values, having sex with your one-night stand is not, as someone else could have satisfied your desire.

Our core values do sometimes change. For example, they may change when our personality or character changes. If you become more introverted, then spending time on your own may become more important to who you are. (We will have a closer look at personality and character in Chapters 3–5).

But changes in your core values can also be the product of what I call a "value adaptation," that is, an adaptation of your core values to fit the limitations of your circumstances. Say having children as soon as you feel financially secure has been one of your priorities in life for years. But time passes, and eventually your chances of becoming pregnant or adopting a child look slimmer and slimmer, until one day it dawns on you that perhaps becoming a parent isn't all that important to you after all.

Such radical shifts in our core values reflect our ability to adapt to our situation. People whose core values are shaped by their circumstances are more likely to be happy with what they have than those of us who hold dear an unachievable childhood dream.

Although value adaptations can change your personality and character, some value adaptations are insignificant. For example, spending time with your spouse may be among your core values until your marriage starts falling apart. But this change in your core values is unlikely to cause any significant change to your personality or character.

Value adaptation is akin to what is known as "preference adaptation."[17] Sour grapes is a prime example of the latter. In the ancient Greek storyteller Aesop's renowned fable "The Fox and the Grapes," from which the expression "sour grapes" originates, a fox finds himself unable to reach the sweet, juicy grapes, which he much prefers to the strawberries that are easily accessible to him. To cope with his frustration, the fox chooses to conceive of the sweet, juicy grapes as sour and distasteful, and on one interpretation of the fable, this change of mindset alters his preferences.

Whether preference adaptation is rational, for example, by being conducive to your overall well-being, has been the subject of substantial debate.[18] In her 2015 book *The Minority Body*, philosopher Elizabeth Barnes discusses the Stockholm Syndrome as an example of preference adaptation that is widely agreed to be irrational:

> [I]n the phenomenon known as Stockholm syndrome, victims of kidnapping or hostage-taking come to prefer being kidnapped—they come to believe that their kidnapper is really on a noble mission, and has rescued them, and that their kidnapping is thus of great benefit to them, etc. It's fairly easy to see how beliefs and preferences such as this could arise. The kidnap victim is put in a traumatic situation from which they see no possibility of escape, so simply in order to cope they (subconsciously or otherwise) lose the desire to escape. Such coping mechanisms may well be an admirable facet of human psychology, but we'd be very reluctant to say that the preferences of a person with Stockholm syndrome are rational, or serve as evidence that being a kidnap victim is a good way to live."[19]

Fans of Álex Pina's television show *La Casa de Papel* (English title: *Money Heist*) (2017–present) may take issue with this assessment of preference adaptation in the case of Stockholm syndrome, as one of the hostesses appears to make the right choice in Season 1 when she cuts her ties to her pathetic coworker and joins the kidnappers. But perhaps this isn't a genuine case of Stockholm Syndrome.

A less controversial case of irrational preference adaptation is that of an abused woman who comes to prefer to stay with her spouse because she depends on him financially.

But other cases are not as easily settled. For example, disabled individuals often sincerely assert that they prefer to have the disability they have to not having it. On the face of it, this may seem to be a blatant case of self-deception. But Barnes makes a convincing case for not dismissing the disability-positive testimony of disabled people up front.

Doing so would be an instance of what philosophy Miranda Fricker calls "epistemic injustice."[20]

Parallel questions of rationality can be asked about adaptive core values. Is it rational to downgrade a core value to avoid regret, disappointment or suffering? This is not the time or place to address this issue. Suffice it to say that I suspect that value adaptations can be rational when they are in your best interest and are not mere tools for increasing your short-term happiness.[21]

We are now in a position to offer an account of a close, or loving, relationship.

> Close (or Loving) Relationship
> A personal relationship between two capable adults is close, or loving, just when:
> It is common knowledge between them that they have a robust desire grounded in a matching core value to promote each other's interests.

This definition may at first seem too rigid. If the bar for the robustness, or motivational force, of the desire is set excessively high, then it doesn't appear to allow for weakness of will (*akrasia*), cases where people succumb to desires against their better judgment. When in the grip of weakness of will, we often prioritize purely selfish pleasure over promoting other people's interests. Say you know that keeping your dinner date with your friend Morgan is important to her. Yet overpowered by weakness of will, you cancel last minute, so you can stay on the couch and watch television. Your weakness of will chips away at the closeness of your friendship with Morgan, but does it compromise closeness altogether?

The answer is no. The occasional bout of weakness of will doesn't compromise closeness altogether, as long as you don't make a habit out of it. The reason for this is that a relationship can be close without being perfectly close. Unlike pregnancies, college degrees, and electoral wins, closeness is not an on-or-off matter. It comes in degrees.[22] This is witnessed by expressions such as "Miranda is Carrie's closest friend,"

"Stanford is equally close with all of his siblings," "Our friendship hasn't been very close the past few weeks," "I feel our marriage is closer than it has ever been," "His parents' relationship would have been closer if his mom hadn't cheated on his dad," "Charlotte is not as close with her coworkers as she would like to be," and "Maria and Sam's relationship is close for a relationship between ex-lovers."

In technical parlance, degree concepts are also known as "gradables." Familiar examples of gradables are "extravagant," "rich," "cold," "tall," "frightened," "honest," and "trustworthy." A home that would be extravagant if located in Camden, New Jersey, would probably not be extravagant if located on Fisher Island in Miami.

The question is what it is for one relationship to be closer than another. Take my parental relationship with my teenage daughter Becky and my collegial relationship with my coworker Risto. To say that my relationship with Becky is closer than my relationship with Risto is *not* to say that Becky and I desire promoting each other's interests with more fervor than Risto and I do, because the felt intensity of desires can vary for reasons quite irrelevant to the question of closeness, and most of the time desires operate below the level of conscious awareness and therefore lack any felt intensity. Nor does it mean that Becky and I desire to promote a higher quantity of each other's interests than Risto and I do, because even if Risto and I aren't as close as my daughter and I, we can still want to promote each other's interests, period, not half of them, or one-third.

Rather, when we speak of differences in closeness, we make reference to our internal hierarchy of core values and matching desires. If it isn't practically feasible for me to promote both my daughter's and my colleague's interests, which—we can assume—are of equal importance, and I act on my value priorities, then I choose to prioritize doing what's in my daughter's interest. Say Becky's swim meet is scheduled to take place at the same time as Risto's book signing, that Becky and Risto both have an interest in my attending their events, and that their interests are comparable in importance. In the envisaged scenario, I am off to the swim meet, because when forced to choose, I prioritize Becky's interests over Risto's, even though promoting Risto's interests is also a core value of mine.

For our relationships to count as close, period, we need not put the other person on a pedestal. Closeness merely requires that the mutual desire to promote one another's interests surpasses a certain threshold. Two individuals who differ in height can both correctly be said to be tall. Similarly, two relationships that aren't equally close can both accurately be said to be close, period. How tall a person needs to be to count as tall depends on a comparison class for tallness. At six feet six inches, Michael Jordan is tall for an American man but not for an NBA basketball player. Likewise, how close a relationship must be to count as close, period, depends on the comparison class for closeness. The friendship between Kim Kardashian and Paris Hilton, for example, was at the time of this writing close compared to other celebrity friendships but not when measured against friendships in general.

Intimacy and Privacy

"Intimacy," in one sense, is a euphemism for "sex." I will set aside this meaning of the term here. In its not purely sexual sense, "intimate" is commonly used synonymously with "close." But a relationship can be close without being intimate.[23] This is often true of relationships between people who are both low in attachment anxiety and high in attachment avoidance.[24] Attachment anxiety reflects the degree to which you are inclined to think that your partner cares about you and is prepared to support you and respond to your needs, whereas attachment avoidance reflects the degree to which you depend on spending time interacting with your partner to feel good about yourself. When low attachment anxiety is combined with high attachment avoidance, this is also known as "dismissive-avoidant attachment."[25] People with this attachment style can be apart for long periods of time without fearing that the other person has lost interest in them. More generally speaking, they don't need to spend a lot of time with their partner to feel good about the relationship. Here is a fictive example:

> Closeness without Intimacy
> Felix and Mateo have been in a romantic relationship for three years. They both have low levels of attachment anxiety and high levels of attachment avoidance. It is shared knowledge between them that they have a strong mutual desire based on core values to promote each other's interests. It is also common knowledge between them that it's in both of their interest to spend very little time together as a couple and shun talk about feelings, old flames, or their commitment to each other. They enjoy "Netflix and chill" a couple of times a week, and they like to go out to restaurants, bars, and clubs on weekends but otherwise they prefer to do things on their own. They are both genuinely happy with the relationship as it is.

Felix and Mateo don't experience the distance between them as dull and aching but as welcoming and invigorating. Because of their mutual strong desire based on core values to promote each other's interests, their relationship meets the criteria for closeness. But setting aside the distinctly sexual meaning of "intimacy," it would be ludicrous to insist that their liaison is intimate. According to *The Oxford English Dictionary*, "intimacy" means "closely connected by personal knowledge; characterized by familiarity; very familiar." It is intimacy of this kind that Felix and Mateo don't want in their relationship.

It is widely agreed among relationship researchers that intimacy requires sharing sensitive information—information of the kind that can make us vulnerable to betrayal, denigration, belligerence, or exploitation by the person we confide in or by people they entrust with the information.[26] It's hard to nail down precisely what counts as the sharing of sensitive information—the kind of information that can make you vulnerable. Parading your best holiday shots on Facebook doesn't count.

Revealing aspects of your past that you are deeply ashamed of to your live-in girlfriend does.

The envisaged scenarios lie at the extremes on the vulnerability scale. Many other types of information can make us vulnerable when shared, even non-verbal information, such as allowing your romantic interest to get a memorable glimpse of you performing "Girls Just Wanna Have Fun" in the shower, inhaling six cream-filled doughnuts in one sitting, or walking around naked in your joint living quarters bloated and gassy.

But sensitive information also encompasses information about your greatest fears, your personality, your character, your core values, your expectations, and so on.

Perhaps the most important mark of intimate or private information is that it's shared only with certain people whom we trust to keep it secret. As philosopher Jeffrey Reiman puts it, "The reality of my intimacy with you is constituted not simply by the quality and intensity of what we share, but by its unavailability to others."[27]

In the 1990s psychologist Arthur Aron and colleagues conducted a series of experimental studies to test the assumption that sharing deeply personal information can create a feeling of intimacy.[28] The researchers aimed at showing that it is possible to make paired strangers develop a mutual feeling of intimacy that mirrors real-life intimacy. They theorized that by making couples engage in "sustained, escalating, reciprocal, personalistic self-disclosure," they would expose their vulnerabilities to each other, which would induce a feeling of intimacy.[29]

The paired strangers were given three sets of twelve questions designed to make them divulge increasingly more sensitive information about themselves. Among the questions were: "Given the choice of anyone in the world, whom would you want as a dinner guest?" "Do you have a secret hunch about how you will die?" "What is your most terrible memory?" "Complete this sentence: 'I wish I had someone with whom I could share . . .'," and "If you were to die this evening with no opportunity to communicate with anyone, what would you most regret not having told someone? Why haven't you told them yet?"

The findings showed that the experimental procedure cultivated intimacy similar to real life intimacy. In 2014 Canadian writer Mandy Len Catron and a male acquaintance tried out Aron et al.'s experimental procedure in a bar and ended up falling in love.[30] But, as Catron notes, they weren't strangers but carried out the experiment the first time they met outside of the gym they both went to, and while they fell in love, they didn't become a couple. The loyalty, dependence, and commitment of real relationships, which the experimental procedure isn't designed to cultivate, are likely among the missing ingredients.[31]

Although a relationship can *feel* or *be regarded as* intimate without reciprocity, true intimacy between capable adults is a two-way street. It requires sharing deeply personal information and jointly recognizing that this makes us vulnerable to betrayal, denigration, belligerence, or exploitation by each other and by other people with whom the information could be shared. It further requires jointly recognizing that the information, by default, is not to be shared with others. Finally, both parties must be motivated by core values rather than coercion. The notion of intimacy can thus be glossed as follows:

Intimate Relationship
A personal relationship between two capable adults is intimate just when:
It is shared knowledge between them that they are motivated by core values to routinely share deeply personal information—information which, by default, is meant to be kept between the two of them.

Intimacy, like closeness, is a gradable concept, which means that some relationships are more intimate than others, and that one and the same relationship can fluctuate in intimacy. But relationships needn't be perfectly intimate to count as intimate as long as they surpass a contextually determined threshold.

Not surprisingly, relationships often fall far below the cutoff for true intimacy, despite appearing intimate to at least one of the parties.

A familiar example is the seemingly intimate relationship you form with a coworker, who unbeknownst to you is the office chameleon. Trojan by nature, the office chameleon initially comes off as friendly, caring, and trustworthy—so much so that sooner or later you entrust her with all sorts of private information pertaining to your romantic relationships, family conflicts, occasional bouts of depression, and even your less than flattering opinions about the company's new leadership. But her enchanting seamless exteriors mask a dark core underneath. Her end is self-gain through character assassination. Her strategy is to win your trust and then exploit it to demolish your reputation, adding serendipitous twists to your words if needed. Her incentive is to satisfy her malicious envy of your accomplishments, ambition, or likeability. You become her favorite punching bag because you are a tad too trusting, assuming from the get-go that others have good intentions.

Trust and Trustworthiness

Closeness and intimacy are tied in interesting ways to trust. Unless we are particularly gullible, we don't trust strangers. We trust that fellow drivers on the highway will not crash into us on purpose, that pedestrians we share the sidewalk with will not snatch our bags when we pass them, and that the person in the airplane seat next to us will not kick us if we accidentally move into their designated space. Trust, in this sense, is a belief-like attitude, a kind of prediction or educated guess.[32] It is also trust in this sense we have in mind when we say things like "I trust that you enjoyed your flight in first class." In fact, you might say this to your guest, even if you secretly hope that she didn't.

When we trust strangers to behave in ways that fit certain general patterns, it's not because we assume that they care specifically about *us*, but rather because we have witnessed other people's behavior fitting those patterns in the past or because we believe that this is how we would behave in similar circumstances.

Similarly, we don't tend to care all that much about what *motivates* strangers to behave as we expect them to, as long as they actually behave that way. If, say, you trust that the pedestrians you share the sidewalk with won't snatch your bag when you pass them, and they live up to your expectations, you most likely won't care why they are meeting your expectations.[33] Whether it's because they are morally obedient, blindly follow the rules of cultural etiquette, or are afraid of getting caught doesn't really matter. What matters is that they don't snatch your bag.

This sort of belief-like trust should be kept apart from the kind of emotional trust we direct toward the people we regard as trustworthy— either in general or as engaged in a specific pursuit, say, as engaged in unclogging your toilet, giving your child her measles shot, or servicing your car. I will use the term "unrestricted trust" (or just "trust" for short) to refer to trust directed at people we regard as generally trustworthy and the term "restricted trust" to refer to trust directed at people we regard as trustworthy as engaged in a specific pursuit.

Restricted trust is similar to restricted respect (or restricted admiration) in being directed toward a person occupying a particular role, such as the role of physician, president, or journalist. Trust of this kind has a dual focus: one is the trustee's competence as engaged in the specific pursuit. The other is the trustee's goodwill toward the truster. For example, if you trust your plumber in matters regarding plumbing but not in matters regarding babysitting, this needn't be because you think your plumber doesn't have your and your child's best interests in mind; you may simply distrust your plumber in the babysitter role because you don't regard her as a competent babysitter.

As philosophers Jacobo Domenicucci and Richard Holton have pointed out, there may also be cases in which we trust someone except in certain narrow circumstances.[34] To borrow one of their examples, you might trust your partner except where alcohol is involved. But I wouldn't consider the envisaged scenario a case of restricted trust, unless your partner's drinking is the source of substantial or repeated betrayals of your trust. Rather, as I see it, although trust is always a matter of degree, our notion of *unrestricted* trust accommodates betrayals of trust that are both infrequent and minute. In other words, unrestricted trust needn't be unconditional; it only needs to surpass a certain contextually determined threshold.

Unlike restricted trust, unrestricted trust is focused exclusively on the trustee's goodwill toward the truster. Expecting the trustee to promote your interests, when reasonable, is essential to unrestricted trust.[35] But unrestricted trust also involves optimism that the trustee cares enough about your relationship to be worthy of your trust.

How then are closeness and intimacy tied to trust? If you trust someone unrestrictedly, you expect them to promote your interests when reasonable, which is to say, you expect them to regard your relationship as close. But the converse does not hold. If you expect someone to promote your interests when reasonable, it doesn't follow that you trust them. It only gives you a reason to trust them. For example, your preoccupation with the possibility of betrayal, however unlikely, could easily create difficulties for you in the trust department. There is, however, a straightforward connection between closeness and trust: a close relationship is one built on mutual trust; it's a kind of trust relationship.

In an intimate relationship, we entrust each other with deeply personal information, expecting each other to safeguard it and not use it against us. An intimate relationship is therefore also a trust relationship, but the trust tied to intimacy is of the restricted variety. If you and I have an intimate relationship, then you trust that I safeguard information you entrust me with, and I trust you to safeguard information I entrust you with. But this does not entail that we trust each other unrestrictedly. I can expect you to promote one of my interests, namely, my interest in you not spilling my secrets. But I cannot expect you to have a robust desire based on core values to promote my other interests. For example, I cannot reasonably expect you to care for me if I'm sick, lend me money if I'm broke, or let me crash on your couch if I'm homeless.

In reality, of course, intimate relationships are often close or have some degree of closeness. A troubling yet touching example of a relationship that began with anger and grief but eventually led to intimacy and some level of closeness is that between Hector Black and Ivan

Simpson, the man who murdered Black's daughter.[36] Some time after Simpson was sentenced to prison, Black decided to write to Simpson. He desperately needed to know what had led this man to commit such a meaningless crime. What followed was an exchange of letters, where Black gradually began to understand Simpson's life. He learned that Simpson was born in a mental hospital, and that his mother suffered from schizophrenia and frequently abused Simpson and his siblings. One day Simpson's mother drowned his sister in a swimming pool while he and his older brother were watching. Later his brother began to regularly rape and strangle him to the point of asphyxiation. The regular exchange of letters between Black and Simpson continued long after Black's desire for closure had been satisfied, and little by little the two men got to know each other better than most people. Their relationship had become intimate, and eventually it even reached some degree of closeness.

While intimacy often coincides with closeness, it's not uncommon for intimate relationships to lack closeness. Secret love affairs between people who are not equal on the family front can be highly intimate while lacking in closeness, partly due to the secrecy of the affair and partly due to the incongruence of core values. Mary Godwin's secret love affair with the dreamy, but very married, romantic poet Percy Bysshe Shelley is often depicted as a series of intimate but highly secret meetings at the grave of Mary's suffragette mother, Mary Wollstonecraft. But when Mary became pregnant with Shelley's child, she was mostly left alone while Shelley visited his wife or went out with Mary's stepsister Claire Clairmont, with whom he was rumored to have a new love affair. Shelley evidently didn't have a robust desire to promote Mary's interests in spite of their intimate secrets.

Just as intimate relationships can fail to be close, so close relationships can fall short of being intimate. We have already encountered one such example. Being dismissive-avoidant, Felix and Mateo thrive in a close romantic relationship with limited intimacy. There are many things they don't know about each other but they don't think that knowing a lot about each other is the only way to have a healthy relationship. It is shared knowledge between them that they have a mutual robust desire grounded in core values to promote each other's interests. They really do care about each other. Indeed, they love each other. But the only way they can thrive in a long-term relationship is by keeping couples time to a minimum.

But there are other more mundane examples of close relationships that don't meet the mark of intimacy. Relationships between family members, such as relationships between siblings or between parents and adult children, are sometimes close but less likely to be intimate. Teenage and adult children often share frustratingly little information with their parents, and most of us, it seems, run our opinions, desires, and core values through a depolarizing filter before sharing them with family. I will never forget Nonno's oft-repeated piece of advice: "*Never* talk about money, religion, morality, or politics." This lesson turns out to be conventional wisdom in America. Close to 60 percent of Americans eschew these topics at Thanksgiving dinner, according to one poll.[37] Despite not sharing sensitive information with certain family members, however, we often care deeply about the very same family members, often going to great length to further their interests at the expense of our own.

It's a Thin Line between Love and Hate

Our desire for close and intimate relationships is the psychological cement of human society. Yet these same relationships are also breeding grounds for hatred and contempt. The reason turns on the special glue that obtains between people in close or intimate relationships.[38] For one thing, we have much greater expectations relating to our close and intimate partners, friends, and family members than we do to mere acquaintances and strangers. For another, we enter into intimate and close relationships with radically different expectations. As culture critic Laura Kipnis chronicles in her 2003 book *Against Love*, some expectations are overwhelmingly culturally determined, such as the presumption of fidelity in long-term romantic relationships, but other expectations are rooted in subcultures or idiosyncratic preferences or core values.

When we open ourselves up to a person we trust or go out of our way to further their interests, this makes us dependent on them. We count on them not betraying our trust by exploiting our willingness to open up to them or help them in their personal pursuits. This dependency can be quite unproblematic when the beloved or trusted person is good-natured. But misplaced trust and love can be soul-crushing.

Exploitations of our willingness to entrust others with deeply personal information or setting aside other things to further their ends are so insidious, not only because such behavior testifies to the other person's ill will toward us or their reckless disregard of our interests and rights, but also because it eats away at our humanity, making us more wary of trusting and caring about others. As the saying has it, once bitten, twice shy.

We expect a whole lot more of the people we trust and care about than we do of strangers and mere acquaintances. If you help a stranger carry their groceries to their car or you give them a handout, you likely count on some formal gesture of gratitude, but you don't expect them to reciprocate. But if you do a close friend a favor, you probably expect her to reciprocate, though not necessarily in kind. Similarly, while we don't ordinarily expect strangers or mere acquaintances to visit us if we get sick, feed us if we are starving, or put us up if we are homeless, this is exactly the kind of goodwill we would expect from a close friend or family member.

What we expect of others can have an enormous impact on what we do, and when and how we do what we do: when we leave for work or pick up our children or go to the gym, when and how much we eat, how long we sleep, how we dress, what we cook for dinner, which invitations we accept, whom we hire, whether we stay in a relationship, whom we marry, and whether we have children. Our expectations shape our thoughts, emotions, and dreams: whether we feel anxious or at ease, what we hope for and fear, where we plan to be in the near future, and whom we plan to be there with.

But we enter into romantic coupledom, in-law relationships, friendships, and collegial relations with radically different expectations about issues ranging from which restaurants to go to and how often to visit one another to how we'll split the bill and whether or not to have children.

Imagine you just embarked on a new romantic relationship. Lovelorn as you are, you are counting on seeing your new love interest most days of the week, but your workaholic girlfriend thinks meeting up once a week is plenty. When you text her, you glance at the phone every two seconds just in case she texted back. You obsessively check your phone, even though you are well aware that your girlfriend hardly ever replies until the following day. When you finally agree to meet up, your expectations once again come into conflict. You have gone to her neighborhood the last five times you guys met up. So this time you expect her to come to you, but when you allude to it, she reminds you that it will be more fun to meet up in her neighborhood, because that's where things are happening. The last few times you guys went out, you grabbed the check, no biggie, but this time you count on her paying, and in the long run you expect to split shared expenses 50/50. But your girlfriend has a different outlook. She tells you that each of you should be responsible for an equal percentage of the expenses proportional to your income. Since you make four times as much as she does, she expects the two of you to split shared expenses 80/20 rather than 50/50.

Needless to say, not all of our expectations are reasonable. Some are outright grotesque. Expecting your partner to pick up the bill every single time you guys go out for dinner, even though you both make good money, is preposterous. So is expecting your partner to join you in clearly immoral pursuits. But once you have weeded out the outright unreasonable relationship attitudes, each of you is left with an endless list of seemingly sensible expectations, preferences, and core values that nonetheless clash with those on the other person's list. This is the kind of friction that could easily wreak havoc on any relationship we fathom as close or intimate.

Philosopher Aaron Ben-Ze'ev has made a strong case for the need to compromise in relationships.[39] Compromises require settling for an option that is inferior to one you envisaged or hoped for. Although compromising requires giving up pursuing what you regard as a better and more satisfying end, close and intimate relationships demand relinquishing some of your autonomy. But balancing opposing expectations, preferences, and core values is challenging and sometimes impossible. How do you compromise if you and your partner disagree about whether you want children or a polyamorous relationship?

Unmet expectations, thwarted desires, and compromised core values are a common source of disappointment, hurt feelings, anger, contempt, vindictiveness, and hatred. The more plans and sacrifices we make to accommodate what we anticipate will happen, the more likely we are to respond with outrage when things don't go our way.

If you and I planned to have dinner Wednesday at nine p.m., you may need to rearrange your life in countless ways to be able to stick to the plan. It is because you rely on us having dinner that you hire a babysitter, reschedule a late-night yoga class, pass on the hors d'oeuvres at the retirement reception, and decline the invitation to join your coworkers for a pint of Guinness at the local pub. You have a lot invested in this expectation.

If I cancel last minute for a good reason, you'll be disappointed. If I cancel for no good reason, you'll probably get upset. If I stand you up, you'll most likely resent me, and if I make a habit out of canceling on you or standing you up, there is a good chance that you will hate me, at least a little. Meanwhile I might expect you to be as carefree as me and hate you for making a mountain out of a molehill.

You might insist that these kinds of conflicts can be eliminated in long-term romantic relationships once the involved parties really get to know each other. I am less optimistic. In today's moral grayscale, our conduct within the bounds of our romantic relationships isn't regulated by the kinds of meticulous regulations that govern the conduct of, say, on-duty military officials. Where would you go to find guidelines for proper conduct in a romantic relationship? Local bookstores are littered with self-help books detailing the rules of romance. But the authors of these books don't agree on what the rules are, and even if they did, this would hardly make them the captains of the relationships that need to stay afloat.

The fact is that we enter into romantic relationships with very different expectations, preferences, and core values, and absent any objective guidelines and rules, couples need to create their own rules as the relationship progresses, which requires a lot of negotiating and compromising. But even once we end up agreeing on some basic relationship rules, these rules are unlikely to help regulate our relationship conduct in most of the situations we will eventually find ourselves in. Perhaps you and your partner have agreed to be monogamous. Monogamy means that you are exclusive. But have you specified exactly what each of you means by "exclusive"? Is flirting acceptable? What about long intimate conversations with people of the opposite sex (assuming you identify as heterosexual)? What about close friendships with people of the opposite sex?

Perhaps you think that after years of getting to know each other, you will eventually have a good sense of what behaviors are and are not acceptable within the bounds of your relationship. But this isn't so. The divorce rate testifies to that. Even if you negotiate and compromise and finally come to an agreement about what exclusivity will mean in your relationship, your jointly engineered guidelines only limit behaviors that relate to infidelity. They offer no guidance on all the other aspects of your coupledom, and if you dare lift the thin veil of law and order guiding your relationship behaviors, you will find yourself face to face with a bottomless abyss of uncertainty.

Add to that all the aspects of romantic relationships that are virtually impossible to regulate. You cannot really make rules about emotional investment. Carrie Bradshaw's relationship with Mr. Big in HBO's hit television series *Sex and the City* is a pitiful example of the kinds of hurt unequal emotional investment can lead to. When Carrie helps Big pack for a business trip, Big casually lets her know he might be moving to Paris for six months or a year. This takes Carrie by surprise. When she asks how long he has known this, he reluctantly admits that it has been in the works for a while. Her question to him about their relationship only makes things worse. Big suggests that Carrie could move to Paris but adds that she should only do it for her own sake. Carrie is taken aback when she realizes that Big has no problem just packing up and leaving; he has little to nothing invested in their relationship; to him she is nothing more than a casual fling. Carrie wonders whether the fact that she repeatedly makes herself vulnerable to Big's putdowns means that she is an emotional masochist.

If you take your partner's failure to meet your expectations to reflect their lack of investment in the relationship, their exploitation of your vulnerability, or their betrayal of your trust, it is only natural for you to develop hatred towards them. Had you known better, you would long ago have abandoned your quiescent relationship.

When your hate completely squashes your love for your romantic partner, it can get ugly. It probably doesn't get much uglier than in the 2008 film *Revolutionary Road*, adapted from Richard Yates' 1961 novel of the same name. When Frank confesses his affair to April in the hope of reconciling with her, she responds with contemptuous laughter, "But I don't [love you]. I hate you. You were just some boy who made me laugh at a party once and now I loathe the sight of you."

Toxic relationships like the one depicted in *Revolutionary Road* are also the theme of the Persuaders' famous lyric "It's a thin line between love and hate." When lead singer Douglas "Smokey" Scott laid those vocals down, it was because his girl had sliced him up like cold cuts after he had stepped all over her night after night, until her love had transformed into hate.

You might wonder how unrequited or uneven love can morph into hate in a matter of days, hours, or even minutes. Where does all the mental and physical energy often triggered by unrequited love go? The likely answer is that the vigor that animates unrequited love and the vehemence that invigorates impassioned hate spring from a single source.

Emotional pain is the bitter fruit of unrequited, uneven, and abusive love. The brain processes emotional pain in much the same way that it processes physical pain. In pain processing, the brain's prefrontal cortex performs an appraisal of the cause, manageability, and intensity of the pain. If the source of the pain is deemed indestructible, this can escalate the pain. This is what happens when sadness turns to despair, hopelessness, or depression. Merely believing that you can destroy the cause of the pain can escalate the norepinephrine and dopamine signaling in the brain's prefrontal cortex.[40] The euphoria of cocaine is triggered by exactly this kind of hyperactivation of the brain's norepinephrine and dopamine systems. Enhanced norepinephrine signaling makes you alert and energetic, whereas hyperactivation of the dopamine system makes you go into a pleasurable manic state.

Pain doesn't usually pave the path to ecstasy. But when your brain is flooded with norepinephrine and dopamine, this lessens your pain and prepares you physiologically to eliminate the source of your pain. This is why the pain of unrequited, uneven, or hurtful love can motivate us to make whirlwind attempts to win over the other person, literally injure them or our rivals, or ghost them—in the juvenile hope of rectifying things.

In the Persuaders' famous lyric, Smokey repeatedly returns home to his girl in the early morning hours. His girlfriend greets him with her sweet voice, tends to his needs, and never questions him about his whereabouts. But, as the lyric has it, "The sweetest woman in the world / Can be the meanest woman in the world / If you make her that way, you keep on hurting her." The girl didn't merely pretend to love him. From inside her cocoon, she desperately tried to win over the bastard. But eventually something inside her changed. Driven by a different strategy for removing the cause of her pain, she was now violently fighting it with a vengeance. What motivated her actions was painful love transmuted into hate.

Neuroscientists Semir Zeki and John Paul Romaya looked at the brains of seventeen subjects while they were viewing pictures of people they hated.[41] They found that while hate activated both cortical and subcortical parts of the brain, it didn't activate the brain's fear-processing center. As low self-confidence correlates with fear processing in the brain, the lack of fear processing partially explains why hate is a confidence booster.

The researchers also found that hate correlates with increased activity in neural areas involved in the guidance and planning of action, including parts of the parietal cortex on the top of the brain and prefrontal areas at the forefront of the brain. This is unsurprising, given that hate prepares people for action.

In the subcortical brain, hatred was found to activate areas in the putamen and the insula that are also activated by aggression, contempt, disgust, and, surprisingly, all-consuming romantic love. While this finding may be surprising at first, there is a natural explanation of the link between love and hate. All-consuming obsessive love is often wholly or partially unreciprocated. Unrequited love is an extremely unpleasant state that can easily trigger disgust, hate, and contempt, especially when rivals are part of the picture. So, unrequited love is associated with antagonistic emotions, including hate and contempt.

Zeki and Romaya identified two key differences between love and hate. One difference lies in their oppositional effects on the fear-processing center. Whereas unrequited love tends to cause anxiety, all-consuming hate is more likely to squash the hater's fear and enhance their self-esteem.

The other key difference between love and hate turns on which brain regions become deactivated when we are in the grip of either emotion. Whereas love is known to deactivate cortical brain regions associated with action planning, hate was only found to inhibit an area in the front of the brain known as the "right superior frontal gyrus." Increased activity in this region has been associated with impulse control and action restraint.[42] So, when this part of the brain suspends its operations, which it does when we are consumed by hatred, we are less likely to be in control of our actions and therefore more likely to act impulsively.

Despite these differences between love and hate, the significant overlap between their neural underpinning is likely part of the story behind the seamless transition from love to hate. While unequal invest-ment in the relationship, exploitations of vulnerability, and betrayals of trust can extinguish our love and leave hate in its place, hate can also swap places with love because we are frightened by the risks associated with our own vulnerability. When we allow ourselves to be vulnerable in a relationship by divulging deeply personal information to the other person and by trusting them, we put ourselves at a significant risk of being intimidated, humiliated, or betrayed.

As psychologist Jerrold Lee Shapiro has pointed out, recognition of the risk of betrayal, intimidation, or humiliation can by itself make us hate the person putting us at risk.[43] The greater our vulnerability to a person's betrayal or abuse of our trust, the more likely we are to hate them. Psychologists Katherine Aumer and Anne Cathrine Krebs Bahn note that, in the envisaged scenario, hate is a response to our recogni-tion of the other person's ability to hurt us.[44] It's a kind of self-protection aimed at making us less vulnerable to potential harm. When we hate others on account of their possible betrayal of our trust, this jeopardizes the possibility of pursuing or continuing an intimate relationship with them.

Jane Austen's *Pride and Prejudice* gives us a memorable glimpse into how hate can serve as a defense against the risks of vulnerability. After being humiliated by the handsome and rich but overbearingly proud Mr. Darcy, the novel's protagonist, Elizabeth Bennet, becomes resentful and contemptuous. But her negative sentiments turn to hate when her acquaintance George Wickham relates to her that Darcy deprived him of a living promised to him by Darcy's late father.

Elizabeth conveys her hatred to her friend Charlotte at a ball at Netherfield after reluctantly accepting Darcy's invitation to dance with him. When Charlotte consolingly suggests that she may find Darcy agreeable, she replies: "Heaven forbid! That would be the greatest mis-fortune of all! To find a man agreeable whom one is determined to hate! Do not wish me such an evil."

Elizabeth regarded Darcy's superbia as despicable but of little con-sequence, but his power to determine the fate of those who are much less affluent or influential than he is makes him dangerous, as far as she is concerned, which is why she is "determined to hate" him. Her determination to hate him serves as a defense against any potential harm he might inflict on her by making her prepared to fight him rather than trust him. As we will see in Chapter 3, hate can indeed be morally justified when its aim is to protect oneself against potential harm.

Until now, we have focused on cases in which hate has taken the place of love. But if you have ever loved, you know that hatred of a person you love doesn't always squash that love. Indeed, we often hate and love one and the same person at the same time. In the Steven Spielberg movie *War Horse*, Rose Narracott says to her husband, Ted, who fears losing her love: "I may hate you more, but I'll never love you less."

But how is it possible for love and hate to co-exist?[45] Although love and hate are both directed at their target because of who he or she is, the two seem like irreconcilable opposites. When we love someone, we wish that they will thrive. When we hate someone, we are more likely to pray for their downfall. So, isn't simultaneously loving and hating a person a psychological state bound to crack up under the weight of its own internal contradictions?

Not quite. But this sentiment is not far from the truth. Like ice cream, love comes in two flavors, chocolate and vanilla, or in trade parlance, compassionate and passionate. Compassionate love includes familial love, friendship love, and love of strangers, also known as "altruism," whereas passionate love includes infatuation, romantic love, and sexual love. However, what we call "romantic love" in everyday language is usually a blend of passionate and compassionate love.

Compassionate love and romantic love in its hybrid form involve what I will call an "attitude of closeness," which is a robust desire based on core values to promote the beloved's interests.[46] Romantic love involves both an attitude of closeness and what I will call an "attitude of intimacy," which is a robust desire for intimacy with your beloved—both sexual and nonsexual intimacy, say, a desire for the two of you to create a space where you can share private information. When you hate someone, you don't desire to promote their interests or be intimate with them. You might even want to impede their interests and go to great lengths to avoid intimacy.

The conjunction of love and hate thus breeds internal inconsistency, or what is also known as "cognitive dissonance." As rationality at a minimum requires internal consistency, cognitive dissonance is an irrational state of mind.[47] We can also say that the attitudes are jointly irrational.[48] Joint irrationality doesn't necessarily distribute to the individual attitudes. But even when we are "blissfully" unaware of harboring inconsistent attitudes, cognitive dissonance almost inevitably results in mental distress and confusion, and an inability to make rational decisions.

Simultaneously loving and hating one and the same person is thus jointly irrational. Or in the words of literary critic Daniel Karlin, it's an opposition of contraries held in a "paradoxical suspension."[49]

A common way of dealing with cognitively dissonant love is to conjure up explanations that can mask the hate, such as "She didn't really mean to humiliate me in front of my friends" or "He only hit me because he's really stressed out about losing his job." In her 2009 memoir *Crazy Love* Leslie Morgan Steiner details the domestic violence she suffered during a four-year long relationship with her ex-husband Conor. He choked her, punched her, banged her against a wall, knocked her down the stairs, broke glass over her face, held a gun to her head, and took the keys out of the ignition on the highway. As Connor's violence becomes more egregious, Steiner's rationalizations become increasingly riven with internal contradictions and efforts to suppress her own anger and hated:

"Do you have any psychology books on domestic violence?" I asked the middle-aged librarian.... She ran her wrinkled index finger along a row of thick, heavy books.... I grabbed four books and ... read the opening to one chapter, looking for some connection:.... Every time a man hits a woman he's saying "I hate you.... Hate? Our relationship was about love, not hate. "I love him beyond words, Winnie," I'd said to her a few days before when she called to check on me. "I am lucky to feel this way. He's brilliant, funny, fascinating. I want to be with him forever. His mother never protected him, Winnie. Who can blame him for being so fucking angry? He needs help, my help. You don't abandon your soul mate."[50]

But these kinds of self-deceptive psychological acrobatics don't dispose of the pain of her growing hatred or the impending realization that her relationship is dysfunctional and extremely dangerous, and eventually she does come to her senses.

Hate as a Parapathic Emotion

Negative emotions like fear, dread, terror, despair, sadness, regret, guilt, shame, disgust, outrage, and hatred are usually unpleasant if not outright painful, unless they hide below the surface of our conscious awareness. It's in large part due to their unpleasant quality that negative emotions can play the biological and social roles they do. For example, fear can help us eliminate or escape from danger, and guilt can help us make amends when we have hurt others. If fear and guilt had been defaulting toward being pleasurable, they would have had quite different biological and social functions.

But when occurring as responses to fiction or the suffering of people we don't fully empathize with, unpleasant emotions sometimes assume a pleasant, thrilling or arousing quality.[51] Emotions embodied in this altered form are also said to be parapathic (from Greek, *para-* plus *pathos*. Literally: resembling the emotional effect).[52]

Parapathic emotions do not completely lose their ordinary unpleasant quality but the protective frame (for instance, the protective frame of fiction) psychologically distances us from the unpleasant, which enables it to become a source of thrill, arousal, amusement, comfort or some other form of enjoyment. Because they are facilitated by a protective frame, parapathic emotions have the depth of their reality-based counterparts but (typically) none of their serious ramifications. Whether we enjoy a tragic novel or watch with fear and fascination as Norman Bates stabs Marion Crane to death in *Psycho*'s renowned 45-second "shower scene," the fear we feel is due to our partial (psychological) substitution of our own identity for the identity of the character or victim. It is because we identify, or empathize, with Marion Crane that we are frightened when Norman Bates shows up in her bathroom, horrified when he stabs her, and pained by her misery. But it's because the fictional frame creates psychological distance between us and the portrayed events that our fear, horror or emotional pain is simultaneously a source of thrill, excitement and pleasure. What makes this balancing act between identity substitution and psychological distance possible is the frame of detachment inherent to the literary, cinematic, and theatrical artforms. The fictional universe captures our attention and becomes the focal point in our stream of consciousness, whereas the depicted events' fictional nature is backgrounded and only diffusely attended. But it is our residual awareness of the fictional events' make-believe nature that builds the protective frame that keeps us grounded in reality and makes it possible for us to enjoy tragedy and horror.

But it's not just fiction that can create a protective frame and allow us to relish in other people's suffering. As long as the victim is not "one of us," we are often in a position to take pleasure in the discomfort that comes with witnessing someone else's suffering. This is what happens when we instinctively slow down on the highway to get a good view of the scene of an accident or find ourselves glued to the television as a news anchor uncovers the gory or tragic details of murder and mayhem. This is also the reason (white) people used to travel long distances to witness lynchings and freak shows.[53]

While disgust, horror, and sadness perhaps are the most common emotional responses to fiction and spectacles, I suspect that all unpleasant emotions could occur in the altered, parapathic form. Even self-reflective emotions like guilt, shame, and loneliness might take on a thrilling quality during immersive play or gaming. During certain sadomasochistic practices, for example, the aim is for the "sadist" to make the "masochist" feel shame that is at once emotionally painful and sexually arousing.

Parapathic emotions are also sometimes employed as a strategy to salvage a dysfunctional relationship from the threats of pain or boredom. As popular wisdom has it, "the two enemies of human happiness are pain and boredom." Parapathic emotions produced by imagined or staged realities can temporarily mask authentic but painful emotions of boredom with a romantic partner or hatred towards them stemming from past unresolved conflicts.

Psychologists Bruce A. Wilson and Lizbeth Luther Wilson call strategic uses of parapathic emotions to camouflage relationship problems rather than addressing them "offense mechanisms."[54] Offense mechanisms serve much the same purpose as psychological defense mechanisms. Both are strategies for distancing ourselves psychologically from events or circumstances that would otherwise be unbearably painful. Although defense and offense mechanisms are deployed for the same purpose, they achieve this aim in different ways. Defense mechanisms are strategies individuals use (often unconsciously) to escape emotional pain. A number of different defense mechanisms have been identified. In projection, for example, a hostile emotion toward another person is camouflaged by projecting that emotion onto the other person. Say you feel bad about disrespecting a coworker. To deal with the discomfort, you unconsciously employ a process that makes you believe that it's your coworker who disrespects you rather than the other way around.

Offense mechanisms are strategies jointly deployed by couples or groups to escape mutual, unendurable emotional pain. Offensive language and behavior is used as a means for replacing shared pain with unpleasant emotions that are simultaneously unpleasant and thrilling but not unbearable.

The relationship between George and Martha in Edward Albee's renowned play *Who's Afraid of Virginia Woolf* is a classic example of a dysfunctional relationship held together by parapathic emotions deployed as psychological offense mechanisms. In the play, the couple's young guests, Nick and Honey, involuntarily become spectators to George and

Martha taking turns putting each other in the hot seat in order to camouflage unresolved pain. Martha makes obnoxious references to Nick's body and then embarrasses George with a story of how he landed in a huckleberry bush at her father's house, who is the president of the university where George works. At this point George points a rifle toward Martha's head. Martha and the guests are deeply terrified. But when George pulls the trigger, an umbrella opens, and Martha's and their guests' sense of horror is replaced with joy and exhilaration.

When the topic of George and Martha's son comes up, Martha makes references to George's problems in the lower "private" compartment and insinuates that their son isn't George's. After George mentions that it's difficult to be married to the president of the university, Martha notes that George "didn't have the stuff" to replace Martha's father as the president of the university, which she insinuates was her main reason for marrying him.

Only in the play's third and final act does the protective frame within which Martha and George can safely make each other feel bad break down. Upon realizing Martha and Nick tried to have sex, George vengefully makes Martha recount details about their son before confessing that he just received some bad news: their son is dead. Martha is crushed, and for the first time one gets the sense that her anguish is real rather than parapathic. At last the truth comes out: they never had a son, but for years they pretended to have one in an attempt to mask the pain of their failed lives.

While George and Martha's relationship is beyond repair, offense mechanisms may sometimes be successful in extinguishing painful conflicts that can otherwise be detrimental to romantic relationships.

Disrespect: The Number One Killer of Relationships

Hate is often proclaimed a relationship killer. For example, philosopher Thomas Brudholm writes: "Hatred lies at the extreme end of the continuum of attitudes at stake in our dealings with one another, and it is tempting to say that the beginning of hatred is the end of a relationship."[55] It is true that hatred can build barriers of steel that must be broken down before hater and hated can reunite and the relationship progress. But research in marriage and relationship psychology spearheaded by psychologist John Gottman and collaborators has shown that contempt and disrespect present greater threats than antagonistic emotions such as anger, resentment, disgust, and hatred.[56] Contempt and disrespect can suck all the air out of the person who has sunk deepest. Enfeebled by oxygen depletion, the contemned or disrespected person is usually in no position to fight his way back up from the disgraced netherworld and prove his true worth. But what is it about contempt that makes it a number one relationship hazard?

Disgust is a close runner-up to contempt, but it's not always a relationship threat. If your partner is suffering from a stomach virus and all it entails, that's not a deal-breaker. It will almost inevitably trigger a disgust reaction. But the focus of your disgust is a transient event, not a permanent feature of your beloved.

Disgust for your partner because of how they look, smell, or behave in a more permanent way can drastically dampen your love for them. But disgust in its pure form is not judgmental. Say your daughter becomes addicted to drugs and enters prostitution. After becoming pregnant and giving birth, she drops off your grandchild in your arms only to return to the streets. Your despair, sorrow, disappointment, and grief may well be tinged by disgust for her, or at least her behavior. But as long as you don't condemn her, your love for her is likely to survive.

Contempt is a deal-breaker because of its disrespect component. Disrespect is also a component of anger, resentment, indignation, and hatred. It's what unifies the antagonistic emotions. But the focus of anger, resentment, and indignation is the wrongdoing, not the person's character. It's only in hate and contempt that we disrespect people for their seemingly flawed character.[57]

But if disrespect is a component of both hatred and contempt, then why is contempt a greater predictor of breakups, divorce, and other forms of relationship disasters than hatred?

The answer is two-fold. In Western cultures, malevolence and potential danger and power are implicitly, or unconsciously, associated in our minds with socially admirable characteristics such masculinity, dominance, creativity, and high intelligence. This association is grounded in a social stereotype. When we are bombarded with stories of malevolent people who are masculine, dominant, and highly intelligent, like Ted Bundy, we become even more prone to associate malevolence with these kinds of positive stereotype features. Mental associations of this kind are also known as "implicit biases."[58] The most commonly discussed implicit, or unconscious, bias is the one that links the concepts *black man* and *dangerous criminal*. While our implicit association of malevolence and positive stereotype features isn't about oppressed social groups, it is nonetheless a prime example of an implicit bias.

But there is a second reason that hatred does not always present as great a threat to relationships as disrespect and contempt. Apprehensive respect, the sort of respect you ought to have for dangerous people and objects, is a component of hatred but not contempt. Apprehensive respect is altogether different from appraisal respect, or admiration. If you have respect for the sea, it doesn't follow that you admire the sea. But apprehensive respect can nonetheless partially conceal the disrespect component of hatred on a psychological level. This is somewhat analogous to the way a fun evening with good friends can temporarily make you forget that you are grieving the tragic loss of a loved one.

Apprehensive respect is likely to augment the attraction created by the positive stereotype features we associate with evil-minded criminals. This is because when an emotional input alters our body's physiology, we bring our perception of our situation to bear on the meaning we attach to our bodily sensations, which means that the same physiological disturbances can educe quite distinct emotions, depending on how we interpret our surroundings.[59] Whether you experience an accelerated heartbeat as panic or thrilling arousal depends on whether you attribute your bodily sensation to a spine-chilling ride in a theme park or the sound of footsteps only a few feet behind you as walk home through a dark alley late at night.[60]

This sort of bias of judgment is part of the lesson of Donald Dutton and Arthur Aron's bridge experiment.[61] In their study, men crossing a fear-arousing suspension bridge or a sturdy walkway were approached by an attractive female interviewer half-way across and were asked to fill out a survey. After the men filled out the survey the woman gave them her phone number and told them to call her if they had any follow-up questions. The researchers found that more participants became infatuated with the interviewer when they were approached on the fear-arousing suspension bridge compared the sturdy walkway. This shows that whether the "fight or flight" response is interpreted as fear or attraction depends on which aspects of our surroundings we take to have caused the response.

Dutton and Aron's findings carry over to our perception of malevolence. As malevolence is associated in our minds with danger, people who seem to be malevolent will tend to trigger a "fight or flight" response in us. But owing to our repeated exposure to the fantasy that malevolent people have various admirable characteristics, we are at risk of misinterpreting our "fight or flight" reaction to a bad person as physical attraction or infatuation. Our physiology screams "attack or run" but our brain yells "attractive mate ahead."

Our proneness to interpret our natural fear response to malevolence as physical attraction may help explain why so many women become obsessed with dangerous killers like Ted Bundy, Jeffrey Dahmer, Charles Manson, and Richard Ramirez, and other violent criminals, which is a well-documented instance of the paraphilia known as "hybristophilia."[62] This term is derived from the Greek words "hubris" (meaning "arrogance, bravado, or overconfidence") and "philo" (meaning "love of or attraction to").

The women who become obsessed with dangerous killers aren't for the most part girlfriends who decide to stay faithful after the killer is caught. Rather, most of them first learn about the criminals once they're on trial or get extensive media coverage. Although other factors, such as attraction to highly controlling men or men who need help or who long for human contact, can contribute to the women's obsession with the killers, the root cause of their obsession seems to be that of mistaking physiological fear for physical attraction or infatuation.

The same mechanism that expounds women's obsession with dangerous serial killers also explains why disrespect is commonly felt more deeply in contempt than in hate. When you hate someone, you perceive them as malevolent and potentially powerful and dangerous. Although hate, conceptually, is a far cry from attraction, our tendency to associate positive stereotype features with malevolence can partially or wholly mask our disrespect for the people we hate.

This raises the question of why the disrespect we harbor in contempt can be a lethal poison to intimate and close relationships. Its fatal blow to relationships appears to turn on its portrayal of its target as "low" and undeserving of respect, or in a worst-case scenario, as subhuman or a nonentity. If you view a relationship partner as inferior overall or in certain respects that matter a great deal to you, not only are you less likely to want to promote their interests or share deeply personal information with them, but you are also biologically primed to want nothing to do with them or to demean and degrade them to the point where they cut the relationship ties.

Hate's Role in Emotional Abuse and Domestic Violence

Personal hate and contempt have different biological action tendencies. Hate is biologically associated with attack, whereas contempt is tied to ridicule, degradation, and social exclusion. These differences in action tendencies are reflected in the types of abuse engendered by hate and contempt in close and intimate relationships.

Emotional abuse is a pattern of behavior used to achieve and maintain power and control over another person by systematically punishing them, damaging their self-confidence, or making them lose trust in their own perceptions. Emotional abusers diminish their partners in an attempt to pull themselves up. Their behavior allows them to remain blissfully ignorant of their own despicable character.

Although emotional abuse doesn't leave physical scars, its victims often describe it as the most emotionally painful and destructive form of domestic violence.[63] The destructive stranglehold the abuse has on its victims reduces their existence and well-being to rubble, leaving them feeling so worthless, paltry, or wicked that they think they deserve the abuse. Others become conditioned to believe that they are crazy because their abuser continues to deny the abuse or uses methods of infliction that make it seem to the victims that they are imagining it. This is also known as "crazy-making" or "gaslighting."

One kind of emotional abuse that often escapes detection is passive aggression, a pattern of indirect hostility that can take the form of subtle insults, sullen behavior, stubbornness, or a deliberate failure to accomplish required or promised tasks. Because passive-aggressive behavior is so subtle in its appearance, it can be hard to tell apart from forgetfulness, distraction, work stress, or ephemeral dysphoria. But the victim may be suffering serious psychological consequences nonetheless.

Hatred and contempt tend to give rise to different patterns of abuse. Because contempt involves disrespect for the target for his or her failings as a person or as engaged in a particular pursuit, the abuser who is motivated by contempt has, or thinks they have, complete power over the partner and intends it to stay that way. To make this happen, they are prone to engage in forms of abuse that further cripple the victim's self-esteem or reminds them of their alleged worthlessness and lowly status.

Condescension is a form of contempt-based emotional abuse. It wears away at the victim's sense of self-worth by trivializing her accomplishments or diminishing her competence, intelligence, youthfulness, or physical appearance. When verbalized, it might sound like this:

- Yeah, sure, your blog post is fine. I just don't see why you needed to spend all Sunday writing it.
- See, that's why I have to be the one to handle the money.
- You are too dumb to understand what I am talking about.
- Hurry up, you old bag, or I'm leaving you in the parking lot!
- Did you remember to brush your teeth?
- Have you considered joining a gym?

Contempt-based emotional abuse can also take the grisly form of public shaming. When Sandy, a resident of Kern County, California, found some of her own makeup in her twelve-year-old daughter Ella's school bag, she callously ordered her daughter into the bathroom, made her lean over the sink, got out the shaver, and shaved off all of her daughter's previously long, thick brown hair while Ella cried convulsively.[64] Sandy made Ella attend school the next day for public humiliation. This (thankfully) resulted in an encounter with Child Protective Services, a child abuse allegation, and a hearing, albeit one that shockingly ruled that the allegation was unfounded.

Jeff Laxamana, a resident of Tacoma, Washington, made use of the same punitive measure, cutting off his thirteen-year-old daughter Izabel's hair. Afterward he uploaded a fifteen-second video to YouTube.[65] The video opens with a shot of a short-haired girl in a black tee staring at the camera. Her father's voice can be heard in the background:

"The consequences of getting messed up, man, you lost all that beautiful hair." The camera pans down to long strands of black hair scattered on the floor. "Was it worth it?"
"No," she replies obediently.
"How many times did I warn you?" the father asks.
"A lot," she responds softly.

Only days after the event, Izabel died by suicide after jumping off a highway overpass.

Cutting off women's hair has historically served as a way of publicly shaming them. When World War II ended in 1945, civilian citizens from France, Belgium, Italy, Denmark, Norway, and Holland rounded up the women who were thought to have had a liaison with a German soldier and shaved their heads.[66] Following the public humiliation of head-shaving, the "traitors" were sometimes paraded through the town, while onlookers spat and urinated on them. Sometimes they were beaten or kicked to death. Women who had had abortions were automatically assumed to have had a sexual encounter with a German soldier.

As we have already seen, although hate, in its narrow sense, also involves disrespect, its disrespectfulness is counterbalanced by apprehension, or fear, which is triggered by the hater's perception of the target as malevolent and potentially powerful and dangerous. Hateful abusers may fear that their partner will leave them, tell friends or family about the abuse, or report it to the authorities. Like contemptuous abusers, hateful abusers want complete power over their partner, but they have a lingering fear that they don't yet have this kind of power. Their abuse is aimed at preempting the feared scenarios and ultimately obtaining complete power over their victim.

Hate-based emotional abuse can take the form of retaliation, angry outbursts, threatening, ordering, name-calling, sarcasm, rude interruptions, or sweeping generalizations intended to define the other person's inner reality. When verbalized, hate-based abuse may sound like this:

- If you file for divorce, then I am taking the kids.
- You can't go out until you've cleaned the dishes.
- You fucking bitch.
- I don't give a shit about your feelings.
- It is none of your goddamn business.
- Shut the fuck up!
- You always feel victimized.

Not all relationship abuse ends (or begins) with emotional abuse. Some abusers are so consumed by hatred that they batter, stalk, sexually assault, torture, or murder their partners, friends, or family. There is a gendered component to this phenomenon. It's almost always men killing women.

In September 2001, Michelle Monson Mosure had endured a decade of abuse from Rocky, her husband and the father of her two children, Kristy and Kyle, when she finally went to the authorities to get a restraining order against him.[67] That day she recounted the physical abuse she underwent at the hands of her husband. He was beating Michelle in front of the children, and threatening to kill them in order to coerce her into obeying him. Yet only days after Rocky was served the restraining order, Michelle recanted her testimony out of fear of retaliation, and the prosecutors were forced to drop the case. Two months later, Rocky shot and killed Michelle, and proceeded to kill their two children, before turning the gun on himself.

It may seem counterintuitive that a person who wants complete power over their partner would willfully kill them. We admittedly say that killers "overpower" their victims, but once the victim is dead, there is no one left to control. So, unless the killer is massively hallucinating, why does the desire to have complete power over another person so often culminate in murder?

One possible explanation is that domestic killers have become so bothered by the victim's residual power that if they cannot seem to wrestle it away from her while she is alive, killing her is the only way to deprive her of it for good.

The domestic killer's distorted reasoning is analogous to the illogical thoughts that motivate the spiteful envier to destroy the envied person's possession. The spiteful envier is under the delusion that she is more deserving of the envied's possession than the envied. The spiteful envier is keenly aware that she is unable to make the possession her own. So, in her unhinged state of mind, she jumps to the conclusion that the only way for justice to prevail is for her to destroy the envied's possession. Say you envy Carly for winning Bruno's love. You know that it's hopeless to try to win Bruno back and come to the conclusion that the only way to restore justice is to deprive Carly of her undeserved "possession." To play it safe, you plan to get rid of Bruno by murdering him. You realize that this means that you definitely will never win him back, but in your deranged state of mind, you take comfort in the fact that Carly will never have him either. As philosopher Sara Protasi points out, "destroying the good is one way of taking the good from the envied."[68] This idea is encapsulated in the saying "Envy spoils the good it covets." In your twisted logic, your successful destruction of Carly's "possession" means that justice has prevailed.

A highly controlling hater may reason in kindred ways. Perhaps Rocky decided to murder Michelle and their two children, Kristy and Kyle, once it dawned on him that his desire to completely dominate her, to annihilate any remnant of instinctual resistance to him, would never be fulfilled while she was still alive. (In reality, of course, her "power" was virtually non-existent and could easily have been circumvented.) Taking his own life after murdering Michelle and their children might also have seemed logical to him from his distorted point of view. He evidently lived for the sick pleasure he took in asserting his power over Michelle, depriving her of the slight semblance of agency she had managed to hang on to. Although Rocky desperately wanted to fully possess Michelle by depriving her of all self-determination, taking her life didn't ultimately satisfy his deviant desire. So, once she had died, his reason to live had died with it.

Like hate, dehumanizing contempt can also motivate battery, sexual assault, torture, and murder, but the hater and the contemner are driven by different motives. Because the dehumanizing contemner sees the victim as less than fully human, brutally assaulting their victim may seem insignificant to them.

When Sara Packer watched her boyfriend rape her fourteen-year-old daughter, Grace, and later choke her to death, the girl had looked to her for help.[69] But rather than coming to her aid, Packer had glanced at her coldly, telling her to just let go. Her dehumanizing contempt for her own child had made Packer incapable of seeing her girl as human. This level of contempt is not only hard to stomach but is also utterly incomprehensible. People capable of such heinous acts harbor dark personalities that are governed by distorted dark "moral" dictums.

The hate-proneness and contempt-proneness residing in people with dark personalities is the topic of Chapter 4. In the next chapter, we will ponder hate's justification and role in our social relationships.

3 | BAD BLOOD

VENGEANCE AND HATE'S JUSTIFICATION

In March 2008, Rand Abdel-Qader, an Iraqi seventeen-year-old girl, was stomped on, suffocated, and then stabbed to death by her father, Abdel-Qader Ali, for becoming infatuated with a twenty-two-year-old British soldier, Paul, in Basra, southern Iraq.[1] Her father went berserk after he discovered that she had been seen in public talking to Paul. She never had any sexual relations with the man.

Pained by what she saw, the girl's mother, Leila Hussein, called her two older sons, Hassan, twenty-three, and Haydar, twenty-one, in the hope that they would intervene. But to her dismay, the two family members simply joined the father's massacre of his own daughter. Police officers initially arrested the father but then released him after two hours, congratulating him on his act.

After witnessing her husband's and sons' gruesome killing of her daughter, Leila Hussein did something that was both unusual and dangerous for a woman in Iraq: she left her husband. She received protection by a women's group but to no avail; two months after her daughter's gruesome murder, Leila Hussein was shot dead by unknown assailants in Basra.

Honor killings, motivated by hatred for one's own kin who allegedly damaged the family's honor, are widely frowned upon in Western cultures. They are paradigm cases of vengeance motivated by retaliatory attitudes. As such, they are morally indefensible.

But what should we say about hate and contempt that aren't accompanied by acts of vengeance? Would it have been appropriate for Abdel-Qader Ali to have felt hatred toward his daughter as long as it didn't motivate him to commit acts of extreme violence? Are there any circumstances in which hate is appropriate? That's the question we will address in this chapter.

Reacting to Perceived Wrongs

In his 1962 landmark essay "Freedom and Resentment," the British philosopher Peter Strawson coined the term "reactive attitude" to refer to our emotional reactions to the wrongdoings or acts of goodwill of people we regard as morally responsible agents.[2] Gratitude, resentment, indignation, forgiveness, reciprocal love, and hurt feelings are paradigm reactive attitudes, and the only ones discussed by Strawson.

Social relationships, or what Strawson somewhat misleadingly calls "interpersonal relationships," are relations that obtain between "people directly involved in transactions with each other."[3] They include personal relationships such as acquaintanceships, friendships, romantic relationships, transactional relationships such as that between you and your dentist or the pharmacist at Walgreens, and stranger relationships such as that between you and the person ahead of you at checkout. We ordinarily have fleeting social relationships with thousands and thousands of acquaintances and random strangers every day, for instance, residents in your apartment building, students in your large lecture classes, baristas at Starbucks, cashiers at Publix, drivers on the freeway, fellow gym-goers, FedEx delivery guys, and so on. Social relationships are the pillars of the socio-moral realm.

Although the reactive attitudes, in Strawson's sense, are natural human responses to other people's conduct, they are not mere bodily reactions, like an allergic reaction to a bee sting, but moral appraisals of others in light of their perceived acts of wrongdoing or goodwill or lawful actions—actions that are neither verboten nor altruistic. The reactive attitudes are more akin to an audience's feedback to a play, such as a standing ovation or a barrage of rotten tomatoes, than to a skin rash.

Reactive attitudes involving negative moral assessments, such as resentment and indignation, address legitimate moral concerns about another person's conduct. For example, resentment is not merely a reaction to a person we think has treated us unjustly but also a moral condemnation of that person's way of interacting with us.[4]

According to Strawson, when we articulate our reactive attitudes in words or action, we convey to other members of society whether we regard their actions as meeting, exceeding, or breaching the moral standards we take to regulate social relationships in our community. Suppose that upon seeing a stranger casually drop their garbage on the street, you feel the familiar sting of indignation. Deciding to confront the person, you pick up their trash and casually walk up to them, saying, "Sorry, is this yours? You just dropped it." Or you pick it up and walk ahead of them to a nearby garbage bin and demonstratively toss it into the bin. Either way, you convey your indignation in response to what you perceive to be a violation of the moral standards governing our conduct and interactions with others. Ideally, the person who was told off in action or words will be less likely to toss garbage on the street in the future. The reactive attitudes thus help uphold the moral norms that govern our interactions and conduct in our moral community. Their absence from everyday life would negatively affect our proper conduct and interactions with others.

We do not always articulate our reactive attitudes, of course. But even when we don't make our feelings known to offenders, responding with, say, anger, resentment, indignation, or praise can help remind ourselves of the moral standards governing our conduct and interactions with others in our moral community.

Strawson contrasts the reactive attitudes, which are based on "involvement or participation in a human relationship," with what he calls "the objective attitude."[5] Strawson doesn't specify which emotional attitudes are "objective." He simply speaks of "the objective attitude," as if there were only one. But I will assume that there can be more than one.

Objective attitudes, for instance, forbearance or humorous amusement, take an uninvolved stance toward the other person, regarding them as a non-participant rather than a participant in the social community. This stance, Strawson argues, cannot include "the range of reactive feelings and attitudes which belong to involvement or participation with others in interpersonal human relationships; it cannot include resentment, gratitude, forgiveness, anger, or the sort of love which two adults can sometimes be said to feel reciprocally for each other."[6] When we take an objective attitude toward another person, we regard them as lacking the capacities required for being a participant in reciprocal, social relationships. Strawson writes:

> To adopt the objective attitude to another human being is to see him, perhaps, as an object of social policy; as a subject for what, in a wide range of sense, might be called treatment; as something certainly to be taken into account, perhaps precautionary account, of; to be managed or handled or cured or trained; perhaps simply to be avoided, though this gerundive is not peculiar to cases of objectivity of attitude.[7]

To adopt the objective attitude toward another human being, Strawson emphasizes, is not the same as looking down on them or completely ignoring them, not initially at least; rather, it's to take "account of them." In other words, an objective attitude is not a dehumanizing or objectifying stance; nor is it by itself a condemnation of the target on account of their appalling practices. So, disrespect, contempt, and hatred, which are not merely "clinically" or "pedagogically" observing their targets, do not qualify as objective attitudes, in Strawson's sense.

Although we don't regard the people we view through our objective lens as moral participants on equal footing with those who become the targets of reactive attitudes, we don't regard them as animals or tools either but rather as humans who lack intact moral capacities and who are therefore in need of training, management, or a cure. For example, Strawson notes, we may "look with an objective eye" on the "tiresome behavior of a very young child."[8] This doesn't mean that we regard them as non-human objects or creatures but only that we recognize that they don't presently have the capacity to understand how to act appropriately. While we do not initially ignore non-participants, Strawson notes that we may eventually refrain from taking account of them, perhaps because we realize that no amount of training, management, or treatment is going to change them.

Strawson's focus is on moral wrongs and acts of goodwill. But reactive attitudes like anger, resentment, blame, praise, and hurt feelings aren't merely targeted at people we take to have acted in a way that is morally criticizable or praiseworthy. We don't just criticize or praise people who have made a moral impact on us. Soccer players routinely blame teammates for bad play, parents scold children for breaking house rules, and bosses' negative evaluations of their underlings' work performance sometimes hurt their feelings. Playing badly, breaking house rules, and feeling hurt by criticism of one's work performance are not *moral* wrongs, yet they nonetheless help maintain order and structure, correct unproductive attitudes and behaviors and encourage productive ones.

Even when people's behaviors and attitudes have no direct bearing on *morality*, it can still be reasonable to criticize or praise the agent. Praising your teammate for his excellent tackling, ultimately resulting in your 1–0 win, is useful, even though good tackling isn't *morally* praiseworthy. Good tackling isn't comparable to jumping into a pond to save a drowning child. Strawson doesn't venture outside of the moral realm. But there is no reason that we shouldn't extend his framework beyond the narrow realm of morality. The reactive attitudes are no less important in helping to sustain norms regulating activities in other areas of our lives, for example, norms for what counts as good art or good jazz music or norms regulating interactions between a private and a sergeant in the Marine Corps. But the reactive attitudes also play a key role in upholding the much more flimsy norms guiding our conduct within the bounds of our personal relationships. It's only by offering praise and criticism in response to one another's relationship behaviors that we will ever get any insight into which kinds of conduct are acceptable to both of us within the bounds of our unique personal relationship.

Dehumanizers as Non-Participants

When we direct reactive attitudes like resentment, blame, gratitude, or praise at other people, we express our criticism or praise
of their conduct. Strawson's pet examples of reactive attitudes—
gratitude, resentment, indignation, forgiveness, reciprocal love,
and hurt feelings—don't make up an exhaustive list, which leaves it
an open question whether hate and contempt should be included
among them.

For an emotion to be a reactive attitude, in Strawson's sense, it must
portray its target in a way that is compatible with the target being a
free agent. This requires honoring Kant's principle of respect, that is,
the principle that states that it's morally indefensible to treat humans
merely as a means to an end, owing to their inherent dignity. Although
Strawson doesn't explicitly appeal to the principle of respect, many
commenters on Strawson's work have made this observation. According
to Stephen Darwall, for example, reactive attitudes like blame and resentment "presuppose respect for the [dignity] of the person blamed or
resented."[9]

Contempt has often been said to fail to respect people's inherent
dignity. Robert C. Roberts, for example, argues that "pure contempt,
unmixed with outrage or anger or indignation, is dehumanizing because it recognizes nothing valuable in its target."[10] If he is right, then
not only would contempt not be a reactive attitude, but it would also
be counterproductive to the kind of civilization Strawson envisages
that the reactive attitudes help uphold. Roberts' portrayal of contempt
rides roughshod over details, however. If you have contempt for a person
you know to be a pedophile, this implies that you disrespect (or condemn) him for his warped character traits (for instance, his perversion
and predatory mentality), and that you disrespect (or blame) him for
the lewdness that is gushing from his moral vices: his lusting after prepu-
bescent children, gazing at them, fantasizing about them, trolling them,
wooing them.

Subjecting pedophiles to contempt can no doubt be morally appropriate. But it's not morally appropriate if the contempt is of the dehumanizing kind that downgrades the target's status to that of a creature without inherent dignity. But contempt need not be dehumanizing. You may feel compelled to try to knock some sense into the person you know to be a pedophile, keep a close eye on him, or alert the authorities yet not wish for him to be subjected to senseless torture or have his freedom revoked without a guilty verdict following a fair trial. Even if your contempt for the pedophile is critical rather than dehumanizing, your attitude involves disrespect for him for his viciousness and the misdeeds that flow from his septic character, yet your critical contempt doesn't portray him as subhuman.

Like contempt, hatred can also assume dehumanizing proportions. Classical examples of all-consuming hate, such as the hate on display in Euripides' *Medea*, are of the dehumanizing kind: destructive, inhumane, and pointless.

Because they present their targets as unworthy of the respect owed to all people, dehumanizing hate and contempt are not reactive attitudes, in Strawson's sense, but nor do they embody the objectivity of perspective that Strawson thinks is an appropriate attitude to adopt toward people who lack the capacity to actively participate in the moral community, such as a very young child or a mentally ill person.

Strawson's objective attitude presents its target as a non-participant, but it doesn't portray her merely as a means to an end. This objectivity of perspective may reveal that the non-participant other is in need of sanction, treatment, or training. But this revelation gives you a reason to help her or notify the authorities, not to disregard her human status or fundamental human rights.

Dehumanizing hate and contempt are thoroughly nasty emotions, not objective attitudes, in Strawson's sense. But those who harbor dehumanizing attitudes toward others thereby become non-participants in the moral community. It's the dehumanizers themselves, not their victims, who are the rightful targets of Strawson's objective attitude. Dehumanizers' inability or unwillingness to play by the rules of society means that we ought to regard them as non-participants in need of sanction, treatment, or training.

This leaves us with the question of whether critical hate and contempt should be included among the reactive attitudes. At the heart of Strawson's theory is the claim that the reactive attitudes play a central role in monitoring and safeguarding the standards that regulate our conduct and social interactions with others in society. Are critical hate and contempt well suited to play this role? In other words, can hate and contempt be a good thing? We turn to this question next.

Two Cheers for Contempt

In her 2003 paper "Contempt as a Moral Attitude," philosopher Michelle Mason argues that contempt can be morally appropriate and deserves to be included among Strawson's reactive attitudes. In support of her view, she offers a critical analysis of Jean-Luc Godard's 1963 French-Italian psychological-drama film *Contempt* (*Le Mépris*), adapted from Alberto Moravia's novel *A Ghost at Noon*. The main character Camille's contempt for her husband Paul, Mason argues, is not only understandable but is in fact morally justified.

In the movie Paul, a young successful French playwright, accepts an offer from the crude American producer mogul Jeremy Prokosch to rework Fritz Lang's adaptation of Homer's *The Odyssey*. After their first disastrous meeting, Prokosch offers Paul's wife, Camille, a ride to his Roman villa in his two-seater sports car, a red Alfa Romeo. Camille looks to Paul to object, but he encourages her to go and follows behind in a taxi with Prokosch's secretary. After that incident, Camille's love for Paul is slowly declining, in part because he took on the lowly film project for the sake of the money and in part because he allows the American mogul to flirt with her to increase his chances of cementing the deal.

During the filming in Capri, Camille's suspicions are confirmed. She allows the predatory producer to embrace her while her husband is watching. When Paul confronts her, she tells him that her respect for him has turned to contempt because he has bartered her sexual services for his own professional advancement. Paul sheepishly offers to end all connections with Prokosch and leave Capri, but Camille has her mind set and leaves with Prokosch in his sports car. When Paul learns that Camille and the producer have been killed in a car crash, he prepares to leave Capri and jettison the dream of writing a movie.

In Camille's own words, Paul's compromise of his artistic integrity and his exploitation of her in order to cement his ties with Prokosch reveal that he is "not a man." But, Mason argues, by saying that Paul is not a man, Camille doesn't intend to convey that Paul is not human, only that he fails to comply with the behavioral norms that apply to husbands and artists. In other words, while Camille has contempt for Paul, her attitude towards Paul isn't dehumanizing contempt, but critical contempt. As Mason puts it, her contempt is a way of expressing that she regards him as "low" relative to society's standards for how a man is expected to behave.

In Mason's opinion, contempt can be a fitting attitude when its target has indeed failed to live up to what can reasonably be expected of them. However, she argues, for contempt to be morally justified, two additional constraints must be satisfied. First, either the agent does not possess a similar fault, or if she does, then she must regard herself and her target as equally contemptible. Second, the contempt must be reason-responsive, that is, it must be malleable enough to taper off if evidence becomes available suggesting that the target doesn't have the presumed repulsive features, or that said features don't flow from a vicious set of character traits.

Camille's contempt is, at least on one interpretation of the movie, morally justified, in Mason's sense. If Paul has indeed compromised his artistic integrity and sold out his wife for professional gain, then Camille's contempt for him is fitting. Her contempt arguably also satisfies the two additional constraints proposed by Mason: she hasn't failed to live up to society's standards for a wife at the time, and we can imagine that she would have forgiven Paul, had he made a greater effort to make amends.

Camille's contempt also serves a morally worthwhile aim, as it becomes a tool for emancipating her from her subservience to her husband. At the beginning of the movie, Camille stands in her husband's shadow. She has no mind of her own, no real self-determination. Her contempt presents Paul as morally inferior to her, and thus presents her as independent of her husband. It is this experience of independence afforded by her contempt that allows her to gain independence. Because anger and resentment are focused on the wrongful action rather than the person's character, they would not have been able to present her as independent of her husband. Camille's contempt thus seems unique in its ability to implore her to view herself as better off without her husband.

In her 2013 book *Hard Feelings*, philosopher Macalester Bell offers a different constellation of arguments for thinking that contempt can be morally defensible. One of the cases she analyzes is Elizabeth Bennet's contempt for the handsome and rich but overbearingly proud Mr. Darcy in Jane Austen's *Pride and Prejudice*. Elizabeth's contempt for Darcy stems mostly from her first impression of him at a ball at Meryton. When Mr. Bingley notices that Darcy is not dancing, he pulls himself away from Elizabeth's beautiful older sister, Jane, to encourage Darcy to dance. Darcy replies he doesn't like to dance with people he is not acquainted with and adds with resentment that Bingley already has claimed the only beautiful girl at the ball. When Bingley points out that Jane's younger sister is available, Darcy catches Elizabeth's eye and remarks loudly enough for her to hear it: "She's tolerable but not handsome enough to tempt me."

Elizabeth stews over the Meryton incident and Darcy's haughtiness for a long time. The attitude she displays toward Darcy is rife with contempt, and her contempt persists, even when Darcy attempts to explain himself. As Austen expert Joan Klingel Ray puts it:

> As abundantly playful as she is, Elizabeth neither forgets nor forgives Darcy's insult. She begins playing the role of Miss Pert

(to borrow Mitford's term) with Darcy in order to pay him back for his mortifying her—all the while oblivious to his trying patiently to explain himself to her.[11]

It is not without irony that Elizabeth's shrewdly displayed contempt for Darcy is what ultimately makes him fall in love with her. When he proposes to her, she responds with bitter scorn, saying: "From the very beginning, from the first moment I may almost say, of my acquaintance with you, your manners impressing me with the fullest belief of your arrogance, your conceit, and your selfish disdain of the feelings of others, were such as to form that the groundwork of disapprobation, on which succeeding events have built so immovable a dislike."[12]

Although Elizabeth later learns that her interpretation of the rumors she has heard about Darcy is mistaken, it is not before she visits Pemberley three months after Darcy's first marriage proposal that she realizes that she no longer despises him but is grateful that he loves her "still well enough to forgive" her "petulance" and "acrimony."[13]

When Elizabeth apologizes for her misperception after accepting Darcy's second marriage proposal, he replies in kind: "What did you say of me, that I did not deserve? For, though your accusations were ill-founded, formed on mistaken premises, my behaviour to you at the time had merited the severest reproof. It was unpardonable. I cannot think of it without abhorrence."[14] Elizabeth agrees that they have both "improved in civility." But Darcy continues his apology. He relates that his parents encouraged him to be overbearing and selfish. "Such I was, from eight to eight and twenty; and such I might still have been but for you, dearest, loveliest Elizabeth! What do I not owe you! You taught me a lesson, hard indeed at first, but most advantageous. By you, I was properly humbled."[15]

According to Bell, not only can contempt be a fitting response to arrogance and superbia, it can also be a superior response to alternatives like anger or resentment.[16] Elizabeth's contempt for Darcy, Bell argues, is a case in point. When Darcy remarks toward the end of the novel that the contempt with which Elizabeth viewed him was well taken, this—Bell writes—illustrates that another person's contempt can provide us with a valuable perspective and make us realize that we ought to change our ways. By forcing us to reevaluate our attitudes and behaviors, being the target of contempt can restore the power balance in one's relationship.

Whether Elizabeth's scornful attitude changes Darcy's moral character as opposed to making him fall in love with her has been the subject of considerable debate.[17] But I agree with Bell that contempt can sometimes help deflate arrogance and superbia. However, anger and resentment can do this as well. As philosopher Robert Solomon has pointed out: "When we get angry, we elevate ourselves into a judgmental position, sort of like a magistrate in court. At first, we felt humiliated, but now we pass judgment on the person who insulted us. Anger helps us save face."[18] But if anger and resentment can also deflate arrogance and superbia, what makes contempt the better response?

The answer can be found in the differences in the focus of concern of resentment and contempt. When you resent a person for a wrongdoing, your focus of concern is the wrongful behavior, not her character. When you hold a person in contempt, by contrast, one focus of concern is her lowly character. Resentment complies with the famous adage "Attack the sin, not the sinner." Contempt challenges it. But for this very reason, contempt may be more effective than resentment in bringing a person down from a position of arrogance and superbia *and* keep them in their proper place. It is because contempt calls attention to vicious character traits, whereas anger and resentment are concerned only with past wrongdoing, that contempt is better suited as a tool for motivating people to change their ways.

Bell argues that contempt has the further virtue of being employable in our efforts to defeat systemic defeaters of social inequality, such as racism. Contempt's usefulness as a tool against racism turns on the arrogance that is built into racism. Bell writes:

> Those who harbor race-based contempt evince superbia: they see
> themselves as having a comparative high status in virtue of their

race, they desire that this status be recognized, and they often attempt to exact esteem and deference from others by dishonoring members of the despised race.[19]

According to Bell, the best way to respond to racial contempt is to "marshal a defiant counter-contempt."

In his 2013 review of Bell's monograph, Roberts offers an objection to this suggestion. According to Roberts, while contempt may be an apt response to superbia, as suggested by Bell, it is less clear that it is useful for overcoming vices of superiority like racism or slavery. A slave in colonial America could not realistically or safely have protested the abominable violation of her human rights by showing contempt for her owner.

Roberts is right, of course, that it's unwise to pour contempt on a violent oppressor. So, he is quite right to say that contempt is unlikely to conquer racial oppression, let alone slavery. But this shortcoming doesn't make it utterly futile to respond to contempt with counter-contempt. Counter-contempt may help alleviate the psychologically damaging effects of being the subject of contempt.[20] As Bell puts it, "if targets of racist contempt can disengage and dismiss the racists as low, then their self-esteem is less likely to be compromised by the racists' contempt."[21]

A similar sentiment has been voiced by philosopher Céline Leboeuf in her influential article "Anger as a Political Emotion" (2018). Leboeuf is particularly interested in the role of anger in disengaging the racist's condescending gaze. When a white person directs a condescending gaze at a black person, this can cause the black person to become disoriented and physically incapacitated. Leboeuf refers to this loss of control of one's own body as "bodily alienation." Bodily alienation is powerfully illustrated in the following two passages written by psychiatrist Frantz Fanon and philosopher George Yancy.

Passage 1, Fanon
And then we were given the occasion to confront the white gaze.
An unusual weight descended on us. The real world robbed us

of our share. In the white world, the man of color encounters difficulties in elaborating his body schema. . . . As a result, the body schema, attacked in several places, collapsed, giving way to an epidermal racial schema. In the train, it was a question of being aware of my body, no longer in the third person but in triple. In the train, instead of one seat, they left me two or three. I was no longer enjoying myself. I was unable to discover the feverish co-ordinates of the world. I existed in triple: I was taking up room. I approached the Other . . . and the Other, evasive, hostile, but not opaque, transparent and absent, vanished. Nausea.[22]

Passage 2, Yancy
Despite what I think about myself, how I am for-myself, her per-spective, her third-person account, seeps into my consciousness. I catch a glimpse of myself through her eyes and just for that mo-ment I experience some form of double consciousness, but what I see does not shatter my identity or unglue my sense of moral decency. Despite how my harmless actions might be constructed within her white racialized framework of seeing the world, I re-main capable of resisting the white gaze's entry into my own self-vision. I am angered. Indeed, I find her gaze disconcerting and despicable. As I undergo this double consciousness, my agency remains intact. My sense of who I am and how I am capable of being—that is, the various ways in which I am able to deploy an oppositional form of self-representation—has not been eradi-cated. I know that I am not a criminal or a rapist. At no point do I either desire to be white or begin to hate my dark skin. And while I recognize the historical power of the white gaze, a per-spective that carries the weight of white racist history and eve-ryday encounters of spoken and unspoken anti-Black racism, I do not seek white recognition, that is, the white woman's recognition. Though I would prefer that she does not see me through the distorting Black imago, I am not dependent upon

her recognition. For me to seek white recognition as a stimulus to a healthy sense of self-understanding is a form of pathology.[23]

The bodily alienation of Fanon's protagonist disrupts his ability to perform skillful action. He sees not just one but two or three empty seats on the train, but he is unable to move, because he no longer has a first-person perspective on where his limbs are in physical space. Ordinary sensory and motor feedback has been disrupted.

In passage 2, Yancy initially internalizes the white woman's gaze and looks down on himself with contempt, because she takes herself to be superior to him. Rather than experiencing his own body and movements from a first-person perspective, Yancy initially sees himself from the contemptuous perspective of the white woman. As a result, he initially becomes alienated from his own body. But rather than letting himself remain in a state of bodily alienation, he becomes angry, which helps him avoid crumbling under the weight of the white woman's scornful gaze.

According to Leboeuf, there is no use in seeking the white person's respect by looking back at them, as is also made clear by Yancy in passage 2. For the black man's movements to regain their skillful quality, Leboeuf argues, he needs to free himself from the restraints of the white gaze. Anger, she argues, can restore ordinary sensory-motor feedback because of its "expansive character." Anger allows the black person to resist the contempt directed at him and assert himself as a black man. He thereby reaffirms his sense of self in the wake of the contempt embodied in the white gaze.

Although Leboeuf's argument convincingly establishes anger as an effective means for members of oppressed groups to reaffirm themselves under oppressive conditions, her argument's focus on the expansive character of anger suggests that the exact nature of the attitude may be less important in restoring the oppressed person's sense of self than its phenomenology. Like anger, contempt is likely to provide the oppressed with the kind of resilience needed when faced with an oppressive person's contemptuous gaze.

To recap: critical contempt satisfies the marks of the reactive attitudes. Because it doesn't portray its target as subhuman, its depiction of its target is compatible with the target being a free agent, which is one of the marks of a reactive attitude. Critical contempt can furthermore be an effective response to the vices of superiority, such as arrogance, vanity, opportunism, and racial contempt. As such, it plays a significant role in upholding the norms regulating social interactions between people in the community, which is the second mark of a reactive attitude. Now, let's move on to the question of whether critical hate is a reactive attitude.

Eye for an Eye

Martha Nussbaum has argued that anger-type emotions like anger, resentment, and hate are never morally defensible.[24] This is because, she argues, the anger-type emotions are conceptually tied to retaliation and retribution. The only form of anger that is free of any retaliatory or retributive elements is what she calls "transition anger," an immediate outrage in response to a wrong that quickly transforms into something more admirable, such as activism for social justice. Transition anger is the kind of anger that would prompt us to exclaim, "How outrageous. Something should be done about that!" All other forms of anger, including resentment, envy, and hate, are morally indefensible, Nussbaum argues, because of their essential tie to retaliation or retribution. She thus disagrees with Strawson that anger and resentment can be appropriate responses to wrongs.

Unlike Nussbaum, however, Strawson did not take retaliation or retribution to lie at the conceptual core of anger and resentment.[25] Strawson argued that a desire for payback is a *common feature* of human responses to wrongs, but he didn't hold that anger and resentment are conceptually bound up with retaliation or retribution.

But hate is much more austere than resentment and blame. So, it might be thought that even if resentment and blame can occur without any retaliatory attitudes in tow, hatred is essentially retaliatory or retributive. I will argue that it is not. But first let's pause to consider what it is that is so bad about retaliation and retribution.

My grandfather was firm in his opinion of what should happen to people who sexually abuse children: they should be strapped to a meat slicer and be cut up like cold cuts, starting with the feet. I suspect that he is not alone in thinking that punishing someone for the suffering they inflicted by making them suffer is at least sometimes acceptable, if not morally justified. The thought is certainly entrenched in popular culture, for example, as encapsulated in the form of sayings such as "What goes around comes around," "You reap what you sow," "An eye for an eye, a tooth for a tooth," "She had it coming!" "Hubris calls for nemesis," "Let her have a taste of her own medicine," "Karma never loses an address," "Karma always strikes back."

"Retribution" is sometimes used as a synonym for "punishment." But this use of the term is somewhat misleading. Punishment is retributive only if its sole or primary aim is to punish the offender in proportion to the offense. In legal theory, retributivism is the view that punishment is justified because perpetrators deserve to be punished proportionally to the crime they committed, up to a limit. The opposing view, also known as "utilitarianism," takes punishment to be justified because it is useful to society, for instance, by deterring would-be offenders from committing crimes.

Legal or institutional retribution should be distinguished from personal retribution, or retaliation, which is the infliction of suffering on someone else to satisfy retaliatory desires. Philosopher Robert Nozick highlights some key differences between institutional retribution and personal revenge. One of the differences he identifies is a difference in pleasure. He writes:

> Revenge involves a particular emotional tone, pleasure in the suffering of another, while retribution either need involve no

emotional tone, or involves another one, namely, pleasure at justice being done.[26]

But what Nozick says here is not quite right. He presumes that the pleasure of revenge derives solely from the suffering inflicted on the aggressor and not from the thought that he deserves to suffer for what he has done. Yet the pleasure of revenge might, and probably often does, derive from the belief that the suffering is "just deserts."

The difference between institutional, or legal, retribution and personal revenge is that only the latter is done for the sake of satisfying a personal desire. Criminals are punished by the state (or the *people*), not by the victim or any other individual. It is true that individuals can, and probably do, feel pleasure when a criminal receives his just deserts, but this is not an intended consequence of criminal justice.

In Western societies, institutional retribution is widely regarded as just, whereas personal retribution, or retaliation, has a bad reputation.[27] But it is hard to put a finger on what exactly is wrong with retaliation.

Extremely cruel retaliation is clearly morally indefensible. In the 2015 American psychological-thriller film *Secret in Their Eyes* (a remake of an Argentinian film by the same title), Jessica "Jess" Cobb (played by Julia Roberts), an investigator for the Los Angeles district attorney's office, finds her eighteen-year-old daughter Carolyn's body in a dumpster, bleached inside and out to destroy DNA evidence of rape and murder. Jess and her friend Ray Kasten (Chiwetel Ejiofor) track down Carolyn's killer, Marzin, but he escapes prosecution when all evidence is destroyed in a fire, and the case is closed. Thirteen years later, Ray finds a man named Clay Beckwith, who he believes is Marzin living under an alias. But Jess insists that he is not her daughter's killer. Later, Ray follows Jess out to her barn and discovers to his dismay that she has kept Marzin in a cage for over a decade. Frazzled and mentally disturbed, Marzin begs Ray to ask Jess to talk to him. Ray leaves his gun behind and walks outside, where he starts digging a grave. In the background we hear Jess shoot Marzin.

Most of us cannot get ourselves to blame Jess for taking revenge against her daughter's killer. This is so, even though Marzin is kept in a cage like a tortured animal under conditions much worse than maximum security prison. But in spite of our sympathy for Jess, most of us would agree that even the most despicable among us have a right to a minimally decent life and that Jess' punishment of Marzin therefore is morally indefensible.

Because Jess' punishment of Marzin is so extremely wicked and cruel, it is easy to make a case for its lack of moral justification. But excessive cruelty is not essential to retaliation. Retaliation can be as "innocent" as asking a classmate who betrayed you to return the textbook you lent him, not because you need it, but because you want to punish him. An act done with a retaliatory attitude is still retaliation even if it merely inconveniences the other person.

What (if anything) is wrong with the more innocent forms of retaliation? Some say retaliation is pointless because it cannot undo the harm already done. In PBS' *Documenting Hate: Charlottesville*, writer and director Richard Rowley interviews the mother of Heather Heyer, who was killed when white supremacist James Alex Fields, Jr., deliberately drove his car into protesters of the Unite the Right rally in Charlottesville, Virginia, in August 2017. When asked what justice would be for Heyer in the upcoming trial of Fields, her mother replies that she didn't know how justice could ever be served, as nothing would ever bring her daughter back. Regardless of how harshly Fields were to be punished, this would never undo the brutal crime he committed. This is not a strike against retributive justice, but a valid point about justice: sometimes justice can never be fully restored.

Retaliation and retribution can both seem pointless. But this is not really the right way to characterize them. As the philosopher Jeffrey G. Murphy has pointed out, because retaliation satisfies retaliatory attitudes, it's not exactly pointless. Whether retaliation is morally defensible or even rational is a different question.

According to Murphy, however, retaliatory attitudes are perfectly acceptable, because they are "encoded in us by our evolutionary history." He writes:

> It certainly *seems* fitting that one strikes back when one has been injured—indeed, such a response seems encoded in us by our evolutionary history—and thus the vindictive person does not seem like the neurotic who does indeed have an emotion that is not fitting to its object—for example, a person who is phobic, who has an irrational fear of objects that are not in fact dangerous.[28]

The view Murphy expresses here is that retaliatory attitudes are fitting, because when we strike back with the aim of getting even, their biological purpose is fulfilled.

But this argument doesn't withstand scrutiny. Murphy is right, of course, that our tendency to avenge against wrongdoers is built into our biology. In the absence of police, courts, and prisons for protecting individual rights, revenge would have been the only feasible way for our ancestors to punish aggressors who violated individual rights. Being revenge-prone must therefore have been evolutionarily advantageous for our ancestors.

But a crucial question here is whether the primary purpose of our ancestors' retaliatory desires was to get even with aggressors. According to an influential hypothesis in evolutionary psychology set forth by my former colleague Michael McCullough and collaborators, getting even wasn't the primary purpose of our ancestors' retaliatory attitudes.[29] Rather, they hypothesize that the cognitive mechanisms for revenge evolved because revenge discouraged the aggressor and would-be aggressors from acting similarly in the future. As a result, revenge-prone individuals would have been treated with greater respect than those who were less revenge-prone and more forgiving, making our revenge-prone ancestors more attractive to potential mates.

But, McCullough and his collaborators argue, revenge also carries costs that can potentially offset its deterrence benefits. Although counter-revenge is an impending risk, revenge can be even more costly when it leads to the loss of a valuable relationship. In such cases, forgiveness may be the less costly path, especially if the aggressor can provide some guarantee that he or she will not be a repeat offender. So, they argue, forgiveness mechanisms evolved to preserve valuable relationships when the cost of revenge was greater than the cost of severing the relationship.

If this hypothesis is right, then the biological purpose of the desire for revenge is not to strike back in order to get even, as Murphy argues, but rather to strike back in order to deter the aggressor and would-be aggressors. So understood, our ancestors' so-called retaliatory attitudes were not aimed at getting even. Their biological purpose wasn't satisfied by an act of vengeance, in Murphy's sense, but rather by an act of deterrence.

But I will not rest my case on the evolutionary purpose of retaliatory attitudes. Instead, I will argue that retaliation is morally indefensible and that retaliatory attitudes are irrational. Retaliation is by definition an act that satisfies a retaliatory desire. Because it is pleasurable when a desire is satisfied, retaliation is a pleasurable infliction of suffering on another person in order to get even. But taking pleasure in another person's suffering is to treat that person *merely* as a means to an end, namely as a means to one's own pleasure. Retaliation thus violates Kant's principle of respect, which states that it's morally indefensible to treat people merely as a means to an end. By treating another person merely as a means to an end, we dehumanize them, which is indisputably wrong. As retaliation infringes on an indisputable principle of morality, it is morally indefensible.

Because retaliation is never morally defensible, asking to get your textbook back from a classmate who borrowed it is wrong if the reason you want it back is that you want to avenge his betrayal. It would not be wrong to ask him to return the book if you really needed it. Nor would it be wrong to ask to get it back because you no longer trust that he will take good care of it. If we cannot trust a person to treat us with decency, then how can we trust them to take care of our things?

What about retaliatory attitudes? Retaliatory attitudes too are irrational. Here is the argument. Not wanting to act on fundamental moral principles is irrational. As the principle of respect is a fundamental moral principle, not wanting to act on it is irrational. So, it's irrational to want to treat other people merely as a means to an end. But if you have a desire to retaliate against your neighbor, say, then you have a desire to treat him merely as a means to an end, namely as a means to satisfy your own retaliatory desire. So, this desire is irrational.

Of course, it might be that you want to retaliate against your neighbor but that you also want to abide by the principle of respect. In this scenario, you both want and don't want to treat your neighbor merely as a means to an end. But this is an instance of cognitive dissonance, an irrational state of mind. So, either way, having a retaliatory desire is irrational.

Because institutional retribution isn't punishment aimed at satisfying anyone's desire, it doesn't fall prey to the same problems as retaliation. But it has been notoriously difficult for retributivists to come up with a valid argument for their position. Perhaps the most convincing defense of retributivism is the social justice argument, developed at length by moral philosopher Jean Hampton.[30] Here is the gist of it. When someone wrongs you, they infringe on your rights and interests. In doing so, they communicate that their rights and interests are more important than yours. Hampton writes:

> If I have a value equal to that of my assailant, then that must be made manifest after I have been victimized. By victimizing me, the wrongdoer has declared himself elevated with respect to me, acting as a superior who is permitted to use me for his purposes.[31]

Hampton's point is that your assailant violates your right to be treated with decency and not to be violated on the basis of ill will or reckless disregard. By infringing on your right, he is sending the message: "Given the circumstances, my well-being is more important than yours. Your right not to be violated by me is therefore temporarily suspended."

Punishing the assailant in proportion to the crime, up to a point, is a fitting response to this message.

Hampton's position is an expressivist variant of retributivism. Expressivism does not justify harsh punishment or even imprisonment. When suffering is inflicted as part of the punishment, this is because of what it symbolizes. For lesser crimes, the corrective claim can be communicated well enough in ways other than imprisonment, for instance, by sentencing the criminal to pay restoration to the victim or do community service.

Critics, such as Murphy and legal theorist Ken Levy, have raised two related worries about Hampton's argument.[32] One worry is this: if we merely need to correct a false claim, why don't we just make a public statement to that effect? Why do we punish criminals?

A related worry is this: if criminals were merely guilty of defaming their victims, then it would be wrong to send them to prison. Defamation is tried in civil court, where a guilty verdict results in victim compensation, usually money, never a prison sentence.

This sort of criticism of Hampton's argument is wrong-headed, however. Her point is not that assault is defamatory. Rather, the assailant's actions reveal information about his attitude toward his victim at the time of the violation. This attitude is bound up with his motive. By harming the victim, the assailant communicates to the public that he regards his own interests as more important than the victim's fundamental human rights. But he doesn't use ordinary speech to convey this message. The vehicle that carries the information is the violation of the victim's fundamental human rights.

The aim of retributive punishment is to provide a fitting response to the assailant's mistaken attitude, revealed by the message he conveys, using a related form of communication, that is, a reduction of his rights. Take rape. A rapist whose ultimate aim is sexual gratification conveys the flamboyantly arrogant attitude: "My interest in sexual gratification is more important than your rights to personal autonomy and dignity." This message, if spoken, is indeed false. But this is not the reason the rapist's rights are reduced by being put behind bars. His rights are reduced because that's a fitting response to his physical violation of the victim's rights.

Hating without Dehumanizing

Because retaliation is dehumanizing, retaliatory hatred is never morally defensible. Whether hate is ever morally defensible thus depends on whether it is essentially tied to retaliatory attitudes, as Nussbaum has argued that it is.

Here I disagree with Nussbaum. Haters need not be fuming with lust for revenge. Hate is a reaction to the hated target's perceived wrongdoing and her apparent malevolence and potential power and threat. When you hate another person, you resent them for their wrongdoing, you disrespect (or condemn) them for their malevolence, and you are apprehensive of their potential power and threat. But only dehumanizing hatred has any close ties to retaliatory attitudes. Resentment, critical disrespect, and apprehension are not essentially tied to retaliatory attitudes. So, hate is not essentially retaliatory.

This leaves us with critical hate as a potential candidate to be a reactive attitude, in Strawson's sense.[33] For this strain of hate to be a reactive attitude, it must at a minimum be fitting. This, in turn, requires that the hated target is responsible for violating the hater or someone in her circle of concern, and that the target is indeed malevolent (or evil) and potentially powerful and dangerous.

It may be argued that these conditions are never satisfied, because there is no such thing as malevolence. One reason for denying that there is such a thing as malevolence originates in skepticism about character traits. Philosophers such as John Doris, Gil Harman, and Mark Alfano have argued that there is no such thing as a stable character trait across all situations.[34] This is also known as the situationist challenge to character traits. In a nutshell, the challenge runs like this (using the specific traits good and bad as an illustration). When good people are put in really bad situations, they tend to act badly. So, both good and bad people sometimes act badly. The distinction between good and bad is therefore meaningless when applied to persons.

By way of reply, it's true that a bad enough situation can make a good person behave badly.[35] But that's just what it is for a person to act "out of character." When situational pressures are the main determinant of your behavior, your personality or character has little influence on your behavior. That's why we say that you're acting "out of character." Good people act badly only in very bad situations, that is, situations that exert an exceptionally strong influence on their behavior. Bad people, by contrast, act badly even in situations that don't exert all that much influence on their behavior.[36] In these situations, they don't act "out of character." Rather, their character traits exert a very strong influence on their behavior.

During the Holodomor, the Soviets' man-made famine, millions of Ukrainians starved to death.[37] Josef Stalin seized their grain and livestock and sealed off the area. People became so hungry that they resorted to cannibalism. Some parents whose children died from starvation survived by cooking and eating them. The Holodomor created situations that were extremely strong determinants of people's food-related actions. Those who refused to steal, enter prostitution, or resort to cannibalism died.[38] Those who shared their food with others died even sooner. Survivors were acting in ways they would never have acted just two years earlier: eating dead bodies, stealing children's food, prostituting themselves, hiding food from people who were starving. But they were not bad people. They were acting "out of character."[39] Bad people act badly even in situations that do not exert much influence on their behavior. The infamous serial killer Jeffrey Dahmer devoured his victims. But he did it because he was evil, not because external forces pressured him into doing it.

It is true that depravity, like other character traits, falls on a spectrum. At one extreme are people like Stalin and Hitler, who ruthlessly murdered millions of people. At the other extreme are people like the workplace bully, who gleefully makes you and your coworkers miserable. Despite being polar opposites, both types of mindset are inimical to the respect we owe one another. Common parlance urges us to reserve strong terms like "evil" and "malevolent" for the most depraved and softer terms like "bad" and "wicked" for those who are not quite as depraved, but this is merely a preference of taste. When used to refer to a point on a spectrum of depravity and not merely to attributes of actions, terms like "evil," "malevolent," "wicked," and "bad" are synonymous.

Absent any reasons to reject that depravity exists, hate can be a fitting attitude. It's fitting when its target's malevolence is the source of their wrongdoing (or plans to do wrong). Thus, it would have been fitting for the parents of Dahmer's victims to hate him for murdering their children, but it would not have been fitting for a Ukrainian during the Holodomor to hate her neighbors for not sharing their scraps of food with her.

But showing that hate can be fitting doesn't suffice to show that it's rational or that it helps monitor and safeguard our normative ideals, which is a mark of the reactive attitudes.

As we saw in Chapter 1, hate that interferes with your ability to function optimally is irrational. So, is hate that doesn't yield to reasons that it is unfitting. Even critical hate—hate that doesn't dehumanize—can be all-consuming and immune to reasons. But critical hate that is more temperate need not interfere with your ability to function optimally, and it will in all likelihood be reason-responsive. If you hate your friend for the egregious act she seems to have committed but then discover that she is innocent, then she would in all likelihood no longer be the target of your hatred.

The question remains, however, whether critical hate can play a role in upholding our normative ideals. Here is an argument that it can. When one person wrongs another, the wrongful act conveys the message: "Given the circumstances, my interests are more important than your rights, and your right not to be violated by me is therefore (temporarily) suspended." Anger's focus is the aggressor's wrongdoing and attitude at the time. So, anger is a fitting response when the situation exerted a significant influence on the assailant's actions. So are blame, resentment, and indignation. But anger isn't a strong enough response when a wrongdoer acts on the basis of malevolence or evil.

The hate-proneness and contempt-proneness that lies at the heart of malevolence and evil reflect a deep-rooted and dehumanizing arrogance that is anchored in an implicit belief to the effect that one's victims or would-be victims are lesser people than oneself and therefore have no right not to be violated. To blame an evildoer for his wrongful act rather than condemning him for his deep-rooted arrogance and abominable beliefs about hierarchies of humans is to silently approve of his mindset: his vicious traits and convictions. Rather than merely being a disapproval of the wrongful act, critical hate is a form of disrespect for the evildoer for his arrogance and abominable beliefs.

Hate also helps safeguard norms and ideals outside the moral realm. As psychologists John Rempel and Siobhan Sutherland have argued, in the context of a relationship, "the communicative aspect of expressions of hate may provide opportunities for both partners to learn potentially important lessons about themselves and each other."[40] As a reaction to a significant offense in the context of a relationship, hate can furthermore communicate to the other person and to yourself how important an issue really is or how much you have been hurt. Because hate is harder to brush aside than blame and resentment, it is a more effective means of engendering guilt, which in turn can prompt the other person to take measures to change for the better. Hate thus serves a worthwhile purpose, not already served by blame or resentment. It is paramount to upholding the norms of a free and just society, both morally and non-morally.

In closing, while dehumanizing hatred is deplorable and insupportable, hate that doesn't dehumanize—what I have called "critical hate"—can be rational and morally appropriate, and it furthermore has an important part to play in monitoring our moral and cultural ideals.

Dehumanizing hate doesn't play any worthwhile role in our lives. It's the attitude fueling the malicious acts of workplace bullies, perpetrators of domestic violence, rapists, imposters, and psychopathic killers. But what's the basis of the dehumanizing hatred that fuels malicious acts? As we will see in the next chapter, a common basis is hate- and contempt-proneness, usually toward certain types of people or groups of people. Hate- and contempt-proneness are components of malevolence, or evil. If, however, malevolent, or evil, people are moved to do bad things by their character or personality traits, this raises the question of whether they should be held liable for their abominable acts. In the next chapter, we will look specifically at whether narcissists, borderlines, and psychopaths are responsible for their actions, but our conclusions also applies to those who hate others on account of their group membership.

4 | BAD TO THE BONE
HATE AS A TRAIT

In 1984, shortly after Elisabeth turned eighteen, her father asked her to help him with a door in the basement of the family home in Amstetten, Austria.[1] She was holding the door so her dad could fit it in its frame when he suddenly grabbed her and placed a cloth over her mouth. She tried to fight him, but her limbs gave way under her, and soon everything went dark.

When she came to, she discovered to her dismay that she was trapped in the dark behind a locked door, her hands tied behind her back. She started screaming and kicking the door and walls, but no one came to her rescue. After she'd been crying out for hours on end, her dad finally showed up. Praying that it was all a terrible mistake, she begged for his help. But he didn't come to her rescue. Instead he chained her to the wall and raped her. After he was done, he told her she would get electrocuted if she attempted to escape.

Josef Fritzl, Elisabeth's dad, had constructed the dungeon over the previous six years with the sole purpose of imprisoning his daughter inside it. The dungeon was a series of connected windowless chambers, less than six feet high, behind a concealed door in the house's basement. The rooms had areas for sleeping, cooking, and washing. Eight doors with conventional and electronic locks separated the dungeon from the outside world. The outermost door was made of reinforced concrete. It was running on steel rails and was secured electronically.

When Elisabeth didn't return that night, her mother reported her missing. But because she was an adult when she disappeared and had run away from home before, the police believed the letter Fritzl provided, allegedly written by Elisabeth, was authentic. The letter stated that she was tired of living with her family and was staying with a friend; she warned her family not to look for her or she would leave the country.

Over the next twenty-four years Elisabeth was kept imprisoned in the dungeon as a sex slave. Several times a week Fritzl would come down to rape her. He bought her skimpy outfits and lingerie to wear in the basement. He also made her watch hard porn and ordered her to reenact the sex scenes. The most violent sessions would last many hours and left her with internal injuries from her dad's oversized sex toys.

When Elisabeth was twenty, she became pregnant for the first time but miscarried after ten weeks. Several miscarriages later, she gave birth to the first of her seven children without any medical assistance or sterile equipment. Fritzl continued to rape and torture her after the children were born.

Three of the children, Kerstin, Stefan, and Felix, were held captive with their mother and never saw daylight. One child died after birth because of lack of medical attention. The remaining three were brought upstairs, where they were raised by Fritzl and his wife, who got approval by the local social services to be their foster parents.

Fritzl's official story was that his missing daughter had joined a religious sect but had returned on three occasions to dump the children on her parents' doorstep. On all three occasions a note that allegedly was from Elisabeth was left saying she was unable to take care of her children. In 1994 Fritzl made a phone call to his wife pretending to be their daughter.

In 2008, the eldest of the imprisoned children, Kerstin, became gravely ill and fell unconscious, and Elisabeth convinced her father to call an ambulance. Her father agreed, and Kerstin was taken to the hospital with a note allegedly written by Elisabeth, stating that she hoped they would take good care of her daughter.

The staff found parts of Fritzl's story suspicious and alerted the police, who reopened the case file on Elisabeth's disappearance. When Elisabeth heard on a radio in the dungeon that the police wanted her to come forward with further details of Kerstin's medical history, she talked her father into taking her to see her daughter in the hospital.

Fritzl agreed and freed Elisabeth and the other two children. This led to Fritzl's arrest, sentencing, and imprisonment.

The magnitude of the contempt and hatred Fritzl must have harbored for his own daughter to bring this level of depravity and suffering upon her is difficult to comprehend. Prior to his trial, his sanity was widely questioned on social media—a debate Fritzl's legal team helped fuel in the hopes that it might allow for an insanity defense. However, it was eventually determined that Fritzl wasn't in the grip of a schizophrenic, manic, or depressive psychosis that made it impossible for him to tell right from wrong, thus ruling out an insanity defense. Indeed, Fritzl had already told the press that he knew what he did was wrong.

Fritzl acted the way he did, not because he was in an altered state of consciousness that made him completely lose touch with reality, but rather because he was infected with the moral rot of a sadistic psychopath.

Psychopathy is a constellation of enduring traits of personality, not a mental illness that causes the person to "act out of character." Dispositional hate and contempt lie at the heart of psychopathy. That is, psychopaths have trait-like tendencies to feel hate or contempt toward other people, especially individuals who make them feel ill at ease.

In this chapter, we will look closer at how dispositional contempt and hate are manifested in narcissism, borderline personality, and psychopathy and what dispositional contempt and hate can tell us about the nature of personality extremes, malevolence and moral and legal responsibility.

The Contemptuous Person

Stable dispositions to harbor emotional attitudes, such as spitefulness, anger-proneness or disgust-sensitivity, are special kinds of personality traits, also known as emotion traits.[2] A personality trait is a stable disposition to respond in a particular way across a range of situations. For example, anger-proneness is a stable tendency to react with intense anger across many different situations. Contempt-proneness and hate-fulness are examples of emotion traits. They are stable dispositions to harbor contemptuous or hateful attitudes toward others. Social psychologist Roberta A. Schriber and her collaborators define contempt-proneness as the tendency to "look down on, feel cold toward, and derogate or distance others who violate their standards and values."[3] Unlike emotions, which are directed at a specific person or event, even when they occur below the level of conscious awareness, emotion traits are stable dispositions that partially determine how readily and strongly a person experiences a given emotion in a triggering situation. For example, a person who is anger-prone is more likely than the average individual to get angry at others across a wide range of different situations.

Antagonistic emotion traits, such as anger-proneness or dispositional contempt, can be dispositions to have the relevant emotion toward people in general or dispositions to have the relevant emotion toward certain types of people or groups of people, for instance, people who are critical of you, women who remind you of your deceptive mother, or people who belong to particular social identity groups, say, blacks, homosexuals, or women.

The dispositional contempt scale, a personality inventory developed by Schriber and her colleagues, is aimed at measuring general contempt-proneness in the normal population. The scale consists of the following ten questions, which must be answered on a five-point scale ranging from 1 (*Never*) to 5 (*Almost always*):

1. I tend to disregard people who fall short of my standards.
2. I often lose respect for others.
3. Feeling disdain for others comes naturally to me.
4. I tend to accept people regardless of their flaws.
5. I would never try to make someone feel worthless.
6. I often feel like others are wasting my time.
7. I hardly ever think others are inferior to me.

8. All in all, I am repelled by others' faults.
9. Others tend to give me reasons to look down on them.
10. I often feel contempt for others.

After determining general contempt-proneness in a group of test subjects, Schriber and her team then administered other personality inventories in order to assess which personality traits are linked to general contempt-proneness.[4] As expected, the researchers found that contempt-proneness is highly associated with tendencies toward exploitativeness, excessive pride, and a feeling of entitlement.[5] More surprisingly, dispositional contempt, despite involving a tendency to look down on others, was found to be associated with a fragile self-esteem.[6]

Although surprising at first, the link between dispositional contempt and a fragile self-esteem can be explained by the fact that not everyone with a fragile self-esteem is your typical self-effacing person. Psychologists Jessica Tracy and Richard Robins point to Willy Loman, the tragic protagonist in Arthur Miller's 1949 play *Death of a Salesman*, as a paradigmatic example of a person with a fragile self-esteem. Loman's sense of self is split between a positive self-image, which is consciously present to him most of the time, and a mostly unconscious negative self-image. According to the positive idealized self-image, he is a successful salesman, who has raised two talented sons. According to the negative self-image, he has failed as a businessman and a father.

Although mostly hidden from conscious awareness, a person's negative self-image is ordinarily readily available to consciousness. Loman, however, has developed a defense mechanism that keeps his negative self-image under the radar most of the time. This protects him against having to face the self-doubt. Loman's defense mechanism is to look at himself and present himself to others in a deceptively positive light; he adjusts his memories to ensure that they paint a picture of him and his sons as successful, and he makes up excuses when necessary to explain failures. Despite these efforts, however, his negative views of himself make their way into his conscious mind every so often, causing his positive self-image to crack. Loman's actual feeling of self-worth is thus highly unstable, ranging from excessive pride and arrogance to pathetic self-pity.

In the scenes where Loman feels good about himself, he is a quintessential contemptuous person: he is exploitative, takes excessive pride in his imagined accomplishments, and feels entitled to special treatment. For example, despite having failed in his current job as a salesman, he is unshakeable in his conviction that his boss will offer him a new position that doesn't require traveling.

Schriber and her team also found that contempt-proneness was associated with the dark triad of personality, which social psychologists Delroy Paulhus and Kevin Williams introduced under that heading in their seminal 2002 paper "The Dark Triad of Personality." "The dark triad" refers to the constellation of narcissism, psychopathy, and Machiavellianism, which are all tendencies toward malevolent, or evil, behaviors that can be spotted in the normal (or subclinical) population.[7] Sadism was subsequently included as a fourth trait in the so-called "dark tetrad."

There is a considerable overlap among the dark personalities. To varying degrees, they all imply a malevolent or evil character with trait-like tendencies toward self-promotion, duplicity, callous exploitation, emotional coldness, contempt, hatred, and aggression.[8] But despite their overlap, the dark traits are distinct personality constructs, and each has its own core facets.

In personality psychology, "Machiavellianism" refers to a duplicitous interpersonal style characterized by tendencies to manipulate, deceive, and exploit others to achieve their goals; "narcissism" refers to an inflated sense of self-importance, an excessive need for admiration, and a lack of empathy; "psychopathy" refers to an unusually high need for excitement and thrills, an impairment in the ability to feel arousal, and a lack of empathy; and "sadism" refers to the tendency to experience pleasure through other people's denigration, discomfort, or pain.[9] The most draconic form of psychopathy includes all the dark personality traits.

In the following section we will look closer at how contempt-proneness is manifested in narcissism, and how certain relationship dynamics can lead to the development of both a narcissistic personality and contempt-proneness.

Two Faces of Narcissism

"Just came from an investor meeting," Nick said, grasping Dr. Malkin's hand firmly in greeting.[10]

The dean had referred Nick for counseling because his parents had become concerned and irate about his absences from class.

"Have a seat." The doctor gestured toward the chair on the other side of his desk. "I assume you know why you are here."

"Yeah, the thing is, I've got bigger fish to fry than going to class," Nick replied, smiling broadly. "I'm starting up a company with a friend. We got the idea one night when we'd been drinking for hours. But it's a great plan."

"Terrific," Dr. Malkin responded. "Congrats."

"I know how to sell myself," Nick said, shrugging. "It's what I do."

Sitting in a classic power position—arms clasped behind his neck, elbows out, Nick looked more like a business executive than a student. He dressed the part, too—a sleek navy-blue suit, gleaming leather shoes, a red-and-blue-striped tie.

"Are you any good at this?" Nick asked. "I don't have much time to waste."

"Guess we'll find out," Malkin replied, feeling sure Nick had already decided. "As I understand it, you might get kicked out because you've missed so many papers and assignments."

"Dean tell you that?" he shot back, snidely. He leaned back, crossing his arms. "Listen, they have to keep me in school. I might be the best thing that's happened to them in a while. The least they can do is try to hold on to me. If they don't, they'll see what a mistake they've made when my idea takes off and I make a killing."

"You can appreciate the dean's position, though?" Malkin asked, curious if he had any perspective on how much jeopardy he'd placed himself in.

"I can talk my parents into anything," he assured the professor. "I can talk pretty much anyone into anything," he added. "They'll convince him just like they did before." He combed his fingers through his hair. "People are making a big deal out of nothing. I can crank out the rest of my work, no problem."

"What made you decide to come to see me?" Malkin asked. "You didn't have to."

"I figured you just need to give me a clean bill of health," Nick answered matter-of-factly.

"Ah," Malkin said. "It doesn't quite work that way, unfortunately. We need to . . ."

"Look," Nick interrupted, "I get that I have to convince the dean's bosses. That's why my parents are paying for this. If you can't help me, I'm sure I can find someone else to get the job done." He started getting up to leave.

"Feel free to leave," Malkin said calmly. "But that isn't going to help you. Part of the problem is you don't think you need anyone's help. You've got a lot of talent and ambition, which is fantastic. But you can't rely on that alone to carry you. If that worked, you wouldn't be sitting across from me now. And the dean wouldn't be meeting with the school next Monday about whether or not this is your last semester here."

That seemed to get Nick's attention. He sat back down.

The case study is adapted from Harvard Medical School psychologist and Huffington Post blogger Craig Malkin's book *Rethinking Narcissism*. As Malkin points out, Nick is a classical narcissist. His attitude smacks of superbia, entitlement, and contempt for other people. He treats Dr. Malkin as his "simple-minded servant," whose only value resides in his presumed ability to get him out of trouble.

It is unsurprising that there is a strong link between narcissism and contempt-proneness. The narcissist looks down on the rest of us mortal beings from his judgmental umpire chair, feeling appalled by our inferiority and weakness. This is the ugly face of contempt-proneness.

The kind of narcissism Nick presents with is a subclinical variant of narcissistic personality disorder. In the fifth edition of the American

Psychiatric Association's *Diagnostic and Statistical Manual of Mental Disorders* (DSM-5), personality disorders and episodic or emerging illnesses of the mind, like depression, schizophrenia, or anorexia nervosa, are listed side by side, masking the key differences between the two varieties of mental disorder.

So-called episodic mental illnesses such as depression, schizophrenia, or anorexia nervosa are ordinarily time- or episode-limited; their successful treatment does not require people to undergo a personality change; and they can typically be successfully treated or controlled with medication or some other conventional form of medical intervention. Personality disorders like narcissism, psychopathy, and borderline personality disorder involve durable personality traits; any successful treatment would require major personality changes; and while personality disorders can sometimes be successfully treated through psychoanalysis or cognitive-behavioral therapy, they cannot be treated with conventional forms of medical intervention.

Personality disorders present a puzzle of sorts. When a person suffers from a personality disorder, their disordered personality is an integral part of who they are—what we might call the "(embodied) person." Successfully treating a personality disorder destroys the person and puts another one in their place, which makes the successful treatment of personality disorders a double-edged sword: it cures by killing. It cures the human being, the living body that serves as the bearer of personality traits. But in the process of curing the human being, it destroys the embodied person and allows an entirely different person to take root. Live and be sick. Or die and get cured.

The destructive nature of personality modification is explored in Anthony Burgess' dystopian 1962 novel *A Clockwork Orange*. In the fictional totalitarian society, a sociopath named Alex, who robs, rapes, and assaults innocent people for his own amusement, is chosen to undergo state-sponsored aversion therapy for his aberrant behavior. Alex is injected with nausea-inducing drugs and is forced to watch graphically violent films. This eventually conditions him to become physically sick at the mere thought of violence. Alex is released from prison, but the treatment has not only cured his violent streak, it has also extinguished what made Alex Alex. Gone are his poetic descriptions of gore, his passion for classical music, even his will to live.

Because a patient's disordered personality is part of who they are, and who they have been as adults, they will usually have desensitized to their own disordered thinking and behavior. Accordingly, the afflicted person does not always experience any clinical symptoms. In fact, personality disorders often cause greater distress to the people who interact with the afflicted person than to the disordered person himself. When the afflicted person does experience clinical symptoms, these symptoms tend to be secondary to the disorder; for example, narcissists and borderlines often present with a depressed mood when seeking professional help. Psychiatrist Robert Michels summarizes the strangeness of personality disorders in DSM-5:

> When a patient presents to a psychiatrist, symptoms are generally those aspects of psychopathology that are easiest to recognize and to diagnose. Anxiety, depression, obsessions, and phobias are seen similarly by patient and doctor and are central defining characteristics of many disorders. Patients with personality disorders are different. Their problems are often more distressing to others than to the patient, and their symptoms are often vague and may seem secondary to their central issue. What determines the diagnosis or defines the focus of treatment is not the anxiety or depression, for example, but rather who the patient is, the life he or she has chosen to lead, and the pattern of his or her human relationships.[11]

The lack of definitive (amoral) clinical symptoms in narcissism and the importance of morally inappropriate behavior in diagnosing the condition has made philosophers question the assumption that the condition is a clinical disorder. Narcissism, it has been argued, is better understood as a moral disorder that can only be successfully treated through moral education and correction. We will ponder the question of the status of narcissism in the next section.

DSM-5 defines narcissistic personality disorder, the clinical variant of narcissism, as a pervasive pattern of grandiosity in fantasy or behavior, a need for admiration, and a lack of empathy, beginning in early adulthood and present in a variety of contexts, as indicated by five (or more) of the following behavioral patterns:

1. Has a grandiose sense of self-importance (e.g., exaggerates achievements and talents, expects to be recognized as superior without commensurate achievements).
2. Is preoccupied with fantasies of unlimited success, power, brilliance, beauty, or ideal love.
3. Believes that he or she is "special" and unique and can only be understood by, or should associate with, other special or high-status people (or institutions).
4. Requires excessive admiration.
5. Has a sense of entitlement (i.e., unreasonable expectations of especially favorable treatment or automatic compliance with his or her expectations).
6. Is interpersonally exploitative (i.e., takes advantage of others to achieve his or her own ends).
7. Lacks empathy; is unwilling to recognize or identify with the feelings and needs of others.
8. Is often envious of others or believes that others are envious of him or her.
9. Shows arrogant, haughty behaviors or attitudes.

Clinical narcissists display co-occurring or oscillating states of grandiosity and hypersensitivity/vulnerability.[12] Accordingly, inventories used to determine pathological narcissism, like the Pathological Narcissism Inventory, encompass hypersensitivity/vulnerability measures alongside measures of grandiosity.[13] In the Pathological Narcissism Inventory, grandiosity is measured by the patient's responses on a five-point scale to questions like "I often fantasize about being recognized for my accomplishments," "I often fantasize about being rewarded for my efforts," and "I want to amount to something in the eyes of the world," whereas hypersensitivity/vulnerability is assessed by the patient's responses on a five-point scale to questions like "It's hard for me to feel good about myself unless I know other people like me," "It's hard to show others the weaknesses I feel inside," and "I like to have friends who rely on me because it makes me feel important." Because of the co-occurrence or oscillation of grandiosity and hypersensitivity/vulnerability in clinical narcissism, there are no officially recognized subtypes of narcissistic personality disorder.

Clinical narcissism is rare. It only affects about 1 percent of the population, and this number appears to stay fairly constant.[14] When a flashy headline exclaims that narcissism is on the rise, the term "narcissism" is used to refer to the more prevalent subclinical, or everyday, variant of narcissism seen in the general population. Upward of 10 percent of people in their twenties are believed to suffer from subclinical narcissism severe enough to compromise their interpersonal relationships.[15]

There are two subtypes of subclinical narcissism: grandiose narcissism, which is continuous with narcissistic personality disorder, and vulnerable (also known as "hypersensitive" or "covert") narcissism. Both subtypes have self-centeredness as a core feature, but the self-absorption is expressed differently in the two cases.

Grandiose narcissism is characterized by extraversion, low neuroticism, and overt expressions of feelings of superiority and entitlement. Owing to their grandiosity, grandiose narcissists believe that they are somehow above the rest of us, and that they therefore are entitled to special treatment. In their view, our job is to cater to their needs. They are true egomaniacs.

Vulnerable narcissism reflects introversive self-absorbedness, high neuroticism, hypersensitivity even to gentle criticism, and a constant need for reassurance. As Malkin points out in *Rethinking Narcissism*, vulnerable narcissists "are just as convinced that they're better than others as any other narcissist, but they fear criticism so viscerally that they shy away from, and even seem panicked by, people and attention."[16]

Owing to the apparent lack of a common core between the subtypes, most personality researchers regard grandiose and vulnerable narcissism as independent traits. However, the fact that the two traits are co-present or oscillate in narcissistic personality disorder, the clinical type, suggests that they do in fact have a common basis.[17]

By controlling for differences in extraversion, psychologist Emanuel Jauk and colleagues were able to show that grandiose and vulnerable narcissists share a common core of narcissistic traits, including contempt-proneness.[18] But the distinct narcissistic styles of the two subtypes was not found to be due merely to differential scores on extraversion. Because of their high neuroticism and hypersensitivity to criticism, vulnerable narcissists are prone to overreact emotionally, always on the verge of bursting open with hatred.

Vulnerable narcissism is associated with a dissociation of the self-image into an explicit, positive self-image and an implicit, negative self-image.[19] The positive self-image is associated with excessive pride, whereas the negative self-image is associated with shame and humiliation. When receiving only positive feedback, the narcissist is able to keep the negative shame-filled self-image hidden below the level of conscious awareness. But when they experience external feedback as criticism, they are forced to confront their negative self-image and endure the feeling of deep-rooted shame.

Whereas the vulnerable narcissist is struggling with internally conflicting self-images, no hidden negative self-representation is threatening to make a dent in the grandiose narcissist's positive self-image. Negative feedback therefore doesn't have as profound an impact on the grandiose narcissist. But the deep shame that negative feedback brings upon the vulnerable narcissist turns her into a combustible compound destined to explode in frightening outbursts of anger or all-consuming fits of hatred.[20] This hostile reaction to insinuations of imperfection in vulnerable narcissists and individuals with narcissistic personality disorder is also known as "narcissistic rage."

Is Narcissism Just Plain Bad Behavior?

Is narcissism a medical condition or a way of being bad? Philosopher Louis Charland has argued that it's the latter.[21] Narcissism, he argues, is a disorder of moral character. His argument targets not just narcissism but all the cluster B personality disorders, as classified by DSM-5.

The cluster B personality disorders, also known as "the dramatic, emotional, and erratic cluster," encompass narcissistic personality disorder, histrionic personality disorder, borderline personality disorder, and antisocial personality disorder. (I am going to set aside histrionic personality disorder in what follows.)[22] There are two other clusters of personality disorders: the odd and eccentric cluster, or cluster A, which encompasses paranoid personality disorder, schizoid personality disorder, and schizotypal personality disorder—and the anxious and fearful cluster, or cluster C, which includes avoidant personality disorder, dependent personality disorder, and obsessive-compulsive personality disorder.

Charland presents two arguments for his claim that the cluster B personality disorders are disorders of moral character: the Argument from Identification and the Argument from Treatment. The gist of the Argument from Identification is this. The cluster B disorders, Charland argues, differ in a crucial respect from cluster A and cluster C disorders: their characterization makes use of moral notions, whereas the characterizations of the other two clusters do not. Narcissistic personality disorder, for example, is characterized using morally laden language such as "interpersonal exploitative behavior," "lack of empathy," "unwillingness to recognize or identify with the feelings and needs of others," "arrogant, haughty behaviors and attitudes."[23] Borderline personality disorder makes use of language that refers to morally disvalued attitudes and behaviors like "manipulativeness," "inappropriate, intense anger," and "proneness to sudden and dramatic shifts in their view of others, alternating between extremes of idealization and devaluation." Finally, antisocial personality disorder is characterized using terms referring to even more egregious moral attitudes and behaviors, such as "deceitfulness," "repeated lying, use of aliases, or conning others for personal profit or pleasure," "lack of remorse," and "indifference to having hurt, mistreated, or stolen from others."

The identifying characteristics of the other two clusters, by contrast, have no moral overtones. Take, for example, schizoid personality disorder, a cluster A disorder. It's characterized by a pattern of detachment from social relationships and a restricted range of emotional expression, as shown by at least four of the following seven characteristics:

1. Neither desires nor enjoys close relationships, including being part of a family.
2. Almost always chooses solitary activities.
3. Has little, if any, interest in having sexual experiences with another person.
4. Takes pleasure in few, if any, activities.
5. Lacks close friends or confidants other than first-degree relatives.
6. Appears indifferent to the praise or criticism of others.
7. Shows emotional coldness, detachment, or flattened affectivity.

Neither the criteria for schizoid personality disorder nor the accompanying narrative differentiating it from other disorders makes use of distinctly moral terminology. The same is true of the other disorders in the A and C clusters.

The reason that moral terminology is used in the diagnostic criteria for the cluster B disorders, Charland argues, is that these disorders essentially involve a defective moral character. If we were to omit the morally laden language, we wouldn't be able to identify and differentiate the cluster B disorders from other psychiatric disorders. People suffering from a disorder in the B cluster often present to health professionals with symptoms like feelings of emptiness, fatigue, trouble concentrating, sleep disturbances, irritability, restlessness, excessive worrying, or work-related stress. But if we were to make a diagnosis solely on the basis of these symptoms, we ought to diagnose the patient with depressive illness or perhaps an anxiety disorder, not a cluster B personality disorder.

Charland's second argument—the Argument from Treatment—trades on intuitions about what it would take to successfully treat or cure the cluster B disorders. There are not currently any effective treatments for most of the disorders in this cluster. Dialectical behavior therapy has been touted as a promising new intervention for borderline personality disorder. But, as we will see, while dialectical behavior therapy can alleviate some symptoms of the disorder, it's extremely rare for any form of psychotherapy to successfully cure borderline, and pharmacological approaches are even less likely to make lasting changes.

Despite the lack of a successful treatment of the cluster B disorders, Charland argues, we have a firm grasp of the minimum requirements a treatment protocol would need to meet to count as successful. To be successful, it would need to specifically target and alter the patient's vicious character traits. If, for example, a new line of therapy for narcissistic personality disorder were to fall short of addressing the narcissist's preoccupation with fantasies of unlimited success, power, brilliance, beauty, or ideal love, then this line of therapy wouldn't qualify as a successful cure or treatment of the disorder.

This concludes Charland's defense of the thesis that the cluster B disorders primarily are disorders of moral character. To say that they primarily are disorders of this kind is not to say that they are not also medical (or clinical) disorders. A medical disorder can be defined as a constellation of symptoms that interfere with a person's ability to function and that together form a specific symptom picture with a clear onset, course, duration, and treatment response, if a treatment protocol is available.

As the cluster B disorders satisfy this definition, they are medical disorders. But the symptoms central to the identification of the disorders in this cluster are rooted in maladaptive character traits. Morally neutral symptoms such as a depressed mood (for instance, a feeling of emptiness) do not matter to the definition of the disorders in cluster B. Or to put the point differently: logically speaking, whether the morally neutral symptoms are present or not is of no consequence to the proper diagnosis of the disorder. This is why Charland insists that disorders in this cluster primarily are disorders of moral character.

Several critics have challenged Charland's argument. We will look at challenges to his argument's applicability to borderline personality later in this chapter. First, let's look at two critical rejoinders to Charland in regard to narcissism, one by the psychologist Peter Zachar and another by the philosopher Marga Reimer.[24]

Zachar questions Charland's premise that moral concepts are required to diagnose narcissistic personality disorder. He grants that narcissism is often frowned upon. This, he says, can be traced back to ancient times, where the narcissistic traits were considered the deadliest of the deadly sins. However, Zachar nonetheless rejects Charland's presumption that moral concepts are essential for the identification of the disorder.

Zachar is hopeful that a factor analysis can help to identify the cluster B disorders. Factor analyses, which include the Big Five model and the Hexaco model, analyze personality in terms of dimensions running from high to low. A particular value on a dimension of personality reflects a trait-like tendency, or disposition, to behave as specified to a low, average, or high degree across different situations. For example, if you are very low on the dimension of *extraversion*, then you probably prefer being by yourself and taking it easy most of the time; you probably avoid large crowds, intense sensory stimulation, and high levels of excitement; and others probably describe you as quiet, serious, and hard to get to know.

Theorists disagree about how many basic factors there are. The five factors of the Big Five model—extraversion, neuroticism, agreeableness, conscientiousness, and openness—are widely recognized as central to the basic analysis of personality.

Each of the five factors of the Big Five model is composed of six aspects of personality, corresponding to the facet scales developed by psychologists Paul T. Costa, Jr., and Robert R. McCrae in 1992.[25]

More recently, research done by psychologists Kibeom Lee and Michael C. Ashton uncovered a sixth fundamental trait. *honesty-humility*, as the trait is called, has four facets: honesty, fairness, generosity, and humility. The four facets of *honesty-humility* capture individual differences in selfishness and self-centeredness. Low scores on *honesty-humility* point to exceptional selfishness and self-centeredness. People who are low in *honesty-humility* think or behave as if they are superior to everyone else and entitled to get what they want by whatever means necessary. They are often deceitful, manipulative, greedy, and arrogant. Lee and Ashton named their six-factor model the "Hexaco model."[26]

If the Hexaco model cuts human personality at its joints, as its proponents allege, then we should expect it to suffice for characterizing narcissism at a more fundamental level. The Big Five and Hexaco factor analyses point to vulnerable narcissism being linked to the facet of high achievement-striving from *conscientiousness*; the facets of high self-consciousness, high angry-hostility, and high vulnerability from *neuroticism*; the facets of low altruism, low cooperation, low modesty, and low empathy from *agreeableness*; the facets of high gregariousness and high assertiveness from *extraversion*; and the facets of low honesty, low fairness, low generosity, and low humility from *honesty-humility*.[27]

But this analysis of narcissism is just as morally laden as DSM-5's diagnostic criteria. Distinctly morally laden facets include: "high-angry hostility," "low altruism," "low cooperation," "low modesty," "low empathy," "low honesty," "low fairness," "low generosity," and "low humility."

Replacing the DSM-5 criteria for narcissism with a factor analysis thus doesn't seem to circumvent the reference to moral character, which supports Charland's point that narcissism is an inherently moral disorder.

Let's move on to Reimer's criticism.[28] According to Reimer, Charland's claim that the cluster B personality disorders are disorders of moral character is cause for concern. It is widely agreed that moral judgments have no place in the practice of medicine. Moral

Facets of the Big Five	High/low sample items from questionnaire
Conscientiousness	
Competence	Complete tasks successfully/Misjudge situations.
Orderliness	Like order/Leave a mess.
Dutifulness	Follow the rules/Break rules.
Achievement-striving	Work hard/Do just enough to get by.
Self-discipline	Get chores done right away/Waste time.
Cautiousness	Avoid mistakes/Rush into things.
Neuroticism	
Anxiousness	Worry about things/Relaxed most of the time.
Angry hostility	Get angry easily/Rarely get irritated.
Depressiveness	Often feel blue/Feel comfortable with myself.
Self-consciousness	Am easily intimidated/Am not embarrassed easily.
Impulsivity	Often eat too much/Easily resist temptations.
Vulnerability	Panic easily/Remain calm under pressure.
Extraversion	
Approachability	Make friends easily/Am hard to get to know.
Gregariousness	Love large parties/Prefer to be alone.
Assertiveness	Take charge/Wait for others to lead the way.
Activity level	Am always busy/Like to take it easy.
Excitement-seeking	Love excitement/Dislike loud music.
Cheerfulness	Radiate joy/Am seldom amused.
Agreeableness	
Trust	Most people have good intentions/people are rarely honest.
Compliance	See no need for pretense or manipulation/Use flattery to get ahead.
Altruism	Make people feel welcome/Look down on others.
Cooperation	Dislike confrontation/Have a sharp tongue.
Modesty	Dislike being the center of attention/Think highly of myself.
Empathy	Empathize with the homeless/People are too demanding of my time.
Openness	
Imagination	Have a vivid imagination/Seldom daydream.
Artistic interest	Believe in the importance of art/Do not like poetry.
Emotionality	Experience emotions intensely/Seldom get emotional.
Adventurousness	Prefer variety to routine/Dislike changes.
Intellectuality	Like abstract thinking/Avoid philosophical discussion.
Progressiveness	Tend to vote for liberals/Believe in one true religion.

judgments can too easily compromise the clinical judgment of the clinician, which in turn could be detrimental to the patient's health. A diagnosis of narcissism requires judging that the patient is deceitful, exploitative, arrogant, and contempt-prone, which is to say, it requires morally judging the patient. But, Reimer continues, casting moral judgment on one's patient compromises one's capacity for empathic concern, which could jeopardize the effectiveness of the therapy.

Reimer agrees with Charland that moral concepts are required for accurately defining the cluster B personality disorders. But she denies that this entails that the disorders in cluster B are disorders of moral character. This is because, she argues, we need to distinguish between morally disvalued attitudes and behaviors, on the one hand, and moral responsibility, or accountability, on the other.

In everyday, non-clinical settings, attributions of morally disvalued attitudes and behaviors usually carry a presumption of moral responsibility, or accountability. Calling someone arrogant, for example, is likely to carry the presumption that they are morally responsible for displaying this attitude.[29] Yet, according to Reimer, the presumption of moral responsibility is not mandatory. For example, we don't hold people with Tourette's syndrome morally responsible for making vulgar vocalizations. Likewise, Reimer argues, we shouldn't hold people with a cluster B disorder morally responsible for their disvalued behaviors and attitudes. She reasons as follows:

> [T]he characteristic symptoms of some mental disorders include morally disvalued traits. This is true of the Cluster B Personality Disorders in particular. Yet if such traits are, quite literally, the symptoms of mental disorder, of psychopathology, it is unclear how we can justifiably hold the (untreated) patient morally responsible for them. More generally, where morally disvalued traits are symptomatic of underlying pathology, patients' moral responsibility for those traits is arguably diminished, even if it is not eradicated. After all, to the extent that personal traits, whether attitudes or behaviors, result from (or are reinforced by) underlying pathology, they do not result from autonomous choice.[30]

So, Reimer thinks it's fairly unproblematic to diagnose a person with a cluster B personality disorder and yet refrain from condemning them for their moral character. She agrees with Charland that people with these personality disorders possess morally bad attitudes and engage in morally bad behaviors, but she denies that they are morally responsible for their bad attitudes and behaviors.

In response to Reimer, let me first say that I grant that if the cluster B personality disorders are like Tourette's syndrome, then people with these disorders are not morally responsible for their bad attitudes and behaviors. But the bad attitudes and behaviors characteristic of, say, narcissism are not at all like the vulgar vocalizations made by people with Tourette's.

It's widely accepted that "ought" implies "can." Also known as Kant's law, this principle says that you don't have an obligation, or requirement, to do things you cannot do. People with Tourette's cannot control their tics and vocalizations. Like hiccups, they are automatic behaviors that are not within their voluntary control. So, people with Tourette's are not morally required to stop their vocalizations or tics.

A plausible variant of Hume's principle states that "responsibility" implies "ability." On this variant, you are not morally responsible for behaviors that you cannot directly control. Because people with Tourette's cannot control their reflex-like behaviors, they are not morally responsible for them.

But the attitudes and behaviors of people with a cluster B personality disorder are not at all like the tics and vocalizations seen in Tourette's. For example, if a narcissist condescendingly tells his spouse, "You don't get it, sweetie, because you're just too dumb," this is not at all like the tics and vocalizations in Tourette's. Unlike the vulgar vocalizations of people with Tourette's, this kind of putdown is not an automatic uncontrollable process. The narcissist's bad behavior is no different from other kinds of bad behavior, such as bumping or ramming the car that cut you off, getting back at a coworker by moving files she needs to access to shelves she cannot reach, or asking out your admirer with the sole aim of copying her homework.[31] Many of the narcissist's bad behaviors, such as his exploitative undertakings and retaliatory pursuits, even require some level of premeditation.

The volition and choice that underpin the narcissist's disvalued attitudes and behavior are, in fact, explicitly mentioned in DSM-5. One of the criteria for clinical narcissism is an *unwillingness* to recognize or identify with the feelings and needs of others. This is what lies behind the common claim that narcissists lack empathy. Narcissists are said to lack empathy, not because they are incapable of taking other people's perspective, but rather because they are unwilling to treat others with empathic concern.[32] So likening narcissism to Tourette's does nothing to support Reimer's allegations that the underlying pathology in narcissism makes the narcissist exempt from moral responsibility.

Here is an argument for thinking that narcissists are indeed morally responsible, or accountable, for their bad attitudes and behaviors. A person is morally responsible for an act, roughly, insofar as they cause the act to occur, and the act realizes their intentions and values.[33] In other words, when a person is morally responsible for an act, she meant to do it. For example, you are morally responsible for breaking your friend's expensive vase, only if you meant to do it. When narcissists behave badly, they do so because they meant to. The narcissist's contemptuous remark, "You don't get it, sweetie, because you're just too dumb," was no accident. He meant to say what he did, which is to say, he is morally responsible for his verbal putdown.

Reimer notes that highly distressing childhood experiences can contribute to the development of cluster B personality disorders. She argues that if you are thrown into a world of poverty, drugs, and crime by parents who abuse you, and you commit a wrongdoing that is strongly linked to the childhood abuse, then you should not be held accountable for the wrongdoing. She writes:

> Brianne [a borderline] was sexually abused as a young child and her misplaced anger is what they call "anger coming out sideways." Her problem is not so much moral as it is epistemic: once

she understands who is responsible for her anger (her abuser),
she will know just where she should be directing it.[34]

But all bad behavior by free agents is due in part to seeds planted during
childhood and adolescence. So if Reimer is right that people's bad up-
bringing can make them exempt from moral responsibility, then no one
whatsoever is morally responsible for their dirty deeds. Not a satisfac-
tory result.

It is true, of course, that you may not be morally responsible for how
your lifelong personality traits have developed. But if you intentionally
act on your bad traits, you are morally responsible for the intended or
foreseeable outcome.

You are not morally accountable if you make a condescending remark to another person while you are asleep or under the influence
of drugs that alter or erase your personality, like cocaine, Ambien, or
Flakka. Nor are you morally responsible if your older brother forces you
to make a condescending remark by twisting your arm, or if you believe
the FedEx guy is a serial killer and therefore slam the door in his face.
But narcissists haven't lost touch with reality. They behave badly because
they choose to do so.[35]

Zachar and philosopher Nancy Nyquist Potter take issue with this
sort of claim.[36] They correctly point out that narcissists often are very
comfortable in their delusions of grandiosity. While some narcissists
exaggerate achievements and talents, others firmly believe that they are
superior to the rest of us.

Zachar and Potter are right that delusions sometimes trap people
in certain unfortunate patterns of behavior. However, narcissists are
not hostage to their positive delusions of grandiosity. They are perfectly capable of restraining themselves when lack of restraint would
cast a shadow of shame on them. Their positive delusions of grandiosity therefore are not of the mind-altering variety that can excuse
bad behavior.

Because narcissists are morally responsible for their ill-behaved manners, it is indeed often difficult for therapists to show empathic concern for

their narcissistic clients. But a good clinician should be able to adopt an impersonal mindset (along the lines of Peter Strawson's objective attitude, as discussed in Chapter 3) when diagnosing people with psychiatric disorders, thus ephemerally bracketing the question of moral responsibility.

Hatred and Self-Hatred in Borderlines

In this excerpt from Paul T. Mason and Randi Kreger's 1998 book *Stop Walking on Eggshells*, the interviewee describes the emotional toll of growing up with a borderline parent:

My mother's love for me was conditional. When I didn't do what I was supposed to—chores or whatever—she would rage, cut me down, and say I was a horrible kid who would never have any friends. But when she needed love, she would become affectionate, hug me, and talk about how close we were. There was never any way to predict which mood she would be in.

My mother got resentful if she felt someone else was taking up too much of my time and energy. She was even jealous of our dog, Snoopy. I always thought I had done something wrong—or that there was something wrong with me.

She took it upon herself to improve me by constantly telling me how I needed to change. She saw something wrong with my hair, my friends, my table manners, and my attitude. She seemed to exaggerate and lie to justify her assertions. When my father protested, she dismissed him with a wave of her hand. She always had to be right. Over the years, I tried to meet her expectations. But whenever I did, they changed.[37]

Borderline personality disorder didn't become an official diagnosable disorder until 1980, when it was included in the third edition of the *Diagnostic and Statistical Manual for Mental Disorders* (DSM-3).

In the current fifth edition of the *Manual* (DSM-5) borderline personality disorder is characterized as a "pervasive pattern of instability of interpersonal relationships, self-image, and affects, and marked impulsivity, beginning by early adulthood and present in a variety of contexts," as indicated by five (or more) of the following:[38]

1. Frantic efforts to avoid real or imagined abandonment. (Note: Do not include suicidal or self-mutilating behavior covered in Criterion 5.)
2. A pattern of unstable and intense interpersonal relationships characterized by alternating between extremes of idealization and devaluation.
3. Identity disturbance: markedly and persistently unstable self-image or sense of self.
4. Impulsivity in at least two areas that are potentially self-damaging (e.g., spending, sex, substance abuse, reckless driving, binge eating). (Note: Do not include suicidal or self-mutilating behavior covered in Criterion 5.)
5. Recurrent suicidal behavior, gestures, or threats, or self-mutilating behavior.
6. Affective instability due to a marked reactivity of mood (e.g., intense episodic dysphoria, irritability, or anxiety usually lasting a few hours and only rarely more than a few days).
7. Chronic feelings of emptiness.
8. Inappropriate, intense anger or difficulty controlling anger (e.g., frequent displays of temper, constant anger, recurrent physical fights).
9. Transient, stress-related paranoid ideation or severe dissociative symptoms.

This is not a comprehensive characterization of borderline personality disorder. This point is worth repeating, as the diagnostic criteria listed in DSM often are treated as the final word on the matter.[39] However, DSM-5 specifically states that "the symptoms contained in the respective diagnostic criteria sets do not constitute comprehensive definitions of underlying disorders" and "diagnostic criteria are offered as guidelines for making diagnoses, and their use should be informed by clinical judgment. Text descriptions, including introductory sections of each diagnostic chapter, can help support diagnosis" ("Use of the Manual").

Indeed, in DSM-5's narrative descriptions of the cluster B disorders, we are told that borderlines and antisocial individuals often are manipulative. But the aims of the manipulation are different in the two cases. Borderlines manipulate to gain nurturance, attention, or positive feedback, whereas antisocials manipulate to gain profit, power, or some other material gratification.

The subclinical variant of borderline personality, while also characterized by deficits in emotion regulation and in the representation of the self and others, is within the normal range of functioning. Borderline personality organization, as the subclinical variant sometimes is called, is one of the vulnerable antagonistic personalities in the vulnerable dark triad, which psychologist Joshua D. Miller and his colleagues brought to the fore of scholarly attention in their 2009 article "Searching for a Vulnerable Dark Triad." The "vulnerable dark triad" refers to the constellation of vulnerable narcissism, borderline personality, and secondary psychopathy.

In their study presented in the article, Miller and his colleagues found that while the borderline trait is genetically linked to antisocial personality disorder, which is the clinical variant of secondary psychopathy, the vulnerable dark traits that were most closely related on the Big Five model of personality were borderline personality and vulnerable narcissism.[40]

Despite having similar five-factor profiles, there are important differences in the underlying deficits of vulnerable narcissism and borderline personality. Whereas the vulnerable narcissist's explicit self-image is vulnerable but positive overall, borderlines oscillate between feeling that they lack a core sense of identity and seeing themselves in an extremely negative light.

Unlike people who don't suffer from a mental illness, borderlines do not have a sense of a stable self across different times and situations. They report feeling like different people depending on where they are and whom they are with, that they are merely pretending to have their own convictions, values, and desires, or that their existence depends on others for cueing on what they should think, want, and like.[41]

As Jerold Jay Kreisman and Hal Straus, the authors of *I Hate You—Don't Leave Me*, put it, borderlines "often adapt like chameleons to the environment, situation, or companions of the moment, much like the title character in Woody Allen's film *Zelig*, who literally assumes the personality, identity, and appearance of people around him."[42]

Borderlines depend on people they know well, such as family members, friends, and colleagues, to provide them with the semblance of a sense of self. But feedback and cueing from others are a double-edged sword. Borderlines run feedback from other people through a Rube Goldberg machine designed to transform the slightest hint of criticism into a punch in the face. The sad irony is that the feedback their very sense of self depends on is what's causing them to feel "misunderstood, mistreated, or victimized or to feel inadequate, inferior, or like a failure."[43]

Negative feedback can trigger violent emotions in borderlines. This emotional consumption of their entire being unhinges their capacity for rational thought and decision-making, impairs their ability to integrate mixed messages into a coherent, nuanced whole, and interrupts their inhibitory control system.[44]

In their stupor, borderlines take criticism to prove one of two things: either they themselves are incompetent and worthless, or their critic harbors ill will toward them. This black-and-white thinking is tied to a related phenomenon known as "splitting." While black-and-white thinking is a reaction to the emotional disruption of the ability to think rationally and make informed decisions, splitting is a psychological defense mechanism.[45] It operates on an unconscious level, where it triggers a saint/devil delusion about others. Splitting results in either self-hatred or other-hatred, or what is also known as "projected hatred," although borderlines usually oscillate between self- and other-hatred.[46]

For borderlines prone to self-hatred, it's more painful to regard other people as harboring ill will toward them than to devalue themselves. So, their splitting induces self-hatred, followed by self-soothing with "drugs" such as alcohol, painkillers, tranquilizers, self-mutilation, or suicide attempts.

For borderlines prone to other-hatred, it's more painful to see themselves as incompetent and worthless than to view their critics as bad people. So, their splitting is a fast track to other-hatred and explosive and uncontrolled anger outbursts.[47] Kreisman and Straus describe splitting this way:

> The world of a borderline, like that of a child, is split into heroes and villains. A child emotionally, the borderline cannot tolerate human inconsistencies and ambiguities; he cannot reconcile another's good and bad qualities into a constant, coherent understanding of that person. At any particular moment, one is either "good" or "evil"; there is no in-between, no gray area.[48]

Borderlines who are consumed by hatred of a person who is critical of them don't recall ever having had any positive attitudes toward that person, or if they do, they feel silly for ever having thought well of them.

They are not in the habit of holding on to their hatred for long periods of time, however. Once they calm down, they tend to undergo a dramatic shift from hate to love and admiration. If their turncoatery doesn't work, it's not beneath them to employ more manipulative tactics, such as feigning illness or threatening suicide, in a desperate attempt to win over the person they pushed away.

If their orchestrated efforts to win over their targets get them nowhere, their ephemeral states of love and hate can crystallize into permanent mental representations. In her 2000 book *Understanding the Borderline Mother*, clinical practitioner Christine Ann Lawson reports on this phenomenon in borderline parents who view their offspring either as the all-good child or the no-good child depending on how validated or rejected the youngster makes them feel. We will look closer at manipulation and cemented hatred in borderline individuals in the next section.

Do Borderlines Have a Flawed Moral Character?

Recall Charland's argument for thinking that the cluster B personality disorders are primarily disorders of moral character. In response to Charland, philosopher Greg Horne[49] has argued that Charland's line of reasoning is unsuccessful for the case of borderline personality disorder.

Horne grants that the attitudes and behaviors characteristic of borderline personality disorder are morally inappropriate. But, he argues, Charland's argument fails to demonstrate that these attitudes and behaviors originate in a morally flawed character.

Horne takes issue with the premise in Charland's argument that it is impossible to imagine successfully treating the cluster B disorders without a change in, or conversion of, moral character. Horne maintains that this premise is false. He reasons as follows. Dialectical behavior therapy, which was originally developed by psychology professor Marsha Linehan for the treatment of suicidal behaviors, has been shown to effectively treat borderline personality disorder by teaching borderlines how to regulate their emotions. Yet dialectical behavior therapy does not require a conversion of moral character. Rather, borderlines are considered successfully treated when they no longer antagonize people in their lives, and they are capable of having stable, interpersonal relationships. According to Horne, since borderline personality disorder can be successfully treated by teaching people afflicted by the condition how to regulate their emotions, the disorder is not a disorder of moral character but a purely clinical disorder.

I have several things to say in response to Horne. The first is that the empirical literature doesn't support his claim that dialectical behavior therapy alone can successfully treat borderline personality disorder.[50] As psychologist Karen R. Scheel argues in her review article, "standard outpatient DBT [dialectical behavior therapy] has been associated with lesser parasuicidal behavior [i.e., a suicidal attempt where the aim is not death], psychiatric hospitalization, anger and psychotropic medication usage, and with increased client retention, overall level of functioning, overall social adjustment, and employment performance."[51]

That's an impressive list. But, as Scheel points out, a long list of psychiatric problems linger after dialectical behavior therapy, including feelings of hopelessness, suicidal ideation, anxious rumination, black-and-white thinking, internalized anger, manipulative tendencies, poor work performance, and low overall life satisfaction.

That's not all that surprising. Dialectical behavior therapy teaches clients a range of techniques they can use to avoid antagonizing other people, quit the drugs they are addicted to, and stay in therapy. Accordingly, they are better socially adjusted and don't get fired from their job. But the therapy doesn't help them develop a core identity. They still depend on other people for cues and feedback on how to behave and what to think and feel. They still hate people who give them negative feedback. They are simply better at stifling the hatred before it sends them into a temper tantrum. They perform poorly on the job and still use manipulation to get attention and approval. They feel just as miserable about themselves and about life in general as they did prior to entering therapy and are preoccupied with fantasies about ending it all.

There are anecdotal accounts of borderlines who have been cured of the disorder after therapy. In her 2002 memoir *Get Me Out of Here*, Rachel Reiland tells her story of how she recovered from borderline personality disorder. But what she and her therapist consider successful treatment goes far beyond a change in attitudes and behaviors. After being in psychoanalysis three times a week for several years, Reiland emerges on the other side as a new person, free of black-and-white thinking patterns, manipulative tendencies, and proneness toward self- and other-hatred. As the reader discovers, building a new personality is a slow and painful process.

Dialectical behavior therapy is far from the breakthrough in the treatment of borderline personality disorder that it has been made out to be. Horne examines other promising therapies. But the alternatives are even less reliable at diminishing borderline symptoms than dialectical behavior therapy.[52]

But perhaps Horne's argument can be restated without the assumption that borderline personality disorder can be successfully treated. Horne argues that the disorder is rooted in "cognitive and emotional deficits that obscure the expression of an otherwise intact moral character."[53] If borderlines did indeed have what he calls "an intact moral character," that would certainly be a blow to the hypothesis that the condition primarily is a disorder of moral character. But evidence suggests that they don't. Before turning to that evidence, however, we need to have a closer look at moral character and its relation to personality.

As we saw in Chapter 1, the moral character of a person is a cluster of character traits that make an individual the sort of ethical person he or she is.[54] A character trait is a stable trait-like disposition to react in certain characteristic ways in particular situations. In virtue ethics, character traits are assessed on the basis of excellence. A virtue is a perfectly excellent trait of character, whereas a vice is a completely flawed trait of character. Trait-like dispositions such as honesty, generosity, good temper, fairness, temperance, humility, courage, friendliness, and wittiness are usually counted as virtues.

On Aristotle's virtue ethics, to possess a virtue is not simply a matter of regularly behaving in a certain way. For example, a person who regularly tells the truth isn't necessarily an honest person. If you regularly tell the truth because you are afraid of getting caught in a lie, you are not really honest.

People who are tactless or indiscreet also lack honesty, as far as Aristotle is concerned. If you tend to publicly reveal what friends have told you in private because doing so amuses you, you are not honest. An honest person is someone who uses reason to determine how truthful they ought to be and who acts accordingly in the particular situation they are in.

Possessing a virtue is a matter of degree. Most of us do not possess any of the virtues to perfection. For example, if you tend to get angry only when there is good reason to get angry but occasionally get angry for no good reason, then you possess the virtue of good temper to a high degree, but you don't possess it to perfection. As it is unlikely that any of us possesses all the virtues to a perfect degree, the notion of a perfectly virtuous person is an ethical ideal.

If you possess the virtue of good temper to a high degree, you have a stable (virtuous) disposition, even if it falls short of reaching the ethical ideal. Likewise, if you possess the virtue of good temper to a low degree, you have a stable (vicious) disposition, even if it falls short of reaching complete imperfection. This is because having a stable disposition requires predictability, not perfection or imperfection. If, however, it is unpredictable whether you get angry or remain calm when you are in a situation that calls for a calm attitude, then you do not have a stable disposition in regard to temper.

There is a certain parallel between the Aristotelian virtues and vices and the personality traits of personality psychology, although not by any means a perfect one. While the six factors of personality on the Hexaco model are too coarse-grained to be able to serve as virtuous or vicious traits, the facets seem better suited for this role. The facets themselves are not traits; rather, a trait is the degree to which you have the facet across a range of different situations, for example, the degree to which you are cheerful, assertive or altruistic.

To a first approximation, we can say that well-adjusted personality traits are virtuous character traits, whereas maladaptive (or maladjusted) personality traits are vicious character traits.

Virtues and well adjusted traits are both *stable* dispositions to behave or think in ways that are appropriately adjusted to the situation, whereas vices and maladaptive traits both are stable dispositions to behave or think in ways that are not appropriately adjusted to the situation. For example, if you tend to be cheerful when things are going well and cheerless when you face hardship, then your disposition to be cheerful is stable and well adjusted—and is therefore a virtuous trait. If, on the other hand, you tend to be cheerful when you face hardship and cheerless when things are going well, then your disposition to be cheerful is stable but maladaptive—and is therefore a vicious trait.

An *unstable* disposition that makes your behavior and attitude radically unpredictable is also maladaptive, but in that case the disposition cannot really be said to be a trait. If, for example, it's unpredictable whether you will be cheerful or cheerless both when things go well and when they don't, then we cannot really say that you have a personality trait along the facet of cheerfulness.

Whether a trait is maladjusted is itself a matter of degree. Just as most of us do not possess any virtues or vices in the highest degree, so most of us do not have any completely adjusted or maladjusted traits. What we ordinarily call a disordered trait is a trait that is maladaptive to a high degree. A trait that is maladaptive to a low degree would be considered within the range of normal population-wide variation.

There are limits to how far we can take the analogy between the virtues and vices and the facets of personality. But the standard objection to assimilating personality traits to character traits, namely that only character traits bear on morality, is a non-starter.

First, we have to remember that Aristotle used the term "moral" in a much wider sense than we do today. For him, moral behaviors and attitudes include prudential behaviors and attitudes.

Second, most of the facets of personality wear their moral or prudential relevance on their sleeves. Examples include the facets of competence, order, dutifulness, self-discipline, and cautiousness from the Big Five dimension of *conscientiousness*; the facets of hostility and impulsivity from the Big Five dimension of *neuroticism*; the facets of morality, altruism, modesty, and empathy from the Big Five dimension of *agreeableness*; and the facets of honesty, fairness, generosity, and humility from the Hexaco dimension of *honesty-humility*.

Let's now return to Horne's claim that borderlines have what he calls an "intact moral character." I assume that what Horne means by "intact moral character" is a character that falls within the normal range and involves possessing the moral virtues to a moderately high degree. This, however, isn't true of borderlines.

In their study of the vulnerable dark traits (borderline personality disorder, vulnerable narcissism, and secondary psychopathy), Miller and his colleagues found that these traits were linked to high neuroticism and low extraversion, low conscientiousness, and low agreeableness, where low agreeableness was manifested in "self-centered, dishonest, and callous attitudes toward others."[55] This suggests that borderlines possess many of the virtuous character traits to a very low degree, suggesting that they have a rather flawed moral character.

So in spite of their vulnerability, borderline individuals don't have an "intact moral character" whose expression is obscured by cognitive and emotional deficits, as Horne would have it. Rather, their cognitive and emotional deficiencies underpin their disordered moral traits.

Are Psychopaths Mad or Bad?

Ferdinand Waldo Demara, Jr., who came to be known as "the Great Imposter," posed at various times of his life as a trauma surgeon, a sheriff's deputy, an assistant prison warden, a civil engineer, a hospital orderly, a doctor of applied psychology, a lawyer, a child-care expert, a Benedictine monk, a Trappist monk, an editor, a cancer researcher, and a teacher.[56] He often borrowed the names and credentials of living people, he forged documents, and he once faked his own suicide.

During his most famous stint as a trauma surgeon and medical doctor onboard a navy ship during the Korean War, he successfully performed major surgery, including amputations and major chest surgery, on some sixteen Korean combat casualties. He had already performed a handful of surgeries on his fellow crew mates during his first few months on the navy ship. But when he received news of the wounded Korean combatants, he knew the task ahead of him would be significantly more difficult. To buy some time, he ordered the personnel to transport the patients into the operating room and prep them for surgery. Gifted with a high IQ and a photographic memory, he was able to speed-read a textbook on the various surgeries he needed to perform. He then went to work on the patients. One of the surgeries, which required removing a bullet close to the heart, brought him local fame when it was reported in a regional newspaper.

Demara, who died in 1982 at the age of sixty, was a psychopath. In popular culture, psychopaths are often portrayed as serial killers. But in reality, few psychopaths are killers, let alone serial killers. Some are CEOs of large companies. Others are blue-collar office bullies.[57] Yet others are doctors or lawyers who never earned a degree.

DSM-5 does not recognize psychopathy as a disorder in its own right, but it is mentioned as a specifier (or subtype) of antisocial personality disorder. The latter is characterized by its persistent pattern of disregard for and violation of the rights of others since age fifteen, manifested in one of seven ways:

1. A failure to conform to social norms with respect to lawful behaviors, as indicated by repeatedly performing acts that are grounds for arrest.
2. Deceitfulness, as indicated by repeated lying, use of aliases, or conning others for personal profit or pleasure.
3. Impulsivity or failure to plan ahead.
4. Irritability and aggressiveness, as indicated by repeated physical fights or assaults.
5. A reckless disregard for the safety of self or others.
6. Consistent irresponsibility, as indicated by repeated failure to sustain consistent work behavior or honor financial obligations.
7. Lack of remorse, as indicated by being indifferent to or rationalizing having hurt, mistreated, or stolen from another.

The main form of psychopathy is linked to thrill-seeking, impaired capacities for empathy and remorse, low neuroticism, low conscientiousness, and proneness to hatred and contempt. This form of psychopathy is also known as true, or primary, psychopathy. When people speak of psychopathy, it is usually this strain of psychopathy they have in mind. People with extreme variants of primary psychopathy often have all the traits of the dark tetrad, including Machiavellianism, narcissism, and sadism.

Secondary psychopathy, one of the vulnerable dark traits, overlaps considerably with borderline personality disorder and vulnerable narcissism. While linked to antisocial behavior, low conscientiousness, and proneness to hatred and aggression, it is also associated with high neuroticism and hypersensitivity to negative feedback.

A special inventory for (primary) psychopathy, the so-called Psychopathy Checklist–revised (PCL-R), originally developed in the 1970s by Canadian psychologist Robert D. Hare, lists twenty characteristics of (primary) psychopathy, including some narcissistic and Machiavellian traits:[58]

1. Excess glibness or superficial charm.
2. Grandiose sense of self-worth.
3. Excess need for stimulation or proneness to boredom.
4. Pathological lying.
5. Cunning and manipulative behavior.
6. Lack of remorse or guilt.
7. Shallow affect, for instance, in the form of superficial emotional responsiveness.
8. Callousness and a lack of empathy.
9. A preference for a parasitic lifestyle, for example, living off of borrowed money.
10. Poor behavioral control.

11. A history of sexually promiscuous behavior, such as a long list of one-night stands.
12. A history of early behavior problems.
13. Lack of realistic long-term goals.
14. Excessive impulsivity.
15. A high level of irresponsible behavior, for instance, not keeping promises or consistently showing up late for work.
16. Failure to accept responsibility for own actions, for instance, by blaming others or circumstances.
17. Many short-term romantic relationships or marriages.
18. Juvenile delinquency.
19. Punishment fails to deter repeat offenses.
20. A history of versatile criminal behavior, for instance, animal torture, theft, rape, murder.

Primary psychopaths have an unusually high need for excitement and thrills because of an impairment in their ability to feel arousal and anxiety. Only the most extreme among high-risk activities are able to make them feel bodily arousal. Moderately high-risk activities bring neither fright nor delight.

Psychopaths are able to plan high-risk actions in meticulous detail, but they lack the emotional capacity needed to avoid taking high risks or to worry about the outcome. Their attitudes toward risky activities are more akin to the value judgments of a disengaged spectator than the visceral bodily reactions of fear or excitement experienced by their fellow human beings. If a psychopath were to lose a huge amount of money on the stock market after a highly risky investment, he would regard the loss as a negative outcome, but he would not feel any anguish related to the loss or any regret related to his decision.

The inability of psychopaths to feel bodily arousal except when engaging in exceptionally high-risk activities may explain their addiction to dangerous endeavors. But it doesn't explain why they tend to commit violent crimes, sometimes even sadistic murders. If they are addicted to extraordinarily high-risk activities, why don't they do what other adrenaline junkies do? Why don't they go bull riding, free climbing, or big-wave surfing?

There is probably no decisive answer to this question. But there is widespread agreement among researchers that psychopaths committing sexual homicide are motivated by hatred, broadly construed.[59]

Despite the sexual component, sexual homicide is not primarily about the sex. Even sexual sadistic tendencies can be satisfied in safe and legal ways. But sadistic sex done safely is lacking that one ingredient the sex killer is after: it doesn't involve the kind of complete control over another human being that the psychopathic killer craves.

Forensic psychologist J. Reid Meloy has argued that many sexual homicides are displaced matricides, driven by maternal hatred. This, he argues, is suggested by the risk factors for sexual homicidal tendencies, which include a history of mistreatment of women or fantasies of assaulting women; hatred or contempt for women, or fear of women; and fetishism for female underclothing and destruction of female clothes.

Though Ted Bundy thrilled at inflicting pain on his victims and evidently was erotically drawn to death, misogyny appears to have been his primary motive. Despite Bundy's claim that he simply was powerless to resist the urge to kill, the loudness of his actions leaves little doubt about his hatred toward women, or at least certain types of women.

Bundy's hatred toward women was likely planted in early childhood. He grew up thinking that his mother was his sister and that his grandparents were his parents. By the age of ten, he had had three different names and had lived in three different houses in three different states. He only discovered that his "sister" was really his mom in college, or perhaps at the end of high school. He never knew who anyone around him really was. The women closest to him had lied to him his entire life, which is likely to have opened an especially rich vein of hatred.

Bundy's killing sprees do indeed look like misogyny run amok, but misogyny of a personal nature. Unable to loosen the suffocating grip of the past, his violent hatred compelled him to torture and murder women who reminded him of his mother or other women who had betrayed him.

Many other serial killers—almost always male—seem to have been driven by misogyny. The television series *Mindhunter* highlights this motive behind the murders of famous psychopaths, such as Richard Speck, an American mass murderer who systematically tortured, raped, and murdered eight student nurses from South Chicago Community Hospital on the night of July 13 into the early morning hours of July 14, 1966; Monte Rissell, an American serial killer and rapist who raped and murdered five women between 1976 and 1977 in Alexandria, Virginia; Jerry Brudos, an American serial killer and necrophile who committed the murders of at least four women in Oregon between 1968 and 1969; and Ed Kemper, an American serial killer and necrophile who murdered ten people, including his paternal grandparents and his mother.

The hatred underlying sexual homicide is not the sort of "blind hatred" that drives classical examples of hate-driven revenge. The hatred that drives Medea to kill her kin in the ancient Greek play and the rancor that inspires sadistic killers like Bundy are poles apart. Whereas the hatred that drives Medea to commit revenge murders causes her great anguish, the hatred that fueled Bundy's killing sprees contributed a great deal to the overall pleasure he derived from catching his "prey" and murdering it. The pleasurable overtones of Bundy's hatred are part of what made killing so addictive for him.

The hatred experienced by psychopathic killers is an exemplar of parapathic hatred. As argued in Chapter 2, a parapathic emotion is a negatively valenced emotion, like hate, contempt, fear, or sadness, that is felt as pleasurable when experienced through a frame of detachment. The fear we experience when watching a horror or thriller movie is pleasurable because we are wearing the lens of detachment provided by the fiction.

The pleasurable hatred that fuels psychopathic killers in their murderous pursuits is not unlike the delightful fear the rest of us experience when Norman Bates stabs Marion Crane to death in *Psycho*'s renowned forty-five-second "shower scene." The main difference between us and them is that we have and they lack a fundamental appreciation of the inherent value of persons. This fundamental appreciation explains why even the thought of crossing the forbidden boundary between fantasy and reality fills most of us with horror and disgust. Lacking this kind of fundamental appreciation, the psychopathic killer crosses that line with considerable ease and enormous pleasure.

A standing question in relation to psychopaths who commit violent crimes is whether they should be excused on grounds of insanity or be punished like other violent criminals.[60] A defense on the grounds of insanity must adhere to the legal criteria known as the M'Naghten Rules:

> [T]o establish a defense on the grounds of insanity, it must conclusively be proved that, at the time of committing the act, the party accused was laboring under such a defect of reason, from disease of the mind, as not to know the nature and quality of the act he was doing; or if he did know it, that he did not know what he was doing was wrong.[61]

The insanity defense is generally not available to psychopaths under U.S. legislation, because psychopaths do not satisfy the conditions outlined in the M'Naghten Rules. They can identify and provide full details of the crimes they committed, and they know that carrying out actions of this nature is legally wrong.

Psychotic criminals differ from psychopaths in this respect. Psychotic criminals don't understand why their actions are wrong. A paradigm example of a psychotic killer is Coral Eugene Watts, who strangled as many as eighty women. Watts was mentally retarded, with an IQ of 75. He basically had the mental capacity of a slow third-grader. In addition to that, he suffered from delusions and hallucinations. When asked about his murders, he insisted that his victims were already dead when he strangled them, because the devil had taken possession of their bodies and had consumed their souls. There is no doubt that Watts' mental impairments compromised his ability to understand the wrongness of his actions.

Unlike psychotics, psychopaths are not in the grip of a hallucination or delusion that causes them to think that someone else is acting through them or that prevents them from seeing the wrongness of their actions.

Courts in the United States allow exculpation from punishment for some of the most mentally disturbed psychotic or retarded criminals on the grounds of insanity, but not for psychopaths, because psychopaths know what they have done and understand why the actions they engaged in are prohibited by law. So, their deficits do not justify a defense on the grounds of insanity.

This line of thought has been challenged. Philosopher David Shoemaker has argued that the nature of the mental impairments observed in psychopaths exculpate them from criminal and moral responsibility. The gist of the argument is this: while psychopathic criminals can provide full details of the crimes they have committed and know what they have done is illegal, they lack the kind of deep moral understanding required to fully comprehend the wrongness of their actions. Deep moral understanding requires empathy. As psychopaths lack the capacity for empathy, they lack the moral understanding required for them to be criminally responsible. So, Shoemaker argues, psychopathy justifies an insanity defense, under the M'Naghten Rules.

However, thinkers like Paul Bloom, Paulina Sliwa and Heidi Maibom have argued that even if psychopaths lack the capacity for empathy, this is not necessarily a good reason to think that they lack deep moral understanding.[62] Here we need to distinguish between two kinds of empathy: cognitive and emotional empathy. Cognitive empathy, also known as "social cognition" or "mind-reading," is the ability to take another person's perspective and make reasonable estimates about what they feel, think, and intend to do. Emotional empathy is the experience of emotional pain in response to another person's suffering, or the experience of pleasure in response to another person's well-being or good fortune.[63]

Psychopaths do not lack cognitive empathy. In fact, they often seem to have particularly well-developed mind-reading skills. The most reliable evidence for their blunted emotions is their reduced skin conductance and startle responses to observing others in distress.[64] But at best their reduced bodily responses to others in distress point to deficiencies in emotional empathy, it doesn't show that they are unable to understand what the other person is going through. Mind-reading suffices for that.

If, however, psychopaths are capable of understanding the suffering their victims are undergoing and the wrongfulness of making them suffer, then they do have the kind of deep moral understanding required for them to fully comprehend the wrongness of their actions. So, the prevailing evidence doesn't back the suggestion that psychopathy justifies an insanity defense, under the M'Naghten Rules, which is to say, psychopaths are bad, not literally mad.

In closing, what psychopaths and narcissists, and to a lesser degree borderlines, have in common is their hate- or contempt-proneness— trait-like tendencies to dehumanize other people, often certain types of people or groups of people. Their hate- and contempt-proneness is rooted in an extreme arrogance regarding their own superior status as humans, or in some cases an excessive need for attention and validation.

The dark personalities of psychopaths, narcissists and borderlines aren't just a source of individual harm. As I will argue in the next chapter, hate crimes, including hate-based mass atrocities, are planned and orchestrated by people with dark personalities who are motivated by their standing hatred and contempt toward certain groups of people.

5 | KILLING IN THE NAME OF
COLLECTIVE INTENTIONALITY AND GROUP HATE

In July 2017, Floridians, and soon the rest of the world, became fired up with outrage when learning that a group of teens had filmed a disabled man drowning.[1] While Jamel Dunn was fighting for his life in a lake, the teens laughed, ridiculed him, and recorded the event on their smartphones for their own perverse entertainment. They displayed a marked unwillingness to help him or notify the authorities. Afterward they posted the video on social media and went on with their lives. Dunn's body wasn't found until three days later. One year later the state of Florida made the decision not to prosecute the teens. Florida has no "Good Samaritan" law protecting disabled people from onlookers filming them drown while exposing them to scorn, ridicule, and laughter.

While the teens' behavior may not be illegal, it violates the basic canons of morality. It displays a callous disregard for human life, or what we called "dehumanizing contempt" in earlier chapters. But the teens' morally incriminating behavior wasn't personal. They didn't carry out a revenge fantasy against Dunn, nor were they provoked by anything he did or said. Dunn was the target of their scorn for the simple reason that he was disabled and happened to be drowning in front of them.

Contempt of this barbarously sickening kind is a prime example of group hate, in the wide sense of "hate." Group hate differs from personal hate by targeting people because of their group membership. Dunn became the target of group hate, not because he was drowning, but because he was a disabled man who was drowning.

There are two strands of hate involving groups: hate executed by groups and hate targeting groups. I will use the term "group hate" to refer to hate targeting marginalized or stigmatized groups or their members because of their group membership and the term "collective hate" to refer to hate mobilized by a group against a common target. Let's look at each in turn.

Group Hate and Group Contempt

Group hate is parasitical on personal hate. It combines resentment for people who belong to a certain group with condemnation of them for their assumed malevolent character. Like personal hate, group hate thus has a dual focus. One is the target's envisioned past or future evil-doing. The other is the target's assumed malevolent character. When we hate people who belong to a particular group on account of their group membership, we resent them for the group's alleged cruelty and condemn them for their malignant character, from which their barbarism allegedly flows.

As we have seen in Chapter 1, blame and condemnation are kinds of disrespect. Hate, however, often doesn't seem to involve the same level of disrespect as contempt. But this is because malevolence, the character flaw that fuels our hatred, is associated in our minds with potential power and danger, capacities that call for apprehension or fear. This fear can mask the psychological effects of the disrespect inherent to hatred. Even so, the actions motivated by group hatred are clearly grounded in disrespect.

Group hatred is commonly exploited by the ruling, or oppressive, class in a society as an instrument for inducing fear in the oppressed group to discourage disobedience. In colonial America, the colonists' hate-fueled treatment of their slaves served as a tool for making slaves fear rebellion or insurrection, which the colonists believed would destroy the economy and civilization.[2] Southern slaveholders, in particular, were extremely cruel to their slaves. Many exposed their slaves to daily whippings and sexual exploitation in order to reduce the risk of rebellion. Disobedient or run-away slaves were frequently chained with shackles made of wrought iron; branded on the palm, body, or face with hot branding irons; forced to wear a metal collar with spikes around the neck; wounded by whipping and then being rubbed with salt, red pepper, and turpentine; raped by masters and mistresses or their sons; having fingers, ears, the tongue, limbs, or genitals cut off; or burned or scalded with hot liquefied animal fat.[3]

After the Revolutionary War, smoldering anti-slavery sentiments resulted in slave owners further escalating their cruelty to avoid internal conflict and maintain cohesion in America and especially in the Southern states. During the Jim Crow era, black men were still commonly thought of as uncontrollable wild beasts who would revert to criminal savagery, unless they were dominated by whites. Lynchings were intended to induce terror among blacks as a "new" way of dominating them, now that they were no longer enslaved.[4] In reality, of course, the use of terror to dominate blacks was equally prominent before the abolition; the main difference was the extremes to which the hatred now needed to be taken to be effective.

Group contempt is another form of group condemnation on account of group members' alleged flawed character.[5] In contempt, the attributed character flaw is not malevolence, but vices such as a lack of integrity and restraint, an impaired sense of hygiene, low intelligence, and animal instincts—the sort of character flaws that ground practices that tend to trigger social disgust, such as petty crimes, excessive lust, incest, and bad hygiene.

As Martha Nussbaum notes in her 2018 book *The Monarchy of Fear*, the unequal treatment of blacks in Jim Crow America was driven, in part, by social disgust, or what she calls "projective disgust." Blacks were prohibited from sharing swimming pools, drinking fountains, dinner plates, and hotel beds with whites, because people assumed that black bodies were sources of contamination.

Disgust by itself, however, does not explain the scornful caricature of blacks as lacking in sophistication, intellect, and integrity. The
source of this caricature was contempt. Indeed, group contempt is
commonly exploited by the ruling class in a society as an instrument
for "naturalizing" social inequality and oppression, because of its emphasis on the oppressed group's inherent vices. If the oppressed group
is thought to be naturally inferior to the ruling class, it can come to
seem to members of both groups that oppression and social inequality
are a mere consequence of the natural order of the universe. We will
look closer at the political roles of group hate and group contempt in
Chapters 6 and 7.

What Is So Collective about Collective Hate?

Group hate and contempt—hatred toward oppressed groups—should
be distinguished from collective hate of the sort seen in organized hate
groups. Although collective hatred typically targets oppressed groups
or their members, it can also be directed at individuals without being
fathomed as an attack on their group identity. For example, the Saudi
officials' brutal murder of *Washington Post* journalist Jamal Khashoggi
was likely motivated by hatred grounded in his criticism of the Saudi regime. Khashoggi is far from the only critic of the Saudi regime who has
been killed by Saudi officials. But the critics of the regime do not constitute a single socially recognized group. So, while the Saudi government's
murder of Khashoggi was the result of collective hatred, it doesn't count
as group hate.

Collective hate, as the term indicates, is hate or contempt that is
had collectively or jointly by a group of people. It is not reducible to an
aggregate of the hate each group member may experience toward the
target. Rather, collective or joint hatred is a special case of collective
(or joint or shared) intentionality, the capacity of minds to be jointly
directed toward objects, people, values, or goals.[6] This is the kind of

intentionality we attribute to group members when we say, "Aleks and Brit are planning to go to Art Basel Miami Beach together," "Otávio and Anjan want to learn to sing in canon," and "The students agreed to surround the White House in protest."

Collective hatred presents the hated group or person in much the same way as individual hatred. For example, the alt-right's hatred toward Jews presents its target as malevolent and guilty of conspiracy and other serious wrongdoings. Similarly, the attitudes of the Saudi officials who killed Khashoggi presumably also presented Khashoggi as malevolent and guilty of serious wrongdoing. These portraits of Jews and Khashoggi are not very different from the one Medea's hatred painted of her husband Jason. The difference between collective and individual hatred doesn't lie in the content of the attitude but rather in the coordination of many people versus the self-determination of a single hating party.

Philosopher Christian List has drawn attention to three kinds of collective attitudes: aggregate, common, and corporate.[7] Aggregate attitudes are attitudes that are held by, say, the majority of a group but that don't require any communication or coordination among group members. Common attitudes are attitudes that are held by all group members, where it's common knowledge that everyone holds the view. For example, all individuals supporting the Black Lives Matter movement are committed to the same cause, which is that of bringing justice to black people, and everyone who supports the movement is aware that everyone else who supports the movement is committed to this cause. Finally, corporate attitudes are attitudes held by groups which, like the U.S. Supreme Court, Hitler's Nazi Party, and Facebook, have the organizational status needed for the group to make genuine group decisions that may not reflect any single individual's opinion.

All three types of collective attitudes will play a role in the chapters to come. But collective hatred of the kind I am mostly interested in is what List would call "common hatred." I prefer the term "joint hatred," however. Joint hatred is characteristic of most hate groups that lack codified organizational structure, such as Stormfront, a Florida-based white supremacist group. But even loosely structured hate groups have outliers who join but don't really harbor any hatred toward the identified target.[8] As List points out, group attitudes that mimic common attitudes can have the same effect on social coordination. But I think something else is going on in the case of joint hatred.

I propose to model joint hatred on the account of joint commitment proposed by philosopher Margaret Gilbert.[9] If you and I agree to go to the Art Basel Miami Beach together, we make a joint commitment to do so. This commitment does not require that individual minds are integrated to form a single, collective mind. Groups do not have minds of their own. Group consciousness is at best a metaphor. Rather, by making a joint commitment to go to the Art Basel Miami Beach together, each of us is obligated to act accordingly and expect the other to act accordingly, and each of us is entitled to hold the other to what we agreed to do.

If we model joint hatred on Gilbert's account of joint commitment, then joint hatred requires a joint commitment to hatred of a more or less well-defined target. But how is it possible to make a commitment to hating a target, whether a person or a group? It is certainly not possible to commit oneself to *feel* hate. We cannot commit ourselves to do something we cannot directly control.

I would like to propose that hatred typically is manifested differently in collectives than it is in individuals. If you are consciously aware of having an emotional reaction to another person, you can usually tell what kind of emotion it is by its distinct focus and feel. This is not how collective emotions operate. Groups of people do not have a single joined body whose physiological changes can somehow be made available to a collective consciousness. When we speak of an idea lingering on in our collective consciousness, that's a metaphor for the idea's widespread and persistent influence.

But if there is no collective consciousness to serve as the subject of joint emotions, how are we to understand the concept? On the view I favor, collective emotions are joint commitments of group members to act as if they have the corresponding emotion. Group members who have the corresponding emotion can honor their commitment by acting accordingly, whereas those who don't can honor their commitment by engaging in a kind of make-believe. They commit themselves to acting as if they were feeling that way.[10]

We emotionally commit ourselves in this way in many aspects of social life. The wedding vow that has taken root in American popular culture is a prime example of a joint emotional commitment: "I promise to be your faithful partner in sickness and in health, in good times and in bad, in happiness as well as in sadness. I promise to love you unconditionally, to support you in your aspirations, and to honor and respect you. This is my solemn vow." It would make no sense to make a mutual commitment to love and respect each other if "love" and "respect" referred to their individual emotional counterparts. We cannot promise to do something we have no direct control over. What we can promise each other is to act as if we love and respect each other. If you genuinely love and respect your spouse, you can honor this commitment by acting on your feelings. But if you realize that you have fallen out of love with them, then acting as if you love and respect them will do just fine in terms of honoring your commitments. Acting-as-if includes such things as saying that you love them or at least not saying that you don't, showing them affection, and treating them with respect. Unless you are a professional actor, you can probably only act as if you love and respect your spouse if your views of them are predominantly positive. If you thought the person you married were a creep, it would be highly unlikely that you would be able and willing to honor your commitments to love and respect them.

Something similar is going on in the case of collective hate. We can understand collective hate as a joint commitment of fellow group members to act as if they harbor individual hate toward the agreed-upon target. People partaking in collective hatred can appropriately hold each other to the expectations generated by the joint commitment and disapprove of behaviors that are not in the spirit of the pledge.

Some hate groups have their own wedding vows of sorts. Although the Ku Klux Klan keep most of their nefarious practices a secret, fragments of their initiation rituals have leaked to the public over the years. Allegedly, during the Klan's initiation rituals new members pledge themselves to hate blacks, Jews, Muslims, and homosexuals.[11]

Although most hate groups don't have the equivalent of wedding vows when new members join, there are many other ways that members can make a commitment to hatred when joining. Simply agreeing to become a member of a group you know is committed to hating a particular target suffices for you to join the joint commitment to hatred.

Collective hatred, of course, need not begin with a group of people already jointly committed to hatred of a specific target. It can also take root in groups initially committed to less abysmal causes. The National Socialist German Workers' Party, or Nazi Party, is a telling example of a political group that grew into a hate group under the leadership of Adolf Hitler. Frustrated with Germany's defeat in World War I and the subsequent economic depression and political instability of Germany, Hitler joined the German Workers' Party, a newly founded nationalist party, in 1919. The party was then a small political organization with only a few dozen members. The subsequent success of the party was largely due to Hitler's charismatic political speeches in which he blamed big businesses and capitalism for the country's hardship. In 1921, Hitler was elected the leader of the party, which by then had been rebranded as the National Socialist German Workers' Party. Hitler's anti-Semitism became the focus of the rebranded national-populist party's agenda, and party members were ordered to act in accordance with Hitler's anti-Jew extremism. While joint hatred was required of members of Hitler's Nazi Party, the party also had the codified organization needed for it to count as corporate, in List's sense.

What Is Dehumanization?

Group hate and group contempt often co-occur. Hate's entanglement with contempt is likely to give rise to a vacillation between resenting the outgroup because of what people of their kind are assumed to have done to us in the past, condemning them on account of their assumed deviant character, and fearing them because of their potentially powerful and dangerous nature, and humiliating them because of their inferior and disgusting nature.

Because emotional vacillation is inevitable when group hate is entangled with group contempt, group hate, in the wide sense of *hate*, may seem paradoxical. At one moment, the ingroup may torture or rape the outgroup because of their resentment for them. At another, the ingroup may hide or run away from the outgroup because of their fear of them. At yet another moment, they may poison them or slaughter them, because of the dehumanizing disrespect they have for them.

The seeming paradoxical nature of group hate is reminiscent of what philosopher David Livingstone Smith has called the "paradox of dehumanization."[12] To dehumanize an outgroup, Livingstone Smith argues, is to regard them as being essentially less than human, which silences our natural inhibitions against harming humans. However, Livingstone Smith argues, this is inconsistent with the fact that dehumanizers implicitly, and often explicitly, acknowledge the human status of their victims. For instance, during the 1994 Rwanda genocide, the Hutus characterized the Tutsis as cockroaches and snakes, suggesting that they regarded them as being essentially less than human, but they also subjected them to humiliation, rape, and torture and referred to them as their "enemies," suggesting that they also regarded them as human.

As Livingstone Smith points out, Morgan Godwyn, an Anglican clergyman advocating for the humane treatment of Indians and African slaves, made a similar point in his 1680 book *The Negro's and Indians Advocate Suing for Their Admission into the Church*. He argued that although slave owners explicitly regarded their African slaves as subhuman, their treatment of them indicated an implicit acknowledgment of the slaves' humanity. For example, by holding them morally responsible for their actions, slave owners treated their slaves as moral agents.

Our tendency to treat dehumanized people as simultaneously human and subhuman has also been noted by philosopher Kwame Anthony Appiah in his 2008 book *Experiments in Ethics*. He writes:

The persecutors may liken the objects of their enmity to cockroaches or germs, but they acknowledge their victims' humanity in the very act of humiliating, stigmatizing, reviling, and torturing them. Such treatment—and the voluble justifications the persecutors invariably offer for such treatment—is reserved for creatures we recognize to have intentions and desires and projects.[13]

Appiah adds that genocidal killers "tell you why their victims—Jews or Tutsi—*deserve* what's being done to them."[14] Their attribution of "just deserts" to their victims, he argues suggests that they recognize their victims' humanity.

Livingstone Smith argues on the basis of these kinds of considerations that genocidal killers don't regard their victims as fully human and also don't regard them as fully subhuman. Rather, in dehumanizing others, they categorize victims simultaneously as human and subhuman and therefore take them to have an "uncanny" or "transgressional" nature. They belong to a species that transgresses our ordinary categories of living things and indeed transgresses what is biologically possible. Dehumanizers, Livingstone Smith argues, regard their victims as particularly deplorable because of their apparent human form, that is, their victims look like humans. As he puts it, "paradoxically, then, part of what makes such dehumanized people so loathsome and menacing is their seeming humanity."[15]

This picture is compelling, but I fear it doesn't accurately capture the attitudes of the perpetrators of genocide and other aggressors untroubled by conscience. Livingstone Smith is one with Appiah in thinking that the fact that dehumanizers humiliate, rape, and torture their victims is evidence that they recognize the humanity in their victims. But this is not how we ordinarily think of such brutal acts. For example, the torture methods that Americans used to break down prisoners held at the Guantánamo Bay detention camp after the 9/11 terrorist attacks—methods that included rectal exams with "excessive force"—are widely characterized as "inhumane" and "barbaric," not as evidence that brutalizers recognized their victims' humanity.[16]

Dehumanizers do realize that their victims are human beings, but this is not evidenced by their brutal acts. Granted, we don't put snakes, rats, and cockroaches in detention camps, or mistreat them in order to make them feel humiliated. But dehumanizers who refer to their victims as "snakes," "rats," or "cockroaches" don't believe their victims are really snakes, rats, or cockroaches. They know that they are not, that they are human beings. Their acts of cruelty are evidence that they don't think their victims are worthy of the respect owed to all people. Their brutality conveys that they think that human beings can lack the person status that demands our respect.

But this is not a belief held exclusively by genocidal killers and American executioners of torture. Appiah's observation that genocidal killers consider their gruesome acts "just deserts" suggests that they view their victims the way we view sadistic serial killers like Ted Bundy and Jeffrey Dahmer. This is particularly salient in comments, such as "He is a monster and *deserves* to be fried," made by the public during Bundy's trial. But the public didn't think Bundy was literally the kind of creature your child claims is hiding under his bed. They knew he was human. Rather, they thought he wasn't entitled to be treated as a person with dignity. The view implicit in this line of thought is that some human beings have personalities that are so dark that they lose the protections that befall other humans. Understood this way, to dehumanize is to treat someone one regards as human in a way that violates the principle of respect, for instance, by avenging against their past evildoing.

As argued in earlier chapters, dehumanizing attitudes are irrational exactly because they violate the principle of respect, and acts of vengeance are morally indefensible because the sole motive of avengers is bloodlust.

The seeming paradoxical nature of dehumanization is thus due to its irrationality rather than to its attribution of an "uncanny" nature to its victims. Similar remarks apply to dehumanizing hatred and dehumanizing contempt.

Hate and contempt, however, focus on distinct character traits. So, they are rationally consistent. For example, a parent of one of Dahmer's victims can feel contempt for Dahmer because of his cannibalism and hatred for him because of his malevolent acts without this amounting to any internal inconsistency.

Dehumanizing hatred and contempt are inherently irrational. But the question remains whether critical group hate and group contempt could be rational. Isn't it rational to hate the Nazis or members of other organized hate groups?

In most cases, probably not. Although organized hate groups are committed to disseminating hatred and encouraging violence against the hated groups, it doesn't follow that all members of such groups are evil or malevolent. Oskar Schindler, a German Nazi, is a paradigm example of a member of an organized hate group who wasn't evil.[17] We can, of course, conjure up cases where critical hatred of people on account of their group membership might be rational. Imagine a group that only accepts members who have committed a crime so barbaric that it alone testifies to the member's malevolence. In the envisaged scenario, hating all members of the group could perhaps be rational. But such cases, if they exist, are rare.

Collective hate is not typically a rational attitude either. Contrary to what philosopher Thomas Szanto has argued, this is not because collective hate takes the form of a joint commitment and therefore isn't a genuinely affective attitude.[18] Rather, collective hate tends to be irrational because it tends to target marginalized or stigmatized social groups. But here again, we can conjure up cases where collective hatred could be rational. Imagine that a group of siblings discover that their much younger sister has been sexually molested by their neighbor for many years. The siblings make a joint commitment to hate the child molester, knowing that it will motivate them to help the police and state prosecutor put the neighbor behind bars. In the envisaged scenario, collective hate could be rational. But in reality, collective hatred tends to have an ugly face.

The Reality of Evil

During the Holocaust, hundreds of thousands of ordinary Germans who had previously lived side by side with Jews and other ethnic minorities willingly carried out, assisted with, or otherwise facilitated sadistic human experimentation and mass slaughter,[19] and a significant number of those who didn't participate were passive bystanders who knew about the mass killings and the intentions of the Nazi regime.[20] In fact, German newspapers continuously printed reports on how the regime punished the unworthy, which would have left very few Germans ignorant of what was transpiring, if not in detail, then in broad strokes.

Ordinary Germans' willing participation in or acceptance of the Holocaust was not primarily a result of a special German psychopathic or sadistic trait. Although—as we will see—dark traits were a driving force in some instances, the vast majority of active German participants and passive bystanders had quite unremarkable personalities before Hitler came to power. Their family lives were quite similar to those of average middle-class Americans today. They had jobs to support their families, they sent their children to school, they donated to local charities, and they socialized with friends and family on weekends. Neither participants nor passive bystanders showed signs of having psychopathic or sadistic dispositions prior to the Nazi era.[21]

Nor is there any evidence that Germans participated exclusively out of fear of retribution from the Nazi state. Although anti-Nazi speech and obstruction of "justice" were punishable by death, no one was coerced to actively contribute to the "Final Solution." Even when explicitly given a chance to opt out, most recruits went on to participate in the killing and torture of Jews and other ethnic minorities. For example, out of the 500 ordinary men in Germany who were recruited to do roundups of the 1,800 Jews in the village of Józefów, only 15 decided not to participate after being told by Mayor Wilhelm Trapp that they were to shoot everyone, including women, children, and the elderly, but that they could step aside if they didn't want to be part of the mass killing. Only 15 out of 500, a mere 3 percent, opted out!

But while the ordinary Germans' willingness to participate in mass killings was not the result of exceptionally psychopathic or sadistic traits, there is evidence to suggest that mid-level and top Nazi officials responsible for the most atrocious acts during the Holocaust were for the most part rather dark personalities. These officials include not just the likes of Heinrich Himmler, Josef Mengele, and Adolf Eichmann but also deplorable Nazi supporters like Maurice Papon, who was responsible for the deportation of almost 1,600 Jews in the Bordeaux region in France to death camps like Auschwitz; Irmgard Huber, the head nurse at a hospital for mentally ill patients, turned killing center in 1940, who administered lethal injections to at least 14,000 people and falsified their death certificates; and Hermine Braunsteiner, who was in charge of selecting women and children to be sent to the Majdanek death camp's gas chambers and who was infamous for her brutality toward the prisoners.

At the Nuremberg war criminal trials, which lasted from November 20, 1945, to October 1, 1946, a common defense given by former Nazis accused of involvement in the Holocaust was that they were just following orders from their superiors. This was also the defense of Nazi SS-Obersturmbannführer Eichmann, who was in charge of the logistics involved in the mass deportation of Jews to ghettos and extermination camps in Nazi-occupied Eastern Europe during the war. When the war ended, he escaped to Argentina but was caught in 1960 and tried in Jerusalem in 1961. During his trial, he denied being anti-Semitic and insisted that he was just following orders. The court sentenced him to death.

After attending parts of Eichmann's trial, political philosopher Hannah Arendt published a controversial analysis of what led ordinary Germans like Eichmann to become active participants in the Holocaust.[22] Arendt argued that Eichmann was just an ordinary, rather boring, bureaucratic conformist, who was "neither perverted nor sadistic," but "terrifyingly normal." Eichmann's only motive was to diligently advance his career in the Nazi bureaucracy. He was too thoughtless and disengaged from the reality of his own evil acts to realize that he did anything wrong. What he did was evil, but, Arendt argued, he did it without evil intent. Arendt called the fact that evil acts can be committed by conformist shallow "joiners" who have no evil intent "the banality of evil." In the postscript to the second edition of *Eichmann in Jerusalem* (1964), she wrote:

> When I speak of the banality of evil, I do so only on the strictly factual level, pointing to a phenomenon which stared one in the face at the trial. Eichmann was not Iago and not Macbeth. . . . Except for an extraordinary diligence in looking out for his personal advancement, he had no motives at all. . . . It was sheer thoughtlessness. . . . He *merely*, to put the matter colloquially, *never realized* what he was doing.[23]

Many details of Arendt's theory have since then been overturned by historical evidence and empirical studies. But it initially enjoyed seemingly strong support from a famous experiment conducted by psychologist Stanley Milgram in 1961.[24] Milgram found that volunteers were willing to administer increasingly more severe electric shocks to a "learner" when egged on by an authoritative scientist in a white lab coat. When participants stopped and questioned the experiment or expressed a wish to check on the "learner," the authoritative scientist in the white lab coat would simply reply with: "The experiment requires that you continue. Please go on." A significant number of participants continued after being encouraged to do so, and some went all the way to 450 volts. "It may be that we are puppets—puppets controlled by the strings of society," Milgram lamented.

A second experiment that initially seemed to support Arendt's conclusion is the Stanford prison experiment, which was conducted by psychologist Philip Zimbardo in 1971.[25] Twenty-four male students were assigned random roles as prisoners or guards in an enclosure in the basement of the psychology building. During the experiment, both prisoners and guards adapted to their roles well beyond Zimbardo's expectations. One-third of the guards began acting like sadistic dictators, whereas many of the prisoners increasingly tolerated psychological abuse. Zimbardo subsequently argued that since the roles of guards and prisoners were arbitrarily assigned, the actions were unlikely to be the result of the students' personality traits but were situationally determined. Zimbardo called the hypothesis that good people turn evil when put in bad circumstances "The Lucifer Effect," a hypothesis detailed in his 2007 bestseller by the same name.

If the findings from Milgram's experiments and the Stanford prison experiment had reflected Eichmann's situation in the Third Reich, then the unique situation Eichmann found himself in may indeed have been the driving force behind his willful participation in mass murder.

But there is a problem. Arendt's theory of the banality of evil is highly inconsistent with what we know about personality. How you behave depends not only on the particular situation you are in but also on your personality. Situations vary in how strongly they tend to influence our behavior. Situations heavily governed by social norms and expectations tend to be very strong determinants of behavior. They are also sometimes called "strong situations."[26] For example, it's a good (though not infallible) prediction that you won't spot a naked person out in public this week. This means that population-wide variation in personality doesn't make much of a difference to whether we decide to wear clothes in public.

The Nazi regime, rife with rules and rituals, created situations that were more likely to influence people's behavior than many of the situations that you and I tend to find ourselves in. But these restrictions didn't marginalize personality as a strong determinant of behavior. For example, most Germans didn't join the Nazi Party, let alone the Schutzstaffel, or SS—Hitler's paramilitary force. At the start of the war in 1939, 6 percent of the German population had joined the Nazi Party.[27] The party membership total rose to 10 percent of the 80 million Germans at its peak in 1945. The SS employed 0.01 percent of the

German population at its peak. Eichmann was evidently part of a very small minority of Germans who decided to work for the SS.

As these numbers testify to, the vast majority of Germans didn't elect to actively participate in the Holocaust. This reflects rather vast differences in German people's personalities and to a much lesser extent differences in physical or social circumstances. So, in spite of the Nazi regime's influence on people's behavior, their personalities were nonetheless still a strong determinant of how they acted. Indeed, a reassessment of the empirical evidence that initially seemed to lend support to the banality of evil coupled with historical details about Eichmann's life tell a more sinister story about why people like Eichmann do evil things.

Psychologist Thomas Blass, the author of *The Man Who Shocked the World* (2004), conducted a meta-analysis of twenty-one versions of Milgram's experiment to determine whether there were any significant differences in personality between participants who went all the way and those who quit before it went too far. Blass found that the volunteers who continued delivering the shocks were significantly more likely to be supporters of authoritarian regimes than volunteers who refused to go all the way. They were also significantly more trusting of others and inclined to follow the lead of others. These findings suggest that if Eichmann did what he did because he was following orders, as Arendt argued, then he wasn't all that ordinary.

However, more recently uncovered historical evidence suggests that Nazis like Eichmann weren't simple pen-pushing bureaucrats only following orders. In his 2006 book *Becoming Eichmann*, which challenges Arendt's conclusions, historian David Cesarani writes:

> Eichmann's Nazi convictions and his unquestioning obedience to orders were part of the same ideological package. His prejudices and predilections had become so ingrained by 1945 that they surface in the marginalia he wrote in books while in Argentina. But does this also mean that he had been a helpless marionette in the Nazi hierarchy? Was Eichmann merely a robotic subordinate, which was the image he tried to construct while in

captivity? Again, he himself provides evidence to the contrary. He averred to [Willem] Sassen [who interviewed Eichmann about his involvement in the Holocaust] that "I am an idealist." Another time he told him: "When I reached the conclusion that it was necessary to do to the Jews what we did, I worked with the fanaticism a man can expect from himself." Obedience can certainly coexist with zeal, but the self-denying portrait Eichmann gave of himself while on trial is belied by evidence of his aptitude for power games within the Third Reich and his willingness in 1944, at least, to play one power centre against another.[28]

Eichmann wasn't a killer or a thug or even particularly anti-Semitic when he first joined the Nazi Party in 1933, Cesarani argues. He only morphed into a monster after he became a member of the Nazi Party. His initially mundane work of collecting information on "the Jewish Question" for the Nazi police would eventually turn him into a fanatical anti-Semite, but, Cesarani concludes, prior to becoming the Nazi's confidant, Eichmann was indeed quite ordinary. So, when it comes to the question of whether we could all have become Eichmann had we been in the same kinds of circumstances, Cesarani and Arendt aren't miles apart. Their answer to this question is a loud and clear yes.

But is that right? The evidence overwhelmingly suggests that it's not. Eichmann was no ordinary paper-pushing bureaucrat. But neither was he just an average man who radicalized while working for the Nazis. Like most of the top officials responsible for carrying out the "Final Solution," Eichmann had a sinister personality. Until 1944, he often bragged about supposedly being the one to hit on the idea of the "Final Solution," and toward the end of the war he notoriously said that if Germany lost, he would "leap laughing into the grave because the feeling that he had five million enemies of the Reich on his conscience would be for him a source of extraordinary satisfaction."[29]

The most compelling reason to doubt that Eichmann turned evil under Nazi influence is that, absent major injuries to the brain, radical personality changes are rare and don't happen overnight or even in a single decade. This overwhelmingly suggests that Eichmann was no ordinary man, not even prior to joining the Nazi Party, but already possessed dark traits that, once unleashed, played a role is his becoming a mass murderer. This is not surprising from the point of view of personality. It is common sense that we all have personality traits that only make a significant difference to our behavior once some situational or "triggering" factor kicks it into gear.[30]

The implication of this is that it simply isn't true that we all would have done what Eichmann did, had we been thrown into the same circumstances. What is true is that corrupt governments have the power to create the circumstances that will harness the sinister inclinations of the 10 to 15 percent of the general population who have dark personality traits.

This conclusion is also consistent with meta-analyses of the Stanford prison experiment. Psychologists Thomas Carnahan and Sam McFarlan conducted a study that looked at whether there are significant differences in the personalities of people who sign up for "a psychological study of prison life," like those in the original prison study, and people who sign up for a psychology study in general.[31] They found that there were indeed shocking differences. People who volunteered for the "prison study" were on average:

- 27 percent more likely to be hostile or aggressive.
- 26 percent more likely to approve of and enforce social hierarchies.
- 12 percent more likely to consider themselves superior to others and scorn others.
- 10 percent more likely to be authoritative or submit to an authority.
- 10 percent more likely to manipulate others for personal gain.
- 7 percent less likely to show empathy.
- 6 percent less likely to be considerate or altruistic.

This suggests that Nazis like Eichmann were more akin to the participants in the Stanford prison experiment than the obedient 65 percent who delivered the fatal shocks in Milgram's experiment.

Eichmann's dehumanizing contempt-proneness toward Jews and his lack of remorse reveal that a dark personality loomed large beneath his banal appearance. While his dark traits may not have been of the magnitude that inspired the most sadistic and callous among the SS officers, medical doctors, and camp leaders to torture and kill, it was forceful enough to prompt him to knowingly and willingly deport millions of Jews to death camps.

Even Arendt noticed that Eichmann was greedy, dishonest, deceitful, power-hungry, and had an inflated sense of self long before the Holocaust. It was his fondness of bragging and basking in his own glory that eventually landed him in trouble. In Argentina, he proudly revealed to fellow Nazis that he had resisted Himmler's last-minute orders to stop the gas chambers, determined to see the genocide through to the end.[32] Perhaps Eichmann wasn't a psychopath or a sadist but rather a Machiavellian or a narcissist, most likely the latter. Regardless of the particular nature of his darkness, there is little doubt that he had malevolent character traits long before being trained by the Nazis.

To become a member of the SS—Hitler's paramilitary force—you had to undergo military training, which included a hardening process. While the hardening process helped desensitize those who would become active executioners, its primary aim was to weed out those who didn't have the dark traits necessary to willingly participate in mass murder. For example, women training to enter the SS were routinely given a puppy as a companion.[33] After the women and their puppy had grown fond of each other, the SS officers in command would order the women to use their own knife to kill their puppy. Non-compliance meant that the person was unfit for the SS and would be dismissed.

Looking beyond the narrow confines of Eichmann's venality, we are still faced with the mind-numbing question of why Germans who, ultimately, inhabit the same moral universe as us never muttered the tiniest peep of protest and even appeared relatively unfazed by the atrocities they knew were unfolding. Let's not forget, of course, about the admirable and courageous Germans who risked their lives to save Jews or other ethnic minorities wanted by the Nazis. But superheroes aside, the question remains of how the Nazis managed to "silence" so many Germans who didn't have it in their hearts to actively do evil.

The answer turns on their dark souls' skillful manipulation tactics. To maximize compliance and minimize resistance among ordinary Germans who didn't have it in them to do evil, the Nazis capitalized on the Germans' long-standing anti-Semitic sentiments and feelings of despair.[34] From the time Hitler came to power in 1933, the population was bombarded with information from the authorities seemingly proving that "the Jewry" were duplicitous, malevolent, and powerful. By the time the war started in 1939, the Nazis had managed to persuade most Germans that the Jews had intentionally destroyed the economy and were secretly scheming to seize control over Germany by enacting a Communist coup, which would lead to their demise.[35]

Once the German people were manipulated into resenting the Jews for World War I and the poor economy, it was easy for the Nazis to create a scapegoat out of the Jews and turn the old anti-Semitic sentiments into full-on hatred.

All-consuming hate is coupled with a retaliatory mentality that makes the hater inclined to regard suffering inflicted on the target as justified. The fear or apprehension component of hate will tend to elicit a survival response, also known as a "fight or flight" response. Since flight often isn't feasible in political contexts, fighting back to eliminate the threat may seem like the only live option. So, by bolstering the German population's anti-Jew prejudices and their feelings of despair, the Nazis were able to make the Germans who might otherwise have resisted look the other way while the Holocaust ran its course.

Political Propaganda

Genocidal killers get away with their atrocities in part by inciting people to hatred and contempt. But how do they incite whole populations to hatred and contempt of the magnitude seen in historical atrocities, such the transatlantic slave trade, the Soviet Ukraine Holodomor, the Holocaust, the Cambodian genocide, and the Rwandan genocide?

Part of the answer is that propaganda works in just this way, that is, propaganda is a tool strategically employed to elicit strong emotions, such as hatred, contempt, fear, and pride, in the targeted group. These emotions can then help unleash people's dark traits or prep those disinclined to do evil for their future role as passive bystanders.

Propaganda is speech that is used with the purpose of manipulating public opinion. "Speech" is here meant to refer broadly to all manners of communication, including spoken language, written language, sign language, non-linguistic symbols like the swastika, pictures, posters, plays, films, television programs, and radio programs. Although the aim of physical violence may have the same aim as propaganda, violence doesn't count as speech. Nor do protests, marches, or riots.

Propaganda need not be political. The goal of advertising is to manipulate public opinion, for example, by appealing to consumers' needs or fears. So, advertising intended to sell a product is a form of propaganda. But the focus here will be on political propaganda.

How does propaganda succeed in manipulating public opinion? In his 2015 book *How Propaganda Works*, Jason Stanley, a political philosopher and philosopher of language, sets out to explain how ordinary people in the grip of a flawed ideology unknowingly can become producers and consumers of propaganda.

Stanley draws a distinction between supporting and undermining propaganda. Supporting propaganda capitalizes on people's emotions, such as nostalgia, sentiment, or fear, to increase the realization of an explicit political ideal.[36]

Donald Trump's 2016 campaign promise to "make America great again" is an example of supporting propaganda. The slogan is intended to invoke a feeling of nostalgia about a mythic past where white men willing to commit themselves to hard work were able to move up the socio-economic hierarchy. The mythic past idealized by the slogan made upward movability possible by endorsing a racist and sexist ideology that rationalized slavery, segregation, and social inequality. The slogan aims at mobilizing support for a political agenda that promotes a return to this kind of society, rich in career opportunities for white men.

Undermining propaganda, the second kind discussed by Stanley, appeals to a political, economic, aesthetic, or rational ideal to mobilize support for a political goal that in fact contradicts that very ideal. One of Stanley's examples comes from the war on drugs in the 1980s that resulted in the passage of the Anti-Drug Abuse Act (ADAA) in 1986. Politicians argued that to secure law and order, or criminal justice, possession and sale of the highly addictive crack cocaine should be punished much more harshly than possession and sale of the purer and less addictive powder cocaine. The harsher punishment for possession and sale of crack doesn't reflect differences in how addictive the drugs are. Crack is only slightly more addictive than powder, and only when the powder is snorted rather than injected. If the powder is dissolved in water and injected, it's just as addictive. Yet the new drug legislation that was passed created a 100-to-1 ratio between how large a quantity of crack versus powder in your possession triggers a minimum prison sentence, as well as a 5-to-1 ratio in the length of the maximum prison sentence. This law resulted in gross social injustice. This is because crack is almost exclusively used by blacks, as only wealthy whites and Latinos can afford to buy powder. So, the sentencing disparity between crack users, who are mostly black, and powder users, who are predominantly white and Latino, contradicts the political ideal of "law and order," or criminal justice.[37]

Stanley is primarily concerned with the latter kind of propaganda, the kind that appeals to political ideals to mobilize support for a goal that undermines the ideal, which he sees as particularly problematic for liberal democracies.[38] Liberal democracies strive for social equality. Yet, Stanley argues, undermining propaganda perpetuates social inequalities by exploiting flawed ideologies that have prevailed throughout most of the society's history.

The beliefs that constitute flawed ideologies are unreflective and built on convention. They make social inequalities seem legitimate to us by misrepresenting social reality, for example, by presenting hierarchies of different groups of people as a natural order or as a necessary evil while playing up the inherent worth of the privileged class. As Stanley notes, during the drug war, politicians failed to see the contradiction between blacks being punished more harshly for the same kind of crime, and the ideal of law and order, or criminal justice, because it was masked by their flawed ideological belief that black people have an addictive personality that can only be controlled by sending them to prison.

The widely publicized photograph of the alt-right protest in Charlottesville, Virginia, a few months before the rally on August 12, 2017, that left thirty-two-year-old Heather Heyer dead and dozens more injured is another example of undermining propaganda. The photograph depicts angry young men holding flaming torches. According to media researcher Joan Donovan, the photograph is "an expert piece of white supremacist propaganda, an image staged by a racist provocateur to generate exactly the kind of media coverage that it received."[39] The photo's apparent message is that the rise in hate is troublesome. But the hidden message, aimed at the would-be supremacists who haven't yet come out of the closet, is that more haters are needed. The photograph thus appeals to the liberal ideal of finding a solution to the troublesome uptick in hatred. But its secret aim is to encourage more hatemongers to break out of their shell, which undercuts the liberal ideal.

Part of the power of undermining propaganda, Stanley argues, lies in its special design. It's engineered to appear to convey an innocuous message. But the real message is concealed, because only then will people buy into it. The "innocent" message conveyed by undermining propaganda is what Stanley calls the "at issue content," and the hidden information is what he calls the "not-at-issue content."

If, for example, you want the public to support stricter immigration laws, referring to non-citizen immigrants as "aliens" can seem harmless, as "alien" is a legal term with just that meaning, but "alien" evokes images of an unwelcome, strange, hostile, humanoid-like creature. This derogatory information is the not-at-issue content. It's the presence of hidden information that makes the propaganda manipulative, according to Stanley.

The strength of Stanley's account lies in its ability to account for how propaganda can make people support a political goal by strengthening their pre-existing ideological beliefs. Its weakness lies in its inability to explain what motivates people to take action. For example, it doesn't explain what makes people engage in political protests or commit hate crimes, or what secures a whole nation's active participation in or tolerance of the implementation of extremist ideologies or "final solutions."

As Hume once noted, beliefs by themselves do not spur action.[40] Your belief that it's wrong to eat meat doesn't suffice for you to be motivated to stop eating meat. If, however, you strongly desire not to eat meat, perhaps because you don't like it, or because you believe it's morally wrong to eat other animals, that will motivate you to take action.

According to Stanley, our ideological beliefs mask the contradiction in the hidden content of undermining propaganda, which makes us less likely to question the information. Uncritically accepting an unsound political argument as sound may be all it takes to persuade us to support the political goal it advances, but it doesn't automatically prompt us to take action.

People become involved in political activism, not because they have flawed ideological beliefs and have been fed a piece of propaganda, but because they have a strong desire to see things change and intend to contribute toward that end. But how do you bring people to the point where they want things to change so badly that they willingly engage in political activism, or are prepared to do almost anything to further a political cause?

The natural answer is that you provoke strong emotions in them, such as disgust, fear, contempt, hate, or pride. The only way that propaganda can motivate people to fight for a political cause is if it tugs at our emotions. This is true even if the propaganda is a coverup of an inconsistency, that is, speech of the kind Stanley calls "undermining propaganda." Propaganda that doesn't hide its true message, that is, speech of the kind Stanley calls "supporting propaganda," appeals to people's emotions, but so does undermining propaganda.

In colonial America, pro-slavery propaganda served to "naturalize" the cruel exploitation of blacks. For example, in *Slavery, as It Relates to the Negro, or African Race* (1843), American writer Josiah Priest argued that it was God's intention for blacks to live in servitude to whites.[41] This, he argued, was evidenced by their durable physical stature and skin, inferior intellect, and irrational behavior, which made them suitable as servants. Priest writes:

> God formed and adapted every creature to the country and elements suited to their natures, so as to compete with difficulties, and to enjoy their being; wherefore, from the facts of the case agreeing with this opinion, the negro was created as he is, and has not been produced and modeled by circumstances and accidents.[42]

All humans, Priest alleged, are created with a purpose, and the purpose of blacks is to serve white men. Priest rewrote and reinterpreted Bible passages to create the appearance that black enslavement was consistent with the humane values promoted by Christians. Noah's three sons, he conjectured, were all of different races. Ham, who Priest claims was black, was destined from birth to act sinfully, which created a natural need for pietist white men to enslave him. The same fate befell all of Ham's black descendants.

In Nazi Germany, propagandists engineered propaganda speeches, posters, and films portraying the Jews as disease-spreading rats feeding off the host nation, poisoning its culture, and polluting the Aryan race. Images of a disease-spreading rat would ordinarily provoke disgust. But a rat of the size that can feed off a nation, poison its culture, and kill off the white race is more likely to provoke contempt that can motivate dark personalities to extinguish the "parasite" to save the nation and hatred that can make mass murder seem justified and necessary to those disinclined to become active executioners.

Appeals to disgust, however, can also help strengthen a pre-existing prejudice against an outgroup. This was the strategy used by Trump when he warned a rally crowd in Pennsylvania in August 2018 that "the fake, fake disgusting news" was out to get him.[43] Appeals to disgust are aimed at making the crowd associate the enemy with bodily decay, weakness, and destruction.

Propaganda works by stirring up emotions in people, but its success in provoking all-consuming contempt and hate depends on the fact that people in groups behave in predictable ways. The predictability of groups is the secret weapon of propagandists.

Homogeneous groups left to their own devices or nudged along by their leaders in devious ways tend to undergo spontaneous polarization. Under the right conditions, this ingroup force can complete the work of the propagandists with subtle or no intervention. The orchestrators can lean back and watch, and then strike once social nature has taken its course.

Spontaneous Group Polarization

Group polarization or ingroup/outgroup polarization, also known as the risky shift and the choice shift phenomenon, is the tendency of group deliberation to move individual group members toward the most fanatical, sometimes the riskiest and sometimes the most cautious, versions of the viewpoint they initially held.[44] For example, after deliberation, people in groups opposed to Obamacare are likely to be still more opposed; people in groups who believe there are no salary inequities in an institution or company are likely, after discussion, to discontinue investigations into its existence; people who think that sexual assault at universities is a serious problem are likely, after discussion, to insist on still more severe measures to prevent it.[45] Group polarization shapes the collective opinion and conduct of schools, colleges, companies, unions, juries, political parties, and governments.

Group polarization toward group extremes is different from attitude polarization. Attitude polarization is individual polarization toward group extremes, which is what we sometimes call "peer pressure."[46] Attitude polarization is consistent with the group's final collective opinion being no more outraire than the initial collective opinion.

Suppose that all but one juror is ready to recommend life without parole for a suspect, whereas the remaining juror is leaning toward life with the possibility of parole. To avoid a hung jury, the other jurors try to bring her around. In the envisaged scenario, the juror's viewpoint has become polarized, whereas the viewpoint of the jury stays more or less the same. That is attitude polarization.

In group polarization, the opinion of the group as a whole moves to a more extreme version of the viewpoint held by any of the individual members. For example, if a jury comes to the verdict of life without the possibility of parole, even though the most extreme juror initially thought life with the possibility of parole would be "just deserts," this is group polarization.

I use the term "group deliberation" as an umbrella term that can refer to the structured, rule-based deliberation of established political or governing entities, the exchange of ideas among activists on blogs or social media, casual sociopolitical chats among friends at local hangouts, and unstructured interactions among people at a golf club, the gym, a church, or a workplace.

The initial research on group polarization was at first met with surprise and skepticism in the scientific community as it was at odds with the theoretical principles of group reasoning that prevailed at the time. It was thought that group decisions would reflect an average of opinions and norms, which is quite intuitive for a group of like-minded individuals. You would expect like-minded individuals to find a compromise that reflects the mean position of the group. The result that overall group opinions move to extremes after deliberation is surprising and counterintuitive.

Despite the initial opposition, research in the area picked up in the 1960s, and group polarization was confirmed as a possible effect of groups on individual decision-making, even in trained decision-makers. Since the 1960s, hundreds of studies have confirmed the phenomenon. For example, in their seminal 1973 piece "Choice Shift and Extreme Behavior," psychologists Eleanor Main and Thomas Walker looked at decisions made by federal district court judges sitting either alone or in groups of three and found that group discussions strongly influenced the judges' decisions.[47] Only about 30 percent of the cases where the judges were alone resulted in extreme verdicts. When the judges were part of groups, deliberation led to radical verdicts in 65 percent of cases.

But not all groups are equally likely to move toward an exaggerated version of the initial opinions of individual group members. In their 1999 piece "Bringing Deliberation to the Democratic Dialogue," political theorists James Fishkin and Robert Luskin report on findings that group polarization is considerably less likely to influence decision-making within highly diverse groups where group members have rights to deliberate and vote. The greatest effect on decision-making has been observed in groups of similar-minded individuals, particularly when the group is new, takes on new tasks, or develops new strategies for implementing their pet cause.[48]

Group polarization is not intrinsically bad. It could well be the psychological force required for people to change in the context of a social support group. Alcoholic Anonymous (AA) is an example of a social support system where group polarization is highly likely to occur. Alcoholics tend to develop extreme viewpoints about alcohol and abstinence. Some of these beliefs are exaggerations of true beliefs, for example, that for an alcoholic one drink is too many and one thousand are not enough, that there is no such thing as making a normal drinker out of an alcoholic, and that alcoholism is a progressive illness which can never be cured (or: "Once an alcoholic, always an alcoholic").[49] These statements are exaggerations of truths, used for rhetorical purposes to make alcoholics adopt a mindset that can help them stay sober.[50] Spawned by exaggerations of the truth, the ideology of AA is in one sense false. But in a setting like AA, it doesn't matter whether the group's extremist beliefs about alcohol are true or false. It is far more important that alcoholics receive the group support they need to quit their addiction. So, in support groups that have an admirable and worthwhile aim, group polarization can actually be a means to good outcomes.

The problem with group polarization is that it is an unreliable method for forming true beliefs. Even if group polarization in a slut-walk protest might lead to new legislation preventing rapists from being acquitted on the grounds that the survivor wore a miniskirt, which surely is a good thing, group polarization is far more likely to be used in devious ways to propagate rumors, bad-mouth opponents, orchestrate smear campaigns, control election outcomes, sustain social inequality, and justify mass killing and genocide.

Someone Like Me

That group polarization occurs is a fact. Why it occurs is more puzzling. What drives this phenomenon is not as simple as the latent desire to conform that we all have. If a desire to conform were the sole force governing group polarization, we should expect the end result of the group to be no more extreme than the most extreme viewpoints of the majority of group members. But we know that group polarization can radicalize groups, even when the majority of group members start out with rather moderate viewpoints.

Cohesive groups of like-minded individuals united by a passionate commitment to a joint cause are considerably more likely to polarize than diverse groups or groups that are not committed to a joint cause.[51] For example, people with pre-existing misogynistic sentiments who regularly read and contribute to the subreddit Red Pill are considerably more likely to polarize than a group of au pairs in Paris who meet up for drinks every Saturday night. The crucial factor in group radicalization is the shared sense of group identity that group cohesiveness and commitment to a joint cause facilitate, not group cohesiveness as such. Let's call these conditions the "optimal starting conditions."

In colonial America the cultivation of a shared identity provided the conditions needed for group polarization to radicalize the colonists' pre-existing anti-black and anti-brown sentiments. Although the first colonists were largely British, and many arrived to escape religious persecution, the colonists were not initially a cohesive group with shared ideals. One factor that helped unite them was, ironically, the colonists' resistance to "enslavement" by the British. While still under British rule, the colonists grew increasingly disenchanted with the British control, as new taxes and policies were imposed to ensure that the colonies paid off their "debt" to the mother country and respected the Native Americans in the West. This eventually led the (by then) thirteen colonies to form a united front against the authority of the British Empire. Their coalition and joint efforts to win the Revolutionary War against the British reinforced the colonists' sense of belonging to a single cohesive group with shared values and rights—values and rights most Americans still cherish today.

It is not without irony that the American identity that gradually materialized in the years leading up to the American Revolution in 1775 escalated the colonists' contempt and hatred for Natives and blacks.

A similar sense of belonging to a single cohesive group also provided the ideal conditions for group polarization to occur in Nazi Germany. Although the "Aryan" German people were already a fairly cohesive group, they were not initially prepared to accept the use of extreme measures to eliminate their alleged enemy. Prior to the war, most Germans had Jewish neighbors, friends, employers, employees, or relatives through marriage, even Eichmann. Two key factors that helped unite the German people were the Great Depression and the perceived threat of a Communist uprising, which had left them feeling frightened and helpless. Nazi propaganda capitalized on these negative feelings, which reinforced the Germans' sense of belonging to a single cohesive group with shared values and rights and a shared enemy.

Social Comparison, One-Upmanship and Normative Bootstrapping

Once the optimal starting conditions are in place, polarization tends to occur spontaneously as a result of a number of psychological factors.

One type of psychological force behind group polarization is confirmation bias. When people deliberate, they take turns offering reasons and arguments for and against the issues under discussion. This is ordinarily a good thing. However, as law professor Cass Sunstein points out in his seminal 2002 article "The Law of Group Polarization," when the majority of group members or some particularly convincing or powerful group members are already leaning in a particular direction on an issue, the group is prone to cherry-pick arguments that further bolster their viewpoints while turning a blind eye to counter-evidence. The result is a disproportionate number of pro arguments. This limited argument pool, which is skewed in a particular direction, can then end up convincing group members who were previously undecided on the issue or who were leaning in the other direction.

This kind of polarizing confirmation bias is particularly vividly illustrated in Sidney Lumet's classic courtroom-drama film *12 Angry Men*. In a New York county courthouse, a jury deliberates on the case of an eighteen-year-old on trial for stabbing his father to death. In a preliminary vote, all but one of the jurors vote "guilty." Juror 8, who votes "not guilty," then questions the reliability of the two witnesses, as well as the prosecution's claim that the murder weapon, a switchblade, is uncommon by producing an identical knife. After a secret-ballot vote, Juror 9 reveals that he has changed his mind. Hours of deliberation ensue, and by the end of the movie, all the jurors are persuaded that there is reasonable doubt about the defendant's guilt, and the jury returns to the courtroom with a "not guilty" verdict.

What makes this movie a particularly strong example of how confirmation bias can result in spontaneous polarization is that most of the jurors' arguments are well-known logical fallacies, such as false cause, hasty conclusion, appeal to ignorance, and appeal to hypocrisy, whereas other persuasion tactics used would be disallowed in a real-life jury situation, such as bringing a copy of the murder weapon into the room from outside. But fallacious reasoning and illegitimate persuasion tactics are often more convincing than logically sound reasoning.

Another type of force propelling group polarization forward is one-upmanship, the "art" of continually outdoing ingroup rivals.[52] Group members will be inclined to outdo each other as long as the increasingly more radical viewpoint continues to be regarded as admirable. One-upmanship can shift the stance of the group as a whole to one that is far more extreme than any group member's initial opinion. Social psychologists Glenn Sanders and Robert Baron describe one-upmanship as follows:

> This realization either "releases" the moderate members from their fear of appearing extreme or motivates moderate members to "compete" with the extreme members to see who can come closest to espousing the most admirable position. In either case, the moderates are motivated to adopt more extreme positions, while there is no corresponding pressure on extreme members to moderate their opinions (although, of course, simple conformity pressure may lead to some small amount of moderation by extreme members). The net result is an overall polarization of opinions, that is, a choice shift.[53]

One-upmanship is a result of social comparison. We are constantly motivated both to be seen and to present ourselves in a socially desirable light. To do this, we must continually process information about how those we compare ourselves to present themselves, and then adjust our own self-presentation accordingly. Many of us implicitly desire to be seen in a more favorable light than the average of those we compare ourselves to. Once we figure out how other people present themselves, we present ourselves in a slightly more favorable light. When all members of a cohesive group engage in this kind of social comparison, the result is a shift of average self-presentation in a more extreme direction.

If a moderate opinion in one direction about a social issue is already seen as favorable by most members of a cohesive group of like-minded individuals, a slightly more radical opinion is likely to be seen by most people as still more favorable. So, after deliberation, the group can come to favor a more radical version of the group's original opinion.

A variation on polarization by one-upmanship is polarization engendered by a misperception of which ingroup values are regarded as ideal by the majority of group members or group leaders and hence a misperception of which group values we should strive toward to be perceived favorably by those we compare ourselves to. This, together with one-upmanship, can move group members to an increasingly more extreme position.

Interestingly, once a group reaches the limit of extremity as a result of a misperception of group values, the initially misperceived group values thereby become the new norm. We can refer to this phenomenon as "normative bootstrapping." By adhering to a misperceived norm, that misperceived norm thereby becomes the new norm for the group.

A striking example of how misperceived group norms can play a role in radicalizing group opinions is the long-term abidance by the trans-woman-exclusion policies governing large queer and feminist events such as the Michigan Womyn's Music Festival. For many years festival organizers and festival goers have abided by an informal policy that only women who were assigned the female sex at birth could attend the event. This is also known as "the intention." The intention is captured by the slogan "womyn born womyn."

The official explanation of why trans women are not welcome at the festival is that they have experienced the male privilege during their up-bringing and that some of them still have a penis. Festival organizers argued that experiencing the male privilege, albeit involuntarily, made trans women fundamentally different from "womyn born womyn." They added that including festival attendees with a penis at the event constituted an impending threat to the "womyn born womyn" both physically and psychologically.

But this is not the real explanation. As Julia Serano, trans activist and author of the bestseller *Whipping Girl*, has argued on numerous occasions, festival organizers endorse the exclusion policies because of traditional norms in queer and feminist groups as well as plain old sexism and misogyny.[54]

Traditionally, discrimination against trans women from these corners consisted in derogatory anti-trans-woman remarks and "witch hunting" by prominent feminist writers, including attempts to prohibit hormone therapy and sex-reassignment surgery.

The endorsement of the exclusion policies at events like the Michigan Womyn's Music Festival is based on disgust and contempt for trans women. As Serano remarks, lesbians who have no problem with trans men and who might even "lust after trannybois" find trans women "creepy" and "effeminate" and don't hesitate to openly air their misogyny.

Festival goers and supporters adopted the far more radical viewpoints because they mistakenly thought that contemptuous attitudes toward trans women reflected core feminist values when in reality they were nothing other than female misogyny, which feminists officially oppose. Group polarization really does work in mysterious ways. As if by magic, the imagined feminist core values became the new group norm for supporters of the "womyn born womyn" ideology.

A second variation on polarization by one-upmanship is what we can call polarization by "outgroup distancing." While people in coherent groups have a desire not to deviate too much from other group members, they also have a desire to be as different as possible from the outgroups they regard as enemies.[55] If the norms, values, or positions of a particular outgroup become salient during ingroup deliberation, this can polarize group opinions in both directions. For example, a group of vegetarians who are deliberating the vices of eating meat may move closer to vegans in their positions on food ethics, but if they are then discussing the fanaticism of vegans, their positions on food ethics may move closer to those of meateaters.

As political scientists Shanto Iyengar and Sean J. Westwood have argued, outgroup distancing also automatically enhances ingroup favoritism and outgroup hostility. They call this group phenomenon "affective group polarization." The researchers looked at the special case of the partisan divide in American politics. Americans are divided when it comes to race and gender, but social norms routinely put a lid on overt expressions of hostility toward women, non-whites, and members of the LGBTQ+ community. However, there are no similar norms to constrain hostility against people who vote for politicians on the other side of the aisle. In fact, hostility toward political opponents is often encouraged and even applauded by political leaders.

To determine the extent of this political divide, the researchers asked research participants to first select a Democrat and a Republican for a scholarship, and then make a selection between a white and a black American. In each selection task, participants were asked to read the résumés for a pair of graduating high school seniors whose achievements were randomly varied. As a cover story, participants were told that an anonymous donor had contributed $30,000 to a scholarship fund but that the selection committee had deadlocked over two finalists and commissioned a survey to decide the winner.

Despite the explicitly apolitical nature of the task, political affiliation had a greater impact than race on which candidate was selected. This indicates that political affiliation influences decision-making outside of politics, making political affiliation both a social and a political divide.

In another study the team used trust and dictator games to test participants' outgroup animosity. In the trust game, the participant, who is Player 1, is given $10 and instructed that she is free to give some, all, or none to Player 2, who she is told is another participant. She is furthermore told that the researcher will triple the amount transferred to Player 2, who can then decide to transfer some, all, or none of the amount she is given back to the participant.

In the dictator game, the amount transferred is not tripled by the researcher, the participant is instructed that there is no opportunity for Player 2 to return funds to her, and she has no opportunity to observe the strategy of Player 2. So, variation in the amount the participant gives to Player 2 in the dictator game is attributable only to her animosity toward the group she is told Player 2 belongs to.

Participants were randomly assigned to play four rounds of the dictator game or four rounds of the trust game. For each round of the game, participants were provided with a description of Player 2, including information about the player's age, gender, income, race/ethnicity, and party affiliation. To give them an incentive to perform well, participants were told that the amount of money they had at the end of the study would determine their success.

In this study, Iyengar and Westwood found that players were more generous toward people with the same political affiliation as themselves, but that ethnicity didn't affect their generosity. If they were told that Player 2 had the same political affiliation as themselves, participants gave 10 percent more than average to Player 2 in the trust game and 24 percent more than average in the dictator game. The results suggest that political affiliation elicited greater ingroup favoritism and outgroup animosity than other social divides in American society.

Group Polarization and the Internet

Although group polarization was flourishing long before the age of the internet and social media, the internet and social media have the propensity to lead to an exaggeration of this phenomenon because there is a greater propensity for politically and socially like-minded people to form online groups in which discussion and deliberation take place. Sunstein made this observation as early as the late 1990s.[56] The internet facilitates the creation of the optimal conditions for group polarization.

As we saw earlier, diverse groups that deliberate in order to reach a joint decision are highly unlikely to polarize, because they don't have a sense of a shared group identity. But when a majority of people, or a few powerful group members, have similar agendas, then we have optimal conditions for group polarization.

Blogs, online forums, social-media sites, and internet groups tend to be frequented by people with very similar agendas. For example, while liberals might read the white supremacy website American Renaissance, its dominant readership will tend to be white supremacists; while an older white woman may join a Facebook group for young black philosophers, the majority of members will tend to be young black philosophers; and while people with no interest in feminism may end up reading the feminist blog Feministing, the majority of the readership will tend to be people with a strong interest in, and inclination toward, feminism.

Online groups are echo chambers where beliefs are amplified or re-inforced by communication and repetition inside the group's closed system. The internet makes it easy to exit a platform if a contributor is unhappy with the direction in which the discussion is headed. This can further increase the sense of a shared identity among the remaining group members, not least when they see themselves in opposition to the online platforms of their targets and enemies.

The anonymity that the internet affords erases individual differences and draws attention to the group rather than individual group members, which can further augment people's sense of a shared identity and the likelihood that the group polarizes.[57]

Orchestrated group polarization is also greatly facilitated by the structure of the internet. Propaganda and deception can help generate cohesive groups of like-minded people, not by identifying the like-minded and then creating a group, but rather by making them like-minded. Once people have been made to feel like they have a shared group identity, spontaneous group polarization can run its course. In the age of the internet, it doesn't take more than one person to get the ball rolling. A girl in high school who is envious of another student's success can exploit existing social networks on Whatsapp, Instagram, or TikTok to spread rumors about the other student or use deception to set her up for humiliation. The internet didn't invent the phenomenon of bullying, of course. Bullying is likely to have existed just as long as culture and society have. But prior to the age of the internet, bullying outside of the school day was limited by the difficulty of people meeting up to conspire. With the pervasive online access, scheming children can meet online any time they choose to plan their attack and reinforce each other's opinions.

People who become radicalized online are particularly dangerous when they leave the internet to express their hatred in brutal mass murders. Wade Michael Page, who murdered six people at a Sikh temple in Wisconsin in 2012, had been an active contributor to online forums dedicated to white supremacy. Dylann Roof supposedly "self-radicalized" online before he went on to murder nine people at a black church in South Carolina in 2015. Robert Bowers had been a prolific contributor to an online platform used by white supremacists before he went on to kill eleven people at a Pennsylvania synagogue in 2018.

Sunstein's prediction in the late 1990s that group polarization would only get worse as the internet expanded and became more readily accessible has now been backed by empirical studies looking at online communities and Twitter.[58] In 2010 social media researchers Sarita Yardi and Danah Boyd analyzed 30,000 tweets on Twitter about the shooting of George Tiller, a late-term abortion doctor, on May 31, 2009, in Wichita, Kansas, and found that conversations between like-minded individuals quickly led to a strengthened group identity within both pro-life and pro-choice groups. Conversations between people from different groups, on the other hand, widened the gap between the opposing communities.

In the age of "fake news," it will hardly come as a surprise that because group polarization is more prevalent for online groups, beliefs formed as a result of online sparring or the airing of opinions on blogs, social-media sites, and group forums are unreliably formed and hence do not have a great propensity to be true overall.

Yet the scariest aspect of the increase in "fake news" is that group polarization triggers a greater ingroup commitment to the truths of wildly distorted scientific theories, subjective opinions, unfounded rumors, and old folk tales; for example, the folk theory that raw onion can absorb harmful bacteria and prevent you from getting sick—a scientifically unfounded story—is still making its rounds on the internet.

While the raw-onion tale probably is relatively harmless, "fake news" can have disastrous consequences. The tales told by anti-vaxxers are a case in point. Although decades of research show that vaccines are safe and effective and that serious side effects are rare, anti-vaxxer parents refuse to get their children vaccinated, owing to the vaccines' alleged severe adverse side effects, which they claim can cause diabetes, autism, or worse. One tactic used by anti-vax advocates is to target grieving parents whose children died after getting vaccinated. Evee Clobes—a poster child for the anti-vaccine movement—died thirty-six hours after getting vaccinated. Although forensic evidence showed that the girl accidentally suffocated while co-sleeping with her mother, anti-vaccine crusaders, including Evee's mother, continue to spread the myth that her death was caused by the vaccines.[59] These conspiracy theories have devastating consequences. Childhood diseases like measles and polio—which once were almost eradicated—were listed among the top ten health threats in the world in 2019 by the World Health Organization.[60]

As Sunstein argues in his 2006 book *On Rumors*, by helping to cement false information in the mind of the public, group polarization is the best-kept secret of conspiracy theorists and propagandists, whether their aim is to crusade for a pet cause, mess with election results, cover up political corruption, or strengthen existing prejudices against members of marginalized groups. For example, spontaneous group polarization helped launder and legitimize the widespread falsehoods that the CIA was responsible for the assassination of John F. Kennedy, that Barack Obama was not born in the United States, that Sarah Palin believed Africa was a country, that Hillary Clinton suffered from a serious illness prior to the 2016 election, and that 5G technology was linked to the spread of COVID-19.[61]

The claim about Palin, which appeared on MSNBC, was eventually traced back to a Martin Eisenstadt, an alleged John McCain policy adviser. But Martin Eisenstadt didn't spread the rumor. Martin Eisenstadt is entirely fake. The think tank where he was claimed to work, the Harding Institute for Freedom and Democracy, is merely a website, and his blog and the online TV clips of him are all fake.

The hoax was put on by filmmakers Eitan Gorlin and Dan Mirvish. They had previously fooled Jonathan Stein, a reporter for *Mother Jones*, and a *Los Angeles Times* political blogger. They subsequently claimed that they weren't the source of the Palin rumor. Whoever was the source of it is not the only person to blame for its popularity. The journalists and bloggers who didn't vet the incoming information are guilty of propagating the rumor and making it seem credible.

Group polarization is crucial for making even the most absurd rumors and tales seem credible. People believed the Palin rumor, because they already thought she was an airhead who "was hot and got ratings." So, the optimal starting conditions that greatly increase the likelihood of group polarization were already in place. Spontaneous polarization pushed the views shared by Palin contemners to the extreme.

When people's conviction in the truth of a tale or rumor is strengthened due to group polarization, not only can this result in political corruption, but it can also have tragic consequences for the targeted individuals, as anyone who googles a person's name typically will have immediate access to the falsehood and may never find out that it isn't true. Many Americans still believe the Palin story. But this is nothing out of the ordinary. Some still believe Clinton orchestrated a child-trafficking ring from the basement of a Washington, D.C., pizza parlor.

The tendency for groups of like-minded individuals to undergo group polarization is the chief reason that propaganda and fake news are such powerful ways of manipulating public opinion, dividing populations, concealing political corruption, and turning pre-existing antipathies toward targeted groups into full-blown hatred.

Extremist leaders avail themselves of the very same tactics in order to carry out mass atrocities, often without ever being held accountable.

Extremist leaders are driven by dark traits and a deep-rooted hatred of the targeted groups. But they cannot orchestrate large-scale mass atrocities unless they can persuade the general public that the targeted groups are responsible for some real or imagined social regress and that the groups' continued presence in society will result in society's downfall. By planting false beliefs in the public imagination about today's oppressed groups and creating conditions enabling group polarization, extremist leaders are able to recruit supporters willing to oppress, torture, or eliminate members of the oppressed groups.

In the next chapter, we will explore how demagogues and hatemongers capitalize on two antagonistic ideologies about the "female essence" as a way of rationalizing hate-based violence against women.

6 | BABY, IT'S IN YOUR NATURE

MISOGYNY, FEMININITY, AND FEMALE FILTH

Ever since I first wrote about misogyny, or hatred of women, back in 2015, I have been greeted daily by a relentless parade of hot-button responses from misogynist readers.[1] Email is a source of anxiety that quickly morphs into full-blown email phobia when your inbox routinely is spammed with sickening messages crafted by an army of women-hating internet trolls. Here is a small sample of the venom that awaits me when I sign in:

> "You're probably one of the nastiest cunts ever conceived. Plz kill urself."

> "Fuck you bitch! i'm gonna find you and fuck u and i wont stop till you hurt bad and regret writing this bullshit."

> "fuck you degenerate cunt your fucking ugly slut. man hater . . . the only thing i hate more than whores like you are the faggots . . . fucking spineless pussies."

> "I read your article about misogyny. I feel i am a bit of a misogynist too. Only because whenever women say men are trash and bash men that is when i somehow feel the need to hurt that person. Now i feel like hurting you."

Another type of reaction I regularly encounter comes from readers who have experienced misogyny firsthand, like the following: "Thank you [. . .]. I just emailed your empowering piece to my 20 year old son. My highest intention is to empower women in thus that they may further teach their sacred sons by sanest example to own their power. Raped by a convicted Child Rapist/Murderer on parole at age 18 1/2 and the second time—after he found me again—at 19. I know 'my stuff!' Ha. [...] Grateful for Strong Women such as bravest you. KM."

I grieve for every woman who has been raped, sexually assaulted, verbally abused, ridiculed, or punched in the face by men—or women for that matter. The mounting sexual and non-sexual violence against women is truly depressing.

The misogynistic comments I have received in response to my *Psychology Today* posts haunt me, but I try to keep in mind that they are empty cyber attacks from cyber trolls I'll never encounter in real life. Fingers crossed. But I too have a story. More than one. But the one I feel least uncomfortable sharing with you is about my closest encounter with a rather surreptitious yet highly toxic form of workplace misogyny.

Many years ago, I was happily employed in a tenured position at a university in the United States, when the College of Arts and Sciences hired a new dean. Let's call him Wyatt. I first suspected something was off when he made his first visit to our department. At the meeting, he started off by performing an autobiographical monologue about his accomplishments as a researcher and administrator. This was followed by his vision for the college. Not once did he ask us about our department, interests, hopes, or dreams.

Despite my gut feeling that something was amiss, I had not anticipated what came next. I was up for promotion. Everyone thought it was a slam dunk. But then I received the anticipated letter from the dean. I could not believe my eyes. He was denying my promotion, because of a "lack of administrative service to the university and the profession." The promotion materials my department chair had submitted for evaluation summarized not only my research and teaching but also many years of administrative service. That year alone I was Director of Graduate Studies, a member of the Faculty Senate, the chair of two college-level committees, and a journal submissions editor.

Was the dean's perception of my administrative service contributions just an innocent oversight? Hardly. It's hard to miss seven pages of bullet points listing a decade's worth of administrative service and a mandatory narrative essay detailing them.

I was allowed to write a letter of appeal, which I did, reiterating my administrative service contributions. Dean Wyatt replied promptly. Surprisingly (or in hindsight, unsurprisingly), he stood by his decision. There was no mention of his "oversight." But he apparently had gone on a mission to locate every typo and grammatical error he could find in the promotion materials submitted by my department chair. That was his new justification for denying me the promotion.

Luckily, college deans aren't dictatorial powers. The provost, the Faculty Senate, and the president all voted in my favor, and the Board of Trustees, who have the final say, concurred, and I was promoted against the dean's wishes.

But that's not the end of the story. Dean Wyatt was now determined to get back at me, with a vengeance. That's the only way I can explain what happened. One of his revenge tactics was to enter micromanagement mode regarding all my public appearances. On one occasion, he called the media outlet that had featured my Perception Lab and demanded that they add a retraction stating the lab didn't exist. You see, unbeknownst to everyone, Dean Wyatt had a new rule that required all labs to be named after the principal investigator. My lab was to be called the "Brogaard Lab." So, as far as Wyatt was concerned, the Perception Lab didn't exist, only the Brogaard Lab did. But he conveniently neglected to mention the Brogaard Lab in the erratum he crafted for the venue.

There were numerous other incidences. There was that time when he had my YouTube videos about the nature of love taken down. He also demanded that I remove my university affiliation from my blog dedicated to the discussion of the nature of love. His reason was that it was too scandalous for a philosophy professor to make comments about love in public. "After all," he said, with chilling arrogance, "what does a philosopher know about love?"

For the longest time, I thought it was a personal vendetta. But then a wave of stories began to appear. There was the political science professor who had been denied the position of department chair because, as Wyatt told her, "You ought to spend your free time taking care of your young boy." Then there was the college journalist who was asked to provide the contact information for all the sources she had used in a press release, and yes, Dean Wyatt did call her sources "just to ensure that they had consented to being cited." They all had, of course. Then there was the female junior faculty member, who had been forced to cancel an international conference trip, because she had forgotten to fill out the "travel form" Wyatt suddenly required for all conference travel.

There were hundreds of narratives in the same spirit, almost exclusively from female employees. Eventually we compared workplace diaries and found the courage to file a complaint with Human Resources.

While waiting for the complaint to be processed, a slew of other stories started popping up, this time about the dean himself. First, we learned that Wyatt's academic accomplishments consisted of two co-authored articles, and that the department that ought to have been his home while he was serving as dean had voted against his affiliation with them. Then we heard from multiple sources that Wyatt had been "let go" at the previous two universities where he had served as a dean. This wasn't public information because he had signed a non-disclosure agreement when resigning. I didn't stick around to see the end of this nightmare. I took a job elsewhere. But I later learned that Wyatt is no longer in academia.

Luckily, not all employers are so blatantly, albeit covertly, misogynistic as Dean Wyatt. For the most part employers strive not to hate women for bursting into the old boys' club and not to judge their employees on the basis of extraneous attributes like gender. We have many generations of feminist activists to thank for that. But how much progress have we actually made since the birth of feminism in the early to mid-nineteenth century?

Not nearly enough!

In July 2018, a video was posted on YouTube of a shocking scene showing Marie Laguerre, a twenty-two-year-old architecture student, being physically attacked by a man outside a café in Paris.[2] She had told the man to "shut up" after he had made sexually explicit comments about her. He then threw an ashtray at her and walked back and punched her in the face. The video of the assault prompted international outrage after it went viral. French police arrested the man in August 2018. After the court proceedings he was sentenced to six months in prison and ordered to pay a €2,000 fine.

French lawmakers subsequently passed a new law, the *outrage sexiste* law, imposing on-the-spot fines of up to €750 on catcallers, wolf-whistlers, and aggressively lecherous people.[3] In September 2018, a thirty-year-old man in France became the first person to be fined under the new law after slapping a twenty-one-year-old woman on her behind, and then telling her, "You have big breasts."[4]

Verbal, physical, and sexual attacks on women are not simply the result of the archaic prejudices and sexist ideologies that are still lingering in today's society. They are expressions of misogyny, defined as hatred of women.

Misogyny is thriving like never before. Sociolinguist Louise Mulla and her collaborator Loretta Trickett, a legal theorist, conducted a study of women's experiences of misogyny in Nottinghamshire in the United Kingdom.[5] They found that 93.7 percent of the 700 residents they interviewed reported having experienced or witnessed misogynistic hate speech or hate crimes. Only 6.6 percent of the respondents who had been a victim of a misogynistic hate crime had reported the incident to the police.

While the public condemnation of the café incident in France enjoyed widespread international support, some people—mostly men—think it's outrageous that men could be fined for giving a woman a "sexual compliment" or "flirting with her."[6] "Sexual compliments" and "flirting" are the opposite of hatred, they insist.

However, this backlash against the *outrage sexiste* law betrays a confusion about the meaning of "misogyny." Slapping a woman on her behind and then telling her "You have big breasts" is not a compliment. It's a paradigmatic example of unadulterated misogyny, born from a false sense of entitlement.

Misogyny is a particular kind of unjustified hatred or unjustified contempt for women in a man's world. By "a man's world," I mean a society where men have more power and privileges than women. The United States is a man's world, or a "patriarchal society" as it's also called. A few pieces of evidence: In 2019, 127 women held seats in the U.S. Congress, making up only 23.7 percent of the 535 members. We, the American people, have never elected a female president. Although some women are legally entitled to equal treatment by their employer, statistics still show a wage gap between men and women. In 2018, a full-time employed woman earned about eighty cents for every dollar a full-time employed man earned in 2018, according to census data. In academia, things don't look much better. In the STEM disciplines and philosophy, women are outnumbered by men, and studies show attrition of women faculty as they move up the academic ranks. In all the STEM disciplines, women make up 42 percent of assistant professors, 34.2 percent of associate professors, and 23.4 percent of full professors.[7] In philosophy, it is estimated that women hold 19 percent of the available tenure/tenure-track positions. Here too there is a pay gap. Across all disciplines in the United States, male faculty make about $18,000 more annually than female faculty.[8]

The one-million-dollar question is, why in the world would men hate women in a man's world? This is the main question I hope to address in this chapter. The short answer is that misogyny, when widespread, can serve as a tool in a patriarchal society for hindering progress for women or increasing the power and privileges of men.[9]

Misogyny falls into two broad categories: hate-based and contempt-based. Hateful misogynists are prone to conjure up excuses if challenged, saying, for instance, "I don't hate women. I love my mom and my sister. They do everything for me." When they say this, they may well be speaking the truth. They don't hate women who conform to the ideology they subscribe to. But the "I don't hate all women" defense misfires, because it's a near-truism that hateful misogynists don't hate all women.

As I argued back in 2015, hate-based misogyny is not simply hatred of women.[10] In fact, you can hate women without being a misogynist.

You can even hate all women without qualifying for the title. Suppose that in some distant future, there are only ten women left on earth. Suppose further that those ten women continually bully Caleb, one of the male inhabitants. Quite understandably, Caleb soon comes to hate the ten women. But they are all the women there are. So, Caleb hates all women. Yet he is not thereby a misogynist.

Conversely, you can be a hateful misogynist without hating any woman. Imagine a society in which all women are subordinate, doting wives, much like in the movie *The Stepford Wives*. In this society, men don't hate women. They love them! They love them, because they behave like the "wives" of the 1950s commercials. They cook, bake, scrub, dress like Barbie dolls, and dote on their men. It's only once the wives object to their subordination that they become the target of the misogynistic husbands' hatred.

As noted, misogyny can be used to perpetuate or escalate the oppression of women in patriarchal societies. Hateful misogyny and contemptuous misogyny, however, are typically used for different ends.

In the contemporary cultural landscape, hateful misogyny is hatred of women who do not conform to the misogynist's ideals about how women ought to behave. Misogynists, of course, have different belief sets, or ideologies, about how women ought to behave. But they agree that there are unwritten rules that women are expected to follow. One such rule is that women shouldn't talk back to men. Hateful misogynists are prone to hate women who disagree with them or tell them off. When the French student Marie Laguerre told the man who was harassing her to "shut up," this released his hatred and she got hit in the face. As philosopher Kate Manne points out in her 2017 book *Down Girl: The Logic of Misogyny*, women who step out of the traditional nurturing, caretaking role to take on a more masculine position—of ambition, or requesting power—are far more prone to misogynist attacks. So are women who step out of the traditional role as "men's sex toys." In South Africa, lesbians are commonly subjected to "corrective rape," intended to "cure" them of their homosexuality. Lydia Smith from the *Telegraph* reports that survivors of corrective rape have said their attackers wanted to show them "how to be real women and what a real man tasted like."[11]

The idea of correcting misbehaving women to turn them into real women is a common theme in the nineteenth-century Victorian poet and playwright Robert Browning's works. In *The Ring and the Book*, Count Guido Franceschini is testifying in court after murdering his young wife, Pompilia:

> Pompilia was no pigeon, Venus' pet,
> That shuffled from between her pressing paps
> To sit on my rough shoulder,—but a hawk,
> I bought at a hawk's price and carried home
> To do hawk's service—at the Rotunda, say,
> Where, six o' the callow nestlings in a row,
> You pick and choose and pay the price for such.
> I have paid my pound, await my penny's worth,
> So, hoodwink, starve and properly train my bird,
> And, should she prove a haggard,—twist her neck!
>
> (v. 701–710)

Guido's apparent defense is that he paid good money for his young wife ("callow nestling") and subjected her to harsh training, but she turned out to be a haggard, which means a hag or witch, or an unchaste woman, so he twisted her neck. But as English professor Daniel Karlin points out, the more disturbing interpretation is not that Pompilia turns out to be unchaste or a witch, but that "Guido turns her into one, 'properly trains' her for that role, because what he really wants is to twist her neck."[12]

Hateful misogyny can be found all over the online "manosphere," to borrow an expression from the Southern Poverty Law Center.[13] The blog Boycott American Women characterizes American women as "generally immature, selfish, extremely arrogant and self-centered, mentally unstable, irresponsible, and highly unchaste."[14] The site advises men to find their mate in countries where women have been raised to be subservient to men. This is also the sentiment expressed on Marky Mark's blog, where Eternal Bachelor advises men not to "get involved with American women; they're sluts, skanks, and disease ridden whores. Besides, if you marry an American woman, she'll just divorce you and screw you over anyway."[15] (This blog has no connection to the actor Mark Wahlberg, who also used to be known as Marky Mark.)

Unlike its hate-based cousin, contempt-based misogyny of the kind most salient in today's society targets women in general. Contemptuous misogynists regard women as inherently inferior to men because their "female essence" is permeated by negative qualities, for instance, the contemner may view women as contaminated, morally corrupt, irrational, incompetent, or ignorant.

Contemptuous misogyny runs rampant in the lyrics of hit songs.[16] One of the most famous anti-women tunes is Robin Thicke's hit song "Blurred Lines," a number one song in 2013. Mocking sexual consent and endorsing rape culture, it portrays women who don't freely submit to men as animals, telling us that they need to be taken by force: "Okay, now he was close / Tried to domesticate ya / But you're an animal / Baby, it's in your nature." A similar message can be gleaned from Dr. Dre's 1992 hit song "Bitches Ain't Shit," when the chorus informs us that women ought to serve men sexually: "Bitches ain't shit but hoes and tricks / Lick on these nuts and suck the dick / Gets the fuck out after you're done / And I hops in my ride to make a quick run." In the 1987 song "It's So Easy," Guns N' Roses' Axl Rose also lets out that he thinks women have nothing better to do than to please men, when he growls, "Turn around bitch I got a use for you / Besides you ain't got nothin' better to do / And I'm bored."

Although conceptually distinct, the two strains of misogyny that rear their ugly heads in contemporary culture are often intertwined, as is apparent in this ugly rant by white nationalist Andrew Auernheimer from *The Daily Stormer*:

Don't sit here and pretend you're a nice traditional girl when you fight against any implementation of traditional values. Say aloud what you are, on the streets, to your families, on social

media: "I'm a despicable whore." Do it before it is too late, because I swear to whatever gods may be that when the purge comes
if you have been using traditionalism as a cloak for your revolting
degeneracy your name is going on a list and we will be coming to
make you pay for it. You will feel the punch to your throat first,
but the hours afterwards at the hands of a WHITE SHARIA
gang will make that seem as just a brief and gentle touch against
your skin. Your ribs will be broken. Your face will be broken.
Some of you will not live to tell about it. This I promise: a
much needed correction is coming for you soon, you disgusting
skanks.[17]

Auernheimer's language, alive with scorn, picks out women as lowly and
disgusting, using slurring expressions like "despicable whores" and "disgusting skanks." For good measure he throws in threats of excessive violence, thereby admitting that he thinks that women are powerful and
present a potential danger to low-lives like himself.

Misogyny runs thick in the veins of contemporary American culture. American culture, of course, is far from the only misogynistic culture and far from the worst—hatred of women is widespread in other
conservative cultures, particularly in the Islamic world.

But how did we get to that point? In its new guidelines to help
psychologists address male violence, sexism, and misogyny, the
American Psychological Association (APA) suggests that misogyny
stems from the masculinity ideology our culture adheres to.[18] The
APA defines "masculinity ideology" as "a particular constellation of
standards that have held sway over large segments of the population,
including: anti-femininity, achievement, eschewal of the appearance
of weakness, and adventure, risk, and violence."[19] It is no doubt correct that the masculinity ideology is a key contributing factor to male
misogyny. But, I will argue, two other equally prevailing ideologies
contribute to the persistence of misogyny and sexism in American
culture today, what I will call "the feminine ideal" and "the myth of
female filth."

Shut Up and Smile: The Feminine Ideal

Misogynistic hatred for nonconforming women has its roots in the historical ideal of femininity. Remnants of that ideal still exist in society today, or so I will argue. This is the ideal the French existentialist and feminist Simone de Beauvoir criticized in her 1949 book *The Second Sex*, which is said to mark the beginning of second-wave feminism.

The suffragettes who spearheaded the feminist movement that came to be known as "first-wave feminism" in the late nineteenth and early twentieth centuries helped give (white, middle-class) women fundamental political rights, specifically the right to vote in public elections, but also greater opportunities in education and employment and the right to own property. They also challenged society's perception of women as matrimonial goods and convenient incubators of the men of the future. For example, in her 1898 book *Women and Economics*, feminist writer Charlotte Perkins Gilman argued that women were passive commodities for men to choose. Men provided economically for their wives in exchange for their domestic and sexual services. Marriage, Gilman wrote, was just prostitution under another name.

But by the post-war years, when de Beauvoir was writing, society's perception of women as destined to serve men was still largely unchanged. De Beauvoir is in search of an answer to the question of why women are oppressed, why they are "the second sex." Her answer is that women, from the very beginning of their lives, have been trained to become secondary to men. Brainwashed by parents, educators, suitors, and later their husbands and nudged along by society's systems of oppression, they come to believe that they are confined to a particular feminine role. De Beauvoir took pains to explain two of the systems that she thinks are central to the continued oppression of women: marriage and motherhood.

As an institution, traditional marriage is oppressive along several dimensions. According to de Beauvoir, although it doesn't make a woman the legal property of a man, it keeps her in a state of childhood, with the diminished rights of a child, yet without the legal protection against her husband sexually violating her. Entrapped by her marriage vows, she is passive in determining whether she wants to get pregnant, and once she is pregnant, she is in servitude to motherhood.

A key instrument for perpetuating the oppression of women is what de Beauvoir calls "the eternal feminine," a term she borrows from Goethe's *Faust*, Part Two.[20] The eternal feminine is the alleged core "essence" of women, according to prevailing attitudes. Women who are in touch with their eternal femininity are modest, proud, extremely delicate, nurturing, selfless, child-like, subservient, and sexually passive.

The cult of the eternal feminine wouldn't have taken hold in society, de Beauvoir argues, had it not been for the mystery it bestows on girls as they grow up. As girls grow up to become women, their own authentic motives and desires are covered by a veil of false consciousness that makes them invested in beliefs and practices that enable their own oppression. "It is because women are mystified," de Beauvoir writes, "that useless and charming qualities such as their modesty, pride, and extreme delicacy flourish."[21] Men disseminate the tale of the eternal feminine to cultivate "useless" feminine qualities in women and lull them into thinking that their deepest desire and purpose in life is to be appealing to men and to serve them and please them. By keeping women "mystified" and preventing them from questioning the role assigned to them, the male oppressors are able to keep the sexual caste system intact. De Beauvoir's overarching goal in *The Second Sex* is to demystify women, to lift their veil of false consciousness, so they are able to see the reality of their oppression and rise up against it.

When *The Second Sex* first appeared in translation in the United States in 1953, four years after its publication in France, it didn't have any noticeable impact on the feminist movement. But it was the main source of inspiration for feminist writer Betty Friedan's 1963 book *The Feminine Mystique*, which sparked the second wave of feminism. Friedan coined the term "the feminine mystique" as a label for the patriarchal attitudes perpetuated by advertising, women's magazines, educators, and Freudian psychologists: "truly feminine" women would be unable to find fulfillment in higher education, careers, or politics; rather, to achieve happiness they should submit to male dominance and not attempt to destroy the bliss by questioning their traditional roles as wives and nurturers.[22] In reality, this media-idealized "happy suburban housewife" image left many women feeling inadequate and deeply unhappy. But the "diagnosis" they were given was that they were at fault for failing to adjust to their instinctual "feminine role" as subservient housewives and nurturing mothers. As Friedan put it:

> [The feminine mystique] says that the great mistake of Western culture, through most of its history, has been the undervaluation of this femininity. It says this femininity is so mysterious and intuitive and close to the creation and origin of life that man-made science may never be able to understand it. But however special and different, it is in no way inferior to the nature of man; it may even in certain respects be superior. The mistake, says the mystique, the root of women's troubles in the past is that women envied men, women tried to be like men, instead of accepting their own nature, which can find fulfillment only in sexual passivity, male domination, and nurturing maternal love.[23]

To compensate for their feelings of inadequacy and emptiness, many women self-medicated with alcohol and tranquilizers, immortalized by the Rolling Stones in their song title "Mother's Little Helper." Although Friedan's book received widespread criticism for its feminist parochialism, it was a wakeup call for many women who had been enthralled by the feminine mystique.

A lot has changed since de Beauvoir wrote *The Second Sex* in 1949, and Friedan sounded her "wakeup" call to women in the early 1960s. But is the ideal of femininity a thing of the past? Or does it still haunt us today?

It's complicated. Women today have choices that weren't available to the trailblazers who fought for our legal rights. We (women in Western cultures) don't put up with "prostitution marriages," sexist jokes, catcalling, invasions of our personal space, nonconsensual squeezes, rubs, and kisses, and we have pursuits that vastly transcend that of attracting a man and becoming his subservient housewife.

That much seems clear. Yet we still live in a world that suffocates us with gender norms, norms we desperately try to squeeze into. As American culture critic Laura Kipnis points out:

> One way or another, women just seem to end up defined by their bodies, or defining themselves by their bodies: a source of self-worth, a site of craziness, most likely both. For every bodily advance wrested from nature or society or men, another form of submission magically appears to take its place; for every inch of progress, a newfangled subjugation. And now, most of them self-inflicted! Take the current mania for thinness, the quest for fitness, the war on cellulite. Freed from compulsory childbearing, women have chained themselves to the gym. Once women suffered under whalebone corsets; now your skeleton must show through the skin for that fashionable look.[24]

Today's prevailing feminine ideal portrays the ideal woman as thin, trim, youthful, pretty, alluring, mild-tempered, nurturing, compassionate, non-promiscuous, not too ambitious, and ladylike in manners and presentation.[25] In certain segments of the population, women should also be domestic and subservient to live up to the standards. Not every little boy and girl grows up thinking the feminine ideal is an immutable truth. Yet most of us endorse a vast array of its demands.

To that end, there are still gaping disparities between what is socially acceptable for men and women to do. In 2015, Mic, a digital news site where "society's change makers" post norm-challenging videos, posted a YouTube video exploring the question of whether people in transit will react differently toward a woman who sits with her legs wide apart on the subway in New York compared to a man.[26] As the video shows, the answer to the question is yes. When the woman in the video is "manspreading," she gets a lot of stares and glares, far more than when a man does it.

I can't say that I have never seen a woman "manspread" in public, but it's exceedingly rare. While writing this book, I spent an entire day riding the train from University of Miami to Brickell and back looking for female "manspreaders." No such luck. Keeping our legs chastely tight in public, it seems, is just one of the many ways that we women try to live up to society's gender norms.

Reversed gender roles are also the theme of French filmmaker Eléonore Pourriat's 2009 short film *Majorité Opprimée*, or *Oppressed Majority*. When the short was first released, it barely received any public attention. Then in 2014, Pourriat uploaded it to YouTube, and it went viral. In 2018, Netflix released a feature comedy film *Je Ne Suis Pas un Homme Facile*, or *I Am Not an Easy Man*, also directed by Pourriat and based on the same concept as her short.

In both films, the world is a matriarchy, where women are naturally thought of as superior to men. Men are naturally more nurturing than women and are in charge of childrearing. In this universe, it's not your mom who asks you when you're gonna give her some grandchildren, it's your dad who keeps bugging you. Women still give birth, but they do it upright while holding onto a pull-up bar, like warriors in a training camp, and as soon as the infant is out, he or she is handed over to the father.

The male characters who work part- or full-time jobs occupy positions that are more commonly occupied by women in our world. The working men are employed as secretaries, assistants, nurses, and pre-school teachers. Career women hold leadership positions as CEOs, investment bankers, chief advisers, and politicians. The women who are not at the very top are house painters, police officers, truck drivers, or criminals.

In this imaginary world, women frequently sexually harass or assault men, which sadly happens to Pierre in the short film, but not in the feature. Unsurprisingly, perhaps, my absolute favorite scenes in the feature film show women "manspreading," and men keeping their legs chastely together.

The gender norms that govern the reversed gender roles in Pourriat's insightful, cinematic thought experiment is not our society's ideal of masculinity, because that's something else altogether. Rather, the ideal the men in the movie are striving to satisfy is just our actual ideal of femininity, the ideology that drives today's hatred for women who cannot or do not want to comply with it or who choose to poke holes in the Barbie doll fantasy.

The Myth of Feminine Filth

Whereas hateful misogynists take nonconforming women to be deliberately breaking with the norms for how women should behave, it's their allegedly malevolent wrongdoing that stirs up the hatred. Contemptuous misogynists, by contrast, regard women's choices as limited by their biology. They see us women as inherently inferior to themselves because of our feminine nature. That nature is, according to them, filthy. Yet regardless of how hard we try, we cannot scrub off the filth. We are stuck with it.

Recall that contempt couples social disgust for the target with condemnation of her for her vicious character. In misogyny, the focus of the social disgust is our alleged departure from traditional masculine qualities dating back to the ancient Greek philosophers, qualities such as reason, rationality, intelligence, moral integrity, and the purity and grace of the masculine body. It is in virtue of our aberration from such masculine qualities that contemptuous misogynists disrespect us or judge us as "low." For example, a contemptuous misogynist may take the female body to lack purity and grace because of its inherent link to sexual intercourse, menstruation, pregnancy, and childbirth; or he may think we lack the masculine ideal of moral integrity, due to our alleged inherent mischief, dishonesty, manipulative tendencies, or abilities to cause uncontrollable desire in men.

I will refer to the ideology that we women are inferior to men because of our dirty qualities as "the myth of female filth." Martha Nussbaum cites Jonathan Swift's poem "The Lady's Dressing-Room" as an example of how our tie to bodily "stuff" stirs up masculine angst.[27] In the poem, a man sneaks into his lover's private quarters after she has spent five hours washing and dressing. There he finds all the dirty signs of her female filth:

> [S]not, ear wax, dandruff, hairs plucked from her chin, clothes with sweaty armpits, skin oil, a basin with "the scrapings of her Teeth and Gums," stockings that smell like "stinking toes"—all of which "turn'd poor Strephon's Bowels." The climax of his revulsion arrives when he opens the laundry chest, a veritable Pandora's box of evils—and finds evidence of urine and feces (perhaps also menstrual fluids, "Things, which must not be exprest").
>
> "Thus finishing his grand Survey, / Disgusted Strephon stole away / Repeating in his amorous Fits, / Oh! Celia, Celia, Celia shits!"[28]

Female filth is incarnate in our womanhood, in the eyes of the filth-fearing misogynist. It is in virtue of our inherent female filth that he sees us as "low." We are by our very nature inferior creatures, because of the unbreakable tie between us and bodily "stuff," manipulation, irrationality, or other dirty traits.

The nineteenth-century German philosopher and arch-misogynist Arthur Schopenhauer is one of the best-known supporters of the idea of the feminine as aberrant and filthy. In his essay "On Women," he argued that women are "by nature meant to obey" as they are "childish, frivolous, and short sighted," and that no woman had ever produced great art or "any work of permanent value."[29] He also held that women are kind of ugly, or unaesthetic:

It is only a man whose intellect is clouded by his sexual impulse that could give the name of the fair sex to that under-sized, narrow-shouldered, broad-hipped, and short-legged race; for the whole beauty of the sex is bound up with this impulse. Instead of calling them beautiful there would be more warrant for describing women as the unaesthetic sex.[30]

The myth of female filth derives from the pseudo-scientific theory that the divergence between men and women largely has its roots in their distinct genetic blueprints. We women are by nature considerably less intelligent, competent, rational, conscientious, self-reliant, and honest than men but more caring and nurturing. Our alleged impulsive, emotional, clingy, manipulative, and dishonest tendencies and flair for childrearing are encoded in our genes, not learned or cultivated.

The doctrine that there are dirty differences between men and women that are rooted in our genetic makeup is also known as "biological essentialism." Essentialism in its filthy form maintains that our female sex chromosomes and our pesky female hormones is the cause of our bodily nature, our irrational minds, and our uncontrollable impulses. Our female filth is essential to our womanhood. Mother Nature made us that way. End of story.

Needless to say, this is utter nonsense. Like other strains of biological essentialism, gender essentialism has been repudiated ages ago. Women cannot be essentially filthy, because there is no "female essence"—or "male essence," for that matter.

Misogyny or Sexism? What's the Difference?

How does misogyny differ from systemic sexism? In *Down Girl*, Manne argues that the difference between the two is that the sexist takes the patriarchal social arrangement for granted, whereas the misogynist "attempts to force women back into it, or to punish them for desertion."[31] For example, a sexist might think that there are natural differences between men and women that justify a certain division of labor, or that a patriarchal society is more desirable and less fraught than the alternatives. A misogynist, by contrast, would be more likely to make sweeping generalizations like "Women are too dumb to deserve equal pay."

Manne grants that the same sort of ideologies used by sexists to justify their biased viewpoints also can be "used in service of misogynist ends in practice."[32] But whether the act is sexist or misogynistic, she argues, depends on whether the agent uses the ideology to justify patriarchal social arrangements, or to police or punish women who don't conform to these arrangements. As Manne puts it, misogyny is the "law enforcement branch" of the patriarchy.

I am in broad agreement with Manne, but our accounts diverge in at least two ways. First, Manne's framework is best suited as an account of hateful misogyny. It isn't applicable to misogyny that takes the form of contempt for women on account of their feminine filth. Consider Joseph Swetnam's attack on women in his 1615 pamphlet *The Arraignment of Lewd, idle, froward, and unconstant women*. According to Swetnam,

> If [a woman] be honest and chaste then commonly she is jeallous [. . .] [women] are ungratefull, perjured, full of fraud, flouting and deceit, unconstant, waspish, toyish, light, sullen, proude, discurteous and cruell.[33]

Swetnam's pamphlet wasn't intended to force women into submission, as he didn't think women were capable of change. Nor was it intended to punish women. It was a warning to young men, advising them to think twice before marrying because of women's filthy nature. Manne's account of misogyny as policing or punishing can't account for this form of misogyny.

Second, unlike Manne, I will argue that misogyny and sexism are overlapping categories. To get a better grip on the difference between sexism and misogyny, it's helpful to look closer at the original usages of the terms. Although the term "misogyny" didn't find a foothold until recently, it actually predates "sexism." "Sexism" was coined by college student Pauline M. Leet in her contribution, "Women and the Undergraduate," to a Student-Faculty Forum at Franklin and Marshall College in 1965. She defined "sexism" by comparing it to racism, stating:

> When you argue . . . that since fewer women write good poetry this justifies their total exclusion, you are taking a position analogous to that of the racist—I might call you in this case a "sexist." . . . Both the racist and the sexist are acting as if all that has happened had never happened, and both of them are making decisions and coming to conclusions about someone's value by referring to factors which are in both cases irrelevant.

The word "misogyny" is much older. As Christine E. Hutchins, a professor of English literature, explains in her article "In a Word: The True History of 'Misogyny,' " a cognate of the word "misogyny" was coined as early as 1615 in response to Swetnam.[34] In his 145-page pamphlet, Swetnam uses anecdotes, rhetoric, and Bible quotes to support the view that women are inherently corporeal, manipulative, mischievous, emotional, and irrational. Swetnam's monograph, misogyny dripping from its pages, leaves a bitter aftertaste in your mouth. But rather than crushing their spirit, the pamphlet prompted critics of both genders to author letters, playscripts, and books repudiating his attack on women, and it was in this context the term "misogyny" was first coined and entered the English language.

When Leet, the student at Franklin and Marshall, introduced the term "sexism," she was referring to disrespectful attitudes toward women based on flawed reasoning or mistaken ideologies about women or certain types of women. Actions based on those attitudes can also properly be called "sexist." As we saw in Chapter 1, the disrespectful attitudes include righteous anger, resentment, envy, disgust, contempt, and hate. Sexism and misogyny, as defined, are not polar opposites. Sexism can take the form of, say, an unjustified disrespectful belief, disgust for women's bodies, or full-on misogyny.

Misogyny is thus a subtype of sexism. But, to avoid confusion, I'll use the term "misogyny" to refer to contempt or hatred for women and reserve the term "sexism" for other types of unjustified disrespect for women, such as disgust, resentment, envy, and disrespectful beliefs.

Leet, in introducing the term "sexism," was hammering down on the flawed reasoning other students had flaunted in their attempt to wrench history to their shabby purposes. To mobilize support for disrespecting women in academia, sexists routinely cite the fact that more men than women have demonstrated excellence in traditional male fields throughout history as a reason for cherry-picking men for academic anthologies, conferences, or prestigious awards. The flaw in this argument lies in the inference from the observed historical disparities between men and women in, say, academic accomplishments to the conclusion that men are academically superior to women. This is a hasty conclusion, because a far more plausible explanation of the gender differences in demonstrated excellence in traditional male areas is that women were prevented or discouraged from entering those areas.

It is worth taking a moment to dwell on the logical fallacies used to justify sexism, because the mere appearance of logic can camouflage even the most palpable sexist attitudes. Appeal to historical gender disparities in demonstrated excellence in traditional male disciplines is far from the only fallacy sexists are fond of wielding in the hope of covering up their shameless promotion of gender inequality. Besides the historical fallacy, the following are some of the logical fallacies routinely deployed to legitimize sexism:

- *Appeal to ignorance.* Justifying sexism on the basis of lack of evidence showing that women's intellect is not inferior to men's. Example: "There is no evidence to show that women have the same capacity for problem solving as men."
- *Ad hominem.* Justifying sexism on the basis of the attitudes or behaviors of a single woman or a small group of women.

Example: "I don't think we should hire a woman. Have you forgotten what happened when we hired Ellen?"

- *Appeal to popularity.* Justifying sexism by appealing to its prevalence in society. Example: "Why should we pay women the same as men for the same work when none of our competitors is doing it?"

- *Begging the question.* Making sexism seem "normal" by asking a question that presupposes women being inferior to men. Example: "When does the rest of society realize that female college professors don't have what it takes to accomplish as much as men?"

- *False dilemma.* Justifying sexism by pretending we only have two options. Example: "Either I need to agree with everything feminists say, or I take a firm stance against all of their views."

- *Genetic fallacy.* Justifying sexism by appealing to genetic differences between men and women.

- *Non sequitur.* Justifying sexism by citing evidence that doesn't support one's conclusion. Example: "It has been shown that women have smaller skull circumferences than men. So, they clearly cannot be as smart as men."

- *Red herring.* Justifying sexism by diverting attention from the main subject. Example: "A lot of my female acquaintances have confided in me that giving up their career greatly reduced the stress they felt when they were trying to juggle career and parenthood. So, women shouldn't try to do both."

- *Slippery slope.* Justifying sexism by showing that equality between the sexes has disastrous consequences in today's society. Example: "If we elect a female president, then before long people will push for electing people who belong to other minorities. Maybe next time they will argue that there has never been a severely mentally disabled president. Then they will argue that there has never been a president who has been in a maximum-security prison. And the next thing we know, our country will be run by serial killers and child molesters." This is also a common form of argument against gay marriage and other kinds of social progress.

- *Straw man.* Justifying sexism by attacking feminists, attributing to them an absurd view that is easily defeated, even though it has never been held by feminists. Example: "Feminists are saying that there are no differences between men and women. That's obviously false. We know that on average, men have more muscle mass than women."

To recap, the misogyny that prevails in America and elsewhere is unjustified hatred of women who stray too far from the feminine ideal or unjustified contempt for women on account of their alleged inherent filthy nature. Sexism is unjustified disrespect for women inspired by the very same misguided ideologies and routinely backed by logical fallacies.

It Takes One to Know One: Female Misogynists

Men tend to take the lead in far-reaching misogynistic movements. But very many women are misogynists too. They are zealous converts to the same ideology as their male counterparts and deploy similar, and occasionally worse, hateful tactics. In fact, empirical evidence suggests that on social media, women are more misogynistic than men.[35]

Like their male counterparts, female misogynists are driven by either hate for women who stray from the feminine ideal or contempt for women in general on account of their alleged inherent filthy nature, for instance, their association with bodily stuff or their manipulativeness.

The female misogynists who are most salient in America today fall into four categories, which I will call: the Puritan, the Self-Hater, the Self-Contemner, and the She-Devil. Like the hateful male misogynist, the Puritan regards the ideal woman as thin, trim, youthful, pretty, alluring, mild-tempered, nurturing, compassionate, non-promiscuous, not too ambitious, ladylike in manners and presentation, and sometimes also as domestic and subservient to men. She takes herself to be pretty darn close to the ideal, possessing the feminine qualities she believes to be the most important ones.

What makes the Puritan a misogynist is not her support of the feminine ideal but her hatred toward women who purposely distance themselves from conventional femininity and traditional gender norms, such as feminists, career women, and working moms. She targets these kinds of women because in her opinion, they are bad women who willfully or recklessly offend against the natural order of things.

Despite regarding themselves as domestic goddesses, Puritans are often public provocateurs who have made it their life's mission to discipline their "lost sisters" and eventually get them back on the "right track." Some are celebs with their own glittery YouTube channels, flashy podcasts, on-fire mommy blogs, or star reality television shows; the rest tend to be actively involved in bullheaded antifeminist groups like Women against Feminism or Women for Christian Domestic Discipline (a.k.a. wife spanking).

Michelle Duggar, a submissive and holier-than-thou housewife and reality-television star, is a prime example of a Puritan female misogynist. She advocates for complete female submission. In a blog post for newlyweds, she shares advice on how women can keep their husbands happy:[36]

> And so be available, and not just available, but be joyfully available for him. Smile and be willing to say, "Yes, sweetie I am here for you," no matter what, even though you may be exhausted and big pregnant and you may not feel like he feels.

Duggar's good-subservient-girl misogyny is not as rare as one might have hoped. Prior to the 2016 presidential election, a number of women tweeted the hashtag #repealthe19th to demand the repeal of women's voting rights after a Donald Trump win was shown to be the certain outcome if only men were to vote in the upcoming election.

The misogynistic Self-Hater, the second type of woman-on-woman hater, is also prone to hatred of women who purposely distance themselves from the feminine ideal and the traditional gender norms, for example, women who are competitive, controlling, prone to anger, or who behave in a manner that isn't ladylike. She pays homage to traditional gender norms and uses any opportunity she sees to preach their social virtue. Men should be dominant alphas, women should be soft and compliant. But unlike the Puritan, the Self-Hater regards herself as one of the badly behaved women and despises herself for lacking the willpower to become more feminine. Self-haters tend to be in denial about their own self-hatred and sometimes also about their hatred toward other women who purposely go against the feminine ideal.

Suzanne Venker, the author of *The Alpha Female's Guide to Men and Marriage: How Love Works*, falls into this category, at least in the way she looks back at her past ways as an alpha wife. "Women have become too much like men," Venker writes. "They're too competitive. Too masculine. Too *alpha*."[37] She attributes modern women's "inability to find lasting love" to their need to dominate and overpower. Women who want to find lasting love, she argues, need to be soft instead of hard. They need to uncover their femininity. She relates how she used to resent having to be feminine to get along with her husband. But her "alpha ways were bumping up against his alpha nature," she writes. "We were like two bulls hanging out in the same pen together, and there was too much friction." So, she decided to embrace her femininity. She reports on what she learned in the following passage:

> It's liberating to be a beta! I'm an alpha all day long, and it gets tiresome. I concede that I thrive on it; but at the end of the day, I'm spent. Self-reliance is exhausting. Making all the decisions is exhausting. Driving the car, literally or figuratively, is exhausting. It took me a ridiculously long time to get it. But once I did, once I accepted that the energy I exude and the way I approach my husband directly affects his response and behavior, I changed my tune. And when I did, something happened. The tension disappeared overnight. Just like that. Well, almost like that. It was a lot of stop and go at first. First I'd handle something the

"right" way—i.e. by not arguing with him, or by not directing his traffic, or by being more service-oriented—and marvel at the response. Then life would get busy, and I'd resort to my old ways. Sure enough, I'd get a different response. So I'd make a mental note of how I messed up and make sure to get it right the next time. Eventually, it became second nature.[38]

Venker preaches misogyny disguised as well-meant advice. Her theory that "women have become too much like men," that women are "too competitive. Too masculine. Too *alpha*," and that this explains their "inability to find lasting love" is grotesquely hateful toward women who are not very feminine, whether it's because they choose not to be or because they are just bad at being girls.

When disclosing why she decided to embrace her femininity, Venker briefly mentions that she "had zero interest in [her] husband adopting a more feminine role." This may at first seem like a logical reason to change. But if we dig a little deeper, Venker's remark turns out to reflect a more depressing fact about her psychology.

Her claim that she "had zero interest in [her] husband adopting a more feminine role" implies that she wanted her husband to be the person in charge, the alpha. She clung to this desire, even while embracing her alpha ways in her marriage. But this means that her excuse for changing her ways wasn't logical after all. Cognitive dissonance prompted her to adjust: she wanted both herself and her husband to be the alpha leader. Something had to give.

As we saw in Chapter 2, cognitive dissonance is a psychologically distressing state of internal inconsistency. Research shows that people typically deal with internal inconsistencies by suppressing the attitude that is culturally frowned upon and then rationalizing their choice to advocate for, and act on, the more culturally acceptable attitude.[39]

By her own account, Venker's internal conflict, that is, her desire for both her and her husband to be the alpha leader, was a great source of distress. The only feasible way for her to soothe her agony was to silence one of her dissonant desires. But there is little sympathy in our society for powerless men who cave to dominant women. So, it's only natural that Venker's wish to be the alpha in her marriage inspired self-hatred. She conquered her self-hatred by muzzling her craving for the alpha role, and to legitimize her choice she then embarked on her book-writing journey.

The misogynistic Self-Contemner, one of the two contemptuous female misogynists, has internalized the myth of female filth. As a result, she has adopted a general attitude of contempt toward everyone of her own "filthy" kind, including herself. She regards women as inferior to men. In her view, women are inferior to men because of their inherent negative qualities, for instance, their promiscuity, manipulativeness, dishonesty, irrationality, incompetence, or stupidity. She tends to be in denial about how her own self-contempt underlies her judgmental attitude toward other women.

I have heard people insist that the idea of self-contempt is in-coherent. If you have contempt for me, you look down on me, because you see me as inferior to yourself. But just as you cannot be shorter than yourself, you cannot be inferior to yourself, or so the objection goes.

Although it is true that you cannot literally be shorter than, or inferior to, yourself, we can see that the objection to self-contempt must go wrong somewhere, because by the same token, we can infer that we cannot blame ourselves, because in blame we also take the judgmental high road and look down at the target with disapproval. But viewing yourself as superior and also looking down on yourself with a judgmental attitude is scarcely less contradictory than having contempt for yourself.

The fact is that we can and do blame ourselves. All the time. In fact, self-directed judgmental attitudes are deeply ingrained in our culture. This is encapsulated in the form of sayings such as "You have only yourself to blame," "Don't be so hard on yourself," and "Don't make yourself a victim of yourself!"

We are able to cast judgment on ourselves by playing distinct roles that reflect different aspects of ourselves. We can and do often play the roles of both the judge and the accused. If you talk to yourself, you may be familiar with this sort of role playing. (Note to self: "My God, you're a despicable piece of shit. A fucking pathetic looser. Get your shitty act together!")

When we cast judgments on ourselves, our conscience plays the role of the cynical unfeeling judge, and the part of us that feels bad plays the role of the accused. The division of labor is one between reason and passion.

Self-contempt is what we sometimes refer to as self-loathing. It materializes when your conscience is cast in the role of the contemner, and your emotions play the role of the contemned, who is made to feel low and appalling. Adolf Hitler allegedly struggled with self-contempt on account of the shame he felt about his Jewish roots.[40]

Hulu's dystopian television series *The Handmaid's Tale*, adapted from Margaret Atwood's novel of the same name, offers several examples of misogynistic Self-Contemners. It tells a frightening tale of the brutalities committed inside the Republic of Gilead, an eerily plausible dystopian America that was the product of religious alt-right supporters in response to drastically declining birth rates in the West. Inside the authoritarian regime, the remaining fertile women are enslaved as "handmaids" by the commanders and their wives to ensure the survival of the white race. (In the novel it's explicitly stated that blacks have been relocated to an area in the Midwest that is set up like South African–style apartheid "homelands." But this aspect seems to have been erased in the television series.)

The television series follows the plight of June/Offred (played by Elisabeth Moss) a handmaid owned by Commander Fred Waterford (Joseph Fiennes) and his wife, Serena Joy (Yvonne Strahovski), two of the alt-right supporters who seized power. The most important part of Offred's job as a handmaid is to carry a child for the commander and his wife. During a monthly act of ritualistic sexual violence called "the ceremony," Offred is shown lying with her head in Serena's lap while Commander Waterford rapes her.

Serena is one of the story's female accomplices who actively participate in contemptuous dehumanization of their own gender.[41] But the
privileged wives are not the only female misogynists. Early on in the
story we learn that one of Gilead's enforcers, Aunt Lydia (Ann Dowd),
who trains, disciplines, punishes, and, if necessary, tortures and kills the
handmaids, is a pro-life extremist who sees herself as saving the women
from sin (or, in Aunt Lydia's words, from "murdering babies," "orgies,"
and "Tinder!").[42]

Serena and Aunt Lydia are prime examples of Self-Contemners.
Although their self-contempt often masquerades behind their cruelty,
we do occasionally get a glimpse of their shame and self-contempt.
Serena was one of the planners of Gilead. She is the author of a best-
selling book about her conservative beliefs, titled *A Woman's Place*, and
was apparently a sought-after speaker prior to the coup. She is also a
control freak with no real power beyond her power over those residing
in her home. She is beaten by her husband in front of Offred when he
returns home after being injured in a terrorist attack and learns that she
has drafted new policies with Offred's help.

Initial appearances to the contrary, commander wives and enforcers
have no real power. The commanders are ultimately in control. Why
then do Serena and Aunt Lydia side with their oppressors and participate in the contemptuous dehumanization of their own gender?
Perhaps their hostility toward their own "kind" gives them some semblance of control in an incomprehensible and unjust world. Or perhaps
they are both dark vulnerable personalities who thrill at inflicting pain
on women, periodically pausing to self-punish and rid themselves of the
built-up shame.

The misogynistic She-Devil, the second strand of contemptuous female misogynist, sees herself as superior to other women and on level
with, if not above, the top alpha males in her world. Other women are,
in her opinion, inferior to men because of their inherent filthy traits,
for instance, their association with bodily stuff or their incompetence,
but somehow she was miraculously born without those vices. The She-
Devil might possess some stereotypical feminine virtues like beauty and

slenderness. But she perceives herself as instantiating stereotypical mas-culine qualities such as intelligence, strength of character, and ration-ality, and her behavior can at times be more manly than that of her male coworkers, classmates, or friends. Don't be surprised if you find out that she can outdrink all of them.

She is in constant competition with other women and would rather kick a woman off the career ladder or out of school than help her prog-ress. But she masterfully escapes detection and punishment for her bad behavior. As you wait for the elevator with your box of personal effects and your withering office plant, your rival is looking down on you from her vocational high chair, her triumphant laughter hanging in the air.

Vivienne Parry, a British science journalist and broadcaster, describes her mother as a misogynist of this type.[43] When Parry revealed to her mother that she wanted to study science at the university, her mother responded, "Whatever for?" Parry was taken aback. But it made her wonder: "Why was my mother so against helping anyone of her own gender climb to the same heights as she did? Why was she so loath to laud female achievement—even when the female forging ahead was her own daughter?" When looking at the past through her contemporary lens, the answer to her question turned out to be terrifyingly simple: "I fear my mother was a misogynist," she writes.

A cut-throat career businesswoman, Parry's mother was more manly than the men and could easily outdrink any of them. Parry writes that her mother thought of herself as the sole woman who deserved a spot at the company's top. She looked down on other women with con-tempt and would rather stab a female coworker in the back than help her progress.

According to Parry, female misogyny is even more prevalent today than in her mother's day. Male misogyny runs rampant in today's so-ciety. But, as Parry points out, female misogyny can be even more toxic. Women may not punch you in the face, though that once happened to me, but if you get in their way or you rise to stardom faster than they do, watch out. Before you have time to blink, they may have gotten you fired, run off with your husband, and adopted your kids. According to

Parry, "when there are so few women at higher levels, many of them think they must behave like a tigress, using every weapon at their disposal to protect their position against other 'sisters.'"

Fierce competition for leadership positions or popularity is no doubt a key factor driving female misogyny. But women who take themselves to be superior to virtually all other women are in all likelihood also host to dark personality traits like narcissism, borderline personality, or psychopathy. Such a woman's firm belief that she is above the usual female inferiority points most strongly to narcissism. But narcissistic traits are also routinely present in borderlines and psychopaths. In the general population dark traits tend to be subclinical, which means that they are not associated with the level of dysfunction seen in clinical cases. But mixing high functionality with sinister character traits is more likely to give you a Molotov cocktail than a Cosmopolitan.

The four types of female misogynists salient in our patriarchal culture are not meant to be an exhaustive categorization of woman-on-woman hatred rooted in patriarchal ideologies. Other types of female misogynists include women who hate or have contempt for all and only black women, women who hate or have contempt for all and only poor women, and so on. We will discuss these forms of misogyny in the next section.

It's worth noting that woman-on-woman hatred rooted in non-oppressive ideologies doesn't count as misogyny, as the term is ordinarily used. But to say that some forms of woman-on-woman hatred don't count as misogyny is not to say that the hatred is acceptable. The so-called Mommy Wars are a case in point.[44] The term "Mommy Wars" is commonly used to refer to contempt- or hate-based cyberbullying mom-on-mom combats between stay-at-home moms and working moms.[45] When the combats are contempt-based, stay-at-home moms launch attacks on working moms whom they regard as inferior to themselves because of their choice to leave their children in the care of strangers in order to focus on their careers, whereas working moms attacks stay-at-home moms whom they regard as inferior to themselves because of their endorsement of a patriarchal arrangement.

When these battles are hate-based, stay-at-home moms view working moms as malevolent and potentially powerful and dangerous because of their contribution to the downfall of traditional gender norms, whereas working moms regard stay-at-home moms as malevolent and potentially powerful and dangerous because they supposedly contribute to an oppressive patriarchal regime. Stay-at-home moms of the envisaged kind are thus misogynists, because they subject other women to unjustified antagonism rooted in oppressive patriarchal ideologies. But nonconformist working moms who target stay-at-home moms don't adhere to a patriarchal ideology. So, their hate should not be labeled "misogyny." But this is not to say that their hatred is acceptable. The hater's focus of concern is her target's malevolent misdeed. Yet it's obviously not a malevolent misdeed to be a stay-at-home mom. So, hating moms because they choose to stay at home is indefensible.

The Good, the Bad, and the Ugly

Women who belong to multiple socially oppressed groups are particularly prone to misogynistic attacks. They are multiply burdened, discredited twice, thrice, or more. Trans women, that is, women who were assigned the male sex at birth but who identify as women, often look a lot more masculine than the average cis woman, especially prior to hormone therapy. Their tendency to deviate from the feminine ideal and the incorrect view in the general population that trans women have chosen to become women make them frequent targets of hateful misogyny.

They are also frequent targets of contempt-based misogyny. As author and trans activist Julia Serano has argued, trans women and others who transgress our culture's gender norms, such as feminine boys, are sexualized in the media, which routinely provide intimate details about the bodies of trans women or transitioning or depict them as perverts who want to become women to fulfill some twisted sexual fantasy. Although trans men are also sometimes objectified by the media, they are not typically sexualized in the way that trans women are.[46] To be recognized legally as women, trans women are often forced to undergo sterilization.[47]

Trans women are also significantly more likely to be the victims of hate crimes than trans men, black trans women being the most vulnerable. According to the Human Rights Campaign, since 2013, 128 trans people have been victims of fatal violence in the United States, and the vast majority of them were women.[48] In April 2019, a brutal attack on Muhlaysia Booker, a trans woman, made national news. According to the *New York Times*, Booker had been involved in a minor traffic accident, and the other driver apparently offered twenty-nine-year-old Edward Thomas $200 to beat her up.[49] The beating was filmed on a cell phone, showing Thomas putting on gloves and then repeatedly punching and kicking Booker while she is struggling on the ground. Other men also started kicking her while other bystanders were passively observing the assault. The attack continued until three women helped Booker get away. The following month, however, Booker's body was found in the street after sounds of gunshots had been reported to the authorities.[50]

Society's greater antagonism toward trans women, Serano argues, "reflects the societal-wide inclination to view masculinity as being strong and natural, and femininity as being weak and artificial."[51]

Other women who belong to multiple socially oppressed or stigmatized groups are also at a greater risk than more privileged women of becoming the targets of hateful misogyny. Blacks, Natives, queer women, sex workers, obese women, career women, and women who are just bad at being girls, for example, are at a particularly high risk at being seen as speaking too loudly, being too hot-headed, laughing too much, being too rough around the edges, being too large, having too much sex, making too much money, having too much confidence, or simply being too masculine to satisfy today's prevailing feminine ideal.

Other women who belong to multiple socially oppressed or stigmatized groups are also at a greater risk than more privileged women of becoming the targets of contempt-based misogyny. Blacks, Latinas, Natives, disabled women, sex workers, and obese women, for example, are particularly prone to be associated with "filthy" vices like promiscuity, laziness, "system milking," or low intelligence.

Black women, for example, are still the victims of historically rooted negative stereotyping in American culture today. Whereas the Mammy stereotype, which characterizes black women as asexual, unattractive, large, domestic women who work for rich white people and babysit their children, is slowly fading, the Jezebel stereotype is alive and kicking. As the Jim Crow Museum points out, the modern-day Jezebel stereotype has widened over the years:

> K. Sue Jewell (1993), a contemporary sociologist, conceptualized the Jezebel as a tragic mulatto—"thin lips, long straight hair, slender nose, thin figure and fair complexion" (p. 46). This conceptualization is too narrow. It is true that the "tragic mulatto" and "Jezebel" share the reputation of being sexually seductive, and both are antithetical to the desexualized Mammy caricature; nevertheless, it is a mistake to assume that only, or even mainly, fair-complexioned black women were sexually objectified by the larger American society. From the early 1630s to the present, black American women of all shades have been portrayed as hypersexual "bad-black-girls."[52]

The modern-day Jezebel stereotype portrays black women as lewd, hypersexual, and promiscuous. This stereotype makes black women more prone than white women to be associated with bodily "stuff," making them even more susceptible to contempt-based misogyny.

Newer pejorative stereotypes of black women include the myth of the welfare mama and the angry black woman. The welfare mama is a lazy overweight black woman past her youth with multiple children in tow living off of hard-working Americans' tax dollars. Finally, the angry black woman stereotype characterizes black women past their youth as hostile, illogical, overbearing, and ignorant.

The welfare mama and the angry black woman stereotypes make us even more prone to associate black women with alleged inherent female vices like promiscuity, laziness, or low intelligence, which puts black women at an increased risk of becoming the targets of contempt-based misogyny.

Pickup Artists, Incels, and Red Pillers

Some of the most extreme and most dangerous misogynists gather in online communities with such fanciful names as "The Red Pill," "incels," and "pickup artists." The Red Pill is a misogynistic subreddit message board, hosted on Reddit, where men who have "swallowed the red pill" go to vent about women. The phrase "to swallow the red pill" comes from the 1999 film *The Matrix*, in which the protagonist, Neo, must choose between swallowing the red pill, which will allow him to see the dark, uncomfortable truth behind the Matrix, and the blue pill, which will allow him to continue living in blissful ignorance inside the fake reality of the Matrix.

The subreddit's Red Pillers claim to have taken off the blindfold and opened their eyes to the reality of the power dynamic between men and women. There are different levels of misogyny among the subscribers.

The "pickup artists" take women to be reacting with arrogance and self-sufficiency to men who are too soft and who don't give women what they really want, which allegedly is to be dominated and controlled by men. According to the pickup artists, women put up a facade in order to test which men are men enough to break it down, not by using old tricks, but by becoming real alpha males. As a subscriber who writes under the handle Angry Atheist puts it, "Women want men to have the power in the relationship. Women want to be dominated. They want you to pass their shit tests. What they don't want is for some beta to know the 'cheat codes' to their system. They want a real alpha, not some beta who studied some RP [Red Pill] book and has learned how to act like one."[53]

Another strand of misogynists call themselves "men's rights activists." They are angry, feel unfairly treated, and place the blame for their problems on feminists. As the *Guardian*'s columnist Gary Younge puts it, "Unable to take advantage of the male privileges they believe they are owed, they feel inadequate and grow resentful, and a handful become violent. Often awkward, shy and unconfident, they cannot meet the standards of machismo that patriarchy demands. They think feminism will destroy them."[54]

Men who frequent the Red Pill subreddit have been unlucky with women in the past, like filmmaker Christian Tafdrup, who directed the 2018 dark Danish comedy-drama *A Horrible Woman* (*En Frygtelig Kvinde*). The movie is said to be a satirical reflection on the nature of women in heterosexual relationships as seen through the eyes of a man. But despite being advertised as a satirical character study, its hateful misogynistic overtones are unmistakable. Through his depiction of women's tyrannical entrapment of the "weaker sex," Tafdrup artfully invites us to detest the movie's female characters.

The film begins with Rasmus and his buddies getting drunk and behaving as obnoxious and uncivilized as they can. Like frat boys. Civilization returns when the wife of one of his friends returns home with a group of female friends. One of them is Marie, the woman villainized in the movie's title. Rasmus and Marie fall in love and begin to see each other. If it were not for the film's ill-intentioned title, we might have let Marie's initial pushiness pass for relationship jitters. But we have an idea of what awaits Rasmus (and us).

Before long, even Rasmus realizes that the woman he fell in love with is a manipulating control freak who is slowly robbing him of his manhood. At first, she exerts her insidious control using the voice of a parent as she calmly explains to him why he needs to change his ways. Everything from his apartment decor and music collection to his diet and workout schedule is molded to fit her ego. When Rasmus' self-confidence hits rock-bottom, Marie's tactics change from paternalistic to contemptuous. As we watch on with horror as Rasmus' autonomy is being stripped away, we are driven toward feelings of hate not just for Marie but for all the women she symbolizes, women who entrap men in this underhanded way in long-term heterosexual relationships.

Throughout the movie we get glimpses of other cruel women and their obedient husbands. When Rasmus shows up at his buddy's house for advice one late evening, his buddy turns him away to appease his nagging wife. Later, in a bar scene, his friends leave Rasmus behind with a round of beer he has just purchased, because their wives and girlfriends expect them to be home on the dot.

Rather than being a cautionary tale of a dysfunctional relationship, *A Horrible Woman* is a troubling piece of pro-misogynist propaganda. In interviews Tafdrup has revealed that the film is loosely based on his own frustrated relationship experiences.

The most jarring and scary of the Red Pillers are those who openly adopt contemptible attitudes toward hard-to-get women. Groups of young men calling themselves "incels," which is short for "involuntary celibates," feel victimized by beautiful girls who won't "give it up." They frequent the subreddit Reddit.com/r/Incels, where they complain about women who deny them their "rightful" sexual experience as the reason why "they're not getting laid."

Like the pickup artists, they also exchange advice on how to game women into having sex with them. But they are darker, more self-centered, and more violent. Their posts are rife with revenge fantasies, and some are prepared to carry them out in real life, as we have seen several examples of in recent years.

Motivated by hatred of women, Alek Minassian, a self-professed incel, repeatedly drove a van into a crowd of people in Toronto in April 2018, killing ten people, eight of whom were women. A message that Minassian had posted on Facebook suggested that he was inspired by Elliot Rodger, who channeled sexual frustration into a shooting rampage in Isla Vista, California, in May 2014.

Rodger left behind a 137-page manifesto and video footage of himself pretentiously announcing the "Day of Retribution." "Well, now"—a theatrical pause—"I'll be a god compared to you."

Rodger's hackneyed script, phony laugh, and rehearsed delivery are telltale signs that his misogyny is rooted in his narcissistic personality. As we saw in Chapter 4, the diagnostic criteria for this disorder include haughty behaviors and attitudes, a grandiose sense of self-importance, a sense of entitlement, a need for excessive admiration, and a preoccupation with fantasies of unlimited success, power, brilliance, beauty, or ideal love. Rodger easily satisfies all the criteria. As my co-blogger Amy Broadway puts it:

[Rodger] idealized a relationship with a beautiful, blonde, white girl. A virgin who had never held a girl's hand, he fantasized about what other people's love lives were like but had a shallow understanding of love. He was baffled that girls didn't swoon over his $300 sunglasses and BMW. Rodger explains that once you hit puberty, life is either "heaven on earth" or a "living hell." According to him, whether or not his life was good depended on how many girls liked him. By basing his life's worth on whether girls liked him, he made women into objects instrumental for feeling self-worth.[55]

The Red Pill subreddits play a big part in the recent rise in misogynistic attacks on women. Frustrated young men, often with no really bad intentions, start following a message board, and eventually they become radicalized.

Demagogues and hatemongers capitalize on antagonistic ideologies about the ideal woman and the filthy woman to attract a certain type of misogynistic follower, spread their own misogynistic beliefs in the general population, and provoke group polarization. As we saw in Chapter 5, group polarization is an efficient way of turning pre-existing antagonism into full-blown hatred. Once the misogynistic followers are fired up with hatred of women, they are more inclined to carry out misogynistic attacks, or even commit mass murder, as in the cases of Rodger and Minassian.

The Red Pill subreddits have become a home for other hateful beliefs. These subreddits are among the places where far-right supporters recruit young blood. The most socially frustrated, lonely, and desperate incels leave their old online forums to join the subreddit Red Pill Right. With a gentle push from far-right hate groups, incels quickly transition from seeing women as the source of all their problems to seeing everyone but white cis heterosexual men as the root of all evil. I turn to the far-right movement and its role in the current hate crisis in our society in the next chapter.

7 | KEEP THE CHANGE, YOU FILTHY ANIMAL

RACIAL HATRED AND THE AMERICAN PHANTASY

On July 6, 1946, in a hospital in New York City, Sylvester Gardenzio Stallone was about to be born when he got stuck in his mother's birth canal. The midwife had no choice but to use two pairs of forceps to pull him out. Unfortunately, she used the forceps incorrectly, and the metal tools ended up causing nerve damage to baby Stallone's face, which left him permanently paralyzed in the lower left side of his face, including parts of his lip, tongue, and chin. His snarling look and the slurred speech for which he eventually became world-famous are not make-believe but actual evidence of his birth defects.

Stallone had a troubled childhood. After the birth of his younger brother, his parents were constantly fighting. Stallone and his brother were put in foster care. When his parents got divorced, Stallone was eleven. After the divorce Stallone lived with his father in Maryland for several years. But he was getting into a lot of trouble and was expelled from several schools. Stallone then moved to Philadelphia to live with his mom and her new husband. He was enrolled in a high school for troubled youth. After graduation he went to the American College in Switzerland to study drama. He then enrolled in the University of Miami in southern Florida to study theater but dropped out before finishing and decided to move to New York to pursue his dream, which was to become an actor.

To make ends meet he worked various odd jobs until he got some minor roles, first in an adult movie and then in Woody Allen's 1971 comedy film *Bananas* and Alan J. Pakula's 1971 neo-noir crime thriller *Klute*. He was subsequently offered a more substantial role playing a tough guy in the 1974 independent film *The Lords of Flatbush*.

Stallone married Sasha Czack, who soon became pregnant. Desperate to support his family, he wrote the movie script for *Rocky* in less than four days. But it wasn't an easy sell. To be able to put food on the table, he had to sell his dog for cash.

After a long series of heartless rejections, Stallone finally received good news. Film producers Irwin Winkler and Robert Chartoff were interested in buying his script and let him play the lead but on a reduced budget. As soon as Stallone received his advance for the film, he bought back his dog, which also got a role in the film.

The finished feature *Rocky* went on to be nominated for ten Academy Awards, including Best Actor and Best Original Screenplay nominations for Stallone. It won an Academy Award for Best Picture and Best Film Editing.

In addition to becoming a successful screenwriter and actor after years of hard work, tenacity, and sacrifices, Stallone has also gone on to become an internationally acclaimed producer and director. He turned scraps into a fortune. Today his net worth is supposedly $400 million.

Despite facing endless failures, sacrifices, and rejections decade after decade, Stallone never gave up but had the guts to stick with his dream to become an actor, and eventually he rose to stardom. The possibility of rising from the gutter and achieving personal wealth through risk-taking, sacrifice, and hard work in the Land of Opportunity is what we call "the American Dream."

This was not the original meaning of the phrase, however.[1] As Sarah Churchwell, the author of *Behold, America* (2018), writes, the phrase originally referred to the equal opportunity that white people have to make a better life for themselves. Although America was founded on this idea, the phrase was first coined in 1931 by historian and Pulitzer Prize winner James Truslow Adams in his book *The Epic of America*, where he argued that America's downfall during the Great Depression was due to the country's obsession with material wealth and its negligence of the higher aspirations of a liberal democracy.[2] The American dream, he wrote, is "that dream of a land in which life should be better and richer and fuller for everyone, with opportunity for each according to ability or achievement."[3]

Despite Adams's aspirations, in the minds of the public the "American Dream" has probably never been a belief in the possibility of leading a rich and full life but rather a belief in the possibility of upward mobility in material wealth for anyone who is willing to work hard, make sacrifices, and take risks.[4] This is the American Dream entrenched in the American psyche, the dream we cling to for dear life.

Yet today strenuous physical labor is more likely to go hand in hand with a minimum wage than with economic prosperity. And affluence is more likely to emanate from inheritance or corruption than from hard work. Indeed, as research conducted by economist Raj Chetty and co-authors has shown, most Americans lack the opportunities essential to upward mobility, with only half of the population earning more than their parents at the same age.[5] A college degree is increasingly touted as the engine of social mobility. On average, people with a bachelor's degree make $1 million more than folks with a high school diploma over the course of their lifetime.[6] This definitely helps the average college-educated person climb a bit further up on the socio-economic ladder. The problem is that 70 percent of the population never get a college degree. And like cars, most people don't move very far without an engine. America's most cherished dream—success follows on hard work—is pie in the sky.

"Sadly, the American Dream is dead," Donald Trump proclaimed when he announced his presidential candidacy for the 2016 election.[7] His promise to his predominantly white voters was to resurrect the dream by freeing them from the shackles of their oppression: immigrants, politicians, professionals, unfair trade deals, and heavy taxation. In his acceptance speech after winning the election, he once again stressed that the American Dream is dead, but that it would be alive and kicking before long. Yet three (going on four) years into his presidency, the American Dream is still six feet under. A tax cut for business owners, stricter immigration policies, a Muslim travel ban, border fences, and cuts in Medicaid spending aren't exactly reviving the dream.

The real reason upward mobility for everyone willing to work hard, make sacrifices, and take risks has become pure fantasy is a rise in socio-economic inequality, a growing gulf in wealth, income, and opportunity between rich and poor, as well as between the wealthy and the middle class. A very small number of people control most of the wealth in the country. It used to be the top ten; now it's down to 1 percent. The top 1 percent who control the country's wealth also dominate the student bodies of the best colleges in the country. As history professor Nelson Lichtenstein recently called to our attention in the *Chronicle of Higher Education*, if you pick a random student attending a college ranked among the thirty-eight best in the country, that student is more likely to be from the top 1 percent than from the bottom 60 percent.[8]

According to America's growing far right, however, the American Dream's demise is the evil work of American liberals, who enabled the Civil Rights Act, the sexual revolution, the influx of immigrants from south of the border, and the ironclad convention of political correctness. American liberals, they argue, assassinated the national ethos of the United States.

The far-right conspiracy theory has it that the social safety nets and equal opportunity acts that bleeding-heart liberals cooked up poisoned America's most cherished trademark, because when we promise people our goodwill regardless of what they do and how they behave, those who are lazy and opportunistic have no incentive to work hard and make the sacrifices needed for upward mobility in society. They learn that if they do nothing, the state jumps to their rescue with welfare, food stamps, Medicaid, and affordable housing.

Another social change the far right lists as evidence for its view that liberal policies squashed "upward mobility for all" is that women's relatively recent interest in having careers of their own allegedly has created bitter job competition, a scarcity of well-paid jobs, unhappy men, frazzled women, and insecure children left by their mothers to be raised by strangers.

Those in the grip of the far-right conspiracy theories paint a rosy image of the luxurious lifestyle of 1950s white middle-class families, or Southern families living in peaceful agrarian communities in the eighteenth and nineteenth centuries.[9] In each imagined society traditional white American nuclear families led satisfying, meaningful lives, which they had built through honest hard work. The traditional values they adhered to offered clear guidance on how to move up through the ranks of society. Unburdened by people of color, Jews, Muslims, Natives, illegal immigrants, asylum seekers, homeless, or other "inferior free-riders," anyone willing to put in the effort and delay short-term gratification could achieve the American Dream.

The fundamental flaw in these glorious utopian visions still lodged in the public imagination is that they don't accurately depict American society at any point in the past. The 1950s ideal white family was a mirage depicted by the glittering magazine ads and flashy television commercials that big businesses used to exploit psychologically pained housewives. Desperate for change, they let themselves get talked into buying the newest life-changing products and merchandise, while secretly praying that one more useless contraption or bottle of Mother's Little Helper would heal their psychic wounds.

Popular culture has primed us to crave regular shots of Western country living in all its confounding glory. A family farm, situated in a small agrarian white community, perhaps dating back to the 1800s, replete with open prairies, fields of harvestable crops, freshly baked bread, livestock, and thick raw milk with cream on top. Think Laura Ingalls Wilder's *Little House on the Prairie*, later immortalized in the 1970s-era *Little House* television show, about a white family living on a farm in Kansas in the 1870s and 1880s. So sweet is the nostalgia that it's hard not to smile just a little—at least until we are reminded that *Little House* wasn't quite as immaculate as we remember it to be. After some run-ins with the local Osage Indians, Pa tells Laura:

> When white settlers come into a country, the Indians have to move on. The government is going to move these Indians farther west, any time now. That's why we're here, Laura. White people are going to settle all this country, and we get the best land because we get here first and take our pick. Now do you understand?[10]

As English professor Francis Kaye shrewdly observes in her 2000 article titled "Little Squatter on the Osage Diminished Reserve," "Wilder, writing as honestly as she knew how, spun a tale that, because of her very decency, makes 'ethnic cleansing' appear palatable."[11]

Let's call the self-serving delusion that America once was, and once again can become, an idyllic nation of white people for whom upward mobility is the rule rather than the exception, where traditional gender norms prevail, and where white people dominate non-whites or live without them entirely "the American Phantasy."

The reason for the archaic spelling of "Phantasy" is two-fold. First, using "Ph" instead of "F" indicates not only a shift in meaning but also the speaker's disapproval of what the term picks out, sometimes for satirical effect, as in "phishing," which refers to an internet scam that baits people into giving out passwords, credit-card numbers, and other personal information, and "phood," an amalgam of "pharmaceutical" and "food," which refers to industrially enhanced food products.

Second, the term "phantasy" spelled with "ph" has been repurposed by psychoanalysts to refer to an imaginative fulfillment of frustrated, conscious or unconscious, wishes. It's a kind of psychological defense mechanism that transiently masks self-destructive emotions, such as feelings of shame, regret, dejection, or powerlessness.[12]

The American Phantasy unites and incentivizes far-right hate groups, fuels their recruitment efforts, and facilitates their "normalization." Trump promised to revive the American Dream. Instead (and perhaps deliberately), he nurtured the imaginative fulfillment of the frustrated wishes of far-right supporters with a tapestry of falsehoods.

The American Phantasy at the Far Right

The far right, also known as white nationalism, the new right, the dissident right, and the alt-right ("alternative right"), is an extremist-conservative political ideology that seeks to change current socio-economic structures on the basis of the claim that whites are superior to non-whites. The two main strands of the far right are white supremacy and white separatism (sometimes called "white identitarianism").

White supremacists promote the view that whites are inherently superior to non-whites and should dominate other ethnic groups and be the primary beneficiaries of political, economic, and social policies. While their ultimate political agenda is a white-dominance caste system, white supremacists routinely opt to voice their views in ways that make them sound virtually indistinguishable from separatists. This strategy is commonly employed by Richard Spencer, president of the white supremacy think tank National Policy Institute and originator of the term "alternative right." Spencer occasionally alleges that his prime goal is to preserve white European American culture in the United States. But a closer look at this political agenda reveals that this kind of talk is nothing more than a prettification of his darker conviction that whites are entitled to dominate non-whites. Unclothed, Spencer's grisly phantasy would be off-putting to website hosts and potential recruits.

White separatists embrace the ideology that whites are superior to non-whites. But rather than pushing for white power, they officially promote the view that whites and non-whites should be separated, for example, by prohibiting "interracial" marriage and procreation, by removing non-whites from existing communities, by establishing a white ethnostate elsewhere, or, in extreme cases, by completely eliminating non-whites.

For example, Matthew Heimbach, a white separatist and neo-Nazi, has expressed a desire to create a National Socialist ethnostate by the name of "Avalon," the hate group Aryan Nations has advocated for building a white republic in the Pacific Northwest, and the hate group Occidental Dissent has expressed a desire to build a "Jew-free white ethnostate in North America" that would re-establish "white supremacy."

Although many white nationalists promote aspects of both far-right ideologies, the two are conceptually distinct. Supremacists advocate the view that white people should dominate other races, for example, by introducing legislation that gives priority to white people, whereas separatists plug a complete separation of whites and non-whites on the basis of white people's alleged superior humanity, intelligence, or integrity. In practice, however, the two doctrines are hard to tease apart. Some separatists maintain that they don't believe that any race or ethnic group should dominate another, and that all races and ethnic groups have the right to develop their own culture separately. Separatists such as Patrick Casey, the leader of the American Identity Movement (formerly Identity Evropa), even insist that they don't preach the inferiority of others. But these assertions have been dispelled as myths.[13]

White nationalism goes beyond merely promoting political ideologies or wallowing in the imaginative fulfillment of the American Phantasy. Its crusaders look down on non-whites with contempt and express their hatred toward ethnicities who fail to acknowledge their alleged inferior humanity, intelligence, or integrity. The exception to their anti-whiteness is their complimenting attitudes toward light-skinned Asians, whom they regard as model minorities. Almost all far-right hate groups target Jews, who they think are conspiring to seize control of the world or to eradicate "the white race."

Hate groups like White Socialist Movement, National Alliance, Stormfront, and the Rise Above Movement have openly encouraged and applauded hate crimes against non-white ethnic groups. Far-right organizations like White Revolution and Identity Evropa have promoted the view that non-whites are a threat to their "white identity," and allege that this gives them license to use radical means to "protect or save" people of Anglo-Saxon or northern European descent. In his 2018 documentary *Documenting Hate: New American Nazis*, Richard Rowley reports that the American military-affiliated neo-Nazi group Atomwaffen Division calls for lone-wolf acts of violence.[14] Victorious lone-wolf killers are subsequently praised as "saviors of the white race." Atomwaffen Division was the inspiration of the British hate group Sonnenkrieg Division, which was exposed by the BBC and found to be connected with five murders.[15]

When the lone-wolf gunman who killed eleven people at the Tree of Life synagogue in Pittsburgh shouted, "All Jews must die," he apparently thought of himself as a savior of the white race. Just prior to the massacre he had posted on social media that he wasn't going to sit by and watch white people get slaughtered by the non-white immigrants, immigrants whose presence could only be blamed on the Jews. He was subsequently glorified by neo-Nazi hate groups, as was the man who stands accused of killing fifty-one Muslims in Christchurch, New Zealand, in March 2019.

White supremacists and white separatists have demonstrated that they are willing to turn to violence in their fight for the American Phantasy, whether it's acted out in hate rallies, neo-Nazi riots, or lone-wolf massacres.

While extremist violence predominantly is the horrid deed of hate groups and their pupils, the narratives promoted by white nationalists are not fringe ideologies.[16] Many current and former government officials, such as senior White House adviser Stephen Miller, Congressman Steve King, former White House chief strategist Steve Bannon, and former attorney general Jeff Sessions, are deeply immersed in white nationalist ideology.[17]

Who Is White?

White nationalists operate with different conceptions of who is white. They generally take their whiteness to consist in their alleged descent from Anglo-Saxon cultures, Nordic cultures, or other white European civilizations.[18] This is not an ironclad rule. Although it firmly locates blacks, Hispanics, Native Americans, and people of Islamic descent in the non-white category, it leaves it open for extremists to stipulate whether Jews are white.

Jared Taylor, the president of the New Century Foundation, a U.S.-based white extremist group that describes itself as a "race-realist, white advocacy organization," defines Jews as white and has referred to them as the "conscience of society."

But Jews are more commonly regarded as non-white. This is the view advocated by the psychology professor Kevin B. MacDonald, one of the directors of the American Freedom Party, a political party founded by skinheads in January 2010 in response to the financial crisis. MacDonald gained popularity in white nationalist circles when he gave his fellow extremists a reason not to deny the fact that Ashkenazi Jews score significantly higher than non-Jews on standardized IQ tests. In his 2004 book, *Understanding Jewish Influence: A Study in Ethnic Activism*, MacDonald argued that because Jews have a higher-than-average verbal intelligence and have lived relatively isolated from other ethnic groups, they have developed a special Jewish competence in outcompeting non-Jews for resources. Numerous Jews, he argued, have used this advantage deliberately to undermine the power of European-derived majorities in the Western world.

Far-right supporters uniformly regard Asians as non-white, but the vast majority of them consider them a model minority group because of their reputation as hard-working, high-achieving, highly intelligent, family-oriented, and capable of easily assimilating into American life and achieving the American Dream, or Phantasy.[19]

Consistent with their misogynist and anti-feminist narratives, many white nationalists also fetishize East Asian women, whom they perceive as naturally inclined to serve men, light their torches, and please them sexually. Their stereotypical physical appearance is also in sync with the feminine ideal: the stereotypical East Asian woman is small, slim, "tight," light-skinned, and cute in a girlish kind of way.

Some white nationalists happily couple up with East Asian women. As Audrea Lim points out in her *New York Times* opinion piece "The Alt-Right's Asian Fetish," far-right figures like Andrew Anglin, Richard Spencer, Mike Cernovich, and Kyle Chapman have been romantically involved with women of Asian descent.[20] White supremacist John Derbyshire is married to and has children with an Asian woman. When he was still working for the *National Review*, he published a list of racist things to tell your children about black people when you have "the talk" with them, but emphasized that the list was intended for both white and Asian parents.

The far right's tolerance and in some cases worship of Asians is a fetish they share with Adolf Hitler. "I have never regarded the Chinese or the Japanese as being inferior to ourselves," Hitler wrote in his testament. "They belong to ancient civilizations, and I admit freely that their past history is superior to our own."[21] Although Germany and Japan were enemies in World War I, Hitler's pro-Asian attitudes contributed to their alliance, which officially began when they consolidated their mutual interests in 1936. At this point the Nazi government officially included the Japanese in its league of "honorary Aryans." Hitler's fondness for Japan peaked following its attack on Pearl Harbor in 1941. When briefed in his headquarters later that night, he exclaimed delightedly: "We can't lose the war at all. We now have an ally which has never been conquered in 3,000 years."[22]

While the white nationalists' Asian fetish is reminiscent of Hitler's pro-Asian attitudes, the model minority myth is not a revival of his concept of "honorary Aryans." Nor is it a white nationalist invention. It's a myth that Asian Americans themselves helped promote during the civil rights movement. The image of the hardworking Asians was quickly co-opted by white politicians who saw it as a convenient way to deny the demands of blacks and Latinos.

The far right's pro-Asian attitudes may look like an odd exception to its hatred toward non-whites. Isn't there a friction between their "Asian fetish" and their core ideology that whites are superior to all other ethnic groups? Not really. White nationalists' pro-Asian attitudes sit well with their inclination to adopt a mindset of tolerance or muffled contempt rather than hatred toward women and non-whites who quietly curl into passive obedience and don't try to contest white male dominance.

But far-righters don't just idealize East Asians who reside in America. They glorify Japan, which—as a result of its political nationalism—has maintained a population of which 98 percent are ethnic Japanese. Ultra-strict immigration policies are partly responsible. Even under the Trump administration, the United States admitted 99,000 refugees from January 2017 to January 2019.[23] Over the same time period the number of refugees resettled by Japan was 48.

Are You a Racist?

In July 2019, President Trump's social-media madness sparked weeks of feverish debate about the definition of "racism."[24] Trump shamelessly tweeted in his usual bully-esque idiolect that the ethnic-minority Representatives Ayanna Pressley, Alexandria Ocasio-Cortez, Ilhan Omar, and Rashida Tlaib should "go back" to the corrupt and crime-infested countries they originally came from.

Donald J. Trump ✔
@realDonaldTrump

So interesting to see "Progressive" Democrat Congresswomen, who originally came from countries whose governments are a complete and total catastrophe, the worst, most corrupt and inept anywhere in the world (if they even have a functioning government at all), now loudly......

♡ 211K   8:27 AM · Jul 14, 2019   ℹ

💬 123K people are talking about this   〉

Donald J. Trump ✔
@realDonaldTrump

Replying to @realDonaldTrump

....and viciously telling the people of the United States, the greatest and most powerful Nation on earth, how our government is to be run. Why don't they go back and help fix the totally broken and crime infested places from which they came. Then come back and show us how....

♡ 186K   8:27 AM · Jul 14, 2019   ℹ

💬 71.6K people are talking about this   〉

Donald J. Trump ✔
@realDonaldTrump

Replying to @realDonaldTrump

....it is done. These places need your help badly, you can't leave fast enough. I'm sure that Nancy Pelosi would be very happy to quickly work out free travel arrangements!

♡ 188K   8:27 AM · Jul 14, 2019   ℹ

💬 71.2K people are talking about this   〉

At a rally in North Carolina a few days later, Trump's criticisms of Representative Omar, one of the four congresswomen, led to the crowd chanting "Send her back!" A week later, Trump added fuel to the fire, stating that the representatives were "not capable of loving the US."[25]

This stirred an international debate about whether Trump's Twitter storms were racist or "just" off-the-cuff xenophobic indiscretions and whether journalists should be in the business of labeling things "racist" as opposed to "racially insensitive" or "racially charged." To many, this debate has been sending a message of its own, namely, that far from being a relic of a bygone era, racism is the ugly truth of modern society. It's about time we identify what lies at its heart.

Philosopher Jorge L. A. Garcia has taken a hard stance on racism. Racism, he argues, is at a minimum a malicious form of racially based disregard for the welfare of people who belong to certain racialized groups.[26] In its most vicious manifestation, racism is hatred of people on account of their designated race. As he puts it:

> In its central and most vicious form, it is a hatred, ill-will, directed against a person or persons on account of their assigned race. In a derivative form, one is a racist when one either does not care at all or does not care enough (i.e., as much as morality requires) or does not care in the right ways about people assigned to a certain racial group, where this disregard is based on racial classification. Racism, then, is something that essentially involves not our beliefs and their rationality or irrationality, but our wants, intentions, likes, and dislikes and their distance from the moral virtues.[27]

According to Garcia, defining "racism" in terms of irrational beliefs about people on account of their designated race fails to capture the hostility that lies at the heart of racism. Even when racists don't have any ill will toward the people they target, a flawed moral character nonetheless underpins their attitudes. At a minimum, racists lack a desire to treat their targets with the decency with which they treat people of their own race.

There is much to be said for Garcia's line of argument. I don't dispute that all racism is antagonistic at its core. My quarrel is with his claim that racism is always underpinned by ill will or malicious disregard. That goes too far. An ignorance-based belief in the inferiority of certain racialized or ethnic groups is a racist attitude, even if it is not premised on ill will or malicious disregard. However, Garcia insists that racism has nothing to do with irrational beliefs. Apparently, he is of the opinion that beliefs by themselves cannot be antagonistic. That doesn't seem quite right, however. The belief that certain racialized or ethnic groups are inferior to other groups is unjustly disrespectful, even if not intended as such. Beliefs of this kind violate Kant's principle of respect for persons, which demands regarding all humans as inherently valuable. It is this kind of dehumanizing racial disrespect incarnate in a person's attitudes or actions that makes that person a racist, a point that has also been made by philosopher Joshua Glasgow.[28]

As we saw in Chapter 1, disrespect is the component that unifies the antagonistic emotions: anger, resentment, envy, disrespect, blame, disgust, contempt, and hate. Defining "racism" in terms of "dehumanizing disrespect" thus entails that dehumanizing racial hatred and contempt are proper forms of racism, as Garcia argues. But they are not the only ways in which racism can be instantiated. Any disrespectful attitude toward others on account of their designated race can bludgeon the humanity out of them. The anti-black disgust that prevailed in the Southern states during the Jim Crow era (late nineteenth century to 1965) is a prime example. As philosopher Martha Nussbaum reminds us:

> In our recent Jim Crow era, which has not entirely disappeared, African American bodies were regarded with disgust, as sources of contamination. Drinking fountains, lunch counters, swimming pools, hotel beds—none of these could be shared. People otherwise intelligent and civilized believed that black bodies carried a powerful taint. As a child of a racist father from the

Deep South (though living in the North), I was told that African Americans smelled differently, that they would spread disease by using the same toilet facilities, that if they used a drinking glass, you had better not drink from that glass again, even after washing it. Although this disgust was based in fantasy, it took on bodily reality: thus, during Reconstruction one hears of people who, having moved from the South to the North and then being seated at a mixed-race table, literally vomited.[29]

During the Jim Crow era, the stereotype that black bodies were sources of contamination, which even heavy cleaning could not remove, elicited a primitive disgust response in whites, discouraging them from sharing drinking fountains, lunch counters, swimming pools, toilet facilities, dinner plates, and drinking glasses, even after thorough cleaning. Primitive disgust was in this way repurposed by the propaganda-disseminating mob as a tool for upholding the existing system of oppression and segregation.

The African-American writer James Baldwin, details his encounter with this primitive form of racism in his 1955 nonfiction book *Notes of a Native Son*: "I learned in New Jersey that to be a negro meant, precisely, that one was never looked at but was simply at the mercy of the reflexes the color of one's skin caused in other people."[30]

The racial violence orchestrated by the lynch mob in the Southern states was fueled by a rather different species of disgust—a perverted, parapathic disgust toward the black body. This very theme of racism as sexualized disgust lies at the heart of Baldwin's short story "Going to Meet the Man," which was published ten years later in 1965. In his exposee, Baldwin masterly demonstrates the perverted, deviant nature of Jim Crow racism, which is revealed as an abnormal, sexual fetish—one that is designed to alienate the reader from the racist characters and their repulsive racial practices.[31] At the outset of the story, Jesse, a racist deputy sheriff, is lying in bed with his wife Grace, initially unable to achieve an erection. Jesse's mind wanders back to a lynching he witnessed as a young child. The black victim—who is viewed by young Jesse as "the most beautiful and terrible object he had ever seen till then"—is approached by a knife-wielding chieftain, who erotically weighs, cradles, stretches and caresses his testicles before he proceeds to brutally castrate him.[32] By recounting the various horrifying and violent racist acts he has witnessed and participated in both as a child and as an adult deputy sheriff, Jesse eventually becomes so sexually aroused that he forces himself on his wife, whispering, "Come on, sugar, I'm going to do you like a nigger; just like a nigger, come on, sugar, and love me like you love a nigger." While raping his wife, "labor[ing] harder than he ever had before," he returns to the morning after the lynching, once again hearing the sounds of "the first cock crow, and the dogs bark, and the tires on the gravel road."[33]

The mob's simultaneous attraction to and fear of black bodies is revealing for what it tells us about the logic of racism: black people do not have human status or inherent worth; their value resides in their utility as tools for alleviating the retaliatory and sexual urges of white men. The lynch mob's treatment of blacks in Jim Crow America is thus a paradigm example of racism embodied in the form of dehumanizing racial disrespect.

The definition of "racism" in terms of "dehumanizing disrespect" accurately reflects both the original and the contemporary usage of the term. According to the *Oxford English Dictionary*, the first recorded use of the word "racism," which was a shortening of the term "racialism," dates back to 1902, but it didn't enter widespread use until the late 1930s.[34] According to James Myburgh, the editor of Politicsweb, the word was "popularized through Mussolini's public embrace of razzismo (racism) in the second half of 1938—and the implementation of severe anti-Jewish race discrimination that followed."[35] The Fascist Party in Italy had earlier condemned racism as unjustified. Their subsequent about-face was fueled by envy of the Jews' perceived privilege and social influence. Endorsing the view that Jews had an inferior racial status was an easy way of justifying the sentiment that their social privilege was undeserved.

Let's return now to the two questions with which we began this section. The first was about the racist status of Trump's July 2019 tweets.

Trump's allegation that the four congresswomen are foreigners is plainly false. They are all citizens of the United States. Representative Omar is the only one of the four not born in the United States. She left Somalia when she was six and settled in the United States four years later. But it's not this misattribution that makes Trump's tweets racist. Rather, it's his claim that if the four elected representatives are unhappy with our government, then they can go back to where they came from. Our president is basically saying that owing to their non-white ancestry, their dissent is not welcome here. They don't have the right to speak freely, at least not until they have fixed the problems in their "own" countries. Apparently, the right to dissent and hence the right to speak freely is reserved for Americans with white European ancestry. This is a shameful example of disrespect for people on account of their ethnic origin. It's not simply a failure at racial etiquette. It's full-blown, in-your-face racism.

This was duly noted by acclaimed journalists, which, however, invited further heated debate: do journalists who use the word "racist" to describe racist acts like Trump's violate the basic tenets of their profession? Surprisingly, even reputable news outlets like NPR, which prides itself on political neutrality, thought so.[36] However, discouraging journalists from using the word "racist" sends the message that "racism" is an epithet, like the N-word, or perhaps a swear word like the F-word. But "racism" is neither an epithet nor a swear word. Yes, calling someone a racist can be offensive. But so can calling someone a criminal or a sex offender. Yet it would be absurd to discourage journalists from using the latter terms.

While Trump's tweets had "racism" written all over them, less blatant forms of racism can be much harder to spot. This is the case for the systemic racism woven into the cultural fabric of America and other societies in which white people enjoy a structural advantage, or privilege, over other ethnic groups. Systemic racism is a system of oppression rooted in history, economics, politics, and culture. When societies publicly condemn explicit acts of racism, as America did in 1968 following the Black power movement, this tends to bring about lasting social change to how we act in public. The majority of us no longer publicly flaunt our racist prejudices in public. We might even convince ourselves that we don't have any prejudices. But we would be wrong. We can't ever fully eliminate the residues of history. Racial prejudices become lodged deep within our psyche long before we graduate from kindergarten, and they continue to leave their marks on our actions.[37] Actions marked only subtly by racist prejudices are also known as "microaggressions." Suppose that on your evening stroll in your secure suburban neighborhood, you spot a black man approach you on the sidewalk, and you instinctively cross the street. Only minutes later you spot a white guy approach you. But rather than crossing the street, you happily greet him as you pass each other. This is a paradigm example of a microaggression. But racial prejudices often lead to much more blatantly racist actions.

Studies conducted by researchers at Harvard University have shown that the majority of Americans, even non-white Americans and social justice crusaders, harbor anti-black prejudices.[38] The perhaps most prevalent prejudice in America today is animosity that results from our automatic mental association of black men with danger and crime. As Harvard sociologist Charles Ogletree has pointed out, "99 percent of black people don't commit crimes, yet we see the images of black people day in, day out, and the impression is that they're all committing crimes."[39]

Not only do our racial prejudices mold our behaviors and attitudes, they even alter our perception. Studies have shown that when volunteers are exposed to images of people holding either a gun or another object, they are much more likely to see the object as a gun when the person is black.[40]

Our prejudices against black men make us prone to interpret and remember information that strengthens our mental association between the concept of a black man and that of a dangerous criminal. This is evident from testimony and eyewitness reports of police shootings of unarmed black men and boys. The police officer who shot and killed Michael Brown, an eighteen-year-old black kid, in Ferguson, Missouri, on August 9, 2014 described him as "demon-like." And the Cleveland police officer who shot and killed Tamir Rice, a 12-year old black child who was playing with a toy gun, on November 22, 2014, testified that he thought the threat to his partner and himself was "real and active."[41]

Mere days before I was getting ready to send in the corrected proofs of this manuscript, tragic reports of racist-infused killings once again surfaced in the media. On February 2020, a former police officer Gregory McMichael and his son Travis McMichael shot and killed Ahmaud Arbery, a 25-year old black jogger, who allegedly matched the description of someone seen on a security camera at a neighbor's construction site.[42] The killing didn't come to the attention of the public until a disturbing video of the shooting emerged online on May 5, 2020. The McMichaels were arrested two days later, and it subsequently came to light that William "Roddie" Bryan Jr., the man who recorded the fatal shooting of Arbery, had assisted the McMichaels by blocking Arbery with his car. Bryan was subsequently arrested on felony murder charges.

On May 25, 2020, another deeply disturbing video recorded by a teenage bystander emerged online.[43] In the video, a Minneapolis police officer is seen pinning George Floyd, a 46-year old black man, to the ground with his knee on his neck, compressing his airway. In a deja vu of the police killing of Eric Garner in 2014, Floyd repeatedly gasps "I can't breathe," and then "I'm about to die."[44] Seven minutes into the video, Floyd's pleas for help go quiet, and a person nearby can be heard saying, "They just killed him." The officer keeps his knee on the unconscious Floyd for almost two more minutes. When paramedics arrived on the scene, no attempts were made to revive Floyd. He was simply put on a stretcher and was taken to a nearby hospital, where he was pronounced dead. Floyd was arrested after officers responded to a 911 call reporting an alleged attempt to pass a counterfeit $20 bill. Surveillance video shows a calm Floyd being led away in handcuffs and in full compliance.

There is no denying that racial prejudices were the driving force behind these killings. We all have the parasite of racism living inside of us, although this is only rarely evident to us when we examine our own minds. Paying close attention to how we behave when we interact with members of oppressed groups could, however, yield insight into our racist inclinations. But prone as we are to self-deception, we often blithely ignore evidence of our own racism or conjure up a creative rein-terpretation of our seemingly racist behavior.

Since the racial prejudices prevalent in our culture are not readily available to our conscious awareness, people who act on their prejudices rarely admit to being racists. This denial is not a conscious attempt to cover up their racism. People sincerely reject the claim that they are racists. This widespread denial is sometimes said to lead to the bizarre phenomenon of racism without racists.[45] But the idea of racism without racists is bordering inconsistency. The unconscious racial biases against black Americans are inherently racist. We can fend off the absurd idea of racism without racists by drawing a distinction between explicit and im-plicit forms of racism.[46] Whereas explicit racists are aware of their racist attitudes, implicit racists are unaware of their inner bigot and their ac-tive contribution to the oppression of marginalized groups.

To be sure, systemic racism is not simply the sum total of people's explicit and implicit racial prejudices. Rather, it is first and foremost constituted by existing norms, laws, and regulations that breed social injustice. However, systemic racism persists in our society because it's tolerated by those of us who benefit from its existence.

Social Darwinism and the Denial of a Common Humanity

The racial hatred and contempt that prevail among far-right supporters are rooted in social Darwinism, a theory first advocated by the nineteenth-century British philosopher Herbert Spencer. Social Darwinism is the application of Darwin's theory of natural selection to social, political, and economic issues. While its core claim, the idea that whites are superior to other ethnicities and therefore are destined to rule over them, predates Darwin's *On the Origin of Species* (1859), social Darwinism was the first theory that attempted to ground the claim in real science.

In eighteenth-century colonial America, white supremacy was backed by pseudo-scholarship advanced as a way for the colonists to justify keeping human beings as slaves while fighting for emancipation from their own "enslavement" by the Brits. The need for justification of the institution of slavery made the patriots capitalize on the latent public opinion that blacks were inherently inferior to white men and perhaps not even human.

They promoted this attitude by endorsing the publication of pseudoscience and pseudo-scholarship claiming that science, the scriptures, or logic proved the inferior status of blacks or their intended purpose as being in the servitude of whites.

In his infamous *History of Jamaica* (1774), the British-born West Indian planter and slave owner Edward Long relied on his own opinionated observations of "Negros" as a basis for a "scientific proof" of their hereditary inferiority. According to Long, "Negros" and white men belonged to different species. The "Negros," he claimed, were "void of genius," incapable of civilization, and without any moral sense. They were portrayed as ignorant, lazy, buffoonish, superstitious, stinky, bulky, shameless, uncontrollably lustful, and sexually promiscuous.

While Long's virulent white supremacy disguised as science is shocking to us today, his views were common among educated people at the time. They had already been widely disseminated by philosophers such as Immanuel Kant and David Hume. Even freedom advocates like Thomas Jefferson, who advocated for freeing the slaves and letting them resettle outside British America, maintained that white men and enslaved blacks constituted "separate nations."

While Long's publication is unlikely to be referenced in furtherance of white supremacy today, social Darwinism is still widely invoked for this purpose by far-right supporters—probably because, on the face of it, it looks very similar to Darwin's theory of natural selection. As we will see, however, social Darwinism is deeply flawed.

Darwin's core idea in *On the Origin of Species* was that the members of the different species are in competition with each other for survival in a habitat with limited resources. The outcome of the struggle for survival is the survival of the fittest. The organisms that are better able to adapt to the habitat are more likely to reproduce and pass on their physical and behavioral traits to offspring. The physical and behavioral traits that were passed on to us from our ancestors in this process of natural selection are characteristics that afforded an advantage for our ancestors in their struggle for survival. Advantageous, or adaptive, traits are traits that help organisms escape or hide from predators, get sufficient nutrition, and reduce injury. The spots on a leopard's fur and the white color of the fur of polar bears are examples of adaptive traits that make predators less likely to spot them in their natural habitat.

Social Darwinists accept Darwin's theory of natural selection but argue that physical and behavioral traits are not the only characteristics that can help organisms survive. Psychological traits like artistic, intellectual, and moral capacities, they argue, can also be advantageous for reproduction and survival. These traits are among the adaptations that have enabled us humans to survive and reproduce, and to progress further than other species on the evolutionary scale. But, they continue, the "human races" have not always been in competition with each other for survival. They have evolved in geographically disparate regions of the world. So, they are not all equally far along the scale of human evolution. People of color, Natives, and Jews—social Darwinists maintain—are at earlier stages of evolution, whereas whites are farthest along. Non-whites are therefore inferior to whites with respect to uniquely human adaptations, such as artistic, intellectual, and moral capacities—adaptations that allegedly explain why whites evolved much further and faster than any other race or species.

Until around 1900, social Darwinists thought of the hierarchy of races as akin to that between adults and children of different ages. This meant that inferior races, much like children, could in principle develop independence and maturity over time, but they would always lag behind the white race in how far they would have evolved. Moreover, because people belonging to the inferior races were like children in their deficient psychological capacities, white subordination and tutelage were necessary means for securing their well-being.

After the emancipation of the slaves in America, proponents of so-cial Darwinism pronounced that black people now had advanced as a race, so much so that enslaving them was now inappropriate, but, they added, blacks had not advanced enough to have the same rights and privileges as whites. For example, Joseph Le Conte, the president of the American Association for the Advancement of Science and the author of *The Race Problem in the South* (1892), wrote that while slavery was no longer appropriate for blacks, who had evolved further under strict dis-cipline, they were still unable "to walk alone in the paths of civilization. [...] In particular, they should not expect to vote."[47]

Although social Darwinism is loosely based on Darwin's theory of evolution, the argument for the superiority of whites is packed with logical fallacies. First, there is no statistically significant correlation between how evolved a species is along the evolutionary scale and its artistic, intellectual, or moral capacities. The most corrupt and blood-thirsty species could easily be the star of the survival game because of its willingness to exploit and manipulate members of other species.

Second, the assumption that the overall group differences in the ar-tistic, intellectual, and moral capacities of whites and non-whites are de-termined by differences in biological inheritance is an instance of the genetic fallacy (like other instances of biological essentialism). In fact, the overall group differences in artistic, intellectual, and moral capacities between whites and non-whites can be fully explained by white people's immoral choices: the fact that whites first kept blacks as slaves and then enforced segregation made it virtually impossible for a black person to demonstrate his or her artistic, intellectual, or moral virtues in the public realm, leaving the false impression that only whites, and white men in particular, had the abilities needed for artistic expression, moral behavior, and rational argumentation.

Third, social Darwinists are confounding "race" as an evolutionary-biological category of the same kind as "species" with "race" as a socio-cultural category with boundaries that change as society is changing.

Although these criticisms were advanced in academic circles around the turn of the century, advocates of the eugenics movement post-1900 reinforced the notion of race as a question of biological inheritance over social environment. This theory was finally discredited in academic circles after World War II.

When contemporary white supremacists, such as Stefan Molyneux, a self-proclaimed "racial realist," employ social Darwinism to legitimize their hateful narratives, they are relying on a discredited theory, repeating the same logical fallacies as its originators did.

But contemporary social Darwinists are not alone in putting whites on a pedestal. As political philosopher Thomas McCarthy points out, theorists in academic circles still make the dubious assumption that white people have superior artistic, intellectual, and moral abilities. The main, admittedly important, difference is that academic theorists tend to attribute social-group differences to social, cultural, or economic factors. As he puts it:

> What is striking about the American discourse of racial difference in the two centuries following the Revolution is how constant the assumptions of superiority and inferiority and policies of domination and deferral remain throughout the many vicissitudes of theory.[48]

Theorists who promote social-group theory take the presumed ethnic, social, and cultural differences between whites and non-whites to call for "paternalistic" intervention. This is highly problematic, as is the underlying presumption of white superiority and the superiority of Western civilization.

But where academic social-group theorists are moved by goodwill and compassion, contemporary social Darwinists are driven by hate and contempt that squash any remnants of goodwill and compassion and wear away at the capacity for rational argumentation. Driven by antipathy, social Darwinists are confounding "different from us" with "deficient" or "defective." Non-whites, they argue, are defective, and their defects are encoded in their genetic blueprint and are therefore resistant to change. So, social Darwinists conclude, only permanent white domination can restrain the unruly dispositions of non-whites and prevent the destruction of the white Nordic-American race.

The far right's appeal to social Darwinism in support of white power is not without irony. White nationalists claim to be victims of Jewish success or immigrants replacing them. But the mantra of social Darwinism is "the fittest social groups survive and thrive." It follows that they ought to accept their defeat in the social survival game.

The Renewal of the "Jewish Question" and the "Great Replacement"

Hitler may have been the one to bring the "Jewish question" to the awareness of the public. But the expression dates back to around 1750, where it was introduced as a euphemism during political debates in Great Britain revolving around the question of the appropriate status and treatment of Jews.

The expression popped up again in discussions in France after the French Revolution in 1789. With his 1843 treatise *Die Judenfrage* (*The Jewish Question*) German historian and theologian Bruno Bauer introduced the term to German intellectuals. In the book, he argued that since religion was incompatible with the secularism of Germany, founded on human rights, the Jews could become assimilated into German secular culture only by relinquishing their religion. The "Jewish question" became the subject of widespread intellectual and public anti-Semitic debate in Germany during the nineteenth and early twentieth centuries, and the allegedly socially dominant Jews were increasingly seen as a racial threat to the purity of the German nation and the cause of the country's erosion. Anti-Semites argued that resettlement, deportation, and laws prohibiting marriage between Jews and Aryans were the only realistic solutions to *Die Judenfrage*.

This culminated in the Nazi interpretation of the "Jewish question" as the question of how to solve the problem of the existence of Jews. Hitler issued his first written comment on this question in 1919, proposing "removal of the Jews altogether" as its ultimate solution.[49] The year Hitler took office as president, Nazi ideologues and party members Johann von Leers and Achim Gercke were contemplating whether resettlement of the Jews in British Palestine would be feasible, as originally proposed by Austro-Hungarian Zionist Theodor Herzl in 1898 in his booklet *Der Judenstaat*. Leers and Gercke both concluded that Jewish resettlement in the Middle East would cause too much unrest and proposed to relocate the Jews to Madagascar or somewhere else in Africa or South America,[50] a proposal that was revisited by the Nazi government in 1938 and launched in 1940. By then, fifteen years had passed since Hitler published the first sketch of his "final solution" to the question: the Holocaust.[51]

The "Jewish question" has gained renewed interest among contemporary white nationalists, alt-righters, and neo-Nazis, who refer to it as "JQ." In the spirit of the Hitler regime, members of anti-Semitic hate groups imagine that a Jewish conspiracy has secured the Jewish people's "undue" social dominance of academia, intellectual life, news outlets, and politics in America. Bob Whitaker, author of "The Mantra," a 221-word attack on multiculturalism, and the American Freedom Party's presidential nominee in the 2016 presidential election, coined the term "white genocide" to refer to the alleged declining percentage of whites in the United States, which he says is a result of deliberate exploitation of white people by American Jews.[52] This Jewish influence has allegedly been instrumental, not only to their success as leaders and thinkers, but also to the popularity of liberal-leftist values and policy preferences that are antithetical to the alt-right's white-power politics.

Jordan Peterson, the clinical psychologist and right-wing provocateur, hit, if not the nail, then the white supremacist on the head when he argued that the "overrepresentation" of Jews in positions of authority, competence, and influence is what we ought to expect given the significantly higher-than-average IQ of Ashkenazi Jews.

The Ashkenazi Jews are the population to which the vast majority of the American and European Jews belong.[53] Although the term "Ashkenazi Jews" refers to Jewish settlers in northern Europe, the settlers can be traced back to a small Jewish population in the Roman Empire who migrated north due to religious persecution. Their higher-than-average IQ is evident from their IQ test scores, which lie eight to fifteen points above the mean.

People with high IQs are significantly more likely to score high on the personality dimension known as *Openness to Experience*, which, Peterson maintains, is "what you are referring to when you describe someone as thoughtful, smart, artistic or philosophical." A high IQ also happens to correlate with a trait-like disposition toward political liberalism. So, the evidence points to a high IQ and its correlation with traits like *Openness to Experience* and *Liberalism* as the reason behind Jewish influence and success, not Jewish conspiracy. "Is the fact that smart people are working hard for our mutual advancement really something to feel upset about?" Peterson asks rhetorically.

Apparently it is. Peterson's post was met with outrage from right-wing commenters, attempting to show that IQ alone cannot account for the disproportionately greater number of successful Jews and that the missing ingredient therefore must be Jewish conspiracy. But this inference is deeply flawed. It is true, of course, that success cannot be read off of an IQ test. But an IQ eight to fifteen points higher than average can contribute to success, not least when combined with other important factors, such as belonging to a culture with a strong emphasis on the value of education, like the Jewish culture.

The notion of the "Jewish question" takes on distinct meanings in the hands of different white-power advocates. This tainted piece of rhetoric is increasingly being used as a stand-in for questions about the appropriate status and treatment of non-whites more generally. In his 2012 essay "Is Black Genocide Right?" Colin Liddell, the editor-in-chief of AltRight.com, wrote, "Instead of asking how we can make reparations for slavery, colonialism, and apartheid or how we can equalize academic scores and incomes, we should instead be asking questions like,

'Does human civilization actually need the Black race?' "[54] By asking whether we actually need the black race, Liddell is elevating his "kind" to the status of judges of life and death, judges who have the power to determine whether black people are "needed." The implied message is that black people have a proper place in society only if they are useful to white people. Liddell's concern is of a kind that could reasonably be expressed about the usefulness of a tool or a machine, as in "Do we really need a juicer in this household?" This is dehumanizing contempt par excellence.

Like the "Jewish question," the idea of a white genocide takes on distinct meanings in the hands of different far-right extremists. In his 2011 book *The Great Replacement*, French far-right extremist Renaud Camus coined the term "genocide by substitution" to refer to the conspiracy theory that white people in France, and in Europe more generally, are gradually being replaced by Muslim immigrants.[55] Camus's book was inspired by the French writer Jean Raspail's 1973 novel *The Camp of the Saints*, which depicts the "end of the white world" as a result of being overrun by a "tidal wave" of Third World refugees. Brenton Tarrant, the gunman who, in March 2019, killed fifty-one people and injured forty-nine at two mosques in Christchurch, New Zealand, paid homage to Camus's theory in a manifesto titled "The Great Replacement."[56] Likewise, Patrick Crusius, the shooter who, in August 2019, killed twenty-two and injured twenty-four at a Walmart in El Paso, Texas, said Camus's book inspired his belief that white Americans are gradually being replaced by Hispanic immigrants.

Camus's "genocide by substitution" is not a fringe conspiracy theory. As revealed in a report by the Southern Poverty Law Center, the conspiracy theory has played a prominent role in shaping the U.S. government's hardline immigration policies.[57] A series of emails that senior White House adviser Stephen Miller wrote to journalists for the far-right news network Breitbart in 2015 and 2016 reveal that Miller promoted *The Camp of the Saints*, the book that inspired Camus, to Breitbart journalists and encouraged them to print news from a white supremacist website promoting the great replacement theory.

This is alarming, considering Miller's role in shaping American politics. The book's anti-immigrant images are hard to stomach. For example, the novel describes the immigrants as "kinky-haired, swarthy-skinned, long-despised phantoms," "teeming ants toiling for the white man's comfort," and "Trash. Nothing but trash. Arabs, criminals, tramps from the street."[58]

The book's influence on U.S. and European politics is evident from the anti-immigrant rhetoric disseminated by political leaders. President Trump has demonized refugees and undocumented immigrants as "filthy animals," "snakes," "thugs," "criminals," and "rapists," who "pour into and infest our Country."[59]

Anti-immigrant rhetoric is equally prominent in Europe. Inspired by Camus's idea of the "great replacement," far-right populist parties paint immigration as "population displacement," "massive invasion," and "substitution."[60] Hungary's prime minister, Viktor Orbán, paints a picture of Europe as a victim, forced to watch with their hands in the air as non-white refugees "kick in their door" and "invade" their land; Germany's far-right Alternative for Germany, the largest opposition party in the country's federal parliament, promotes "remigration," a large-scale resettling of immigrants to their native lands; and the leader of Austria's far-right Freedom Party, Heinz-Christian Strache, who served as the country's vice chancellor from 2017 to 2019, has announced that his party is fighting against "replacement of the native population."

A similar worry about "replacement" underpinned American eugenicist Madison Grant's book *The Passing of the Great Race* from 1916, in which he bemoans the dilution of the pure Nordic-American race by non-Nordic immigrants.[61] A spin-off of the First International Eugenics Congress that took place in London four years earlier, with attendees from several European countries and the United States, Grant's book helped propagate the idea of racial purity across the globe.[62]

"Eugenics" derives from Greek and literally means "well born." It refers to an ideology that promotes social efforts to buttress natural selection with artificial selection aimed at improving the inheritable traits of humans. The eugenics movement was thriving in the first four decades of the United States, with more than thirty states passing forced-sterilization laws. The same fear of replacement that caused the eugenics movement to take root in the United States in the early 1900s lies behind today's white-power movement and its fretting over the endangerment of the white race.

Hatred and Social Immobility

The million-dollar question is why we are witnessing the rise in hatred now. A whole slew of factors ranging from the viscosity of history to political corruption undoubtedly have a role to play. But I think two factors stand out. One is that upward mobility is no longer feasible for most people, making the lower classes easy targets of the far right's manipulation and misinformation. The other is that young people today are much more likely to be hate-prone and desperate for affirmation compared to past generations, making them more susceptible to influence by extremist ideology.

Upward mobility is becoming increasingly difficult for most people in the United States. Even people who belong to the middle class are living from paycheck to paycheck with no hope of ever climbing the socio-economic ladder. Stagnant and struggling, it's shockingly easy for them to succumb to the American Phantasy, whether it's by spraying the internet with hate speech, wielding a semi-automatic weapon at a fast-food restaurant, or voting for a presidential candidate who touts the greatness of our country's mythic past and blames its downfall on non-whites, women, immigrants, and non-gender-conforming individuals.

But how exactly is lack of upward mobility linked to hatred? Public health scientist Maimuna Majumder analyzed two data sets on hate incidents in the United States, one from the FBI and another from the Southern Poverty Law Center, both showing that hate crimes adjusted for variation in population size are not uniformly distributed across the fifty states.[63]

To find out why not, Majumder collected data on key socio-economic factors for each state, including percent non-whites, percent non-citizens, percent population in cities, percent voters for Trump in 2016, percent population with at least a high school degree, seasonally adjusted unemployment, median household income, percent poverty among whites, and income inequality.

After controlling for these variables, she found that income inequality was the most significant determinant of hate incidents per capita.[64] The greater the income inequality, the greater the hate incidents per capita. The only other variable that was significant was percent population with at least a high school degree. The more people with at least a high school degree, the greater the hate incidents per capita.

According to Majumder, this indicates that how likely people are to commit hate crimes may have more to do with how much money they make compared to others in their community than with their objective situation. Those hit hardest by the income inequality—typically those without a high school diploma—are more likely to take out their frustration on non-whites and immigrants.

Majumder is right that the rise in income inequality is a key factor in explaining the rise in hate incidents, but that's unlikely to have much explanatory power independently of considerations of upward mobility. If you are struggling financially compared to your neighbors and you are economically stuck, fighting an uphill battle, you are more likely to become resentful than if you know you are headed down a well-trodden path to economic success.

Feeling resentful about being stuck economically obviously doesn't *make* people violent. But the propaganda and conspiracy theories disseminated by the far right are designed to stoke the resentments of the lower classes among white people. Pre-existing resentments and prejudices among disadvantaged and socially immobile whites make them particularly vulnerable to far-right rhetoric, misinformation, and manipulation. Keeping underprivileged whites where they are on the socio-economic ladder helps the far-right garner support and strengthen its ascendance.

But a second social trend may be contributing to the hatred we are witnessing today. We turn to that next.

Hooked on the Drug of White Nationalism

Throughout history, organized hate groups have been devoted to the recruitment of the youth. The reason is simple: young people are far more susceptible to influence than mature adults. As part of their preparation for the Holocaust, the German Nazis indoctrinated the "Aryan" youth by designing Nazi schoolbooks for use in all disciplines, even those unrelated to politics, social science, or history. The books were aimed at subtly acclimating the kids to mass murder by building up their hostility toward Jews and other ethnic groups. The indoctrination strategy was to desensitize the youth and inflame their smoldering fear and hatred by exposing them to fictive scenarios of mass murder in the guise of homework assignments. The following are two examples of math problems from the high school math book *Mathematics in the Service of National-Political Education* (1935 edition):

Problem 199.
A 1000 kg poison gas bomb contains 70% of poison gas. (1) How many bombs of this kind are needed for the gassing of an area of 2.2 square kilometers (town center of Berlin) if (a) 10,000 kg of mustard gas is necessary for 1 square kilometer, and if (b) 20,000 kg of phosgene is necessary for 1 square kilometer? (2) How many planes would have to be in operation if every plane carried three bombs of this kind? (3) At what intervals of time must the bombs be dropped if the planes have a speed of 50 meters per second and fly in single-file echelon? (4) How

great must the distance between two neighboring planes be?
Solutions:

(1a) 57 bombs	(1b) 114 bombs
(2a) 19 planes	(2b) 38 planes
(3a) 13 1/3 secs	(3b) 13 1/3 secs
(4a) 105 m	(4b) 52 m

Problem 200.
According to statements of the Draeger Works in Luebeck in the gassing of a city, only 50% of the evaporated poison gas is effective. The atmosphere must be poisoned up to a height of 20 meters in a concentration of 45 mg/m³. (a) How much phosgene is needed to poison a city of 50,000 inhabitants who live in an area of four-square kilometers? (b) How much phosgene would the population inhale with the air they breathe in ten minutes without protection against gas, if one person uses 30 liters of breathing air per minute? (c) Compare this quantity with the quantity of the poison gas used.

Solutions:
(a) 7.2 T
(b) 675 g
(c) 0.009%.

The nature and order of these two problems exemplify the Nazi indoctrination tactic for winning over young people. By focusing on the town center of Berlin, where many of the students lived, the first math problem was likely to generate anxiety and fear that an enemy might be gassing the city as well as hateful feelings toward anyone who would do such a thing. The second problem then provides the "solution" to the great danger presented by the enemy.[65]

As today's far-right hate groups borrow many of their tactics from the German Nazis, it should come as no surprise that they put a lot of resources into converting the youth. Schools, colleges, and universities around the United States along with "hip" internet message boards—like the various subreddits dedicated to hatred—are "fertile recruitment grounds," as neo-Nazi Andrew Anglin smugly noted.[66]

The use of "faddy" white nationalist newspeak—like "14 words," "88," "28," "WP," "≠," the "echo," the quadruple hashtag symbol, Pepe the Frog, and the white-power hand sign—which teachers and parents are less likely to recognize, makes recruitment efforts easier, especially on the internet.[67]

One reason young people are more susceptible to influence than mature adults is that, on average, it takes the human brain twenty years to fully mature. This means that the adolescent and the adult brain are wired differently. While the brain becomes more interconnected during puberty, it still relies more on the limbic system, the center of emotion and memory control, than on the prefrontal cortex that is essential for rational decision-making. The result is poor impulse control, a thirst for risk-taking, susceptibility to addiction, and a limited ability to think in the abstract. In other words, the average teenager is better prepared for the zombie apocalypse than the third quarter's Spanish test.

In her 2016 book *White Rage*, Carol Anderson, argues that far-right extremism, like a chemical drug, can be addictive. As she puts it in an opinion piece in *the Guardian*:

> [W]e are seeing the effects of far too many Americans strung out on the most pervasive, devastating, reality-warping drug to ever hit the United States: white supremacy. Like all forms of substance abuse, it has destroyed families and communities and put enormous strains on governmental institutions. It has made millions of Americans forsake their God and jettison their patriotism just to get a taste. High on its effects, its users feel powerful, heady, even as they and everything around them disintegrates. And, as with most drug crises, while not everyone may be strung out, everyone is very surely affected. In 2017, millions of Americans are hooked on this drug. As clearly as track marks in the arms, the most visible signs are all around us.[68]

Is Anderson's suggestion that white supremacy is a drug more than an effective metaphor? Sadly, the answer is yes. As noted in Chapter 2, all-consuming hate is coupled with a brain chemistry reminiscent of the effects of cocaine and methamphetamine. Like coke and meth, profound hate is accompanied by hyperactivation of the brain's norepinephrine and dopamine systems. Hyperstimulation of the norepinephrine system creates a feeling of alertness and stamina, whereas hyperactivation of the dopamine system boosts confidence and the feeling of pleasure and deactivates the amygdala, which is involved in processing fear, pain, and social emotions such as empathy. The hyperstimulation of the dopamine system is also responsible for hate's addictive properties. Addiction is a response to an under-stimulated dopamine system, which is far more common in people with low self-esteem. Over time, the brain adapts to constant excitation of the norepinephrine and dopamine receptors, which means that more potent and frequent doses of the hate drug are needed to achieve the same stimulating effect.

It's understandable, then, that young people, attracted to adrenaline rushes and dopamine highs, soak up the thrills offered by far-right extremism like superabsorbent sponges.

But this is not why youngsters today are more susceptible to influence by extremist ideology than past generations. After all, the slow maturation of the human brain is not an artifact of modern society but a biological adaptation that has been proved to equip us with a survival advantage in the game of evolution.

But young people are not generally treated the same way today as they were even just a few decades ago. In the late 1970s and 1980s, children, tweens, and teens were roaming free till dinnertime or bedtime, playing, biking, and roller skating on the neighborhood streets. A checklist meant to help parents in 1979 decide whether their kids were ready for kindergarten included the question: "Can he travel alone in the neighborhood (four to eight blocks) to store, school, playground, or to a friend's home?"[69]

Parental estrangement made many kids, who felt alone and lost, easy recruits for far-right movements, as Christian Picciolini, former neo-Nazi skinhead and founder of the organization Life After Hate, tragically details in his 2017 memoir *White American Youth*.

The rest have dealt with their own fears and insecurities by over-engaging in their own children's lives. Parents who are hyper-present in their children's lives are also known as "helicopter parents." To the helicopter parent, parenting a child means hovering over their heads, watching their every move. They whir and fret relentlessly and hyper-vigilantly over their precious pearls, oversteering and micromanaging their lives. They secretly want to wrap their children in bubble wrap, hide them in a hermetically sealed safe, and swallow the key.

Over-parented children often grow up without the ability to be in-dependent or grapple with life's ordinary ordeals. They are still attached to their parents by the umbilical cord. Lacking a sense of independence, they often struggle with mood disorders or emotion dysregulation.

Psychologists Holly Schiffrin and colleagues from the University of Mary Washington looked at how helicoptering affects the self-determination and well-being of college students.[70] They asked 297 American undergraduate students, ages eighteen to twenty-three, to describe their mothers' parenting behaviors as well as rate their own autonomy and competence, how well they get along with other people, their level of anxiety and depression, and their overall satisfaction with life. Helicopter parenting was found to correlate with higher levels of anxiety and depression and decreased life satisfaction among kids, as well as lower levels of perceived autonomy, competence, and ability to get along with others.

But that's not all. Helicopter parents also tend to overcompensate for their own insecurities by affirming their children for any achieve-ment, however small. This has fostered a breed of people significantly more likely than the population average to have one of the vulnerable dark personalities: borderline, vulnerable narcissism, or secondary psychopathy.[71] Studies conducted by psychologist Jean Twenge and collaborators have shown that approximately 70 percent of students today score higher on narcissism and lower on empathy than the average student thirty years ago.[72] Significant changes have even been observed within the same generation. In a study comparing early and late Millennials, psychologists Julia Brailovskaia and Hans-Werner Bierhoff found that late Millennials were scored higher on narcissism and sensation seeking than early Millennials, even when the effects of age were controlled for.[73] Entitlement, egotism, and non-compliance—the hallmarks of both grandiose and vulnerable narcissism—were correlated positively with reliance on social media for self-presentation and affirmation. Other studies have shown that late Millennials are more likely than previous generations to present with indicators of vulnerable psychopathy and borderline, such as impulsivity, risk-taking, irritability, aggressiveness, self-absorption, unstable romantic relationships, attention-seeking, low self-esteem, and a strong need for affirmation.[74] Two studies conducted by psychologist Brad Bushman and colleagues found that the current generation of young adults have become so addicted to affirmation that they prefer moments that boost self-esteem to having sex, eating sweets, and drinking.[75]

This should hardly come as a surprise. Many of these kids have been showered with affection. But not unconditional affection. The affection served a purpose: to help the little pearls achieve worldly success. It's merit-based. As David Brooks from the *Houston Chronicle* puts it: "Parents glow with extra fervor when their child studies hard, practices hard, wins first place, gets into a prestigious college."[76]

Children can experience a lack of love and care even when there are no obvious explicit indicators that parents are cold, aggressive, or neglecting. Many over-involved parents use expressions of love and affection as a parenting tool. This is also known as "symbolic rejection," often expressed verbally in the form of implicit potential punitive measures or encouragement: "I don't love you when you throw a hissy fit like this," "I love you, especially when you behave as nicely as you did tonight," "You received an A in Spanish! I love you so much."[77]

Children and adolescents hear these avowals of "love" as declarations of a lack of real love of them for who they are—the kind of love that is meant to be oblivious to achievement and good behavior. From the youngsters' point of view, the best they can hope for on the love front is transient love, meritocratic love, low-tariff love, love that must be earned—but not unconditional love.

Thirsty for accolades, young people with vulnerable dark personalities are highly susceptible to the spell cast by extremist groups committed to bolstering the youngsters' ego as part of their recruitment efforts. Hate groups offer many of the attractions of classic cults, including a higher purpose, a secret lingo, adrenaline highs, and a sense of belonging.

Even hardcore hate groups like the Atomwaffen Division have targeted college campuses as recruitment sites.[78] Joining a militaristic hate group with a strong commitment to hatred of a particular target may quench young people's thirst for approval by creating what Hitler called "blood cement" (*Blutkitt*)—a bond of collective guilt stronger than that between blood relatives and capable of silencing any lingering moral qualms. Hitler allegedly picked up the expression "blood cement" from a book on Genghis Khan (1162–1227), the founder of the Mongol Empire.[79]

In short, two factors seem unique to today's hate culture. (i) Deprived of the opportunity of moving up the socio-economic ladder, lower classes among whites are left searching for scapegoats to blame for their situation, making them easy targets of the manipulation and misinformation of the far right. (ii) A greater proportion of today's youth have vulnerable dark traits compared to past generations. Prone to hatred and craving affirmation, young people of our time are more susceptible to the lure of extremist fringe groups.

The question is what can be done about today's hate crisis. In the next chapter, we will explore some options for curtailing hatred.

8 | ... AND JUSTICE FOR ALL

HATE SPEECH, GROUP LIBEL, AND RATIONAL DISCOURSE

On Sunday, April 15, 2018, a video titled "U Street" with a Face Palm emoji next to it was posted to Twitter showing two males kicking and hitting a man repeatedly while what appears to be a second male victim is seen falling to the ground hard and then lying still in the street.[1]

The victims seen in the video were later identified by their friends on Twitter as the Washington, D.C., residents Michael Creason and Zach Link.[2] Three assailants kicked and punched the two gay men while yelling homophobic slurs.

This was the first of a handful of anti-gay attacks occurring in the same district in D.C. in 2018 alone. Anti-gay attacks, also referred to as gay bashings, became a federal hate crime in 2009 more than a decade after Matthew Shepard, a twenty-one-year-old University of Wyoming student, and James Byrd, Jr., a forty-nine-year-old Texas resident, were brutally murdered, Shepard in a gay bashing and Byrd possibly because he resembled the black inmates who had gang-raped one of his killers in prison.

Named after Shepard and Byrd, the 2009 hate crimes act is an expansion of the 1969 United States federal hate-crime law, which originally permitted federal prosecution of anyone who "willingly injures, intimidates or interferes with another person, or attempts to do so, by force because of the other person's race, color, religion or national origin" while the person is engaging in a federally protected activity, like voting or going to school. In 1994, Congress passed the Violence against Women Act, which contained a provision that allowed victims of gender-motivated violence to sue their attackers in federal court. But six years later, it was struck down by the Supreme Court in *United States v. Morrison*, 529 U.S. 598 (2000), because it was found to violate the Commerce Clause, which allows the government to regulate interstate and foreign commerce but not "State police powers."

The Shepard/Byrd Act removed the 1969 federal hate-crime law's prerequisite that the victim be engaging in a federally protected activity and added crimes motivated by a person's actual or perceived gender, gender identity, sexual orientation, or disability when the crime affects interstate or foreign commerce.

The act reflects the United States' official stance that a motive of group hatred is of a particularly malicious nature and therefore warrants punishing the perpetrator more severely than if the crime had been committed without this motive. Prosecutors and judges rely on factors such as the language used by the accused and the nature and severity of the attack to determine whether the assault was committed with a motive of group hatred.

As of October 2018, the Shepard/Byrd Act had been used to indict eighty-eight defendants in forty-two hate crimes cases, with sixty-four convictions. Twenty states have no hate-crime laws of their own, which means that if a hate crime that occurs in one of those states isn't reported to the FBI or doesn't fall under federal law, assailants will not be charged with a hate crime.

This does not mean that crimes against LGBTQ+ people and other marginalized groups are not punished in those states. All states in the U.S. have statutes criminalizing acts of violence that show a malicious disregard for another person's inherent worth, such as murder, assault, rape, and hijacking.

As a rule of thumb, violent acts are punished more severely the more malicious the motive is. The degree of harm inflicted plays a secondary role. For example, all states in the U.S. treat sexual assault as more severe than almost all other forms of assault, not because it invariably inflicts greater physical injury on the victim, but because the motive behind sexual assault, whether it's to obtain sexual gratification or sexually dominate the victim, is regarded as particularly malicious.[3] The differences in hate-crimes statutes across the United States thus reflect differences in whether state legislators regard a motive of group hatred as particularly malicious.

Where federal and state law come into conflict, federal law prevails, as guaranteed by the Fourteenth Amendment to the Constitution. Even when there are hate-crimes statutes in the state where the crime was committed, the federal hate-crimes law permits federal prosecution of crimes that fall under the law. A federal conviction can carry a harsher sentence that can involve being sent to a federal prison that is much farther away from home than a state prison. The Shepard/Byrd Act therefore is thought to have deterrent effects that go beyond those of state statutes.

Even if the Shepard/Byrd Act should turn out not to provide any extra assurance for protected groups, it has independent practical and symbolic value.[4] Hate-crimes statutes, in general, can help victims feel less marginalized. Victims of sexual violence and LGBTQ+ people who are attacked because of their group membership face a social stigma that often makes them think twice about reporting the attack to the police. The slight comfort of knowing that an act of violence is legally recognized as a hate crime can be what it takes for a survivor to be willing to report it.

Exceptions to the First Amendment

Whereas hate crimes are recognized as a special class of crimes in the United States, hate speech is not legally recognized as a special category of speech. Partly for this reason, hate speech isn't a well-defined type of speech beyond what common sense tells us.[5]

However, to a first approximation, we can say that hate speech is speech that communicates hatred or contempt or incites people to hatred or contempt toward oppressed groups or representative members of these groups on the basis of their group membership.[6] For example, hurling a degrading slur at a black person would tend to communicate contempt toward them because they are black, whereas displaying billboards portraying Muslims as terrorists would tend to incite hatred toward Muslims (or intensify prejudices against Muslims) in viewers.

"Hate speech" is to be understood broadly as referring to all manners of communication used to communicate hate or contempt or incite people to hatred, contempt, fear, or violence, including spoken and written language, sign language, non-linguistic symbols like the swastika or a burning flag, trademarks, pictures, posters, plays, films, podcasts, and television and radio programs.

The United States recognizes the benefits of stricter laws for physical violence and threats motivated by group hate, but this is not the country's official stance when it comes to hate speech. U.S. justices have regarded previous attempts to regulate hate speech as unconstitutional on the grounds that hate-speech laws infringe on the First and Fourteenth Amendments of the Constitution, which compel both state and government to protect the right to free speech.

In recent cases, such as *Matal v. Tam*, 582 U.S. ___ (2017), Supreme Court justices agreed that hate speech is offensive, but they nonetheless maintained that imposing broad restrictions on offensive speech is unconstitutional.[7] The issue in *Matal v. Tam* was an anti-discrimination clause that prohibits registering trademarks that may "disparage" any "persons, living or dead, institutions, beliefs, or national symbols." Pointing out that trademarks are expressive in nature and aren't intended to make factual claims, the justices rejected the anti-discrimination clause as an unconstitutional restriction of speech.

Although hate speech remains unregulated in the United States, not all speech is constitutionally protected. Yes, even in the United States, what you say can land you in jail! Speech that remains unprotected by the First and Fourteenth Amendments includes fraud, perjury, blackmail, bribery, threats of violence, incitement to violence, fighting words, child pornography and other forms of obscenity,[8] speech of strong governmental interest such as unfair trade practices, and speech that isn't of public interest such as defamation and intimidation that occur in the context of a private dispute.[9]

But here is the crux: the laws prohibiting speech like fighting words, perjury, or bribery do not count as hate-speech laws, because they don't offer special protection for marginalized groups. In other words, a motive of group hatred makes no difference to how verbal transgressions such as blackmail, perjury, or threats of violence are classified and handled by the courts. If you tell your coworker who identifies as gay that unless he pays you $1,000, you'll out him to your homophobic boss, that's blackmail. That's a crime but not a hate crime. Saying that it's a crime but not a hate crime means that the courts will regard it as no worse than, and no different from, telling a coworker that unless he pays you $1,000, you'll tell his wife that he cheated on her.

Two recent cases can help shed light on the legal differences between hate crimes and hate speech. On January 21, 2019, a group of teens on bicycles, calling themselves "Bikes Up Guns Down," were blocking traffic in downtown Miami in a protest of the lack of affordable housing in Liberty City, a predominantly black neighborhood. A passerby, Dana Scalione, who had gotten out of her SUV, started screaming at one of the teens and shoving his bicycle for allegedly having run over her foot. Scalione's boyfriend, Mark Allen Bartlett, also jumped out of the car, aggressively approaching, wielding his gun, and repeatedly hurling racial epithets at the kids.

A bystander called the police, and they arrested Bartlett for carrying a concealed firearm without a permit, a third-degree felony.

The teens later filed a civil lawsuit, stating that Bartlett and Scalione violated Florida's hate-crimes statute and demanding a jury trial.[10] The statute provides a cause of action for treble damages, which means that a court is permitted to triple the amount of monetary compensation to be awarded to a plaintiff.

On February 19, 2019, State Attorney Katherine Fernandez Rundle brought enhanced criminal charges against Bartlett, charging him with improper exhibition of a firearm, enhanced to a third-degree felony, and three counts of aggravated assault with prejudice, enhanced to second-degree felonies.[11]

The Florida hate-crimes statute provides increased minimum and maximum penalties for crimes based on the victim's race, color, ancestry, ethnicity, religion, sexual orientation, national origin, homeless status, or advanced age. For example, Florida law increases a charge of improper exhibition of a firearm, a first-degree misdemeanor, to a third-degree felony. Although Florida does not legislate against hate speech under that heading, the fact that Bartlett hurled racial slurs at the teens is not an irrelevant factor in how the criminal case is settled. Because Bartlett threatened the teens with a gun, which is a crime, his racialized speech can be used as evidence that his threatening behavior constitutes a hate crime.[12]

A second case that can help illuminate the legal distinction between hate crimes and hate speech is a federal court decision that took place in November 2018. The Court ruled that a case that had been brought against Andrew Anglin, the publisher of the neo-Nazi website Daily Stormer, could proceed to civil court. Charges were brought against Anglin because he encouraged the readers of his neo-Nazi website to harass Tanya Gersh, a Jewish realtor in Montana, after she became involved in a real-estate dispute with Sherry Spencer, the mother of white nationalist Richard Spencer, in the Montana town of Whitefish in 2016. "Hit Em Up[.] Are y'all ready for an old fashioned Troll Storm? [. . .] Tell them you are sickened by their Jew agenda to attack and harm the mother of someone whom they disagree with," Anglin wrote, according to the suit.

Gersh filed a civil complaint in the spring of 2017, after "she and her family had received more than 700 disparaging or threatening messages in the form of phone calls, voicemails, text messages, emails, letters, social media comments, and Christmas cards." The suit charges Anglin under the "Montana law for invasion of privacy, intentional infliction of emotional distress, and violations of [Montana's] Anti-Intimidation Act."

Anglin initially tried to get the lawsuit dismissed on First Amendment grounds.[13] But in November 2018, U.S. District Judge

Dana L. Christensen ruled that it could proceed, stating that Anglin's call for harassment was not intended to inform the public about a matter of public concern but was instead based on Anglin's "personal hostilities." This is how Judge Christensen explained his ruling:

> "'[N]ot all speech is of equal First Amendment importance,' however, and where matters of purely private significance are at issue, First Amendment protections are often less rigorous." Snyder, 562 U.S. at 452 (quoting *Hustler Magazine, Inc. v. Falwell*, 485 U.S. 46, 56 [1988]). This is so because the regulation of "speech on matters of purely private concern" does not "threat[en] the free and robust debate of public issues" or "potential[ly] interfere[] with a meaningful dialogue of ideas." *Dun & Bradstreet*, 472 U.S. at 760. (*Gersh v. Anglin*, 9:2017cv00050 [D. Mont. 2018])

Judge Christensen added that "The 'inappropriate or controversial character of a statement is irrelevant to the question whether it deals with a matter of public concern.' *Rankin v. McPherson*, 483 U.S. 378, 387 (1987). [. . .] Although Anglin drew heavily on his readers' hatred and fear of ethnic Jews, rousing their political sympathies, there is more than a colorable claim that he did so strictly to further his campaign to harass Gersh."

Marc Randazza, the lawyer who represented Anglin, told the media that the judge's decision was "dangerous for free speech," warning that it could be used to curtail free speech in other forums.[14]

But he is wrong about this. Judge Christensen's ruling has no relevance whatsoever to the free-speech debate. Quite on the contrary. The judge explicitly stated, "The Court cannot find that Anglin's speech is unprotected on the basis that it evinces a morally and factually indefensible worldview." But conversely, the Court also could not and did not find that Anglin was entitled to special federal protection, as his verbal attack on Gersh was personal in character, not fair comment of public concern. Speech that is personal in character is not protected by the First and Fourteenth Amendments of the Constitution.

The Harm in Hate Speech

While there are exceptions to the constitutional protection of speech, hate speech remains unregulated under that heading. But one wonders, is speech really all that different from physical violence or threats of physical violence?

We know that words can injure. If a person verbally abuses you, their words are intended to harm you emotionally. Verbal abuse is emotional violence, or assault. Words can harm others because they are not always used to innocuously describe how things are or ought to be, but also to stir up emotions. Sometimes we use our words to warn others, sometimes we use them to inform, and sometimes we use them to injure. When you make a promise, threaten, apologize, warn, demand, order, joke, tease, belittle, undermine, blame, criticize, humiliate, insult, degrade, and so on, you thereby perform a speech act.

The philosopher John Austin, who developed an influential theory of speech acts, distinguished between three kinds of acts that we perform when we speak, namely, the locutionary act, the act of articulating the words; the illocutionary act, the thing you intentionally do with your words by expressing them; and the perlocutionary act, the change your illocutionary act produces.

Consider this scenario. After a relaxing dinner at your favorite Italian restaurant, you hear an elderly man in the parking lot yell at his female companion, "Hurry up, you old bag, or I am leaving you in the parking lot!" The woman then starts jogging to keep up with him. In this scenario, the locutionary act is the man's utterance. The illocutionary acts are the acts of degrading and threatening. And the perlocutionary act is the act of making the woman move faster. I will use the term "speech act" as short for illocutionary speech acts.

Hate speech is a verbally abusive speech act targeting one or more people on the basis of their group membership. The real motive behind all verbal abuse, whatever its nature, is to retaliate against the target, gain or retain control over them, or prevent them from getting what they deserve.

Hate speech is no different. Hate speakers target representatives of a group or the whole group in order to retaliate against the group, or gain or retain control over the group, or prevent them from getting what they deserve. As retaliation and oppression are morally wrong, hate speech is morally wrong.

The law doesn't prohibit all (or only) morally wrong acts, however. It only proscribes conduct that is threatening, injuring, or otherwise endangering to private property or people's health or safety. Cheating on your boyfriend, for example, wouldn't be legally prohibited, even though it's morally wrong.

But if the law proscribes acts that are threatening, injuring, or otherwise endangering to private property or people's health or safety, why doesn't it automatically prohibit hate speech? Didn't we just establish that hate speech injures people?

Not quite. A person who is verbally assaulted, perhaps repeatedly, does ordinarily suffer emotional harm, but the law tends to shy away from regulating emotionally harmful activities. This is because it is very hard to distinguish between emotional harm that is a direct result of an act and emotional harm that is an indirect outcome of the act, or what is known as a "secondary injury." A secondary injury is trauma, depression, or other mental illness that occurs weeks, months, or years after the initial or primary injury, often brought about by a lack of a proper support system or revictimization. Revictimization typically occurs when the victim is blamed for getting in harm's way. Family members, partners, friends, police officers, prosecutors, judges, social workers, the media, coroners, clergy, and even mental-health professionals can cause secondary injury, which makes attributing secondary injury to the original assailant problematic.

Even when hate speech does not cause long-term emotional damage, it tends to be hurtful. So why don't we simply conclude that hate speech is damaging because it hurts people's feelings? One problem with this suggestion is that hate speech doesn't inevitably hurt people's feelings. A target who is unusually tough, didn't hear what was said, or didn't grasp what was conveyed might not get hurt. But hatred hurled at someone is deeply problematic, even when it fails to hurt anyone's feelings.

Conversely, when "innocent" speech is misinterpreted as hateful, it can hurt people's feelings. Even something as explicit as "I hate you" need not be ill intended. It's not when used as a figure of speech, known as "litotes," to express envy without resentment. This is how it was used in an exchange I overheard between my daughter's classmates Macey and Tanya:

> MACEY: "What did you get on your English paper?"
> TANYA: "A+."
> MACEY: "Really!?! I am so jealous."
> TANYA: "What did you get?"
> MACEY: "A−, which is better than what I got on the history quiz. You didn't get an A+ on the history quiz, too, did you?"
> TANYA (WITH A GRIN): "I did."
> MACEY (SMILING): "I hate you!"

If Macey had said this to someone less familiar with the teen dialect, she might inadvertently have hurt their feelings. But that by itself wouldn't have made Macey's expression legally harmful. Hurt feelings are not a reliable indicator of legal harm.

There are other ways in which the law could classify hate speech as harmful, however. In an influential 2012 book titled *The Harm in Hate Speech*, law professor Jeremy Waldron argues that the harm in hate speech lies in its status as a special kind of libel that defames the members of the targeted group.

Defamation, loosely defined, is the dissemination of a falsehood about a person or group that damages that person's or group's reputation. In legal theory, a distinction is drawn between slander, which is oral defamation, and libel, which is defamation published in print, in writing, or broadcast through radio, television, film, or the public internet. Unlike slander, libel must have a certain permanence of form.

The sort of group libel to which hate speech belongs, Waldron argues, is criminal group libel. Criminal libel used to play a greater role in U.S. jurisprudence than it does today, where libel and slander commonly are treated as torts. But several states continue to keep criminal defamation laws on the books alongside their civil defamation laws, including Florida, Idaho, Kansas, Louisiana, Colorado, Michigan, New Hampshire, and North Carolina. Montana's criminal defamation law was rendered unconstitutional by U.S. District Court Judge Donald Molloy on March 18, 2019, in *Myers v. Fulbright*.[15]

The elements of criminal libel laws are similar to those of civil libel laws. However, a crucial difference between criminal and civil libel is that in civil libel, the damage is to a private or public individual but not to the public as such. In criminal libel, by contrast, the damage is to the public or the state rather than a particular person.

The *target* of criminal libel can be another person, a public official, a social group, a government entity, a public school, and even a deceased individual. While dead people obviously cannot sue others, the defamatory effects on their reputation can sometimes be considered a damage to the state, or the public.

Because the harm in criminal libel is to the state, criminal libel is particularly well suited for Waldron's purposes. If the state is the injured party, there is no need to worry about whether hate speech causes actual damages to particular group members; all we need to worry about is whether smearing group members' reputation harms the public (and not just the individual group members).

How exactly does Waldron think hate speech damages the public? It does so, he argues, because it creates the appearance that members of the targeted group have a diminished social (or legal) standing compared to members of other groups. This change in how society appears to its citizens is a disturbance of public order, Waldron argues, and this is what hate-speech laws offer an assurance against—for all of us.

However, on Waldron's view, the harm in hate speech isn't just a public harm. The public harm of hate speech supervenes on its harm to individual group members. Hate speech harms people, he argues, because it violates human rights, specifically the right to dignity.

Here I will pause for a minute and reflect on the meaning of "dignity," as there appears to be some confusion about this notion. The Universal Declaration of Human Rights proclaims in article 1 that "All human beings are born free and equal in dignity and rights." The human rights are said to derive from the inherent dignity of the human person. Since our inherent dignity is inalienable, so are our rights. They can't be taken away from us. But the Declaration then goes on to state that certain acts, such as torture, are prohibited because we want to "protect both the dignity and the physical and mental integrity of the individual."

But this is incoherent. If our inherent dignity is inalienable, or in-destructible, then why is it in need of protection from destruction? If your beer mugs were made of super-glass, a new material proven to be unbreakable and unscratchable, there would be no need for you to do anything to protect them from breaking.

The inconsistency in the Declaration stems from a common equiv-ocation on the word "dignity." "Dignity" is sometimes used to refer to the inherent, inalienable, and equal worth of all people, a common "es-sence" that entitles all people to be respected as ends in themselves. This is the core idea behind Kant's principle of respect for persons, which renders it morally wrong to treat people merely as a means to an end.

This is not the meaning of "dignity" as it occurs in the passage where the Declaration states that we want to "protect both the dignity and the physical and mental integrity of the individual," because what's inalien-able and indestructible clearly isn't in need of protection.

The confusion arises because, as moral philosopher Remy Debes has pointed out, "dignity" has a multiplicity of meanings most of which have no theoretical substance.[16] Its only substantial meaning derives from translations of Kant's German term *die Würde* ("the worth"), for example, as it occurs in the following well-known quote:

> In the kingdom of ends everything has either a price [*einen Preis*] or a dignity [*eine Würde*]. Whatever has a price can be replaced by something else which is equivalent; whatever, on the other hand, is above all price, and therefore admits of no equivalent, has a dignity.[17]

As a translation of Kant's notion of *die Würde*, "dignity" refers to the inherent or unearned worth all people (and indeed all intrinsically valuable things) share equally.

As Debes points out, the Christian Renaissance writer Giovanni Pico della Mirandola's *Oration on the Dignity of Man* from 1486 is sometimes cited as a historical source of our current use of "dignity." However, *dignitas*, the Latin word for dignity, occurs only twice in his treatise, and in both cases, it refers to the dignified behavior of angels or perhaps God himself. Pico della Mirandola's usage of "dignity" is a likely source of the term's most common colloquial use. Colloquially, "dignity" can refer to the stateliness, gravitas, poise, grace, or other dignified manner we expect of people who are of high rank, who exhibit an extraordinary strength of character, or who lead a highly spiritual life free of bodily depravity. For example, we might say of a person who is moving gracefully that she's moving with dignity.

In colloquial language, "dignity" can also refer to a person's psychological and bodily integrity and wholeness. This is how the expression is used when we speak of a person having a right to die with dignity or a rape victim having been stripped of her dignity.

Conceding that "dignity discourse is cursed by equivocation,"[18] Waldron imbues the term with new meaning. Dignity, on his proposal, lies at the foundation of each person's reputation: a person's dignity is their social standing, which is the general assessment of the person by members of the social community.

People's social standing, Waldron argues, ought to be the same regardless of their membership in a particular group. However, he continues, when we take "dignity" to refer to a person's social standing, their dignity is not immutable or indestructible but needs to be "established, upheld, maintained, and vindicated by society and the law." As members of society, we are all required to "refrain from acting in a way that is calculated to undermine the dignity of other people."[19] This, Waldron argues, is the requirement that hate-speech laws reinforce.

Although Waldron holds that our dignity, or social standing, can be diminished by others, he nonetheless maintains that everyone ought to be regarded as having the same social standing and therefore as having equal dignity regardless of group membership. Human persons are entitled to be regarded as having equal dignity, because they have the same inherent worth. When we portray people as subpar citizens in speech or action, not only do we mistakenly regard them as less worthy than they are, but we also make other members of society likely to see them in this false light.

Is Hate Speech Defamatory?

Waldron's claim that hate speech is harmful because it defames the targeted group seems plausible when the substance of the speech is comprised by disparaging factual claims. Pseudoscientific claims such as white nationalist Gordon Baum's allegation that black people are a "retrograde species of humanity" is an example of a denigrating factual claim about members of a marginalized group.[20] This allegation defames black people by falsely claiming that they are less inherently valuable than whites because of their ethnicity.

Another example of hate speech that makes a disparaging factual claim about members of a marginalized group is speech that attributes a crime to its targets. Such misattribution was particularly prominent in Hitler's speeches. For example, at his table talk in October, 1941, he blamed Jews for the two million deaths in World War I, calling them criminals: "From the rostrum of the Reichstag, I prophesied to Jewry that, in the event of war's proving inevitable, the Jew would disappear from Europe. That race of criminals has on its conscience the two million dead of the First World War, and now already hundreds and thousands more."[21] This is a prime example of group defamation of the sort Waldron has in mind.

The problem with Waldron's proposal is that in many cases, speech that intuitively falls under the concept of hate speech doesn't make a factual claim and therefore is not truth-evaluable, that is, it lacks a truth-value. This automatically disqualifies it from being defamatory, as defamation by definition is the dissemination of a falsehood (plus other conditions).

One type of hate speech that doesn't make a factual claim is slurring speech. There is a growing consensus among philosophers and linguists that slurring speech is not truth-evaluable.[22] Philosopher Renée Jorgensen Bolinger has made a similar point about all kinds of verbal rudeness, including expletives, vulgarities, general pejoratives, and slurs.[23] Expletives are socially disvalued expressions used in outbursts, such as "Goddamnit!" or "Crap!" Vulgarities are tabooed terms that make references to bodily stuff or sexual acts, such as "fuck," "shit," "fart," "dick," and "ass." Pejoratives, or terms of abuse, are used to condemn people for their alleged disvalued behaviors or appearances. "Asshole," "dickhead," "moron," "jerk," "cunt," "cock tease," "fatso," and "liar" all have general pejorative uses. Finally, slurs are pejoratives that make reference to a cultural stereotype associated with a marginalized group. "Nigger," "kike," "faggot," "dyke," "slut," and "cripple" are prime examples. Terms of abuse like "bitch," "whore," "hick," "sissy," and "white trash" have both slurring and general pejorative uses.

Bolinger argues that when it is commonly known that a rude term is linked to a negative stereotype, but a speaker nonetheless chooses to use it rather than a less rude or neutral alternative, she thereby signals that she endorses the negative stereotype. If, for example, Sebastian, who is planning a party, says to his coworker, "I'm not inviting that cunt," referring to his boss who just reprimanded him, then he is signaling that he is endorsing the view that his boss instantiates the negative stereotype associated with the term "cunt," say, that she is a dislikable woman who is exercising hubris and doesn't know her true place in the world. Rude expressions, including slurs, thus convey the speaker's contemptuous or hateful opinion of the targeted person. For example, if a white person uses the N-word pejoratively to refer to a black person, they convey that they think that blacks are lesser humans than whites.

Opinions make a factual claim about the speaker, but not about the target. If I say "I think you are beneath me," I am making a factual claim about what I think, but not about you. So, hurling a slur at another person isn't false (or true) and therefore isn't defamatory.

This criticism of Waldron's framework can be formulated in more general terms within the theory of speech acts. Recall that Austin distinguished among three kinds of acts that we can perform with speech: locutionary, illocutionary, and perlocutionary acts. The locutionary act is the act of uttering the words, the illocutionary act is the act we're intentionally performing by expressing the words, and the perlocutionary act is what we accomplish by expressing the words. If Tim tells Sally to close the door, then the act of uttering the words is the locutionary act. The act of ordering Sally to do something is the illocutionary act, and Tim's getting the door closed by Sally is the perlocutionary act. As noted earlier, I use the term "speech act" as shorthand for the illocutionary speech act.

Which speech acts we perform when we speak (if any) depends on our intentions and sometimes other things as well. If I say "I promise to pay you" but I am insincere, then I have not succeeded in making a promise.

John Searle, Austin's student, developed a classification of speech acts, which will prove useful for fleshing out my objection to Waldron. What Searle calls "representatives" are speech acts, such as statements, descriptions, assertions, allegations, reports, and explanations, that by definition are made with the aim of making the words that are uttered match the world. They have what Searle calls a "word-to-world direction of fit." For example, if you assert that Albany is the capital of New York, your aim is to get things right. But what you assert is right only if your assertion fits the world. As Albany is the capital of New York, your assertion is true.

Searle proposed four additional classes of speech acts, which he labeled directives, commissives, expressives, and declarations. Let's look at each in turn.

Directives are speech acts, such as orders, demands, commands, requests, pleas, permits, invitations, and suggestions, that are aimed at making the hearer do something. They don't aim at making the words fit the world. Rather, they aim at making the world fit the words. They have what Searle calls a "world-to-word direction of fit."[24] For example, if you use "Close the door!" to make Seb close the door, your goal is to get Seb to change the world in such a way as to match your words. You want him to change the world as it currently is and cause it to become a world in which the door is closed. If Seb follows your command and closes the door, then your command is satisfied. But commands and other directives are not in the business of being true or false. The speech act of ordering someone to close the door isn't the sort of thing that has a truth-value. So, it cannot be defamatory.

You can, however, use the language of directives to pretend to be making a directive while sneakily intending to imply a falsehood about the hearer. For example, if I point to you and say, "Pay me right now for the cocaine I gave you. Yup, that bag of powder right there in your pocket," with the intention of conveying that you are guilty of possessing cocaine, that's defamation by implication. Despite the fact that I pretend to order you to do something, I am in fact falsely implying that you are committing a crime.

Let's turn to the class of speech acts that Searle calls commissives. When you make a commissive speech act, such as a promise, a pledge, a vow, an oath, a threat, or a refusal, you commit yourself to some future act. Like directives, commissives don't aim at making the words fit the world. Rather, they aim at making the world fit the words. So, they too have what Searle calls a "world-to-word direction of fit." For example, if

I say, "I promise that I will pay you," and I am sincere, then I intend to change the world in such a way that you have been paid by me.

Commissives make a true claim about the speaker but not about the target. They make a true claim about the speaker because we can only successfully perform a commissive speech act if we are sincere. But that requires that it is true that we promise, pledge, or threaten to do something. For example, if I say, "I promise to pay you," and I am sincere, then I am making a true claim about me. But I am not making any factual claim about you.

The language of commissives can, however, be used with the devious intention of conveying false information about a target. For example, if I were to tell you, "I promise to pay you for the cocaine you gave me," I may succeed in conveying that you have committed the crime of selling cocaine, in which case what I said would count as defamation by implication.

Next, the class of speech acts that Searle calls expressives reveal information about the speaker's emotions. Examples include apologies, congratulations, condolences, forgiveness, and gratitude. Speech acts in this class neither aim to make the words uttered match the world nor make the world match the words uttered. If you thank Seb for babysitting your children or you congratulate Sally on her new job, you don't aim to make your words fit the world; rather, you *presuppose* something, that is, you presuppose that Seb has babysat for you, or that Sally has gotten a new job. When you perform an expressive speech act, your intention is to reveal an emotion, not to say something false about the hearer. So, expressives cannot be defamatory.

But it should come as no surprise at this point that the language of expressives also can be used with the devious intention of making a false claim about the hearer. For example, if I walk up to you and say in a sarcastic tone, "I am so sorry that you got arrested for turning tricks," I am implying that you got arrested for prostitution. But falsely accusing someone of a crime is defamation. So, what I said may count as defamation by implication.

The final class of speech acts in Searle's classification is the class of declarations. Declarations bring a state of affairs into existence. Examples include arrests, baptisms, marriages, divorces, appointments, and excommunications. When you perform a declarative speech act, you are creating something by saying something.

Declarations can only be made by a speaker who is sincere and has the authority to bring about the specified state of affairs. For example, if I say, "You are fired!" "I find you guilty as charged!" or "I appoint you department chair," then I bring it about that you are jobless, guilty as charged, or department chair only if I have the authority to do so, and I am sincere. If I don't have the authority to do so, or I am insincere, then I don't succeed in declaring that anything become the case. I simply fail to make a declaration.

Although the overt content of declarations isn't defamatory, we can intentionally use the language of declarations to make false assertions, which then can have defamatory effects. For example, if I dress up as a police officer and stop you on the street, shouting, "You are under arrest for the murder of your wife!" I have presented you in a false light to other people on the street. That would count as defamation.

In short: we can only defame someone if we intentionally imply a falsehood about them. When we make directive, commissive, expressive, or declarative speech acts without intentionally implying a falsehood, that's not what we do. So, Waldron is unable to account for the harm of hate speech that takes the form of directives, commissives, expressives, or declarations. To see this, consider the following examples of hateful speech acts found online:[25]

- Get off my property, filthy fucking jew! (directive)
- I swear that I will persist until all of you Muslims are dead. (commissive)
- I hate faggots. (expressive)
- You niggers are under arrest for dealing. (declaration)

Extremely nasty examples of hate speech! Yet if the speaker is sincere and is not implicitly conveying any factual claim, then none of them counts as group defamation. This is because they are directive, commissive, expressive, and declarative speech acts, respectively, and these four types of speech acts are not in the business of making false (or true) claims. So, Waldron's account cannot explain why these awful examples of hate speech are harmful.

At the outset of his book, Waldron himself offers an example of a speech act that isn't aimed at describing the world. He writes:

> A man out walking with his seven-year-old son and his ten-year-old daughter turns a corner on a city street in New Jersey and is confronted with a sign. It says: "Muslims and 9/11! Don't serve them, don't speak to them, and don't let them in." The daughter says, "What does it mean, papa?" Her father, who is a Muslim—the whole family is Muslim—doesn't know what to say. He hurries the children on, hoping they will not come across any more of the signs.[26]

The person who posted the sign "Don't serve Muslims, don't speak to them, and don't let them in" is likely making a demand, which is a directive speech act. Because it is not aimed at portraying the world as it is, but rather aimed at demanding that the hearer refrain from doing something, it would be a stretch to call it group libel.

Waldron, however, takes it to "send a message" to the members of the minority denounced on the sign, namely, the following message:

> Don't be fooled into thinking you are welcome here. The society around you may seem hospitable and nondiscriminatory, but the truth is that you are not wanted, and you and your families will be shunned, excluded, beaten, and driven out, whenever we can get away with it. We may have to keep a low profile right now. But don't get too comfortable. Remember what has happened to you and your kind in the past. Be afraid.[27]

And it sends a message to others in the community who are not members of the minority under attack. Waldron continues:

> We know some of you agree that these people are not wanted here. We know that some of you feel that they are dirty (or dangerous or criminal or terrorist). Know now that you are not alone. Whatever the government says, there are enough of us around to make sure these people are not welcome. There are enough of us around to draw attention to what these people are really like. Talk to your neighbors, talk to your customers. And above all, don't let any more of them in.[28]

That's the point of the sign, Waldron says, "that's the point of hate speech—to send these messages, to make these messages part of the permanent visible fabric of society so that, for the father walking with his children in our example, there will be no knowing when they will be confronted by one of these signs, and the children will ask him, 'Papa, what does it mean?'"[29]

The sign, of course, doesn't actually convey complex messages of this sort. Waldron is speaking rhetorically. But couldn't he insist that the sign, while used to make speech acts that are not truth-evaluative, also conveys the claim that Muslims have a lower social status than people from the speaker's group because they are Muslims?

Waldron could indeed insist on this, and that is probably his point, that all hate speech conveys a falsehood of this kind. That might seem to blunt our objection that because the sign is making a demand, it fails to defame anyone.

Upon further scrutiny, however, the proposed fix on behalf of Waldron fails on several counts. One is that the Islamophobe who posted the sign needn't have intended to convey any false claims. Her intention could simply be that of demanding that readers don't serve Muslims, don't speak to them, and don't let them in. This would make her a terrible person, but it wouldn't make her guilty of group libel.

A second reason against the proposed fix on behalf of Waldron is that even if the Islamophobic poster intended her message to be offensive to Muslims, the message she conveys isn't that Muslims have a lower social standing in society than other groups but rather that she endorses a claim of this sort. This follows directly from leading accounts of offensive speech, such as that proposed by Bolinger. But the claim that *the speaker thinks* Muslims have a lower social standing in society than other groups isn't a factual claim about Muslims. It's a true factual claim about the speaker.

A third reason against the proposed fix is that if the Islamophobic sign did in fact send the message that Muslims have a lower social standing than other groups because of their ethnicity, then that message could (sadly) be true, in which case it's not defamatory. Unlike a person's inherent worth, people's social standing in society, their dignity, in Waldron's sense, is not an immutable or indestructible entity, as he himself points out. Their dignity depends on how they are regarded by other members of society. An accomplished scientist who discovered a cure for cancer and a child sex offender who is serving time in prison do not have the same social standing in society, even though they arguably are equals when it comes to their fundamental rights to a minimally decent treatment. Likewise, the Islamophobic poster could argue that because social status depends on how people are regarded by the members of society, and the members of society share her opinions, it is true that Muslims have a lower social standing than the group to which she belongs. If most other members of society are as Islamophobic as she is, then she might be right about this. But in that case, her implied claim that Muslims have a lower social standing in her Islamophobic society is true, not false. So, the Islamophobic person isn't defaming anyone.

The upshot is that Waldron's thesis that the harm in hate speech lies in its defamatory nature only applies to a very limited class of hate speech. However, I will now present a different argument for why even non-factual hate speech should be regulated.

The Argument from Communicative Rationality

In his riveting contributions to political philosophy, German philosopher and sociologist Jürgen Habermas, one of the most influential political theorists of our day, has developed a theory of practical rationality intended as an alternative to a moral philosophy, such as Kant's, which posits fundamental, objective, rationally necessary, and unconditional moral principles.[30] Habermas agrees with Kant that there are objective, rationally necessary, and unconditional moral (and other normative) principles. But he disagrees with Kant that such principles have their special status independently of our faculty of reason. According to Habermas, objective, rationally necessary, and unconditional moral principles have this special status because they cannot reasonably be denied. This approach places Habermas in the pragmatist tradition with respect to normative truth. In the literature on truth, this view is also known as anti-realism about truth.[31]

At the heart of Habermas' theory are the concepts of *communicative rationality* and *communicative action*. Communicative rationality is a normative ideal implicitly underlying the process of reaching uncoerced consensus in communication. A statement offered in a verbal exchange is communicatively rational when it's "defensible against criticism" and is aimed at overcoming merely subjective opinion and reaching mutual agreement "through the medium of reason."[32]

Communicative action is cooperative discourse regulated by the norm of communicative rationality. It's the basis for securing the political legitimacy of democracy. Democracy requires not only that each citizen has a vote but also that they have a voice. Everyone must have had a fair opportunity to engage political authorities and other members of the critical public in legitimate debate. But, Habermas argues, not all forms of communication are legitimate.

Expanding on the theories of speech acts set forth by Austin and Searle, Habermas identifies three classes of (illocutionary) speech acts that satisfy the ideal of communicative rationality: constative, normative, and expressive.

Constative speech acts are sincere assertions about what is true. A statement is sincere only if the speaker believes it is true and is able to defend its truth against criticism. "Elizabeth Warren was running for president," "The Bill of Rights didn't originally apply to the states," "Biofuels are more efficient than oil as an electricity source," and "The jury found McGuire guilty of first-degree murder" are all examples of assertions about what is true.

Normative speech acts are sincere assertions about what is right. "We ought to change the healthcare system," "(You must) stop smoking now," and "It's your turn to make dinner tonight" are all assertions about what is right.[33]

Expressive speech acts are sincere assertions about the speaker's own state of mind, including introspections, emotions, opinions, and perceptions. "I am not sure," "You hurt my feelings," "I think you are being insincere now," and "I heard on NPR that Trump is planning a North Korea–U.S. summit" are prime examples.

When we perform a constative or normative speech act, Habermas argues, we offer what he calls a "legitimacy claim" to the audience, and the audience can then accept, question, or reject the claim. For example, if you sincerely say, "It's your turn to make dinner," you thereby offer a legitimacy claim, which I can accept by making dinner, question by asking "Why?," or reject by citing a legitimate reason. If I question your legitimacy claim, the ideal of communicative rationality requires you to either retract your claim or defend it by providing reasons for it, for example, by reminding me that we agreed to take turns making dinner.

We also offer a legitimacy claim to our audience when we perform expressive speech acts. But unlike constative and normative speech acts, expressive speech acts cannot always be defended using language. But if they are incompatible with the speaker's behavior, they can then be legitimately questioned.[34] For example, if you say that you love animals, but you are cruel to your dog, then we have reason to doubt the sincerity of your claim.

The legitimacy claims we offer when we engage in communicative action, that is, when we perform constative, normative, or expressive speech acts, are thus internally connected with reasons and grounds. This is what makes speech of this kind communicatively rational.

Unlike communicative action, strategic speech isn't intended to abide by the ideal of communicative rationality. Rather than being a tool for attempting to reach consensus or mutual understanding, its sole aim is to coerce others into blindly endorsing ideologies they would otherwise have questioned or rejected.[35] Strategic speech thus vitiates the fundamental human rights to self-determination and autonomy.

Habermas recognizes two kinds of strategic speech: manifest and latent. Manifest strategic speech carries its rotten incentive on its sleeve, so to speak. Examples include *overt* threats (e.g., "Join our movement, or we will make life miserable for you!"), aggressive demands (e.g., "Stop blocking the road!" uttered while the speaker is wielding a gun), hostile questions (e.g., "Are you going to give me the money, or do you want me to tell your wife about your affair?"), and contemptuous expressives (e.g., "I am so sorry that you got arrested for turning tricks").

Latent strategic speech is strategic speech in sheep's clothing, that is, it's disguised as communicative action. For this reason, it can be much more insidious. Example of latent strategic speech that doesn't qualify as hate speech per se include greeting your chronically late coworker with "Hey, you're on time!" with the intention of making him feel bad about his tardiness, and telling your unmarried frenemy "How are *you* still single? You're so pretty!" with the aim of making her think something is wrong with her.

According to Habermas, latent strategic discourse is distorted communication:

> The validity basis of linguistic communication is curtailed surreptitiously; that is, without leading to a break in communication or to the transition to openly declared and permissible strategic action. . . . The confounding thing about "systematic distortion" is that the same validity claims that are being violated

(and violation of which has pathological effects) at the same time serve to keep up the appearance of consensual action.[36]

As law professor Sarah Sorial points out, Holocaust deniers increasingly disguise fact-grubbing as reasonable argument or legitimate historical scholarship. Their favored mode of public engagement is civil and respectable language that appears to conform to the ideal of communicative rationality. Yet by appealing to the democratic ideals of freedom of speech and equal participation in order to coerce adversaries into accepting undemocratic draconian ideals, such as white supremacy and neo-Nazism, they are covertly violating the basic canons of rational communication.

Despite appearances, members of the public who deploy manifest or latent strategic speech in political debate are not engaging in communicative action and therefore are not making legitimate contributions to democratic interaction. In fact, Habermas argues, speech strategically intended to deceive one's adversary is counterproductive to the goal of securing the legitimacy of democracy.

Now, my proposal is to offer an explanation of the harm of hate speech by drawing on Habermas' theory of communicative rationality. As we will see, this will allow us to classify certain forms of speech as hate speech, even if they don't portray anyone in a false light and therefore aren't defamatory. It should be noted that we can embrace this perspective on hate speech without having to endorse Habermas' pragmatist/anti-realist account of objective, rationally necessary, and unconditional principles.

Manifest hate speech is aimed at reaching consensus by silencing targeted group members or convincing would-be bigots to subscribe to the haters' agenda.

The street sign, cited by Waldron, that states "Muslims and 9/11! Don't serve them, don't speak to them, and don't let them in" is an example of manifest hate speech. As we saw earlier, Waldron's claim that this message is an example of group libel is highly questionable, as it doesn't obviously convey any factual claim and hence is not false (or true). Yet it's a very nasty and hateful sign, and there is therefore no doubt that it ought to count as legally harmful. But the sign is harmful, not because it defames, but because it's intended to coerce the public into agreeing with the speaker's Islamophobia. The coercive strategy here is to activate the cultural stereotype (or implicit bias) that Muslims are terrorists. So, the reason the sign should count as a hate speech crime, on my view, is in large part that by posting the sign, the speaker is intending to manipulate or coerce the public into adopting a racist ideology.

Hate speech disguised as reasoned debate may succeed in convincing members of the critical public by making them numb to legitimate concerns. Holocaust deniers, for example, may disguise their unsound arguments and their lack of evidence and pretend to be offering a legitimacy claim to their audience. But the appearance of legitimacy masks a twisted and intractable hinterland of ill intentions. Holocaust denial camouflaged as reasoned debate is not aimed at reaching consensus or mutual understanding. It's a dangerous contagion aimed at infecting the public with Jew-hate. It's a prime example of distorted communication, pretending to honor the ideal of communicative rationality while laughing at it behind its back.

As hate speech, whether manifest or latent, is incompatible with the goal of reaching genuine agreement or mutual understanding in deliberations, it's at odds with the ideal of communicative rationality and is therefore counterproductive to the goal of securing the political legitimacy of democracy.

Let's now look at how this proposal fares compared to Waldron's. A key difference between my proposal and Waldron's is that whereas he takes the speech content to be the key factor in determining whether speech is harmful, I propose to regard hate speech crimes as malice crimes, which is to say, the mindset of the speaker plays a major role in determining whether the speech is harmful. Proof of malice here would require proof of intent to deceive, manipulate or coerce, or reckless disregard for the self-determination and autonomy of other people.

Waldron's proposal has a further serious drawback. Because it ties hate speech to group defamation, it runs the risk of overgenerating.

Indeed, we can look to our allies overseas to adjudicate its success. In Europe, hate-speech laws that treat speech as unlawful when it has defamatory effects have all too often been used to sanction political expressions that are deemed upsetting but which many of us would not regard as hateful.[37] For example, on one occasion several European protesters speaking up against decisions made by the Israeli government were convicted of hate speech crimes. Although the Israli Government and the Jewish population are distinct entities, the reason for the convictions was that the anti-Government signs carried by the protesters were held to defame Jews.[38]

By contrast to Waldron's proposal, my proposal does not trace the harm of hate speech to the speech content, or the manner of expression; rather, the harm of hate speech can be traced to the malicious mindset of people engaging in hateful linguistic practices aimed at silencing, harassing or intimidating members of marginalized groups, or aimed at advertising hatred to young people or others looking for a scapegoat for their struggles.

New Strategies for Combating Hate

Limited restrictions on free speech are not a stop-all-hate tool. Many other strategies for combating hate need to be explored. But simply preaching that we need to become more tolerant is not the answer to today's hate crisis. The million-dollar question is how societies can conquer the hate that lingers even with limited restrictions on hate speech.

A promising strategy for pushing back against the growing white nationalist movement and its hateful narratives is to educate the young before it's too late. Nora Flanagan, a teacher at Northside College Preparatory High School in Chicago, has developed a toolkit to help parents, students, teachers, school administrators, and the wider community combat white nationalism at schools. The toolkit, which is published by the non-profit organization Western States Center in Portland, Oregon, offers concrete advice about what to do when confronted with white nationalist hatred or sneaky recruitment tactics, like placing racist or anti-Semitic flyers inside library books.[39] Suggestions range from learning to recognize the ever-growing number of white nationalist memes, characters, symbols, and phrases to cleaning swastikas off the bathroom wall with an alcohol wipe.

While teaching the young to resist the seduction of hate groups is a powerful way of muzzling the growth of the white nationalist movement, this strategy won't work for the not-so-young or youngsters raised by hatemongers.

But there are other promising strategies for combating extremist movements, some more long-term than others, such as mitigating the massive social inequity among members of society through activism, electing representatives committed to putting an end to political corruption, persuading social-media moguls to refuse to host hatemongers' hateful message boards, enhancing people's opportunity to have their voices heard, and making our voting systems more effective and fair.

I am one with those who argue that merely giving every citizen a vote doesn't satisfy the demands of democracy. Democracy, by its very nature, requires that everyone has a vote as well as a voice. In fact, one of Habermas' main concerns about contemporary society is that political decision-making is increasingly less influenced by rational communication among civil members of society. When we do exchange information, the purpose of the exchange is rarely that of communicating sincere beliefs that are aimed both at being true and at reaching agreement or mutual understanding.

Hate groups use communication platforms to reinforce their own hateful views of non-whites and women or trick others into adopting their ideology. But even those of us radically opposed to their hateful viewpoints all too often use communication platforms for the purpose of flaunting our "fantastic" lives publicly or semi-publicly or engage people whose political views are virtually identical to ours in rational discourse, which defeats the purpose of rational communication as a tool for fair decision-making. Perhaps this is one of the main threats to democracy today.

One reason most of us don't even bother attempting to have conversations with political opponents on online message boards is that the anonymous nature of the internet makes it too easy for trolls to boycott any attempts at rational communication. Events that allow face-to-face communication are more promising places to attempt to engage political opponents in rational communication. But this requires that committed individuals make organized efforts to make it happen. Thus far, there aren't a lot of venues of this kind. One notable exception is Civic Saturdays, which Eric Liu, the founder of Citizen University, started together with his spouse in Seattle and which since then have propagated to other cities.[40] Civic Saturdays are local assemblies where different-minded people from local communities get together to engage in rational communication about social, ethical, and legal issues.

Another strategy that could move us closer to Habermas' ideal of communicative rationality is to change the electoral system in a way that encourages political candidates to engage voters and each other in successful communication, aimed at reaching agreement or mutual understanding. Political scientist Larry Diamond has long been advocating for ranked-choice voting.[41] In this type of electoral system, voters rank candidates in order of preference. The ranked votes are counted differently in different implementations of ranked choice voting. In instant-run-off voting, where there is one winner, the candidate with the majority of first-choice votes wins. If no candidate receives the majority of first-choice votes, the votes for the candidate with the fewest first-choice votes are allocated to the candidate ranked second by those voters, if any. This is repeated in a series of run-off rounds until there is a majority vote. In multiple candidate elections, a common ranked-choice system is to elect the candidates that get the required number of first-choice votes. If there are additional seats available, then the primary candidates' surplus votes are transferred to the voters' next choice candidates. If yet further seats are open, the votes from the candidate with the lowest number of first-choice votes are transferred to the voters' next choice, and so on.

Ranked-choice voting makes it harder for politicians to win simply by catering to their partisan base. To secure as high a rank as possible, they need to engage not only first-choice voters but also, say, second-, third- and fourth-choice voters. Ranked-choice voting thus discourages political candidates from engaging in insincere campaigning, such as character assassinations of opponents, or "mudslinging," and seduction dances in swing states. Because votes for candidates that are unlikely to get a lot of first-choice votes are transferred to the next choices on voters' ballots, this system also makes a candidate's "electability" less of an issue.

Ranked-choice voting is used in parliamentary and local elections in a number of countries around the world. It's been used in Australia for federal lower house seats since 1918 and in Ireland for parliamentary elections since 1937. In the late 1990s and early 2000s, countries like Fiji, Malta, and Papua New Guinea followed suit.[42] In United States, ranked-choice voting was ratified for state and federal elections in Maine in 2016. If the bill is not blocked by Maine Republicans' veto campaign prior to the November 2020 election, this will be the first use of ranked-choice voting in a presidential election in the United States.[43] A number of American cities and counties have implemented or moved to adopt ranked-choice voting for local elections, including New York City, San Francisco, and Santa Fe, among many others.[44] Hawaii, Kansas, Wyoming and Alaska furthermore use ranked-choice voting in primary presidential elections, which has the further advantage that the votes for candidates who have dropped out of the race can be allocated to voters' backup choices.[45]

Depending on how it's implemented, ranked-choice voting may make little or no difference in elections with only two candidates. Here, cardinal voting, where candidates are independently rated, rather than ranked, could be a suitable alternative.

Another alternative to ranked-choice voting is an electoral system that gives the public the power of using their single vote to either support a candidate they like or vote against a candidate they dislike.[46] Call this "Yea-or-Nay voting." This system should not be confused with parliamentary procedures in which voters have the power of verbally approving, disapproving, or abstaining in response to a call for action. As an electoral procedure, Yea-or-Nay voting requires choosing whether you want to use your vote to back your favorite candidate or oppose your least favorite candidate. The winning candidate is the one with the greatest number of adjusted favorable votes.[47] Yea-or-Nay voting gives political candidates and their supporters an incentive not to aggravate an opponent's base to the point of being willing to use their single vote against them. It thus has many of the same advantages as ranked-choice voting but is a more direct indicator of a candidate's relative popularity or unpopularity.

Both types of electoral system give political candidates an incentive to engage voters and other candidates in rational communication during campaigning, and because elected candidates better reflect the support of a majority of voters, not just a plurality of voters, they are more likely to be successful in engaging voters after their election. Because such voting systems promote the ideal of communicative rationality, they could rightly be called "rational voting systems."

Rational voting systems encourage rational communication and discourage hate speech, which is a form of failed communication. This makes it a promising way to curtail the rise in group hatred and political polarization and start engaging with each other across party lines.[48]

Summary of the Book's Argument

Narrow hate and contempt are antagonistic emotions—attitudes that condemn their targets for their supposedly flawed character. In hate, the target is condemned for dark traits assumed to be the source of some moral injury they have inflicted on the hater or someone in the hater's circle of concern. In contempt, the target is condemned for pitiful traits assumed to be the source of appalling practices or conditions.

Condemnation is a form of disrespect rendering the subject as "low" relative to some standard. The disrespect in hatred is often overshadowed by the apprehension or fear we experience in response to the envisioned potential power and danger of evil people.

As disrespect can be dehumanizing or critical, so can hatred. While dehumanizing hatred is deplorable and best avoided, critical hatred can be rational and expressions of it morally appropriate, but only when the hatred is personal rather than being targeted at groups. Personal hate also plays a part in upholding the norms of our personal and social relationships.

Although dehumanizing hate and contempt don't play any worthwhile role in our lives, they are central to explaining evil, mass murder, genocide, misogyny, and the far-right movement in the United States and Europe.

Propaganda and "fake news" are disseminated as means for turning people's pre-existing antipathies toward the targeted groups into full-on hatred and contempt. Spontaneous group polarization, the tendency of groups of like-minded individuals to move to extremes during deliberation, is a group-level force that explains why propaganda and misinformation work.

Demagogues and hatemongers capitalize on misogynistic and white nationalist ideologies as a way of rationalizing hate-based violence against non-whites, immigrants, and women. One factor that may be contributing to the escalation of hatred against non-whites and immigrants is that upward mobility is increasingly more difficult. Deprived of the opportunity of moving up the socio-economic ladder, lower classes among whites are left searching for scapegoats to blame for their situation, making them easy targets of the manipulation and misinformation of the far right. Another potential factor turns on the empirical finding that a significantly greater number of young people have vulnerable dark traits compared to past generations. Prone to hatred and craving affirmation, today's youth are more susceptible to the lure of extremist fringe groups.

But, I have argued, politicians and lawmakers have it in their power to curtail the hate crisis, among other things, through limited legislation of hate speech, as is already done in Europe and elsewhere.

There has been a major backlash against Europe's hate-speech laws. Opponents legitimately point to abuses of this kind of legislation in several European countries.

However, I think the reason European hate-speech laws may do more harm than good is that they focus exclusively on the *effects* of hate speech.

To avoid absurd limitations on speech, we need to make hate speech a matter of speaker intentions or speakers' reckless disregard for the rights of others. Most U.S. states already regulate speech that presents a threat to specific individuals. But when speakers intend to *force* their own views on the public in illegitimate ways, then the speech violates the very ideals the First Amendment aims to protect, and such speech therefore shouldn't be considered free speech.

An obvious worry about making hate speech contingent on specific intent or reckless disregard is that specific intent and reckless disregard are notoriously hard to prove, as the recent presidential impeachment inquiry demonstrated. But proving intent or disregard isn't impossible, especially not when the harmful speech is recurrent. Importantly, creating an obstacle to proof of liability by requiring proof of intent or disregard errs on the side of caution, and thus moots the most forceful criticism of European hate-speech legislation.

CONCLUSION

(OR, THOSE WHO DON'T LEARN
FROM HISTORY ARE DOOMED TO
REPEAT IT)

When Myrtle Vance, the three-year-old daughter of the town sheriff, was found strangled in Paris, Texas, in 1893, suspicion fell on Henry Smith, a young black man. He had been beaten up by the sheriff prior to the child's disappearance, and it was rumored that he wanted revenge and that he had been seen with the girl on the day of her disappearance. The evidence against Smith was, however, circumstantial at best. As anti-lynching activist and investigative journalist Ida B. Wells-Barnett noted in her 1895 pamphlet *The Red Record*, Smith was widely described as a "harmless, weak-minded fellow" with no prior criminal record.[1] He had even volunteered in the search for the body. Desperately wanting a scapegoat to hold accountable for his loss, the sheriff accused Smith. A false charge of rape was added, in Wells-Barnett's words, "to inflame the public mind so that nothing less than immediate and violent death would satisfy the populace."

Smith fled the town, likely with the help of family members, but authorities caught up with him in Arkansas and brought him back to Paris, Texas, where a crowd of more than ten thousand spectators were awaiting his lynching.[2] In the town's main square, Smith was tied to a ten-foot-tall platform, and his clothes were torn off. For nearly an hour, the sheriff, his brother-in-law, and his twelve-year-old son took turns pressing red-hot iron against Smith's skin one inch at a time, starting with his feet and ending with his face. An iron rod was thrusted down his throat, and his eyes were burned out. The crowd cheered and chanted gleefully as Smith screamed in agony. Still fully conscious, Smith was then covered with kerosene and lit ablaze. The fire burned through the heavy rope that held him up, and he fell to the platform engulfed in flames. To everyone's surprise, he scrambled up to his feet, jumped down from the scaffold, and rolled out of the flames. Some spectators looked away, sickened by the sight, but a few men at the front jumped out and grabbed him and threw him back into the fire, where he burned to death.

Extrajudicial violence—or lynching—has a long history in America, stretching back to the colonial era and continuing well into the twentieth century. But as historian Grace Elizabeth Hale notes in her 1998 book *Making Whiteness*, the lynching of Smith was "the founding event in the history of spectacle lynching . . . the first blatantly public, actively promoted lynching of a southern Black by a large crowd of southern whites."[3] The event was widely advertised, the town had chartered excursion trains free of charge for whites, and professional photographs of the lynching were taken and later sold as prints and postcards.

The main purpose of spectacle lynchings was to uphold the ideals of white supremacy: racial "purity," white privilege, and white power. As *New York Times* columnist Jamelle Bouie observed, white supremacy of the time was rooted in a "collective bargain."[4] White laborers received a low wage but were compensated by a "public and psychological wage," which came in the form of free admission to public functions, public parks, and the best schools, leniency by the courts, and social status. As the rights of blacks took on new dimensions, this wage was put in jeopardy. By impressing the power of white supremacy, spectacle lynchings helped curb the threat to the social order and keep the lower classes of whites calm and content.

Many public lynchings were called for by townspeople even when a formal trial of the accused was already scheduled.[5] This was the case in the 1903 lynching of George White, who was accused of raping and murdering Helen S. Bishop, the daughter of a minister. After a guilty verdict by a coroner's jury, White was committed to a jailhouse to await a formal trial three months later. But the townspeople were furious about the delay of "justice," which prompted Reverend Robert A. Elwood of the Wilmington Olivet Presbyterian Church to deliver an ominous sermon, where he declared the justice system broken. Incited by hatred, a mob stormed the jailhouse and demanded a confession from White. After securing a confession, the mob fit a noose around his neck and dragged him from the jailhouse to the place where the assault had occurred. Crowds of townspeople were cheering them along en route. An even bigger crowd was waiting at the lynching site in their carriages to get a "memorable glimpse" of Smith being burned alive.

Why did people opt for, even insist on, such dehumanizing and excessive brutality when given a choice? Research in psychology has shown that when members of groups are competing with an outgroup, they go through a process of deindividuation, which results in a diminished sense of individuality and a suppression of normal reactions and inhibitions.[6] Deindividuation may have contributed to the voyeuristic thrill, an almost Dionysian ecstasy, the spectators experienced at the spectacle lynchings, but it doesn't explain the shockingly violent lust for vengeance and the population-wide push to bypass formal trial and due process.

A more plausible explanation is that dehumanizing attitudes toward a target weaken people's ordinary responses to the target's pain and suffering. But not all dehumanizing attitudes could possibly have this effect. The mere attribution of a subhuman status to some group of individuals doesn't motivate cruelty. We classify dogs and cats as subhuman without being the least bit inclined to cause them pain and suffering.

In this book, I have argued that what moves executioners, and the spectators who cheer them on, to commit indescribably cruel acts is dehumanizing hatred. Unlike purely cognitive acts, such as beliefs and judgments, emotions have motivational force, and all-consuming emotions like dehumanizing hatred can have an almost insurmountable motivational force.

Dehumanizing hatred is morally indefensible in part because of the immense lust for vengeance that pulsates at its core. However, this evident truth may seem to clash with the view that emotions are special kinds of perceptual attitudes—a view I subscribe to.[7] Perception isn't the kind of thing that ordinarily can be subject to normative judgment. If you mistakenly see a dog as a wolf, we might recommend that you see an eye doctor, but we wouldn't ordinarily label your perception as "bad," "wrong," or "nasty." As philosopher Christine Tappolet has pointed out, however, unlike most ordinary cases of perception, emotions involve negative or positive appraisals, and those appraisals may themselves be subject to moral assessment.[8]

When we are possessed by dehumanizing hatred, we regard the targeted individuals as having committed (or intending to commit) an unforgivable act because of their evil character traits. When hatred dehumanizes, it casts our fellow human beings as deserving of inhumane cruel treatment, not *because* the hated individuals are believed to be subhuman (even if they *are* thought of in this way), but rather because profound hate is coupled with hyperactivation of the brain's norepinephrine and dopamine systems.[9] Hyperstimulation of the brain's norepinephrine system increases your alertness and stamina, whereas hyperactivation of the brain's dopamine system boosts your confidence and feeling of pleasure. It also deactivates the amygdala, a small almond-shaped part of the subcortical brain, which is involved in processing fear, pain, and social emotions such as empathy. It is this neurophysiological profile of hatred that deprives dehumanizers of their ordinary resistance to inflicting suffering and pain on others.

How prone people are to become possessed with hatred depends not only on external factors but also on their pre-existing character traits. As we have seen, the key orchestrators of lynchings and genocides possess dark traits that make them far more prone to dehumanizing hatred than passive onlookers and those actively resisting the violence.

Group hatred is often entangled with contempt. This is evident from the way we use expressions like "hate mail," "hate group," "hate speech," and "hate crime." Hate and contempt serve opposite-directed political purposes. Group hate is an effective tool for eliciting fear in the oppressed group to discourage disobedience. Group contempt, by contrast, is a powerful way of shattering outgroup members' sense of self and making them believe they are inferior to their oppressors, thus ultimately ensuring the perpetuation of social inequality and oppression. When group hate and group contempt are widespread in a society, they can also serve as instruments for "rationalizing" racial violence, or the threat of violence sometimes used in ethnic cleansings. In his 2006 book *Buried in the Bitter Waters: The Hidden History of Racial Cleansing in America*, investigative journalist Elliot G. Jaspin argues that at the time of the spectacle lynchings, racial cleansings took place in many counties in the United States, especially in the South. The mob would officially announce a date and a time by which blacks would have to be gone to avoid being killed. Those who owned property were forced to leave it behind without ever being remunerated.

People of color have continued to be a key target of white supremacists ever since spectacle lynchings and racial cleansings were commonplace in America, especially in the Southern states. During the second half of the twentieth century, anti-black and anti-brown hatred seemed to relocate from society's core to its fringes. But group hatred certainly is no longer a fringe phenomenon, if it ever was. Jews, Muslims, women, immigrants, and members of the LGBTQ+ community are also increasingly targeted by hate groups or lone wolves. It's a rare day when we are not bombarded with news of yet another hate crime, often of massive proportions.

Group hatred often takes on dehumanizing proportions, which makes it unfitting, irrational, and morally indefensible, but there is another reason group hatred lacks fit, logic and moral sense: it inaccurately portray all members of a given social group as being engaged in criticizable conduct that flows from their criticizable character traits.

As we have seen, hate can be fitting, rational, and morally appropriate when it is directed at individuals rather than groups and contains no remnants of dehumanization or retaliatory desires. Only critical hate is fit to play this role and only when it's directed at individuals and is not underpinned by a thirst for vengeance.

Critical hatred is morally defensible when it's fitting and rational, *and* its true purpose is to help safeguard personal or social norms and values. To be fitting, its target must be deserving of the hate. But that's not all. Just because the target is deserving of hate, that doesn't mean that the hate is fitting. To be fitting, it must be directed at the target *for* harm they inflicted (or plan to inflict) due to their sinister character. The hatred must also be of the right magnitude.[10]

Both critical hate and resentment involve recognizing other people's inherent worth, which raises the question of what the difference is between critical hate and resentment. In this book, I have argued the main difference between them is that the target's character is a focus of concern of hatred, but not of resentment. Resentment can be rational when directed at people who don't have particularly dark traits but who have acted "out of character." Hatred cannot.

As I use the term, *rationality* is a prudential matter; it concerns the interests of the person who possesses the emotion. An emotion can be fitting and nonetheless still be irrational.[11] Critical hate that is a source of cognitive dissonance or is so all-consuming that it poisons your mind, to borrow an expression from the early-twentieth-century German philosopher Max Scheler, is irrational, even if its target acted wrongly and the wrongdoing is underpinned by dark character traits.

As we saw in Chapters 2 and 3, hate can sometimes help safeguard personal or social norms and values. If, for example, your hatred motivates you to break out of a dysfunctional relationship or avoid contact with a toxic person, then it helps safeguard your interests. In short, not all forms of hate are inherently nasty.

Group hatred is the true villain in our current hate crisis, which raises the question, what can be done to curtail it? Politicians and policymakers, I have argued, have it in their power to address group hatred, for instance, by legislating against hate speech.

There has been a major backlash against European hate-speech legislation. Opponents legitimately point to abuses of this kind of legislation in several European countries.[12] While intended to "curb the incitement of racial and religious hatred," as MSNBC analyst and former Obama official Richard Stengel puts it in his call for hate-speech legislation in the United States,[13] these laws have frequently been used to sanction political expressions that are deemed upsetting but that many of us would not regard as hateful.[14]

Here are just two of many examples. In 2012, a British Muslim teen was arrested after having referenced the killing of innocent Afghans by British soldiers, adding: "All soldiers should DIE & go to HELL! THE LOWLIFE FUCKIN SCUM! gotta problem go cry at your soldiers grave & wish him hell because that where he is going."[15]

In 2015, France's highest court upheld the criminal conviction of twelve protesters for wearing T-shirts with the print "Long live Palestine, boycott Israel."[16] The court ruled that it violated France's restrictions on hate speech.

Neither the British teenager nor the twelve protesters were targeting social identity groups. After all, neither soldiers nor the Israeli government constitute social identity groups.

Such chilling effects of hate-speech legislation doesn't give us reason to become radical free speech crusaders. They merely give us reason not to do what the Europeans do. The reason European-style restrictions on hate speech can have such chilling effects is that European legislators take speech that *appears* hateful to *be* hateful, regardless of the speaker's mindset.

Germany, France, and Iceland specifically mention group defamation—speech that defames groups by stating or implying falsehoods about their members. The view that the harm in hate speech resides in its defamatory effect is the view defended by law professor Jeremy Waldron. We looked at the problems with this view in Chapter 8 but let me quickly summarize the main points. The idea that the harm in hate speech resides in its defamatory effects is overly preoccupied with the subjective consequences of speech. Consider Waldron's prime example of hate speech printed on a sign: "Muslims and 9/11! Don't serve them, don't speak to them, and don't let them in." This is not defamation, in the legal sense, because defamatory speech must at a minimum be false. Legal theory does recognize what is known as defamation by implication. So, perhaps the message on Waldron's sign implies something that is defamatory. But it's not at all clear what exactly that message implies. Presumably, most English speakers today would interpret the sign as conveying that Muslims are terrorists. But interpretation is not implication. Expanding the notion of defamation to include defamation by interpretation leaves it open to interpret nearly any statement relating to social identity groups as hate speech. For example, a harmless statement like "I don't think it's right for the American government to side almost exclusively with Israel" might be *interpreted* as conveying an anti-Semitic message.

We can avoid such absurdities, I have argued, by making hate speech partially a matter of malice. When speakers intend to *force* their own opinions and sentiments about social identity groups upon other members of the public in illegitimate ways, their speech violates the very ideals the First Amendment aims to protect, and such speech therefore shouldn't be considered free speech.

An obvious worry about making hate speech contingent on malice is that malice can be notoriously hard to prove, as witnessed by the recent presidential impeachment inquiry into the "Ukraine affair." But proof of malice clearly isn't unattainable, especially not when the harmful speech is recurrent. Importantly, creating an obstacle to proof of liability by requiring proof of malice errs on the side of caution, and thus avoids the most ludicrous implications of European-style hate-speech legislation.

Long story short, I am not calling for radical restrictions on freedom of expression. In fact, I am a staunch advocate of free speech, free press, and academic freedom. Merely giving every citizen a vote doesn't satisfy the demands of democracy. Democracy, by its very nature, requires that everyone has a vote as well as a voice, which in turn requires freedom of speech and opportunity to speak. Encouraging rational communication that aims at reaching mutual understanding and creating more opportunities for more people to speak and be heard may help preserve the democratic ideal envisioned by the framers of the Constitution and, hopefully, can also help prevent the current hate crisis from spiraling out of control.

NOTES

Prologue

1. Andrew Solomon, "The Reckoning: The Father of the Sandy Hook Killer Searches for Answers," *New Yorker*, March 10, 2014, https://www.newyorker.com/magazine/2014/03/17/the-reckoning, retrieved May 15, 2019.

2. Reclaiming Narrative Truth, "Changing the Narrative about Native Americans: A Guide for Allies," https://rnt.firstnations.org/wp-content/uploads/2018/06/MessageGuide-Allies-screen.pdf, retrieved June 23, 2019. See also Garet Bleir and Anya Zoledziowski, "Hate in America: Native Women Are 10 Times More Likely to Be Murdered," News 21, August 20, 2018, https://newsmaven.io/indiancountrytoday/news/garet-bleir-and-anya-zoledziowski-news21-missoula-mont-native-american-women-across-the-JcYnboa74EqLjuujZLHYzw/, retrieved September 30, 2019.

3. Wray Herbert, "The Anatomy of Everyday Hatred," Huffington Post, May 23, 2014, https://www.huffpost.com/entry/the-anatomy-of-everyday-h_b_5380440, retrieved May 2, 2017. See also Aumer-Ryan & Hatfield (2007).

4. See Sethi (2018).

5. Arendt (2006 [1964]). The book was first published in 1963.

6. Cesarani (2006).

Chapter 1

1. Hume (2000, p. 214).

2. On hate's elusive nature, see Hume (2000, p. 214); Kant (2006 [1798], p. 150); Darwin (2009, p. 249). For discussion of hate's historic reputation as resistant to analysis, see Brudholm & Johansen (2018).

3. The web search, conducted on August 30, 2018, included both the target emotion entry and its cognates, for example, "pride" and "proud." The search didn't include names of emotions that double as proper names, such as "Joy."

4. "Hygge" (pronounced "hue-guh") is an emotion word when used self-reflectively, as in "jeg hygger mig," which is semantically related, but not equivalent, to "I am enjoying myself." However, "hygge" can also be used as an adjective to describe an event or situation that feels cozy, charming, or special.

5. Ben-Ze'ev (2000).

6. Allen (2008, chap. 1, p. 12).

7. For a state of the art take on evaluative perception, see Bergqvist & Cowan's (2018) introduction to their edited volume *Evaluative Perception* as well as the contributions to that volume. For an innovative take on evaluative looks, see Martin (2010). Martin argues that there is a class of evaluatives which track nothing but our responses to the evaluated entity (e.g., "splendid" and "awesome"). The primary use of this class of evaluatives is to characterize visual appearances. So, he argues, "look" sentences containing this class of evaluatives (e.g., "Jacky looks stunning in her pink Chanel suit") have a reading that is not available for most non-evaluative "look" sentences (e.g., "The apple looks red"). Martin takes this as a basis for skepticism about the idea that the semantics of evaluative "look" statements can be exploited as evidence for a particular perceptual model of evaluation uptake. See also the book symposium forthcoming in *Philosophy and Phenomenological Research* on my *Seeing and Saying* with contributions by Alex Byrne, Mike Martin, and Nico Orlandi.

8. Ben-Ze'ev (2002), Mason (2003), Prinz (2004a, 2004b), Nussbaum (2016), and Protasi (2016), among many others, appeal to a similar distinction between an emotion's target and focus (of concern).

9. To identify the target (if any) of an emotion E, you can ask a "Whom" question, for instance, "Whom are you E at?" To identify the focus of an emotion E, you can ask a "Why" question, for instance, "Why are you E?" "Whom" questions about sadness such as "Whom are you sad at?" have no answers, because they are ungrammatical. So, sadness doesn't have a target. The answer to "Why are you sad?" gives you the emotion's focus of concern, for instance, "(Because) Morgan doesn't live close to me anymore."

10. Ekman (1994), Ekman & Friesen (1986).

11. Aragón et al. (2015).
12. See e.g., Lutz (2001), Barrett (2006, 2017).
13. See e.g., Tschalaer (2017).
14. See e.g., Garrido. & Davidson (2019).
15. Lutz (2001).
16. The "five stages of grief" model is further developed in Kübler-Ross (2005). As the model is based on observations made mostly in contemporary Western cultures, it may be that grief itself and not just its expression is culturally variable.
17. Prinz (2004b).
18. Ekman (1994). Gervais & Fessler (2017) make a strong case for thinking that contempt is a complex emotion.
19. Plutchik (2001), Miceli & Castelfranchi (2018). See also Prinz (2007).
20. See Brogaard (2015). The question of an emotion's valence is a tricky one. We often respond with emotional pain when we feel that we are treated unjustly, but antagonistic emotions such as hate and anger can sometimes result in an activation of the brain's dopamine system, which can lead to a pleasurable high that is similar to the euphoria that motivates the recreational use of cocaine and methamphetamine. This pleasurable high is likely to partially numb the emotional pain of feeling unfairly treated. So, even when an emotion ordinarily has a negative valence, its discomfort can be permeated by pleasure. In such cases, the emotion is also said to be "parapathic" (Apter, 1992, 1997; Brogaard & Hernandez, 2020). A paradigm example of a parapathic emotion is the "thrilling" fear we experience when watching a horror movie. We return to parapathic emotions in Chapter 2.
21. Derek de Koff, "Hollywood's Most Arrogant Celebrities," NickiSwift. com, https://www.nickiswift.com/126738/hollywoods-most-arrogant-celebrities, retrieved June 16, 2019.
22. For the role of blame in anger, see also Pereboom (2014, p. 128).
23. As MacLachlan (2010) has argued, the injustice that is the focus of resentment and indignation need not be a *moral* injustice.
24. This distinction between benign and malicious envy has been defended by Protasi (2016), who attributes it to Aristotle. See also Neu (2000, ch. 3), Goldie (2000, ch. 8), D'Arms & Jacobson (2000), D'Arms & Kerr (2008), D'Arms (2009).
25. See Protasi (2016).

26. Protasi (2016, 2017).

27. Ben-Ze'ev (1990), Solomon (2006), D'Arms (2009), Protasi (2017).

28. See also Scheler (1972 [1913]), Darwall (2013).

29. Solomon (2006, p. 38).

30. The wish to have (had) the envied person's advantage must also be (prudentially) rational in order for the envy to be (prudentially) rational.

31. Scanlon (2008, p. 136).

32. At least during Q&As. See also Wallace (2011).

33. Smith (2013).

34. Hieronymi (2001, p. 546).

35. Frank Newport, "Martin Luther King Jr.: Revered More After Death Than Before," *Gallup*, January 16, 2006, https://news.gallup.com/poll/20920/martin-luther-king-jr-revered-more-after-death-than-before.aspx, retrieved July 2, 2019.

36. Darwall (1977, p. 38). See also Darwall (2004, p. 49; 2006).

37. Darwall (1977, p. 42).

38. The view here attributed to Darwall, viz. that recognition respect doesn't involve an appraisal of the target's character, is somewhat contentious. For example, one could argue that the most evil among evil people (think Josef Stalin, Adolf Hitler, and Ted Bundy) don't have what it takes to be worthy of recognition respect.

39. I am going to set aside the tricky issue of whether all humans are entitled to recognition respect. Perhaps extreme depravity testifies to a lack of inner dignity, or worth. But better safe than sorry, we should err on the side of caution and regard everyone as worthy of respect.

40. Kant (1997 [1785]).

41. Rawls (1971, 1980, 1989); Korsgaard (1986, 2008, 2009).

42. Feinberg (1973). See also Dillon (1992, 2018).

43. Feinberg (1973, p. 1).

44. Twain (1996 [1884], chs. 4–7).

45. As cited in Carleheden et al. (2012).

46. Siri Carpenter, "Harvard Psychology Researcher Committed Fraud, U.S. Investigation Concludes," *Science Magazine*, September 6, 2012, https://www.sciencemag.org/news/2012/09/harvard-psychology-researcher-committed-fraud-us-investigation-concludes, retrieved January 3, 2020.

47. Chris Harris, "Mom Admits She Aided in Teen Daughter's Rape, Murder, Dismemberment; Calls Girl a 'Nonentity,'" *People*, March 21, 2019,

https://people.com/crime/mom-admits-she-aided-in-teen-daughters-rape-murder-dismemberment-calls-girl-a-nonentity, retrieved March 22, 2019.

48. Greek Mythology, https://www.greekmythology.com/Other_Gods/Nemesis/nemesis.html, retrieved May 8, 2020.

49. Sher (2005, p. 68).

50. See, e.g., Monteiro & Azevedo (2010).

51. Darwin (2009 [1872], p. 106).

52. Emma Löfgren, "Dog Tries Swedish Fermented Herring for the First Time," TheLocal.se, August 19, 2016, https://www.thelocal.se/20160819/watch-this-dog-eat-swedish-fermented-herring-for-the-first-time, retrieved January 8, 2018.

53. E.g., Nussbaum (2001, 2006, 2018).

54. Nussbaum (2018, p. 104).

55. Rozin's research on disgust can be found in Rozin, Millman, & Nemeroff (1986), Rozin & Fallon (1987), and Rozin et al. (1994). See also Strohminger (2014).

56. Nussbaum (2018, p. 107).

57. See also Kelly (2011), Nussbaum (2018).

58. As noted by Giubilini, the term "moral disgust" is sometimes used to refer to disgust elicited by a judgment to the effect that an act or practice is morally wrong. Since disgust is a reflex-like response, I will assume that the judgment of moral wrongness is subsequent to the disgust. For discussion, see Giubilini (2016).

59. Korsmeyer (2011, p. 122), Nussbaum (2018, p. 105).

60. Bruun Rasmussen, "Danish Avant-Garde," December 6, 2017, https://bruun-rasmussen.dk/m/news/171120_3.html, retrieved December 19, 2018.

61. "My Car Is My Lover," BBC America, https://www.youtube.com/watch?v=ahZTpiayz3I, retrieved January 5, 2010.

62. Rousseau (1978 [1762]).

63. See Boyd (2004).

64. The "I hate your face" memes are tricky. In some of the memes, the hated face is supposedly punch-inviting. This suggests that the person is provoking you with his face to the point of inciting you to violence. Perhaps "I hate your face" is simply an idiom, meaning "seeing your face makes me want to punch you."

65. The case is based on the Jason Niemasz rape case. Jameson Cook, "Soccer coach convicted of raping 12-year-old player," Macombdaily.com, January 26, 2017, https://www.macombdaily.com/news/nation-world-news/soccer-coach-convicted-of-raping-12-year-old-player/article_c53a8476-cd4e-5ad2-9321-354f8b5fb927.html, retrieved January 7, 2020.

66. See also Bell (2005, 2008, 2011, 2013), Cogley (2018).

67. "Disdain," "contempt," and "scorn" are often used synonymously. However, scorn is arguably not an emotion but the behavior accompanying public displays of contempt.

68. Miceli & Castelfranchi (2018) argue that disrespect is a component of both contempt and disgust. But, as we have seen, you can find a person repulsive without thereby disrespecting or judging them for their disgust-eliciting characteristics. For example, if you learn that your coworker get sexually aroused from licking eyeballs (yes, that really is a thing!), you might naturally react with disgust toward him, yet you need not therefore look down on him with withering contempt.

69. See also Bell (2005, 2013).

70. Kant (1996 [1797], 6: 462).

71. Ben-Ze'ev (2000, p. 309).

72. Hall (2010, p. 25).

73. On the difference between anger and hate, see also Ben-Ze'ev (1992).

74. As Thomas Brudholm and Birgitte Schepelern Johansen shrewdly observe: "One does not simply hate someone or something. One hates them or it for being or having done something; one hates it or them for a reason; one believes or judges it or them to be or represent something" (2018, p. 93).

75. Wray Herbert, "The Anatomy of Everyday Hatred," Huffington Post, May 23, 2014, https://www.huffpost.com/entry/the-anatomy-of-everyday-h_b_5380440, retrieved May 2, 2017.

76. Gaylin (2003).

77. See, e.g., Nusbaum (2001, 2016, 2018).

Chapter 2

1. See also Brudholm (2010).

2. LaFollette (1996, p. 10).

3. See, e.g., Sherman (1989, 1993), Thomas (1989).

4. On the relationship between virtue and human flourishing, see also Annas (2011).

5. Cocking & Kennett (2000, p. 287).
6. See also Ebels-Duggan (2008), Koltonski (2016).
7. A similar account of (close) friendship can be found in Friedman (1993, p. 191).
8. See also Helm (2010, 2012, 2014).
9. See also MacIntyre (1999).
10. LaFollette (1996, p. 10). Alfano (2016) makes this point about friendship, or what I would call "close friendship."
11. Alfano (2016, p. 188).
12. Watson (1975, 1993, 1996, 2004).
13. Doris is mostly concerned with a valuational account of (morally responsible) agency but develops a valuational account of the self in Ch. 8. A valuational view of agency can also be found in Watson (1975, 1996). See also Frankfurt (1971), Slote (1980, 1982), Velleman (1992), Bratman (2001, 2007, p. 48), Smith (2005), Schlosser (2015), Sripada (2016, 2017). The kind of agency at stake here is that of autonomous (or "full-fledged" or "deep") agency. This presupposes Davidson's (1980, 1987) notion of agency in terms of intentional behavior. There is some reason to think that the etiology of our informational and motivational attitudes and reasoning capacities can compromise our autonomous agency; Slote (1980), Mele (2001), Fischer & Ravizza (1998), Vargas (2006, 2013a), Brogaard & Slote (2020, forthcoming). For example, if an evil scientist plants an irresistible desire in Mother Teresa that motivates her to torture babies, her actions are nefarious but arguably not fully autonomous. But we can account for the compromised autonomy without appealing to historical factors. If Mother Teresa retains her actual values, she will disown her nefarious desire. The lack of autonomy in desire-inception cases is thus explainable on a valuational account of autonomy, or self-determination. A different question is what to say in response to value-inception cases. Doris has argued that value-inception cases make no difference to agency. As he puts it: "if your action properly expresses your values, it's an exercise of agency, regardless of whence your values came" (2015, 30). I am sympathetic to that idea. But more needs to be said to explain our intuitions in value-inception cases that involve our core values. Changes to our core values can sometimes be the result of changes to our personality or character, or vice versa. Changes to our core values might, if radical enough, make us a different "person" by altering our "self." If an evil scientist makes torturing babies one of Mother

Teresa's core values, then arguably she is no longer the same person as the Mother Teresa we love and admire. Similar remarks apply to questions of moral responsibility. Manuel Vargas (2013b, p. 277) has argued that desire-inception cases undercut moral responsibility, when the desire is irresistible. I think that is right, provided the agent disowns the desire. Agents who truly value their irresistible desire seem morally corrupt regardless of the etiology of their values.

14. Bratman (1987), Doris (2015, p. 27).
15. In previous work, I have argued that when we regard others as irreplaceable, this indicates that we value them in some way, not that we love them (Brogaard, 2015).
16. Doris (2015, p. 28).
17. Sen (1977), Elster (1983), Nussbaum (2001), Barnes (2007, 2015, pp. 123–135), Beach (2015).
18. See, e.g., Sen (1977), Elster (1983), Bovens (1992), Nussbaum (2001), Pettit (2006), Baber (2007), Barnes (2007, 2015, pp. 123–135), Bruckner (2009), Beach (2015).
19. Barnes (2015, p. 127).
20. Fricker (2007).
21. Cf. Elster (1983, p. 125).
22. Helm (2010, p. 284).
23. See also Cocking & Kenneth (1998). For the view that intimacy is essential to friendship, see Thomas (1987, 2013).
24. Bowlby (1969, 1973, 1979), Ainsworth et al. (1978).
25. Leary (2019).
26. Aron et al. (1997).
27. Reiman (1976, p. 32).
28. Aron et al. (1997). They use the term "close" in the sense in which I use the term "intimate."
29. Aron et al. (1997, p. 364).
30. Mandy Len Catron, "To Fall in Love with Anyone, Do This" *New York Times*, January 11, 2015. https://www.nytimes.com/2015/01/11/style/modern-love-to-fall-in-love-with-anyone-do-this.html, retrieved June 1, 2015.
31. See Aron et al. (1989).
32. Baier (1986), Holton (1994), Jones (1996, 2012, 2017), Mullin (2005), Walker (2006), Faulkner (2007a, 2007b, 2011, 2014, 2015, 2017), McGeer (2008), Helm (2014), Darwall (2017), Domenicucci & Holton (2017).

33. Jones (1996), Walker (2006, pp. 76–77), Helm (2014).
34. Domenicucci & Holton (2017).
35. Jones (1996) argues similarly that the expectation that the trustee will be "directly moved by the thought" that the truster is counting on them is a component of trust (p. 10).
36. "Blame," *RadioLab*, NPR, September 12, 2013, https://www.wnycstudios.org/podcasts/radiolab/episodes/317421-blame, retrieved November 15, 2019.
37. Jessica Taylor, "Americans Say to Pass the Turkey, Not the Politics, at Thanksgiving This Year," NPR, November 21, 2017, https://www.npr.org/2017/11/21/565482714/americans-say-to-pass-the-turkey-not-the-politics-at-thanksgiving-this-year, retrieved November 13, 2019.
38. Margalit (2017, ch. 4).
39. Ben-Ze'ev (2011, 2019).
40. See Brogaard (2015, ch. 2).
41. Zeki & Romaya (2008).
42. Hu et al. (2016).
43. Shapiro (2016, p. 156).
44. Aumer & Bahn (2016, p. 137). See also Aumer et al. (2014), and Aumer et al. (2015).
45. For an alternative take on this question, see Dorschel (2002).
46. See also Brudholm (2018, p. 15).
47. Broome (2013), Doris (2015, p. 106). David Chalmers has developed an interesting principle of rationality in terms of self-doubt (Chalmers 2012, ch. 5). Some cases of cognitive dissonance probably are cases of self-doubt.
48. It may be argued that internal inconsistency is purely theoretical rationality with no practical implications. However, cognitive dissonance almost inevitably results in ambivalence about what to do, and internal inconsistency is therefore a form of practical irrationality.
49. Karlin (1993).
50. Steiner (2009, pp. 195–196).
51. Carroll (1990).
52. The theory of parapathic emotions and psychological reversals (also known as "reversal theory") is developed in Apter (1982, 1992, 1997, 2001). See also Hick & Derksen; and Korsmeyer, who she refers to parapathic disgust as the "sublate."
53. Brogaard & Hernandez (forthcoming).

54. For the psychology of offense mechanisms in relationships, see Wilson & Wilson (1999).

55. Brudholm (2010, p. 293).

56. Buehlman & Gottman (1996), Gottman & Silver (1999), Gottman (2003), Gartlan et al. (2006), Gottman (2011), Gottman & Silver (2012), Gottman & Gottman (2018).

57. As argued in Chapter 1, disrespect is a component of blame and condemnation, which are central to hate and contempt.

58. I will assume that the memory-association model of implicit biases is correct. On this model, implicit biases are distributed social-category representations (or category schemas) encoded in long-term memory in the ventral (perception) stream. The encoding is a result of frequent and consistent co-activation of a social-category concept and concepts representing stereotype features, social roles, or social affordances. Implicit biases, as I use the term, do not encompass (implicit) prejudices understood as unconscious emotional responses. I take stereotypes to accommodate evaluative responses, like *Muslims are dangerous* or *Blacks are aggressive*; see Haslanger (2012, 2013). On an alternative model, implicit biases are clusters of co-activating representational and affective components, "Aliefs" in Tamar Gendler's sense; see Gendler (2008a, 2008b). See also Gendler (2011, 2012), Amodio (2014), Madva & Brownstein (2018).

59. See Barrett (2006, 2017).

60. See Barrett (2017).

61. The bridge-arousal study can be found in Dutton & Aron (1974).

62. Kristin Canning, "There's Actually a Reason Why So Many Women Were Obsessed with Ted Bundy," *Women's Health*, May 7, 2019, https://www.womenshealthmag.com/health/a27397635/ted-bundy-hybristophilia-definition, retrieved May 27, 2019.

63. See Evans (1992, 1993).

64. Lois Henry, "Shaving Child's Head Isn't Abuse. Seriously?" *Bakersfield Californian*, August 21, 2011, http://www.bakersfield.com/columnists/lois-henry/2011/08/22/shaving-child-s-head-isn-t-abuse-seriously.html, retrieved June 3, 2015.

65. Anna Merlan, "13-Year-Old Girl Dies by Suicide after Dad Shares Public Shaming Video," Jezebel.com, June 4, 2015, http://jezebel.com/13-year-old-girl-dies-by-suicide-after-dad-shares-publi-1708967488, retrieved July 12, 2015.

66. Antony Beevor, "An Ugly Carnival," *Guardian*, June 5, 2009, https://www.theguardian.com/lifeandstyle/2009/jun/05/women-victims-d-day-landings-second-world-war, retrieved June 10, 2010.

67. Rachel Louise Snyder, "We Prosecute Murder without the Victim's Help. Why Not Domestic Violence?" *New York Times*, May 4, 2019, https://www.nytimes.com/2019/05/04/opinion/sunday/domestic-violence-recanting-crawford.html, retrieved May 28, 2019.

68. Protasi (2016, p. 23).

69. Chris Harris, "Mom Admits She Aided in Teen Daughter's Rape, Murder, Dismemberment; Calls Girl a 'Nonentity,'" *People*, March 21, 2019, https://people.com/crime/mom-admits-she-aided-in-teen-daughters-rape-murder-dismemberment-calls-girl-a-nonentity, retrieved March 22, 2019.

Chapter 3

1. Afif Sarhan & Caroline Davies, "Mother Who Defied the Killers Is Gunned Down," *Guardian*, June 1, 2008, https://www.theguardian.com/world/2008/jun/01/iraq, retrieved August 1, 2016.

2. Strawson (1982 [1962]), Vargas (2004, 2008, 2013a).

3. Strawson (1962, p. 4).

4. Different but related accounts of the function of the reactive attitudes can be found in, e.g., Hieronymi (2001), Darwall (2006), Brudholm (2010), Macnamara (2013a, 2013b), Smith (2013).

5. Strawson (1962, p. 7).

6. Strawson (1962, p. 9).

7. Strawson (1962, p. 7).

8. Strawson (1962, p. 8).

9. Darwall (2006, p. 84).

10. For considerations against strong emotions like hatred being reactive attitudes in Strawson's sense, see also Darwall (2006), Nussbaum (2016, 2018).

11. Ray (2013, p. 39).

12. Austen (2004 [1813], p. 131).

13. Austen (2004 [1813], p. 265).

14. Austen (2004 [1813], p. 411).

15. Austen (2004 [1813], p. 413).

16. See also Kim (1999), Abramson (2009, pp. 199–200), Fischer (2011), Couto (2014), Cogley (2018), Bell (2011, 2018).

17. Austen expert Ray argues that neither Elizabeth nor Darcy changes in character throughout the novel. This interpretation is due to a misunderstanding of Darcy. He is not selfish and arrogant or socially awkward, she argues, but "a remarkably patient, clever man, who at times, unfortunately, manifests ungentlemanly alpha-male grumpiness" (2013, p. 35).

18. Solomon (2006, p. 16).

19. Bell (2013, p. 203).

20. Leboeuf (2018) argues that non-retaliatory anger can have a similar effect.

21. Bell (2013, p. 206).

22. Fanon (2008 [1967], pp. 90–92).

23. Yancy (2008, pp. 847–848).

24. E.g., Nussbaum (2018).

25. Strawson (1962).

26. Nozick (1981, p. 367).

27. See, however, Murphy (2003), Holroyd (2010).

28. Murphy (2003, pp. 22–23).

29. McCullough et al. (2013).

30. Versions of the social justice argument in defense of retributivism have been offered by, e.g., Murphy (2003), Levy (2014). For an overview of the critique of Hampton's argument, see Walen (2016). In moral philosophy, a similar argument formulated in terms of moral equality has been provided in defense of the reactive attitudes. See, e.g., Hieronymi (2001), Brudholm (2010), and Smith (2013), as well as Chapter 1 of this book.

31. Hampton (1988, p. 125).

32. See Murphy (1990a), Levy (2014). For discussion, see also Walen (2016).

33. See also Brudholm (2018, p. 15).

34. See, e.g., Harman (1999, 2003, 2009), Doris (1998, 2002), and Alfano (2013, 2018). See also Doris, J. & Stich (2005, 2006). For the situationist challenge to virtue epistemology, see, e.g., Olin & Doris (2014).

35. For alternative (and complementary) replies to the situationism challenge, see Kristjánsson (2008) and Railton (2011).

36. See also Leary (2019).

37. Eric Margolis, "Seven Million Died in the 'Forgotten' Holocaust," https// rense.com/general44/forog.htm retrieved July 30, 2019. Dominic Sandbrook, "The Forgotten Holocaust: How Stalin Starved Four Million

to Death in a Grotesque Marxist Experiment—Which Many in Russia STILL Deny," *Daily Mail*, September 18, 2017, https://www.dailymail.co.uk/news/article-4897164/The-forgotten-Holocaust-Ukraine-famine-1932-33.html, retrieved July 30, 2019.

38. Snyder (2010, pp. 50–51).

39. This is a partial concession to David Hume, who argued that people should only be blamed when they act on the basis of bad character traits.

40. Rempel & Sutherland (2016, p. 118).

Chapter 4

1. George Pitcher, "Evil, Yes, but Josef Fritzl Is Chillingly Ordinary," *Telegraph*, March 18, 2009, https://www.telegraph.co.uk/comment/5012923/Evil-yes-but-Josef-Fritzl-is-chillingly-ordinary.html, retrieved January 5, 2019.

2. Emotional traits probably can also take the form of dispositions to have specific existential feelings, where an existential feeling is a bodily feeling (e.g., of anger, sadness, or fear) that isn't directed to any specific object. See Ratcliffe (2005, 2008) and Bortolan (2017).

3. Schriber et al. (2017, p. 282).

4. Schriber and her team didn't find contempt-proneness to be linked to disgust-sensitivity, understood broadly to include disgust-sensitivity to disease-causing agents, moral transgressions, and undesirable sexual behaviors. This finding is consistent with the view defended in Chapter 1 that contempt presents its target as "low" in virtue of the target's implicit association with bodily fluids, animal instincts, death, or bodily decay.

5. Tracy & Robins (2007).

6. Schriber and her team found a link between contempt-proneness and low self-esteem, but also between contempt-proneness and vulnerable narcissism, suggesting that the low self-esteem in contemptuous individuals is of the fragile kind described in Tracy & Robins (2003).

7. On the dark triad, see also Jakobwitz & Egan (2006), Chabrol et al. (2009), Miller et al. (2009), Jonason & Webster (2010), Furnham et al. (2013), Jones & Figueredo (2013), Láng (2015), Muris et al. (2017). On the dark tetrad, see Buckels et al. (2013).

8. Paulhus & Williams (2002). See also Paulhus et al. (2001) and Jones & Figueredo (2013).

9. Al Ain et al. (2013), Pincus et al. (2009), Hare et al. (1991).

10. Adapted from Malkin (2015, pp. 40–41).

11. DSM-5, Clinical Cases, 18.7.
12. Pincus & Lukowitsky (2010).
13. Pincus et al. (2009).
14. DSM-5 estimates that 0.5 to 1 percent of the U.S. population suffers from clinical narcissism (50 to 75 percent are men).
15. Sadie F. Dingfelder, "Reflecting on Narcissism: Are Young People More Self-obsessed Than Ever Before?" American Psychological Association *Monitor* 42, no. 2, February 2011, https://www.apa.org/monitor/2011/02/narcissism, retrieved April 2, 2019.
16. Malkin (2015, p. 34).
17. Miller et al. (2017), Jauk et al. (2017).
18. Jauk et al. (2017). Cf. Crowe et al. (2019).
19. The theory that the narcissist's self-image is split into an explicit, positive self-image and an implicit, negative self-image was proposed by Brown & Bosson (2001) and further defended by Tracy & Robins (2003).
20. Bushman & Baumeister (1998), Zeigler-Hill & Wallace (2011), Miller et al. (2013).
21. Charland (2006, 2010).
22. The main reason that I am not including histrionic personality disorder is that I am skeptical for various reasons that it's a separate personality disorder, distinct from borderline personality disorder, rather than a subtype of the latter.
23. The examples of the morally charged language used in the descriptions of the cluster B disorders are taken from DSM-5's diagnostic criteria as well as the accompanying narrative that is used in the identification and differentiation of the disorders.
24. Zachar & Potter (2010), Reimer (2010, 2013).
25. Costa & McCrae's (1992) NEO PI-R facet scale originally listed the following facets. *Neuroticism*: Anxiety, Hostility, Depression, Self-Consciousness, Impulsiveness, Vulnerability. *Extraversion*: Warmth, Gregariousness, Assertiveness, Activity, Excitement-Seeking, Positive Emotions. *Openness to Experience*: Fantasy, Aesthetics, Feelings, Actions, Ideas, Values. *Agreeableness*: Trust, Straightforwardness, Altruism, Compliance, Modesty, Tender-mindedness. *Conscientiousness*: Competence, Order, Dutifulness, Achievement Striving, Self-Discipline, Deliberation.
26. The Hexaco model of Lee and Ashton (2004) lists different facets of the other five factors from Costa & McCrae (1992), who developed the NEO

PI-R facet scale. *Honesty-Humility*: Sincerity, Fairness, Greed, Avoidance, Modesty. *Emotionality (Neuroticism)*: Fearfulness, Anxiety, Dependence, Sentimentality. *Extraversion*: Social Self-Esteem, Social Boldness, Sociability, Liveliness. *Agreeableness*: Forgivingness, Gentleness, Patience. *Conscientiousness:* Organization, Diligence, Perfectionism, Flexibility, Prudence. *Openness to Experience*: Aesthetic Appreciation, Inquisitiveness, Creativity, Unconventionality.

27. For facet-level analyses of narcissism, see, e.g., Samuel & Widiger (2008) and Glover et al. (2012).

28. Marga Reimer's argument against treating the cluster B disorders as disorders of moral character can be found in Reimer (2010) and is developed further in Reimer (2013).

29. Later, Reimer cashes out the presumption of moral responsibility in terms of Grice's conversational implicatures, but the technical details need not concern us here.

30. Reimer (2010, p. 180).

31. Carl Kline, a supervisor in the White House Security Office, allegedly moved files that Tricia Newbold, one of his employees, needed access to shelves she could not reach. Alex Marquardt & Zachary Cohen, "White House Security Official Suspended, Alleges Boss Broke Rules," CNN, January 31, 2019, https://www.cnn.com/2019/01/31/politics/white-house-security-clearance-suspension/index.html, retrieved March 2, 2019.

32. On the differences among cognitive empathy, or mind-reading, emotional empathy, and empathic concern, or care, see, e.g., Bloom (2016) and Slote (2010, 2011).

33. You are morally responsible for the consequences of your actions, if you specifically intended the consequences to occur, or if they occurred as a result of your reckless disregard for other people's rights.

34. Reimer (2010, p. 182).

35. Even on a compatibilist account of responsibility, narcissists are responsible for their nasty acts and attitudes. On Doris' (2015) valuational account of agency, for example, you are accountable for what you are doing, when you act on your values. As the narcissist is under the impression that those she treats with contempt are inferior to her, her actions clearly reflect her values. So, she is responsible for her bad behavior.

36. Zachar & Potter (2010).

37. Mason & Kreger (1998, p. 13).

38. DSM-5 (p. 663).
39. See, e.g., Potter (2006) and Reimer (2010).
40. On the genetic link between borderline and antisocial personality, see Kendler et al. (2008).
41. Waldinger (1993), Mason & Kreger (1998).
42. Kreisman & Straus (2010, p. 12).
43. Bradley & Westen (2005, p. 933).
44. On the borderline's inability to integrate positive and negative representations, see Kernberg (1983 [1975]), Bradley & Westen (2005).
45. On borderline splitting, see also Kernberg (1983 [1975]), Volkan (1988), Beck et al. (1990), Bortolan (2017). On the difference between black-and-white thinking and splitting, see, e.g., Oshio (2009).
46. Kernberg (1983 [1975]) argues that other-hatred is a form of projection that occurs in connection with splitting.
47. Different subtypes of borderline personality disorder may be split along internalizing versus externalizing dimensions. See Bradley et al. (2005).
48. Kreisman & Straus (2010, pp. 13–14).
49. Horne (2014).
50. For reviews of the efficacy of dialectical behavior therapy in the treatment of borderline personality disorder, see Scheel (2000), Stoffers et al. (2012), Cristea et al. (2017), Oud et al. (2018).
51. Scheel (2000) p. 76.
52. Scheel (2000), Stoffers et al. (2012), Cristea et al. (2017), Oud et al. (2018).
53. Horne (2014, p. 216).
54. For an overview of the philosophical literature on moral character and virtue ethics, see Slote (2010, 2011), Hursthouse & Pettigrove (2018), Homiak (2019).
55. Miller et al. (2009, p. 1556).
56. See Crichton's (1959) biography.
57. For a review of the dark triad and workplace behavior, see, e.g., LeBreton et al. (2018).
58. Hare, Hart, & Harpur (1991).
59. For a review of the nature of sexual homicide, see Meloy (2000).
60. This debate about criminal responsibility and punishment parallels the debate about whether people with cluster B disorders are morally responsible for their morally disvalued behaviors and attitudes. For arguments against excusing violent psychopaths from incarceration on the grounds of insanity,

see Maibom (2008, 2005, 2014, 2018) and Ramirez (2013, 2015). For the opposing view that psychopaths are not morally or criminally responsible, or at least not to the full extent, see, e.g., Shoemaker (2015, 2017).

61. Queen v. M'Naghten, 8 Eng. Rep. 718 [1843].
62. See Bloom (2016), Sliwa (2017), Maibom (2018).
63. See, e.g., Bloom (2016).
64. For psychopaths' deviant physiological responses to seeing others in distress, see House & Milligan (1976), Blair (1999a, b), Herpertz et al. (2001), and Birbaumer et al. (2005).

Chapter 5

1. J. D. Gallop, "No Charges for 5 Teens Who Mocked and Filmed Drowning Man, Jamel Dunn, in a Cocoa Pond," *Florida Today*, June 22, 2018, https://www.floridatoday.com/story/news/2018/06/22/no-charges-year-after-teens-mocked-drowning-man-prosecutors-rule-out-filing-charges/723259002, retrieved October 5, 2018.
2. Moore (1980), Finkenbine (2004), Davis (2006).
3. Weld (1839), Mellon (1988), Berlin (1998).
4. Wells-Barnett (1895, The Project Gutenberg Ebook).
5. "Disdain," "contempt," and "scorn" are often used synonymously. However, it is arguable that scorn is not an emotion but the behavior accompanying public displays of contempt.
6. John Searle introduced the term "collective intentionality" in his 1990 paper "Collective Intentions and Actions." The concept of a joint mind, however, dates back to ancient times.
7. List (2014).
8. Roy & Schwenkenbecher (2019).
9. For Gilbert's views of joint commitment, see, e.g., Gilbert (1989, 2001, 2002, 2006, 2009). For other "thick" views of collective intentionality, see, e.g., Cohen & Levesque (1991), Miller (2001), Pettit & Schweikard (2006), Alonso (2009), Bratman (2014a, b), Paternotte (2014), Shapiro (2014), List (2014), Roy & Schwenkenbecher (2019).
10. This raises the question of whether a hate group is collectively responsible for crimes committed by individual members in the name of the group (see Feinberg, 1968). We do sometimes take this to be the case. For example, the Islamic terrorist group al-Qaeda was held collectively responsible for the September 11, 2001 terrorist attacks by against the United States.

11. Cook (2011 [1922]). This list sometimes includes Catholics and immigrants as well.
12. Livingstone Smith (2011, 2016).
13. Appiah (2008, p. 144).
14. Appiah (2008, p. 247).
15. Livingstone Smith (2016, pp. 434–435).
16. Carol Rosenberg, "Lawyer: 'Sodomized' Guantánamo Captive Recovering after Surgery. Prison: No Comment," *Miami Herald*, October 15, 2016, https://www.miamiherald.com/news/nation-world/world/americas/guantanamo/article108484372.html, retrieved December 5, 2019. Editorial Board, "Don't Look Away," *New York Times*, December 5, 2019, https://www.nytimes.com/2019/12/05/opinion/cia-torture-drawings.html, retrieved December 5, 2019.
17. For a contemporary example, see Picciolini (2017).
18. Szanto (2018).
19. Browning (1992).
20. Gellately (2001).
21. Testimony of Franz K., Staatsanwaltschaft Hamburg, 141 Js 1957/62, 2482–87. See Mazower (1992).
22. Arendt (2006 [1964]). The book was first published in 1963.
23. Arendt (1963/2006, p. 287). See also Formosa (2011).
24. Milgram (1963). See also Milgram (1974), written for a mass audience.
25. Haney et al. (1973). See also Zimbardo (2007), written for a mass audience.
26. Mischel (1977).
27. McNab (2011, 2013)
28. Cesarani (2006, p. 361).
29. As quoted in Stangneth (2011, p. 234).
30. Leary (2019).
31. Carnahan & McFarlan (2007).
32. Stangneth (2011).
33. Alexander (1949).
34. D. J. Goldhagen, C. R. Browning, & L. Wieseltier, "The 'Willing Executioners'/'Ordinary Men' Debate," https://www.ushmm.org/m/pdfs/Publication_OP_1996-01.pdf, retrieved August 28, 2016.
35. Adolf Hitler—Speech before the Reichstag, January 30, 1937, http://www.worldfuturefund.org/wffmaster/Reading/Hitler%20Speeches/Hitler%20Speech%201937.01.30.html, retrieved April 15, 2018.

36. Stanley (2015, p. 53).

37. Stanley (2015, pp. 59–60).

38. Stanley (2015, p. 51).

39. Lois Beckett, "The Year in Nazi Propaganda: Images of White Supremacy in Trump's America," *Guardian*, December 27, 2017, https://www.theguardian.com/media/2017/dec/27/the-year-in-nazi-propaganda-images-of-white-supremacy-in-trumps-america, retrieved January 5, 2019.

40. Hume (2000 [1739–1740], book 2). Broome (2013) argues that when we believe we ought to do something, this often motivates us to it. However, it is doubtful that ideological beliefs automatically generate "ought-to" beliefs.

41. Priest, (1843 [1852]), http://babel.hathitrust.org/cgi/pt?id=miun.aev3 898.0001.001;view=1up;seq=7<<<REFC. Bradley (1998) argues that patriot propagandists deliberately omitted the issue of slavery from the agenda listing the goals for freedom for the American Revolution.

42. Priest, (1843 [1852], p. 98).

43. "Trump Calls Media 'Fake, Fake Disgusting News,'" *USA Today*, August 2, 2018, https://www.usatoday.com/videos/news/nation/2018/08/03/trump-calls-media-fake-fake-disgusting-news/37278655, retrieved December 19, 2018.

44. Stoner (1968).

45. Sunstein (2002).

46. Sunstein (2002, 2009a).

47. Main & Walker (1973).

48. For the effect of group homogeneity on group polarization, see also Myers & Lamm (1976).

49. *This Is A.A.: An Introduction to the A.A. Recovery Program*, pp. 8–10, https://www.aa.org/assets/en_US/p-1_thisisaa1.pdf, retrieved April 30, 2018.

50. The group admittedly suggests a definition of "alcoholism" (or "alcohol dependence") as "a mental obsession with drinking, coupled with a compulsive desire to drink." In other words, a form of OCD. These statements are nonetheless exaggerations. For example, a person who abstains from alcohol for a long time may no longer have a desire to drink, as they themselves point out. By their own definition of "alcoholism," then, it is false that people will always be alcoholics, and while it is no doubt true in most instances that one cannot make a normal drinker out of an alcoholic, some

are able to drink socially, just like some ex-smokers manage to have a ciga-rette once in a while without becoming dependent again.

51. John Doris (2015, Ch. 5) cites numerous empirical results suggesting that reasoning is better when collaborative. However, a closer look at the studies he cites reveals that the findings pertain to groups of different-minded individuals.

52. A comprehensive review of one-upmanship can be found in Isenberg (1986).

53. Sanders & Baron (1977, p. 304).

54. Serano (2007).

55. Hogg et al. (1990), Hogg & Reid (2006).

56. Sunstein (1999).

57. Wallace (1999).

58. Jessie Daniels (2009) reports on group polarization in online communities.

59. Brandy Zadrozny & Aliza Nadi, "How Anti-Vaxxers Target Grieving Moms and Turn Them into Crusaders against Vaccines." MSNBC News, September 24, 2019, https://www.nbcnews.com/tech/social-media/how-anti-vaxxers-target-grieving-moms-turn-them-crusaders-n1057566, retrieved December 15, 2019.

60. "WHO Says Anti-Vaxxers Are Global Health Threat," WebMD News from Healthday, https://www.webmd.com/children/vaccines/news/20190117/who-says-anti-vaxxers-are-global-health-threat, retrieved December 15, 2019.

61. Aaron Blake, "A New Study Suggests Fake News Might Have Won Donald Trump the 2016 Election," *Washington Post*, April 3, 2018, https://www.washingtonpost.com/news/the-fix/wp/2018/04/03/a-new-study-suggests-fake-news-might-have-won-donald-trump-the-2016-election/?utm_term=.f20f10fdd1f3, retrieved April 3, 2018. On the origin and spread of the 5G conspiracy theory, see Ahmed et al. (2020).

Chapter 6

1. Berit Brogaard, "12 Ways to Spot a Misogynist: Men Who Hate Women May Not Consciously Realize It. But Their Acts Reveal Them," *Psychology Today*, February 18, 2015, https://www.psychologytoday.com/intl/blog/the-mysteries-love/201502/12-ways-spot-misogynist, retrieved February 18, 2015. Berit Brogaard, "What Is Misogyny, Anyway?" *Psychology*

Today, March 5, 2015, https://www.psychologytoday.com/us/blog/the-mysteries-love/201503/what-is-misogyny-anyway, retrieved March 5, 2015.

2. "Woman Posts Video Online of Man Attacking Her after She Reprimanded Him for Sexually Harassing Her," YouTube video, https://youtu.be/2F0rtJoLzPY, retrieved February 3, 2019.

3. "Combating Sexual and Sexist Violence," Gouvernement.fr, https://www.gouvernement.fr/en/combating-sexual-and-sexist-violence, retrieved February 1, 2019.

4. Kabir Chibber, "The First Man Is Fined under France's New Anti-Catcalling Law," Quartz, September 25, 2018, https://qz.com/1401503/frances-new-anti-catcalling-law-has-prosecuted-its-first-man, retrieved February 1, 2019.

5. Louise Mullany & Loretta Trickett, "Misogyny Hate Crime: New Research Reveals True Scale of Issue—and How the Public Are United against It," The Conversation, July 31, 2018, https://theconversation.com/misogyny-hate-crime-new-research-reveals-true-scale-of-issue-and-how-the-public-are-united-against-it-100265, retrieved February 3, 2019. For the original research, see Mulla & Trickett (2018).

6. Teresa Mull, "Defending Men Who Want to Woo," *American Conservative*, July 17, 2018, https://www.theamericanconservative.com/articles/defending-men-who-want-to-woo/comment-page-1, retrieved February 8, 2019.

7. "Report Documents the Attrition of Women Faculty as They Move up the Academic Ladder," WIA Report, https://www.wiareport.com/2019/09/report-documents-the-attrition-of-women-faculty-as-they-move-up-the-academic-ladder, retrieved September 11, 2019. Sally Haslanger, "Women in Philosophy? Do the Math," *New York Times*, September 2, 2013, https://opinionator.blogs.nytimes.com/2013/09/02/women-in-philosophy-do-the-math, retrieved January 14, 2014.

8. Joshua Hatch, "Gender Pay Gap Persists across Faculty Ranks," *Chronicle of Higher Education*, March 22, 2017, https://www.chronicle.com/article/Gender-Pay-Gap-Persists-Across/239553, retrieved January 13, 2019.

9. See also Manne (2017).

10. Brogaard, "12 Ways to Spot a Misogynist"; Brogaard, "What Is Misogyny, Anyway?"https://www.psychologytoday.com/us/blog/the-mysteries-love/201503/what-is-misogyny-anyway, retrieved March 5, 2015. https://

www.psychologytoday.com/gb/blog/the-mysteries-love/201503/what-is-misogyny-anyway, retrieved January 15, 2019.

11. Lydia Smith, "Corrective Rape: The Homophobic Fallout of Post-Apartheid South Africa," *Telegraph*, May 21, 2015, https://www.telegraph.co.uk/women/womens-life/11608361/Corrective-rape-The-homophobic-fallout-of-post-apartheid-South-Africa.html, retrieved November 5, 2019.

12. Karlin (1993, p. 197).

13. "Misogyny: The Sites," Southern Poverty Law Center, March 1, 2012, https://www.splcenter.org/fighting-hate/intelligence-report/2012/misogyny-sites, retrieved January 4, 2019.

14. Since the time of writing, this blog has been removed. However, the blog owner has repeated his misogynistic commentary in the comment section on various other blogs, for instance, the Female Science Professor blog on February 8, 2011, http://science-professor.blogspot.com/2011/02/advisorstudent.html, retrieved June 21, 2020.

15. "Men Didn't Agree to Feminism, by Eternal Bachelor," Marky Mark's Thoughts on Various Issues, January 3, 2012, http://markymarksthoughts.blogspot.com/2012/01/men-didnt-agree-to-feminism-by-eternal.html, retrieved February 17, 2019.

16. Michelle Lulic, "12 Songs That Are Actually Full of Super Misogynistic Lyrics," Bustle, January 26, 2016, https://www.bustle.com/articles/137558-12-songs-that-are-actually-full-of-super-misogynistic-lyrics, retrieved February 1, 2019.

17. As quoted in Peter Ludlow, "Fascism Doesn't Work Like That: A Review of Jason Stanley's *How Fascism Works*," Politics/Letters, December 20, 2010, http://quarterly.politicsslashletters.org/fascism-doesnt-work-like-that-a-review-of-jason-stanleys-how-fascism-works, retrieved January 3, 2019. The quote is from "Just What Are Traditional Gender Roles?" Daily Stormer, May 19, 2017, https://dailystormer.name/just-what-are-traditional-gender-roles, retrieved January 3, 2019.

18. Tim Fitzsimons, "American Psychological Association Links 'Masculinity Ideology' to Homophobia, Misogyny," NBC News, January 8, 2019, https://www.nbcnews.com/feature/nbc-out/american-psychological-association-links-masculinity-ideology-homophobia-misogyny-n956416, retrieved January 9, 2019.

19. "APA Guidelines for Psychological Practice with Boys and Men," American Psychological Association, August 2018, https://www.apa.org/about/policy/boys-men-practice-guidelines.pdf, retrieved January 9, 2019. See also "Guidelines for Psychological Practice with Girls and Women," American Psychological Association, December 2007, https://www.apa.org/about/policy/girls-and-women-archived.pdf, retrieved January 9, 2019.
20. De Beauvoir (1949, p. 197).
21. De Beauvoir (1949, p. 257).
22. In her book *What Love Is*, Carrie Jenkins defines an analogous ideology, which she calls the romantic mystique, which is the idea that romantic love is elusive and mysterious, and analyzing it or reasoning about the love one has for another person would entail its destruction.
23. Friedan (2001 [1963], pp. 91–92).
24. Kipnis (2006, p. 13).
25. Alia E. Dastagir, "Women Are Now Seen as Equally Intelligent as Men, Study Finds," *USA Today*, July 18, 2019, https://www.usatoday.com/story/news/nation/2019/07/18/differences-between-men-and-women-most-now-say-intelligence-equal/1767610001, retrieved September 1, 2019.
26. "NYC Subways: What Happens When a Lady 'Manspreads,'" Mic, January 5, 2015, https://youtu.be/oo6D4MXrJ5c, retrieved March 12, 2019.
27. Nussbaum (2018, p. 106). For the full text of Swift's poem, see https://www.poetryfoundation.org/poems/50579/the-ladys-dressing-room, retrieved June 13, 2019.
28. Nussbaum (2018, p. 106).
29. Schopenhauer (2015 [1851]).
30. Schopenhauer (2015 [1851]).
31. Manne (2017, p. 87). See also Richardson-Self (2018), who draws an interesting distinction between sexist and misogynistic speech.
32. Manne (2017, p. 80).
33. Swetnam (1615, pp. 7, 16).
34. "In a Word: The True History of 'Misogyny,'" On the Issues, https://www.ontheissuesmagazine.com/2009summer/cafe2.php?id=63, retrieved February 1, 2019.
35. Jose Florez, "Women Are More Misogynistic Than Men on Twitter, Study Found," Mental Daily, October 19, 2016, http://www.mentaldaily.com/

article/2016/10/women-are-more-misogynistic-than-men-on-twitter, retrieved October 1, 2018. Jen Kim, "Are Female Misogynists on the Rise? An Exploration of How the Trump Campaign Encourages Women to Hate Women," *Psychology Today*, October 25, 2016. https://www.psychologytoday.com/us/blog/valley-girl-brain/201610/are-female-misogynists-the-rise, retrieved December 3, 2018.

36. Kendall Fisher, "Michelle Duggar Delivers Sex Advice, Encourages Women to Cater to a Man's 'Special Need' Even When Exhausted or Pregnant," E News, October 12, 2015, https://www.eonline.com/news/705581/michelle-duggar-delivers-sex-advice-encourages-women-to-cater-to-a-man-s-special-need-even-when-exhausted-or-pregnant, retrieved May 20, 2019.

37. Suzanne Venker, "Society Is Creating a New Crop of Alpha Women Who Are Unable to Love," Fox News, February 8, 2017, https://www.foxnews.com/opinion/society-is-creating-a-new-crop-of-alpha-women-who-are-unable-to-love, retrieved March 27, 2019.

38. Venker, "Society Is Creating a New Crop of Alpha Women."

39. Festinger (1962).

40. "Hitler's Antisemitism: Why Did He Hate the Jews?" Anne Frank House, https://www.annefrank.org/en/anne-frank/go-in-depth/why-did-hitler-hate-jews, retrieved March 29, 2019.

41. Emma Dibdin, "Why Women Are the True Gender Traitors of *The Handmaid's Tale*: Without the Likes of Serena Joy and Aunt Lydia, There Would Be No Gilead." *Cosmopolitan*, April 28, 2017, https://www.cosmopolitan.com/entertainment/a9570760/the-handmaids-tale-complicit-women, retrieved February 22, 2019.

42. At least in the first season. In later seasons Aunt Lydia shows signs of sadism. So does Serena. Both of them are, however, highly nuanced characters.

43. Vivenne Parry, "Why Women Are the Worst Misogynists," *Daily Mail*, August 17, 2016, https://www.dailymail.co.uk/femail/article-3745873/Why-women-worst-misogynists-high-flying-mum-never-helped-classic-example-says-VIVIENNE-PARRY.html, retrieved April 28, 2018. See also Hodsden (2018).

44. Kim Lock, "The 'Mommy Wars' Are the Patriarchy's Latest Attempt to Control Women," *Guardian*, October 27, 2015, https://www.theguardian.com/commentisfree/2015/oct/28/the-mummy-wars-

are-the-patriarchys-latest-attempt-to-control-women, retrieved February 3, 2016.

45. Abetz & Moore (2018).

46. Julia Serano, "Transmisogyny Primer," https://www.juliaserano.com/av/TransmisogynyPrimer-Serano.pdf, retrieved May 20, 2019.

47. Emily Hamann, "Solidarity for Our Sisters, Not Just Our Cisters," WIRE, https://www.wire.org.au/feminist-solidarity-transwomen, retrieved May 20, 2019.

48. "Violence against the Transgender Community in 2019," Human Rights Campaign, https://www.hrc.org/resources/violence-against-the-transgender-community-in-2019, retrieved May 15, 2019.

49. Christine Hauser & Emily S. Rueb, "In Attack on Transgender Woman, Dallas Man Was Offered $200, Police Say," New York Times, April 15, 2019, https://www.nytimes.com/2019/04/15/us/transgender-woman-dallas.html, retrieved May 10, 2019.

50. Leah DunLevy, "The Fatal Shooting of Muhlaysia Brooker Is Part of a Larger Trend of Violence against Black Trans Women," Pacific Standard, May 20, 2019, https://psmag.com/news/fatal-shooting-of-muhlaysia-booker-trend-of-violence-against-black-trans-women, retrieved May 21, 2019.

51. Serano's website, https://www.juliaserano.com/outside.html, retrieved May 19, 2019. For her book-length treatments of trans misogyny, see Serano (2013, 2016 [2007], 2016).

52. "The Jezebel Stereotype," Jim Crow Museum of Racist Memorabilia, https://www.ferris.edu/HTMLS/news/jimcrow/jezebel/index.htm, retrieved May 12, 2019.

53. "Why Do Most People Find the Red Pill Misogynistic or 'Morally Reprehensible'?" https://www.reddit.com/r/asktrp/comments/9ulq4v/why_do_most_people_find_the_red_pill_misogynistic, retrieved January 17, 2019.

54. Gary Younge, "Nearly Every Mass Killer Is a Man. We Should All Be Talking More about That," Guardian, April 26, 2018, https://www.theguardian.com/commentisfree/2018/apr/26/mass-killer-toronto-attack-man-men, retrieved April 28, 2018.

55. Amy Broadway, "Elliot Rodger's Narcissism: 'Why Do Girls Hate Me So Much?" Psychology Today, June 4, 2014, https://www.psychologytoday.

com/us/blog/the-mysteries-love/201406/elliot-rodger-s-narcissism, retrieved June 4, 2014.

Chapter 7

1. Anna Diamont, "The Original Meanings of the 'American Dream' and 'America First' Were Starkly Different from How We Use Them Today," *Smithsonian*, October 2018. https://www.smithsonianmag.com/history/behold-america-american-dream-slogan-book-sarah-churchwell-180970311, retrieved November 2, 2019.

2. Adams (1931). The framers of the Constitution, John Adams, Benjamin Franklin, Alexander Hamilton, John Jay, Thomas Jefferson, James Madison, and George Washington, were generally opposed to banking, big corporations, and the accumulation of wealth. The turning point came when opening a national bank, which would make revenue from foreign investment and interest on loans, became the only feasible option for paying back the debt from the Revolutionary War. Hamilton, who led the campaign, won the support of President Washington and Congress. However, Jefferson remained opposed to Hamilton's new vision of America.

3. Adams (1931, p. 214). Adams elaborates as follows: "It is a difficult dream for the European upper classes to interpret adequately, and too many of us ourselves have grown weary and mistrustful of it. It is not a dream of motor cars and high wages merely, but a dream of a social order in which each man and each woman shall be able to attain to the fullest stature of which they are innately capable, and be recognized by others for what they are, regardless of the fortuitous circumstances of birth or position" (pp. 214–215).

4. "Upward mobility" refers to the movement from one social class or economic level to another, for instance, as a result of hard work, risk-taking, sacrifices, connections, inheritance, marriage, or social changes. However, the relevant sense here is upward mobility through hard work, risk-taking, and sacrifices.

5. Chetty et al. (2017).

6. David Kirp, "The College Dropout Scandal," *Chronicle of Higher Education*, July 26, 2019, https://www-chronicle-com.access.library.miami.edu/interactives/20190726-dropout-scandal, retrieved August 7, 2019.

7. Churchwell (2018).

8. Nelson Lichtenstein, "The Ivy League Should Be Twice as Big: The Failure of Elite Private Colleges to Reflect the Nation's Demographic

Transformation Has Reached a Crisis Point." *Chronicle of Higher Education*, October 31, 2019, https://www-chronicle-com.access.library. miami.edu/interactives/20191031-Lichtenstein?cid=wcontentgrid_41_ 5, retrieved November 30, 2019. Lichtenstein's calculations pertain to the top one percent in income, not top one percent in wealth.

9. This point is reminiscent of Stanley's (2018) claim that fascism works in part by invoking nostalgia for a "mythic past, tragically destroyed." In his critical review of Stanley's book, Peter Ludlow argues that this rhetorical strategy is not used exclusively by fascists. In fact, Ludlow writes, "It's hard to think of a conservative American politician who hasn't played this tune," and many liberals have used this kind of rhetoric as well. This point is well taken. However, while it's true that fascists are not alone in harnessing some myth or other about the past, I think it's safe to say that appeals to the American Phantasy run rampant on the far right. Peter Ludlow, "Fascism Doesn't Work Like That: A Review of Jason Stanley's 'How Fascism Works,'" Politics/Letters, December 20, 2018, http://quarterly. politicsslashletters.org/fascism-doesnt-work-like-that-a-review-of-jason-stanleys-how-fascism-works, retrieved January 3, 2019.

10. Wilder (1935, pp. 236–237).

11. Kaye (2000, p. 126).

12. For this use of the word "phantasy" with "ph," see Hayman (1989).

13. For the view that a conceptual distinction should be drawn between white supremacy and white separatism, see, e.g., research by Dobratz & Shanks-Meile (2000, pp. vii, 10; 2006).

14. Richard Rowley, *Documenting Hate: New American Nazis*, Frontline and ProPublica, PBS, November 20, 2018.

15. Daniel De Simone, "Teenage Neo-Nazi Admits Terror Offences," BBC News, April 23, 2019, https://www.bbc.com/news/uk-48027056, retrieved May 7, 2019.

16. Adam Serwer, "White Nationalism's Deep American Roots: A Long-Overdue Excavation of the Book That Hitler Called His 'Bible,' and the Man Who Wrote It," *Atlantic*, April 2019, https://www.theatlantic. com/magazine/archive/2019/04/adam-serwer-madison-grant-white-nationalism/583258, retrieved November 13, 2019.

17. Michael Edison Hayden, "Stephen Miller's Affinity for White Nationalism Revealed in Leaked Emails," Southern Poverty Law Center, November 12, 2019, https://www.splcenter.org/hatewatch/2019/11/

12/stephen-millers-affinity-white-nationalism-revealed-leaked-emails, retrieved November 13, 2019.

18. The violent and irrational Viking culture of pagan Scandinavia would be a good fit for far-right supporters. But this is not usually the culture they openly aspire to return to.

19. For the origins of the model minority myth, see, e.g., Wu (2013); Audrea Lim, "The Alt-Right's Asian Fetish," *New York Times*, January 6, 2018, https://www.nytimes.com/2018/01/06/opinion/sunday/alt-right-asian-fetish.html, retrieved January 3, 2019; Clio Chang, "The Alt Right's 'Asian Exception' Is Cribbed Directly from the White Mainstream," *Splinter*, January 25, 2018, https://splinternews.com/the-alt-rights-asian-exception-is-cribbed-directly-from-1822421189, retrieved January 4, 2019.

20. Lim, "The Alt-Right's Asian Fetish."

21. Adolf Hitler, *My Political Testament*, Note 5, February 1945–April 1945. United States, Office of United States Chief of Counsel for Prosecution of Axis Criminality, Nazi Conspiracy and Aggression, 8 volumes and 2 supplementary volumes (Government Printing Office, Washington, DC, 1946–1948), VI, 259–263, Doc. No. 3569-PS.

22. Kershaw (1999/2000, p. 656).

23. National Immigration Forum, "Fact Sheet: U.S. Refugee Resettlement," January 25, 2019, https://immigrationforum.org/article/fact-sheet-u-s-refugee-resettlement, retrieved February 20, 2019.

24. Matthew Yglesias, "Trump's Racist Tirades against 'the Squad,' Explained: Is There a Method to the Madness?" Vox, July 18, 2019, https://www.vox.com/2019/7/15/20694616/donald-trump-racist-tweets-omar-aoc-tlaib-pressley, retrieved July 18, 2019.

25. Jon Swaine, "Trump Renews Racist Attack on Squad: 'They're Not Capable of Loving the US.'" *Guardian*, July 21, 2019, https://www.theguardian.com/us-news/2019/jul/21/trump-racist-squad-democrats-omar-ocasio-cortez-tlaib-pressley, retrieved July 21, 2019.

26. See also Garcia (1997, 1999, 2011), Fredrickson (2002), and Levy (2016).

27. Garcia (1996, p. 6).

28. Glasgow (2009).

29. Nussbaum (2018, p. 118).

30. Baldwin (1955, p. 93).

31. This interpretation of "Going to Meet the Man" is based on work in progress with Aleks Hernandez. See Brogaard & Hernandez (2020).

32. Baldwin (1965, p. 247).

33. Baldwin (1965, p. 249).

34. Gene Demby, "The Ugly, Fascinating History of the Word 'Racism,'" NPR, January 6, 2014, https://www.npr.org/sections/codeswitch/2014/01/05/260006815/the-ugly-fascinating-history-of-the-word-racism, retrieved January 8, 2015.

35. James Myburgh, "How the Word 'Racism' Was Born, and Why It's Important," Politicsweb, March 15, 2016. https://www.politicsweb.co.za/news-and-analysis/on-the-origins-of-racism. Retrieved August 16, 2017.

36. Keith Woods, "Opinion: Report on Racism, but Ditch the Labels," NPR, July 17, 2019, https://www.npr.org/sections/codeswitch/2019/07/17/413380545/opinion-report-on-racism-but-ditch-the-labels, retrieved July 18, 2019.

37. Brogaard (2020).

38. Greenwald et al. (1998). For a philosophical critique of the implicit association model of implicit biases, see Mandelbaum (2016).

39. Cited in Caryl Rivers, "'Confirmation Bias' Has a Long History of Helping Whites Demonize Blacks." *Los Angeles Times*, December 11, 2014, https://www.latimes.com/opinion/op-ed/la-oe-rivers-confirmation-bias-race-20141212-story.html, retrieved February 2, 2019.

40. For the psychological studies of weapon bias and their implications, see Payne (2001, 2005, 2006) and Payne et al. (2002).

41. Oliver Laughland and Jon Swaine, "Officer Who Killed Tamir Rice Says He Believed 12-Year-Old was in Fact 18." *The Guardian*, December 1, 2015, https://www.theguardian.com/us-news/2015/dec/01/tamir-rice-shooting-cleveland-police-timothy-loehmann-grand-jury, retrieved December 9, 2015.

42. Khushbu Shah, "Ahmaud Arbery: Former Police Officer and Son Charged in Shooting of Black Jogger." *The Guardian*, May 7, 2020, https://www.theguardian.com/us-news/2020/may/07/ahmaud-arbery-former-police-officer-and-son-charged-in-shooting-of-black-man, retrieved May 9, 2020.

43. Jelani Cobb, "The Death of George Floyd, in Context." *The New Yorker*, May 28, 2020, https://www.newyorker.com/news/daily-comment/the-death-of-george-floyd-in-context, retrieved May 28, 2020.

44. Mirna Alsharif, "Eric Garner's Mother Says George Floyd's Death Feels Like déjà vu." CNN.com, May 27, 2020, https://www.cnn.com/2020/05/27/us/eric-garner-mother-reax-floyd/index.html, retrieved May 28, 2020.

45. Thomas Chatteron Williams, "Racism without Racists?" *Atlantic*, September 20, 2011, https://www.theatlantic.com/national/archive/2011/09/racism-without-racists/245361, retrieved April 2, 2019.

46. See Levy (2016).

47. Quoted in Hawkins (1997, p. 201).

48. McCarthy (2007, p. 21).

49. "Adolf Hitler Issues Comment on the 'Jewish Question,'" United States Holocaust Memorial Museum, https://www.ushmm.org/learn/timeline-of-events/before-1933/adolf-hitler-issues-comment-on-the-jewish-question, retrieved December 3, 2018.

50. Achim Gercke, "Die Lösung der Judenfrage," *Nationalsozialistische Monatshefte*, no. 38 (May 1933): 195–197; and, in the same issue, Johann von Leers (1933, pp. 229–231), https://research.calvin.edu/german-propaganda-archive/gercke.htm, retrieved December 3, 2018.

51. Kershaw (1999, p. 258), Yahil (1991, p. 51). Original sources: Hitler, *Mein Kampf*, vol. 1 (1925), Chapter XII: The First Period of Development of the National Socialist German Workers' Party, http://www.hitler.org/writings/Mein_Kampf/mkv1ch12.html, retrieved June 21, 2020; Hitler, *Mein Kampf*, vol. 2 (1926), Chapter XV: The Right of Emergency Defense, http://www.hitler.org/writings/Mein_Kampf/mkv2ch15.html, retrieved June 21, 2020.

52. "White Nationalist American Freedom Party Gears Up for 2016," Southern Poverty Law Center, August 13, 2015, https://www.splcenter.org/hatewatch/2015/08/13/white-nationalist-american-freedom-party-gears-2016, retrieved September 2, 2015.

53. Jordan Peterson, "On the So-Called 'Jewish Question,'" https://jordanbpeterson.com/psychology/on-the-so-called-jewish-question, retrieved December 1, 2018.

54. Quoted in Anti-Defamation League, "From Alt Right to Alt Lite: Naming the Hate," https://www.adl.org/resources/backgrounders/from-alt-right-to-alt-lite-naming-the-hate, retrieved December 3, 2018.

55. Camus (2011).

56. Emma Pettit, "As White Supremacists Try to Remake History, Scholars Seek to Preserve the Record," *Chronicle of Higher Education*, August 5,

2019, https://www-chronicle-com.access.library.miami.edu/article/As-White-Supremacists-Try-to/246876, retrieved August 7, 2019; John Eligon, "The El Paso Screed, and the Racist Doctrine Behind It," *New York Times*, August 7, 2019, https://www.nytimes.com/2019/08/07/us/el-paso-shooting-racism.html, retrieved August 7, 2019.

57. Hayden, "Stephen Miller's Affinity for White Nationalism."
58. Raspail (1975 [1973], p. 306).
59. Tweet by President Donald Trump, June 19, 2018, https://twitter.com/realdonaldtrump/status/1009071403918864385?lang=en, retrieved August 15, 2018.
60. Elaine Ganley, "Far-Right EU Candidates Fan the Flames of Anti-Immigration Rhetoric," *Christian Science Monitor*, May 16, 2019, https://www.csmonitor.com/World/Europe/2019/0516/Far-right-EU-candidates-fan-the-flames-of-anti-immigration-rhetoric, Retrieved June 5, 2019.
61. Leonard (2016).
62. Stepan (1991).
63. Maimuna Majumder, "Higher Rates of Hate Crimes Are Tied to Income Inequality," FiveThirtyEight, ABC News, January 13, 2017, https://fivethirtyeight.com/features/higher-rates-of-hate-crimes-are-tied-to-income-inequality, retrieved February 30, 2017. As Majumder notes, the data sets have various shortcomings, particularly reporting biases. State-level factors such as the likelihood that a reported hate crime will lead to an arrest or that state prosecutors will prosecute hate crimes may also play a role in explaining why hate incidents per capita are not uniformly distributed across the states.
64. See also Browman et al. (2019).
65. Alexander (1949, p. 7).
66. Justin Ward, "Day of the Trope: White Nationalist Memes Thrive on Reddit's r/The_Donald," Southern Poverty Law Center, April 19, 2018, https://www.splcenter.org/hatewatch/2018/04/19/day-trope-white-nationalist-memes-thrive-reddits-rthedonald, retrieved May 9, 2019.
67. David Neiwert, "Is That an OK Sign? A White Power Symbol? Or Just a Right-Wing Troll?" Southern Poverty Law Center, September 19, 2018, https://www.splcenter.org/hatewatch/2018/09/18/ok-sign-white-power-symbol-or-just-right-wing-troll, retrieved September 29, 2018. The

Anti-Defamation League's Hate Symbols Database can be found at https://www.adl.org/hatesymbolsdatabase, retrieved June 24, 2019.

68. Carol Anderson, "America Is Hooked on the Drug of White Supremacy. We're Paying for That Today," *Guardian*, August 13, 2017, https://www.theguardian.com/commentisfree/2017/aug/13/america-white-supremacy-hooked-drug-charlottesville-virginia?CMP=Share_AndroidApp_Facebook, retrieved February 10, 2018.

69. Christine Whitley, "Is Your Child Ready for First Grade: 1979 Edition," Chicago Now, August 1, 2011, http://www.chicagonow.com/little-kids-big-city/2011/08/is-your-child-ready-for-first-grade-1979-edition, retrieved March 29, 2015.

70. Schiffrin et al. (2014).

71. See, e.g., Grubbs et al. (2019).

72. Twenge et al. (2008), Twenge & Campbell (2009), Twenge (2013), Podzimek (2019), Grubbs et al. (2019). See also Jean M. Twenge, "Millennials: The Greatest Generation or the Most Narcissistic?" *Atlantic*, May 2, 2012, https://www.theatlantic.com/national/archive/2012/05/millennials-the-greatest-generation-or-the-most-narcissistic/256638, retrieved December 6, 2015; Rob Asghar, "All Work and No Play Makes Your Child . . . a Narcissist," *Forbes*, February 20, 2014, http://www.forbes.com/sites/robasghar/2014/02/20/all-work-and-no-play-makes-your-child-a-narcissist,   retrieved December 6, 2015. Twenge's research was originally criticized for not controlling for which school the participants attended. But when they controlled for school attended, they still found that Millennials are more narcissistic than past generations; Twenge & Foster (2010). Of course, it would be a mistake to conclude on the basis of a rise in narcissistic features among Millennials that this is how Millennials are.

73. Brailovskaia & Bierhoff (2020). See also Brailovskaia & Bierhoff (2012), Twenge et al. (2019).

74. Erfianti & Mahudin (2019), Fernandes (2019), Grubbs et al. (2019). See Crowe et al. (2019) for the features common to grandiose and vulnerable narcissism.

75. Bushman et al. (2011).

76. David Brooks, "The Dark Shadow of Merit-Based Love," *Houston Chronicle*, April 24, 2015, https://www.houstonchronicle.com/opinion/outlook/article/Brooks-The-dark-shadow-of-merit-based-love-6222833.php, retrieved May 24, 2016.

77. Paula Vasan, "How Parents Express Love in Different Parts of the World," February 3, 2015, https://www.huffpost.com/entry/how-parents-express-love-in-different-parts-of-the-world_b_6511164, retrieved October 12, 2015.

78. Bridget Johnson, "Neo-Nazi Recruitment Video Circulates Online with Goal of 'Accelerating Vengeance.'" *Homeland Security Today*, May 21, 2019, https://www.hstoday.us/subject-matter-areas/terrorism-study/neo-nazi-recruitment-video-circulates-online-with-goal-of-accelerating-vengeance, retrieved June 20, 2019.

79. Breitman (1990).

Chapter 8

1. "Cell Phone Video of Alleged Attack on 2 Gay Men in DC," WUSA9, April 16, 2018, https://www.wusa9.com/video/news/local/cell-phone-video-of-alleged-attack-on-2-gay-men-in-dc/65-8098375?jwsource=cl, retrieved May 8, 2018.

2. Meghan Cloherty, "LGBTQ Community Rattled Following Weekend Attack on U Street," WTOP News, April 19, 2018, https://wtop.com/dc/2018/04/lgbtq-community-rattled-following-weekend-attack-on-u-street, retrieved May 8, 2018.

3. Kahan (2001).

4. David Crary, "Views Are Mixed on Hate Crime Law Named for Matthew Shepard," AP News, October 12, 2018, https://www.apnews.com/a6d811ece9254facbc68df40d20e931a, retrieved October 30, 2018.

5. Corlett & Francescotti (2002) offer an insightful discussion of the trouble with standard definitions of "hate speech," such as the definition proposed by Brison (1998, p. 313). Brison defines "hate speech" as "speech that vilifies individuals or groups on the basis of such characteristics as race, sex, ethnicity, religion, and sexual orientation, which (1) constitutes face-to-face vilification, (2) creates a hostile or intimidating environment, or (3) is a kind of group libel." One counterexample to Brison runs as follows: "Suppose that an European American motorist becomes angry with a Latino motorist and mutters to herself, "Learn how to drive, you stupid spic!" Suppose, moreover, that no one hears this remark (she is alone in her car with the windows rolled up) and no one notices her angry gestures. In this case, the remark is not face-to-face, it does not create a hostile or intimidating environment, and it does not qualify as group libel. But it does

seem to count as hate speech" (pp. 1080–1081). Further, the open-ended phrase "such characteristics as" leaves it wide open which other characteristics can make speech qualify as hate speech; for example, the characteristic of being a member of a hate group seem to satisfy this condition. Corlett & Francescotti (2002) also take issue with the common assumption that only phrases that are used and not merely mentioned can qualify as hate speech. But, they argue, the sentence "You know, the word 'nigger' really applies to you!" might well count as hate speech in spite of the fact that "nigger" is mentioned, not used. Corlett & Francescotti (2002) aspire to conjure up a definition of hate speech that doesn't bear on how we settle the question of whether it should be legislated. In my view, this aspiration is impossible to achieve. So, in this chapter I am going to take for granted that the question of whether to legislate hate speech is inseparable from the question of what hate speech is.

6. Simpson (2013), Greene & Simpson (2017).

7. *Matal v. Tam*, 582 U.S. ___ (2017). https://supreme.justia.com/cases/federal/us/582/15-1293, retrieved January 3, 2019.

8. Langton (1993) argues that pornography in its most common form is a speech act that subordinates and silences women. On this view, pornography in its typical form is a kind of hate speech.

9. In *Chaplinsky v. New Hampshire*, 315 U.S. 568 (1942), the Supreme Court ruled that fighting words are not constitutionally protected, stating that "Resort to epithets or personal abuse is not in any proper sense communication of information or opinion safeguarded by the Constitution, and its punishment as a criminal act would raise no question under that instrument," but the Court has since then limited fighting words to those that are an immediate incitement to violence or fighting.

10. *Joseph v. Scalione,* Filing #84113459,(Fl. 11th Cir. 2019), https://media.local10.com/document_dev/2019/01/30/Youth%20protesters%20vs.%20Dana%20Scalione%20and%20Mark%20Bartlett_1548876638387_18308274_ver1.0.pdf, retrieved March 6, 2019.

11. "Press Release: Enhanced Felony Charges Filed in Mark Bartlett Case," Miami-Dade State Attorney Katherine Fernandez Rundle, February 19, 2019, http://www.miamisao.com/press-release-enhanced-felony-charges-filed-in-mark-bartlett-case, retrieved March 6, 2019.

12. See also Baron (2016) for an argument in favor of the view that the public nature of hate crimes gives society as a whole a reason to push for harsher sentencing.

13. Tanya Gersh vs. Andrew Anglin, Court Order CV 17-50-M-DLC-JCL, U.S. District Court, District of Montana, Missoula Division, filed November 14, 2018, https://www.splcenter.org/sites/default/files/documents/order_on_motion_to_dismiss.pdf, retrieved January 3, 2019.

14. M. Volz & M. Kunzelman, "Neo-Nazi's Attorney Calls Court Ruling Dangerous for Free Speech," Associated Press/*Missoulian*, November 15, 2018, https://missoulian.com/news/state-and-regional/neo-nazi-s-attorney-calls-court-ruling-dangerous-for-free/article_7c0351ee-664c-57fe-8094-65ba59fc560a.html, retrieved January 15, 2019.

15. Eugene Volokh, "Montana Criminal Libel Statute Struck Down." The Volokh Conspiracy, March 18, 2019, https://reason.com/volokh/2019/03/18/montana-criminal-libel-statute-struck-do, retrieved March 19, 2019.

16. Debes argues that the notion of dignity lacks solid historical roots. Remy Debes, "Dignity Is Delicate," Aeon, https://aeon.co/essays/human-dignity-is-an-ideal-with-remarkably-shallow-roots, retrieved March 21, 2019.

17. Kant (1997 [1785], 4:434).

18. Waldron (2012, p. 139).

19. Waldron (2012, p. 60).

20. "Gordon Baum," Southern Poverty Law Center, https://www.splcenter.org/fighting-hate/extremist-files/individual/gordon-baum, retrieved March 31, 2019.

21. "Statements by Hitler and Senior Nazis Concerning Jews and Judaism," https://phdn.org/archives/www.ess.uwe.ac.uk/genocide/statements.htm, retrieved March 31, 2019.

22. The views that offensive uses of slurs don't have truth-values and that the offensiveness of slurs can't be explained by their semantic content have been the dominant views in philosophy of language for some time. See e.g. Hornsby (2001), Richard (2008), Tirrell (2012), Anderson & Lepore (2013a, 2013b), Camp (2013), Bolinger (2017), Anderson (2018), and Gray & Lennertz (2019). Neufeld (2019) argues that slurs are semantically empty kind terms, because they aim at but fail to pick out a

stereotype-related essence of the targeted group, for instance, a blackness essence. However, Neufeld's approach is compatible with various pragmatic accounts of why slurs are offensive. For problems with purely semantic accounts of the derogatory content of slurs (e.g., the one entertained by Hom, 2008) see e.g. Richard (2008) and Jeshion (2013).

23. Bolinger (2017).

24. This is what Searle (1976) calls "a world-to-word direction of fit." Searle credits Anscombe (1957) with the idea of a direction of fit.

25. Because these speech acts contain a pejorative, they are also expressives.

26. Waldron (2012, p. 1).

27. Waldron (2012, p. 2).

28. Waldron (2012, pp. 2–3).

29. Waldron (2012, p. 3).

30. Habermas develops the theory of communicative rationality in Habermas (1984, 1987, 1990, 1993, 1998, 2001a, 2001b, 2003). Useful discussions of the theory of communicative rationality can be found in, e.g., Thompson (1983), Bohman (1986), Dalberg-Larsen (2001, 2007), Niemi (2005), Gelber (2010), Sorial (2015), and Bohman & Rehg (2017).

31. For reviews of pragmatic/anti-realist approaches to truth, see e.g. Brogaard & Salerno (2005, 2019); Brogaard (2016).

32. Habermas (2003 [1962], p. 25).

33. Assertions about what is beautiful can also be legitimate, but, Habermas argues, aesthetic rightness is bound to particular cultures. So, even when we make defensible aesthetic claims, we cannot expect them to be met with unanimity.

34. For discussion of the differences in how we can rationally assess the different kinds of legitimacy claims, see Bohman & Rehg (2017).

35. As Langton (2012, p. 75) notes, there seem to be both "illocutionary and perlocutionary dimensions to hate speech." Habermas' aim, however, is to encourage speech that isn't focused on its perlocutionary effects and also doesn't include illocutionary speech like demands and threats.

36. Habermas (2001b, pp. 154–155).

37. Glenn Greenwald, "In Europe, Hate Speech Laws Are Often Used to Suppress and Punish Left-Wing Viewpoints," The Intercept, August 29, 2017, https://theintercept.com/2017/08/29/in-europe-hate-speech-laws-are-often-used-to-suppress-and-punish-left-wing-viewpoints, retrieved November 10, 2019.

38. Greenwald, "In Europe, Hate Speech Laws are Often Used to Suppress and Punish Left-Wing Viewpoints."

39. *Confronting White Nationalism in Schools: A Toolkit*, Western States Center, https://www.westernstatescenter.org/schools?fbclid=IwAR1ScYLwXw k81hhqLO3QCt9VNOV89Pr7nu_pIjP92nbpKQe5wnlDD6VoJDw, retrieved June 22, 2019. "CPS Teacher Develops Toolkit to Fight White Nationalism," NPR, June 20, 2019, https://www.npr.org/local/309/ 2019/06/20/734155483/c-p-s-teacher-develops-toolkit-to-fight-white-nationalism\, retrieved June 22, 2019. George M. Eberhart "Confronting White Nationalism: How Libraries Can Anticipate and Counter Racist Incidents," *American Libraries*, June 22, 2019, https://americanlibrariesmagazine.org/blogs/the-scoop/confronting-white-nationalism, retrieved June 22, 2019.

40. Liu (2019).

41. Diamont (2019). See also the report recently released by the Commission on the Practice of Democratic Citizenship, *Our Common Purpose: Reinventing American Democracy for the 21st Century*, American Academy of Arts and Sciences, June 2020, https://www. amacad.org/ourcommonpurpose/report, retrieved June 24, 2019.

42. "Where It's Used," Ranked Choice Voting Resource Center. https://www. rankedchoicevoting.org/where_used, retrieved May 6, 2020.

43. Scott Thistle, "Amid pandemic, GOP gathers signatures to kill ranked-choice voting," Pressherald.com, May 18, 2020, https://www.pressherald. com/2020/05/18/amid-pandemic-gop-gathers-signatures-to-kill-ranked-choice-voting/, retrieved June 2, 2020.

44. "Where It's Used," Ranked Choice Voting Resource Center, https://www. rankedchoicevoting.org/where_used, retrieved May 6, 2020.

45. "Ranking Presidential Candidates," *Fair Vote*, https://www.fairvote. org/rcv_for_presidential_nominations#presidential_primaries_2020, retrieved June 4, 2020.

46. These ideas are based on work in progress with Thomas Alrik Sørensen.

47. If a candidate gets 20 percent favorable votes and 9 percent unfavorable votes, whereas a competitor gets 40 percent favorable votes but 31 percent unfavorable votes, then the adjusted favorable votes is 11 percent for the first candidate but only 9 percent for the second candidate.

48. When this book was at the final stages of production, the American Academy of Arts and Sciences' Commission on the Practice of Democratic

Citizenship released a report detailing how to get closer to the democratic ideal in the United States. The Commission, chaired by Danielle Allen, Stephen B. Heintz, and Eric Liu, proposes six strategies for how to achieve this goal, which range from making changes to the voting process and securing equal representation in Congress and to inspiring a culture of commitment to America's constitutional democracy. This is a must-read for anyone who cares about our democracy.

Conclusion

1. Wells-Barnett (1895, ch. 3 in The Project Gutenberg Ebook). On lynchings in America, see also Williams (2001).
2. "Another Negro Burned: Henry Smith Dies at the Stake," *New York Times*, February 2, 1893.
3. Hale (1998, p. 207).
4. Jamelle Bouie, "The Joy of Hatred: Trump and 'His People' Reach Deep into the Violent History of Public Spectacle in America," *New York Times*, July 19, 2019, https://www.nytimes.com/2019/07/19/opinion/trump-rally.html, retrieved November 5, 2019.
5. Miller (2005).
6. Postmes & Spears (1998).
7. Brogaard (2015, Ch. 3).
8. Tappolet (2011). Siegel (2017) argues that perception can be epistemically downgraded, which disqualifies it as an immediate justifier of belief. But this is different from saying that perceptions can be the sole ground of morally indefensible acts.
9. Brogaard (2015, Ch. 2).
10. See D'Arms & Jacobson (2000). See also D'Arms & Kerr (2008).
11. See also D'Arms & Jacobson (2000) who argue that the question of an emotion's fittingness must be kept apart from the question of its appropriateness.
12. Jonathan Turley, "No, the U.S. Does Not Need European-Style Hate Speech Laws," *USA Today*, November 8, 2019, https://www.usatoday.com/story/opinion/2019/11/08/no-us-not-need-european-style-hate-speech-laws-column/4157833002, retrieved November 10, 2019.
13. Richard Stengel, "Why America Needs a Hate Speech Law," *Washington Post*, October 29, 2019, https://www.washingtonpost.com/opinions/

2019/10/29/why-america-needs-hate-speech-law, retrieved November 10, 2019.

14. Glenn Greenwald, "In Europe, Hate Speech Laws Are Often Used to Suppress and Punish Left-Wing Viewpoints," The Intercept, August 29, 2017, https://theintercept.com/2017/08/29/in-europe-hate-speech-laws-are-often-used-to-suppress-and-punish-left-wing-viewpoints, retrieved November 10, 2019.

15. Fahad Ansari, "A racially aggravated prosecution? The case of Azhar Ahmed," Open Democracy, March 21, 2012, https://www.opendemocracy.net/en/opendemocracyuk/racially-aggravated-prosecution-case-of-azhar-ahmed/, retrieved September 13, 2018.

16. Glenn Greenwald, "In Europe, Hate Speech Laws are Often Used to Suppress and Punish Left-Wing Viewpoints," The Intercept, August 29 2017, https://theintercept.com/2017/08/29/in-europe-hate-speech-laws-are-often-used-to-suppress-and-punish-left-wing-viewpoints/?comments=1, retrieved September 13, 2018.

REFERENCES

Abetz, J., & Moore, J. (2018). "'Welcome to the Mommy Wars, Ladies': Making Sense of the Ideology of Combative Mothering in Mommy Blogs." *Communication Culture & Critique* 11: 265–281.

Abramson, K. (2009). "A Sentimentalist's Defense of Contempt, Shame, and Disdain." In P. Goldie (ed.), *The Oxford Handbook of Philosophy of Emotion*. New York: Oxford University Press, 189–194.

Abramson, K. (2014). "Turning Up the Lights on Gaslighting." *Philosophical Perspectives* 28, no. 1: 1–30.

Adams, J. T. (1931). *The Epic of America*. New York: Blue Ribbon Books.

Ahmed, W., Vidal-Alaball, J., Downing, J., & López Seguí, F. (2020). "COVID-19 and the 5G Conspiracy Theory: Social Network Analysis of Twitter Data." *Journal of Medical Internet Research* 22, no. 5: e19458.

Ainsworth, M. D., Blehar, M., Waters, E., & Wall, S. (1978). *Patterns of Attachment: A Psychological Study of the Strange Situation*. Hillsdale, NJ: Lawrence Erlbaum.

Al Ain, S., Carre, A., Fantini-Hauwel, C., Baudouin, J. Y., & Besche-Richard C. (2013). "What Is the Emotional Core of the Multidimensional Machiavellian Personality Trait?" *Frontiers in Psychology* 4: 454. 10.3389/fpsyg.2013.00454.

Alexander, L. (1949). "The Molding of Personality under Dictatorship: The Importance of the Destructive Drives in the Socio-Psychological Structure of Nazism." *Journal of Criminal Law and Criminology* 40, no. 1: 3–27.

Alfano, M. (2013). *Character as Moral Fiction*. Cambridge: Cambridge University Press.

Alfano, M. (2016). "Friendship and the Structure of Trust." In A. Masala & J. Webber (eds.), *From Personality to Virtue*. Oxford: Oxford University Press, 186–206.

Alfano, M. (2018). "A Plague on Both Your Houses: Virtue Ethics after Situationism and Repligate." *Teoria*. In press.

Allen, S. A. (2008). *The Sugar Queen: A Novel*. New York: Random House Reader's Circle.

Alonso, F. M. (2009). "Shared Intention, Reliance, and Interpersonal Obligations." *Ethics* 119, no. 3: 444–475.

American Psychological Association (2007). *Guidelines for Psychological Practice with Girls and Women*.

Amodio, D. M. (2014). "The Neuroscience of Prejudice and Stereotyping." *Nature Reviews Neuroscience* 15, no. 10: 670–682.

Anderson, C. (2016). *White Rage*. London: Bloomsbury.

Anderson, L., and Lepore, E. (2013a). "Slurring Words." *Nous* 47: 25–48.

Anderson, L., and Lepore, E. (2013b). "What Did You Call Me? Slurs as Prohibited Words." *Analytic Philosophy* 54, no. (3): 350–363.

Anderson, L. (2018). "Calling, Addressing, and Appropriation." In D. Sosa (ed.), *Bad Words: Philosophical Perspectives on Slurs*. Oxford: Oxford University Press, 6–28.

Annas, J. (2011). *Intelligent Virtue*. Oxford: Oxford University Press.

Anscombe, G. E. M. (1957). *Intention*. Oxford: Basil Blackwell.

Appiah, K. A. (2008). *Experiments in Ethics*. Cambridge, MA: Harvard University Press.

Apter, M. J. (1982). *The Experience of Motivation: The Theory of Psychological Reversals*. Cambridge, MA: MIT Press.

Apter, M. J. (1992). *The Dangerous Edge: The Psychology of Excitement*. New York: Free Press.

Apter, M. J. (1997). *Reversal Theory: Motivation, Emotion and Personality*. London: Routledge.

Apter, M. J. (ed.) (2001). *Motivational Styles in Everyday Life: A Guide to Reversal Theory*. Washington, DC: American Psychological Association.

Aragón, O. R., Clark, M. S., Dyer, R. L., and Bargh, J. A. (2015). "Dimorphous Expressions of Positive Emotion: Displays of Both Care and Aggression in Response to Cute Stimuli." *Psychol Sci.* 26, no. 3: 259–273.

Arendt, H. (2006 [1964]). *Eichmann in Jerusalem: A Report on the Banality of Evil*. New York: Penguin.

Aristotle. (2012). *Nicomachean Ethics*, R. C. Bartlett & S. D. Collins (eds./trans.). Chicago: University of Chicago Press.

Aron, A., Dutton, D. G., Aron, E. N., & Iverson, A. (1989). "Experiences of Falling in Love." *Journal of Social and Personal Relationships* 6: 243–257.

Aron, A., Paris, M., & Aron, E. N. (1995). "Falling in Love: Prospective Studies of Self-concept Change." *Journal of Personality and Social Psychology* 69: 1102–1112.

Aron, A., Melinat, E., Aron, E. N., Vallone, R. D., & Bator, R. J. (1997). "The Experimental Generation of Interpersonal Closeness: A Procedure and Some Preliminary Findings." *Personality and Social Psychology Bulletin* 23, no. 4: 363–377.

Aumer, K., & Bahn, A. C. K. (2016). "Hate in Intimate Relationships as a Self-Protective Emotion." In K. Aumer (ed.), *The Psychology of Love and Hate in Intimate Relationships*. Cham, Switzerland: Springer, 131–151.

Aumer, K., Bahn, A. C. K., & Harris, S. (2015). "Through the Looking Glass, Darkly: Perceptions of Hate in Interpersonal Relationships." *Journal of Relationships Research* 6: e3.

Aumer, K., Bahn, A., Janicki, C., Guzman, N., Pierson, N., Strand, S., & Totlund, H. (2016). "Can't Let It Go: Hate in Interpersonal Relationships." *Journal of Relationships Research* 7: e2.

Aumer-Ryan, K., & Hatfield, E. (2007). "The Design of Everyday Hate: A Qualitative and Quantitative Analysis." *Interpersona* 1, no. 2: 143–172.

Austen, J. (2004 [1813]). *Pride and Prejudice*. New York: Simon & Schuster.

Baber, H. E. (2007). "Adaptive Preferences." *Social Theory and Practice* 33, no. 1: 105–126.

Baier, A. (1986). "Trust and Antitrust." *Ethics* 96: 231–260.

Baldwin, J. (1955). *Notes of a Native Son*. New York: Beacon Press.

Baldwin, J. (1995 [1965]). "Going to Meet the Man." In *Going to Meet the Man: Stories*. New York: Vintage International, 229–249.

Barnes, E. (2007). "Disability and Adaptive Preference." *Philosophical Perspectives* 23, no. 1: 1–22.

Barnes, E. (2016). *The Minority Body: A Theory of Disability*. New York: Oxford University Press.

Baron, M. (2016). "Hate Crime Legislation Reconsidered." *Metaphilosophy* 47, nos. 4–5: 504–523.

Barrett, L. F. (2006). "Solving the Emotion Paradox: Categorization and the Experience of Emotion." *Personality and Social Psychology Review* 10, no. 1: 20–46.

Barrett, L. F. (2017). *How Emotions Are Made: The Secret Life of the Brain*. New York: Houghton Mifflin Harcourt.

Bauer, B. (1843). *Die Judenfrage*. Braunschweig: Fr. Otto.

Beach, S. (2015). "Adaptive Preferences Are Not Irrational." M.A. thesis, Department of Philosophy, University of Missouri, St. Louis.

Beck, A. T., Freeman, A., & Davis, D. D. (1990). *Cognitive Therapy of Personality Disorders*. New York: Guilford Press.

Bell, M. (2005). "A Woman's Scorn: Toward a Feminist Defense of Contempt as a Moral Emotion." *Hypatia* 20, no. 4: 80–93.

Bell, M. (2008). "Forgiving Someone for Who They Are (and Not Just What They've Done)." *Philosophy and Phenomenological Research* 77, no. 3: 625–658.

Bell, M. (2011). "Globalist Attitudes and the Fittingness Objection." *Philosophical Quarterly* 61, no. 244: 449–472.

Bell, M. (2013). *Hard Feelings: The Moral Psychology of Contempt*. New York: Oxford University Press.

Bell, M. (2018). "Contempt, Honor, and Addressing Racism." In M. Mason (ed.), *Moral Psychology of Contempt*. London: Rowman & Littlefield, 3–16.

Ben-Ze'ev, A., (1990). "Envy and Jealousy." *Canadian Journal of Philosophy* 20, no. 4: 487–516.

Ben-Ze'ev, A. (1992). "Anger and Hate." *Journal of Social Philosophy* 23: 85–110.

Ben-Ze'ev, A. (2000). *The Subtlety of Emotions*. Cambridge, MA: MIT Press.

Ben-Ze'ev, A. (2002). "Are Envy, Anger and Resentment Moral Emotions?" *Philosophical Explorations* 5, no. 2: 148–154.

Ben-Ze'ev, A. (2011). "The Nature and Morality of Romantic Compromises." In C. Bagnoli (ed.), *Morality and the Emotions*. Oxford: Oxford University Press, 95–114.

Ben-Ze'ev, A. (2019). *The Arc of Love: How Our Romantic Lives Change over Time*. Chicago: University of Chicago Press.

Bergqvist A., & Cowan, R. (2018). "Evaluative Perception: Introduction." In Anna Bergqvist & Robert Cowan (eds.), *Evaluative Perception*. Oxford University Press, 1–17.

Berlin, Ira. Many Thousands Gone: The First Two Centuries of Slavery in North America. Cambridge, MA: Belknap Press of Harvard University Press, 1998.

Birbaumer, N., Veit, R., Lotze, M., Erb, M., Hermann, C., Grodd, W., & Flor, H. (2005). "Deficient Fear Conditioning in Psychopathy: A Functional Magnetic Resonance Imaging Study." *Archives of General Psychiatry* 62, no. 7: 799.

Blair, R. J. R. (1999a). "Psychophysiological Responsiveness to the Distress of Others in Children with Autism." *Personality and Individual Differences* 26, no. 3: 477–485.

Blair, R. J. R. (1999b). "Responsiveness to Distress Cues in the Child with Psychopathic Tendencies." *Personality and Individual Differences* 27: 135–145.

Blass, T. (2004). *The Man Who Shocked the World*. New York: Basic Books.

Bloom, P. (2016). *Against Empathy: The Case for Rational Compassion*. New York: Ecco.

Bohman, J. F. (1986). "Formal Pragmatics and Social Criticism: The Philosophy of Language and the Critique of Ideology in Habermas's Theory of Communicative Action." *Philosophy and Social Criticism* 11, no. 4: 331–353.

Bohman, J., & Rehg, W. (2017). "Jürgen Habermas." *The Stanford Encyclopedia of Philosophy* (Fall 2017 Edition), E. N. Zalta (ed.), https://plato.stanford. edu/archives/fall2017/entries/habermas.

Bolinger, R. J. (2017). "The Pragmatics of Slurs." *Noûs* 51, no. 3: 439–462.

Bortolan, A. (2017). "Affectivity and Moral Experience: An Extended Phenomenological Account." *Phenomenology and the Cognitive Sciences* 16: 471–490.

Bovens, L. (1992). "Sour Grapes and Character Planning." *Journal of Philosophy* 89, no. 2: 57–78.

Bowlby, J. (1969). *Attachment and Loss*, Vol. 1: *Attachment*. New York: Basic Books.

Bowlby, J. (1973). *Attachment and Loss*, Vol. 2: *Separation: Anxiety and Anger*. New York: Basic Books.

Bowlby, J. (1979). *The Making and Breaking of Affectional Bonds*. London: Tavistock.

Boyd, R. (2004). "Pity's Pathologies Portrayed: Rousseau and the Limits of Democratic Compassion." *Political Theory* 32, no. 4: 519–546.

Bradley, P. (1998). *Slavery, Propaganda and the American Revolution*. Jackson: University Press of Mississippi.

Bradley, R., Conklin, C. Z., & Westen, D. (2005). "The Borderline Personality Diagnosis in Adolescents: Gender Differences and Subtypes." *Journal of Child Psychology and Psychiatry* 46: 1006–1019.

Bradley, R., & Westen, D. (2005). "The Psychodynamics of Borderline Personality Disorder: A View from Developmental Psychopathology." *Development and Psychopathology* 17: 927–957.

Brailovskaia, J., & Bierhoff, H.-W. (2012). "Sensation Seeking Narcissists, Extraversion and Self-Presentation in Social Networks in Web 2.0." *Journal of Business and Media Psychology* 3: 43–56.

Brailovskaia, J., & Bierhoff, H.-W. (2020). "The Narcissistic Millennial Generation: A Study of Personality Traits and Online Behavior on Facebook." *Journal of Adult Development* 27: 23–35, doi:10.1007/s10804-018-9321-1.

Bratman, M. E. (1987). *Intention, Plans and Practical Reason*. Cambridge, MA: Harvard University Press.

Bratman, M. E. (2001). "Two Problems about Human Agency." *Proceedings of the Aristotelian Society* 2000–2001: 309–326.

Bratman, M. E. (2007). *Structures of Agency: Essays*. New York: Oxford University Press.

Bratman, M. (2014a). "Rational and Social Agency: Reflections and Replies." In M. Vargas & G. Jaffe (eds.), *Rational and Social Agency: Essays on the Philosophy of Michael Bratman*. Oxford: Oxford University Press, 294–343.

Bratman, M. (2014b). *Shared Agency: A Planning Theory of Acting Together*. Oxford: Oxford University Press.

Breitman, R. (1990). "Hitler and Genghis Khan." *Journal of Contemporary History* 25, nos. 2/3: 337–351.

Brison, S. J. (1998). "The Autonomy Defense of Free Speech." *Ethics* 108, no. 2: 312–339.

Brogaard, B. (2015). *On Romantic Love*. New York: Oxford University Press.

Brogaard, B. (2016). "Against Naturalism about Truth." In Kelly Clark (ed.), *The Blackwell Companion to Naturalism*. Oxford: Blackwell, 262–276.

Brogaard, B. (2018). *Seeing and Saying*. New York: Oxford Unversity Press.

Brogaard, B. (2020). "Implicit Biases in Visually Guided Action." *Synthese*. https://doi.org/10.1007/s11229-020-02588-1.

Brogaard, B., & Hernandez, M. A. (2020). "Disgust and the Logic of Racism in James Baldwin's 'Going to Meet the Man.'" Unpublished manuscript.

Brogaard, B., & Salerno, J. (2005). Anti-Realism, Theism, and the Conditional Fallacy." *Nous* 39: 123–139.

Brogaard, Berit, & Salerno, Joe. (2019). "Fitch's Paradox of Knowability." In Edward N. Zalta (ed.), *The Stanford Encyclopedia of Philosophy*. https://plato.stanford.edu/archives/fall2019/entries/fitch-paradox/.

Brogaard, B., & Slote, M. (forthcoming). "Against and for Ethical Naturalism. Or: How Not to 'Naturalize' Ethics." *American Philosophical Quarterly*.

Brogaard, B. & Slote, M. (2020). *On Respect and Disrespect: A Broad Perspective*. Book Manuscript.

Broome, J. (2013). *Rationality through Reasoning*. Oxford: Wiley-Blackwell.

Browman, A. S., Destin, M., Kearney, M. S., & Levine, P. B. (2019). "How Economic Inequality Shapes Mobility Expectations and Behaviour in Disadvantaged Youth." *Nature Human Behaviour*, doi: 10.1038/s41562-018-0523-0.

Brown, R. P., & Bosson, J. K. (2001). "Narcissus Meets Sisyphus: Self-love, Self-loathing, and the Never-ending Pursuit of Self-worth." *Psychological Inquiry* 12: 210–212.

Browning, C. R. (1992). *Ordinary Men: Reserve Police Battalion 101 and the Final Solution in Poland*. New York: HarperCollins.

Browning, R. (1981 [1868–1869]). *The Ring and the Book*, ed. Richard D. Altick. New Haven: Yale University Press, 1981.

Bruckner, D. (2009). "In Defense of Adaptive Preferences." *Philosophical Studies* 142, no. 3: 307–324.

Brudholm, T. (2010). "Hatred as an Attitude." *Philosophical Papers* 39: 289–313.

Brudholm, T. (2018). "Hatred beyond Bigotry." In T. Brudholm & B. S. Johansen (eds.), *Hate, Politics, Law: Critical Perspectives on Combating Hate*. New York: Oxford University Press, 53–75.

Brudholm, T., & Johansen, B. S. (2018). "Pondering Hatred." In T. Brudholm & J. Lang (eds.), *Emotions and Mass Atrocity*. Cambridge: Cambridge University Press, 81–103.

Buckels, E. E., Jones, D. N., & Paulhus, D. L. (2013). "Behavioral Confirmation of Everyday Sadism." *Psychological Science* 24: 2201–2209.

Buehlman, K.T., & Gottman, J. (1996). "The Oral History Coding System." In J. Gottman (ed.), *What Predicts Divorce? The Measures*. Hillsdale, NJ: Erlbaum, OH11–OH118.

Bushman, B. J., & Baumeister, R. F. (1998). "Threatened Egotism, Narcissism, Self-Esteem, and Direct and Displaced Aggression: Does Self-Love or Self-Hate Lead to Violence?" *Journal of Personality and Social Psychology* 75: 219–229.

Bushman, B. J., Moeller, S. J., & Crocker, J. (2011). "Sweets, Sex, or Self-Esteem? Comparing the Value of Self-Esteem Boosts with Other Pleasant Rewards." *Journal of Personality* 79, no. 5: 993–1012.

Camp, E. (2013). "Slurring Perspectives." *Analytic Philosophy* 54, no. 3: 330–349.

Camus, R. (2011). *Le Grand Remplacement* [The Great Replacement]. Neuilly-sur-Seine: David Reinharc.

Carleheden M, Heidegren, C.-G., & Willig, R. (2012). "Recognition, Social Invisibility, and Disrespect." *Distinktion: Scandinavian Journal of Social Philosophy* 13, no. 1: 1–3.

Carnahan, T., & McFarlan, S. (2007). "Revisiting the Stanford Prison Experiment: Could Participant Self-Selection Have Led to the Cruelty?" *Personality and Social Psychology Bulletin* 33, no. 5: 603–614.

Carroll, N. (1990). *The Philosophy of Horror, or; Paradoxes of the Heart.* New York: Routledge.

Cesarani, D. (2006). *Becoming Eichmann*. Essex: Da Capo Press.

Chabrol, H., Van Leeuwen, N., Rodgers, R., & Séjourné, N. (2009). "Contributions of Psychopathic, Narcissistic, Machiavellian, and Sadistic Personality Traits to Juvenile Delinquency." *Personality and Individual Differences* 47: 734–739.

Chalmers, D. J. (2012). *Constructing the World*. Oxford: Oxford University Press.

Charland, L. C. (2006). "The Moral Character of the DSM IV Cluster B Personality Disorders." *Journal of Personality Disorders* 20, no. 2: 116–125.

Charland, L. C. (2010). "Medical or Moral Kinds? Moving beyond a False Dichotomy." *Philosophy, Psychiatry, & Psychology* 17, no. 2: 119–125.

Chetty, R., Grusky, D., Hell, M., Hendren, N., Manduca, R., & Narang, J. (2017). "The Fading American Dream: Trends in Absolute Income Mobility since 1940." *Science* 356, no. 6336: 398–406.

Churchwell, S. (2018). *Behold, America: The Entangled History of "America First" and "The American Dream."* New York: Basic Books.

Cocking, D., & Kennett, J. (1998). "Friendship and the Self." *Ethics* 108, no. 3: 502–527.

Cocking, D., & Kennett, J. (2000). "Friendship and Moral Danger." *Journal of Philosophy* 97, no. 5: 278–296.

Cogley, Z. (2018). "Contempt's Evaluative Presentation and Connection to Accountability." In M. Mason (ed.), *The Moral Psychology of Contempt*. New York: Rowman & Littlefield, 131–150.

Cohen, P. R., & Levesque, H. J. (1991). "Teamwork." *Noûs* 25, no. 4: 487–512.

Cook, E. A. (2011 [1922]). *Ku Klex Klan Secrets Exposed*. Project Gutenberg eBook. https://www.gutenberg.org/files/35976/35976-h/35976-h.htm.

Corlett, J. A., & Francescotti, R. (2002). "Foundations of a Theory of Hate Speech." *The Wayne Law Review* 48: 1071–1100.

Costa, P. T., & McCrae, R. R. (1992). *NEO PI-R Professional Manual*. Odessa, FL: Psychological Assessment Resources.

Couto, A. (2014). "Reactive Attitudes, Disdain and the Second-Person Standpoint." *Grazer Philosophische Studien* 90: 79–104.

Crichton, R. (1959). *The Great Impostor: The Amazing Career of Ferdinand Waldo Demara, Who Posed as a Surgeon, a Prison Warden, a Doctor of Philosophy, a Trappist Monk and Many, Many Others*. New York: Random House.

Cristea, I. A., Gentili, C., & Cotet, C. D. (2017). "Efficacy of Psychotherapies for Borderline Personality Disorder: A Systematic Review and Meta-Analysis." *JAMA Psychiatry* 74, no. 4: 319–328.

Crowe, M. L., Lynam, D. R., Campbell, W. K., & Miller, J. D. (2019). "Exploring the Structure of Narcissism: Toward an Integrated Solution." *Journal of Personality* 87, no. 6: 1151–1169.

Dalberg-Larsen, J. (2001). *Pragmatisk Retsteori*. Copenhagen: Jurist- og Økonomforbundets Forlag.

Dalberg-Larsen, J. (2007). "Jürgen Habermas: Demokrati og Retsstat." *Retfærd* 30, no. 116: 99–104.

D'Arms, J. (2009). "Envy." *The Stanford Encyclopedia of Philosophy* (Spring 2009 Edition), E. N. Zalta (ed.), http://plato.stanford.edu/archives/spr2009/entries/envy.

D'Arms, J., & Jacobson, D. (2000). "The Moralistic Fallacy: On the 'Appropriateness' of Emotions." *Philosophy and Phenomenological Research* 61, no. 1: 65–90.

D'Arms, J., & Kerr, A. D. (2008). "Envy in the Philosophical Tradition." In R. H. Smith (ed.), *Envy: Theory and Research*. New York: Oxford University Press, 39–59.

Darwall, S. (1977). "Two Kinds of Respect." *Ethics* 88, no. 1: 36–49.

Darwall, S. (2004). "Respect and the Second-Person Standpoint." *Proceedings and Addresses of the American Philosophical Association* 78, no. 2: 43–59.

Darwall, S. (2006). *The Second-Person Standpoint: Morality, Respect, and Accountability*. Cambridge, MA: Harvard University Press.

Darwall, S. (2013). "Ressentiment and Second-Personal Resentment." In *Honor, History, and Relationship: Essays in Second-Person Ethics II*. Oxford: Oxford University Press,

Darwall, S. (2017). "Trust as a Second-Personal Attitude (of the Heart)." In P. Faulkner & T. Simpson (eds.), *The Philosophy of Trust*. Oxford: Oxford University Press, 35–49.

Darwin, C. (2009 [1872]). *The Expression of Emotions in Man and Animals*, New York: D. Appleton.

Davidson, D. (1980). *Essays on Action and Events*. Oxford: Oxford University Press.

Davidson, D. (1987). "Knowing One's Own Mind." *Proceedings and Addresses of the American Philosophical Association* 60: 441–458.

Davis, David Brion. (2006). *Inhuman Bondage: The Rise and Fall of Slavery in the New World*. New York: Oxford University Press.

De Beauvoir, S. (1949). *The Second Sex*. New York: Knopf Doubleday.

Diamont, L. (2019). *Ill Winds: Saving Democracy from Russian Rage, Chinese Ambition, and American Complacency*. New York: Penguin.

Dillon, R. S. (1992). "Respect and Care: Toward Moral Integration." *Canadian Journal of Philosophy* 22: 105–132.

Dillon, R. S. (2018). "Respect." *The Stanford Encyclopedia of Philosophy* (Spring 2018 Edition), E. N. Zalta (ed.), https://plato.stanford.edu/archives/spr2018/entries/respect.

Dobratz, B. A., & Shanks-Meile, S. L. (2000). *The White Separatist Movement in the United States: White Power, White Pride!* Baltimore: Johns Hopkins University Press.

Dobratz, B. A., & Shanks-Meile, S. L. (2006). "The Strategy of White Separatism." *Journal of Political and Military Sociology* 34, no. 1: 49–80.

Domenicucci, J., & Holton, R. (2017). "Trust as a Two-place Relation." In P. Faulker & T. Simpson (eds.), *The Philosophy of Trust*. Oxford: Oxford University Press, 150–162.

Dorschel, A. (2002). "Is Love Intertwined with Hatred?" *Journal of the British Society for Phenomenology* 33, no. 2: 273–285.

Doris, J. (1998). "Persons, Situations, and Virtue Ethics." *Noûs* 32: 504–530.

Doris, J. (2002). *Lack of Character: Personality and Moral Behavior*. Cambridge: Cambridge University Press.

Doris, J. (2015). *Talking to Our Selves: Reflection, Ignorance, and Agency*. Oxford: Oxford University Press.

Doris, J. M., & Stich, S. P. (2005). "As a Matter of Fact: Empirical Perspectives on Ethics." In F. Jackson and M. Smith (eds), *The Oxford Handbook of Contemporary Philosophy*. Oxford: Oxford University Press, 114–152.

Doris, J. M., & Stich, S. P. (2006). "Moral Psychology: Empirical Approaches." *The Stanford Encyclopedia of Philosophy* (Winter 2003 Edition), E. N. Zalta (ed.), http://plato.stanford.edu.access.library.miami.edu/entries/moral-psych-emp.

Dutton, D. G., & Aron, A. P. (1974). "Some Evidence for Heightened Sexual Attraction under Conditions of High Anxiety." *Journal of Personality and Social Psychology* 30, no. 4: 510–517.

Ebels-Duggan, K. (2008). "Against Beneficence: A Normative Account of Love." *Ethics* 119: 142–170.

Ekman, P. (1994). "Strong Evidence for Universals in Facial Expressions: A Reply to Russell's Mistaken Critique." *Psychological Bulletin* 115: 268–287.

Ekman, P., & Friesen, W. V. (1986). "A New Pan-Cultural Facial Expression of Emotion." *Motivation and Emotion* 10: 159–168.

Elster, J. (1983). *Sour Grapes: Studies in the Subversion of Rationality*. Cambridge: Cambridge University Press.

Erfianti, L. G., & Mahudin, N. D. M. (2019). "Impulsivity, Online Disinhibition, and Risk Taking among Digital Millennials: Challenges of e-Safety in Industry 4.0." *Journal of Occupational Safety and Health* 16, no. 1: 45–53.

Evans, P. (1992). *The Emotionally Abusive Relationship*. New York: Simon & Schuster.

Evans, P. (1993). *Verbal Abuse: Survivors Speak Out on Relationship and Recovery*. Avan, MA: Adams Media.

Fanon, F. (2008 [1967]). *Black Skin, White Masks*. Trans. Charles Lam Markmann. New York: Grove Press.

Faucher, L., & Machery, E. (2009). "Racism: Against Garcia's Moral and Psychological Monism." *Philosophy of the Social Sciences* 39, no. 1: 41–62.

Faulkner, P. (2007a). "A Genealogy of Trust." *Episteme* 4, no. 3: 305–321.

Faulkner, P. (2007b). "On Telling and Trusting." *Mind* 116, no. 464: 875–902.

Faulkner, P. (2011). *Knowledge on Trust*. Oxford: Oxford University Press.

Faulkner, P. (2014). "The Practical Rationality of Trust." *Synthese* 191, no. 9: 1975–1989.

Faulkner, P. (2015). "The Attitude of Trust Is Basic." *Analysis* 75, no. 3: 424–429.

Faulkner, P. (2017). "The Problem of Trust." In P. Faulkner & T, Simpson (eds.), *The Philosophy of Trust*. Oxford: Oxford University Press, 109–128.

Feinberg, J. (1968). "Collective Responsibility." *The Journal of Philosophy* 65, no. 21: 674–688.

Feinberg, J. (1973). "Some Conjectures on the Concept of Respect." *Journal of Social Philosophy* 4, no. 2: 1–3.

Fernandes, S. (2019). "Prediction of a Rise in Antisocial Personality Disorder through Cross-Generational Analysis." PsyArXiv, January 19, https://psyarxiv.com/zdm32, retrieved October 13, 2019.

Festinger, L. (1962). *A Theory of Cognitive Dissonance*. Stanford: Stanford University Press.

Finkenbine, Roy E. (2004). *Sources of the African American Past: Primary Sources in American History*. New York: Pearson and Longman.

Fischer, A. H. (2011). "Contempt: A Hot Feeling Hidden under a Cold Jacket." In R. Trnka, K. Balcar, & M. Kuška (eds.), *ReConstructing Emotional Spaces: From Experience to Regulation*. Prague: Prague College of Psychosocial Studies Press, 77–87.

Fischer, J. M., & Ravizza, M. (1998). *Responsibility and Control: A Theory of Moral Responsibility*. Cambridge: Cambridge University Press.

Fishkin, J. S., & Luskin, R. C. (1999). "Bringing Deliberation to the Democratic Dialogue." In M. McCombs & A. Reynolds (eds.), *The Poll with a Human Face: The National Issues Convention Experiment in Political Communication*. Mahwah, NJ: Lawrence Erlbaum, 3–38.

Formosa, P. (2007). "Understanding Evil Acts." *Human Studies* 30, no. 2: 57–77.

Fox, R. C. (1962). "Elizabeth Bennet: Prejudice or Vanity?" *Nineteenth-Century Fiction* 17, no. 2: 185–187.

Frankfurt, H. (1971). "Freedom of the Will and the Concept of a Person." *Journal of Philosophy* 68, no. 1: 5–20.

Fredrickson, G. (2002). *Racism: A Short History*. Princeton: Princeton University Press.

Fricker, M. (2007). *Epistemic Injustice: Power and the Ethics of Knowing*. New York: Oxford University Press.

Friedan, B. (2001 [1963]). *The Feminine Mystique*, paperback ed. New York: W. W. Norton.

Friedman, M. (1993). *What Are Friends For?* Ithaca: Cornell University Press.

Furnham, A., Richards, S. C., & Paulhus, D. L. (2013). "The Dark Triad: A 10-Year Review." *Social and Personality Psychology Compass* 7: 199–216.

Garcia, J. L. A. (1996). "The Heart of Racism." *Journal of Social Philosophy* 27, no. 1: 5–46.

Garcia, J. L. A. (1997). "Current Conceptions of Racism." *Journal of Social Philosophy* 28: 5–42.

Garcia, J. L. A. (1999). "Philosophical Analysis and the Moral Concept of Racism." *Philosophy and Social Criticism* 25, no. 1: 13.

Garcia, J. L. A. (2011). "Racism, Psychology and Morality: Dialogue with Faucher and Machery." *Philosophy of the Social Sciences* 41: 250–268.

Garrido, S. & Davidson JW (2019). "Funerals and Mourning Rituals, First Online: 20 March 2019, *Music, Nostalgia and Memory*, Palgrave Macmillan. pp 241-263

Gartlan, A., Gottman, J. S., & DeClaire, J. (2006). *Ten Lessons to Transform Your Marriage: America's Love Lab Experts Share Their Strategies for Strengthening Your Relationship.* New York: Random House.

Gaylin, W. (2003). *Hatred: The Psychological Descent into Violence.* New York: Public Affairs.

Gelber, K. (2010). "Freedom of Political Speech, Hate Speech and the Argument from Democracy: The Transformative Contribution of Capabilities Theory." *Contemporary Political Theory* 9, no. 3: 304–324.

Gellately, R. (2001). *Backing Hitler Consent and Coercion in Nazi Germany*, New York: Oxford University Press.

Gendler, T. S. (2008a). "Alief and Belief." *Journal of Philosophy* 105, no. 10: 634–663.

Gendler, T. S. (2008b). "Alief in Action (and Reaction)." *Mind and Language* 23, no. 5: 552–585.

Gendler, T. S. (2011). "On the Epistemic Costs of Implicit Bias." *Philosophical Studies* 156: 33–63.

Gendler, T. S. (2012). "Between Reason and Reflex: Response to Commentators." *Analysis* 72, no. 4: 799–811.

Gercke, A. (1933). "Die Lösung der Judenfrage." *Nationalsozialistische Monatshefte* 38: 195–197.

Gervais, M. M., & Fessler, D. M. T. (2017). "On the Deep Structure of Social Affect: Attitudes, Emotions, Sentiments, and the Case of 'Contempt.'" *Behavioral and Brain Sciences* 40: e225. doi: 10.1017/S0140525X16000352.

Gilbert, M. (1989). *On Social Facts.* New York: Routledge.

Gilbert, M. (2001). "Collective Remorse." In A. Jokic (ed.), *War Crimes and Collective Wrongdoing: A Reader*. Oxford: Blackwell, 216–235.

Gilbert, M. (2002). "Collective Guilt and Collective Guilt Feelings." *Journal of Ethics* 6: 115–143.

Gilbert, M. (2006). *A Theory of Political Obligation*. Oxford: Oxford University Press.

Gilbert, M. (2009). "Shared Intention and Personal Intentions." *Philosophical Studies* 144: 167–187.

Gilman, C. P. (1898). *Women and Economics: A Study of the Economic Relation between Men and Women as a Factor in Social Evolution*. N.P.: Small, Maynard & Company.

Giubilini, A. (2016). "What in the World Is Moral Disgust?" *Australasian Journal of Philosophy* 94, no. 2: 227–242.

Glasgow, J. (2009). "Racism as Disrespect." *Ethics* 120, no. 1: 64–93.

Glover, N., Miller, J. D., Lynam, D. R., Crego, C., & Widiger, T. A. (2012). "The Five-Factor Narcissism Inventory: A Five-Factor Measure of Narcissistic Personality Traits." *Journal of Personality Assessment* 94, no. 5: 500–512.

Godwyn, M. (2003 [1680]). *The Negro's and Indians Advocate Suing for Their Admission into the Church*. Whitefish, MT: Kessinger Publishing, LLC.

Goldie, P. (2000). *The Emotions: A Philosophical Exploration*. Oxford: Oxford University Press.

Gottman, J. (2003). *The Mathematics of Marriage*. Cambridge, MA: MIT Press.

Gottman, J., & Gottman, J. S. (2018). *The Science of Couples and Family Therapy: Behind the Scenes at the "Love Lab."* New York: W. W. Norton.

Gottman, J., & Silver, N. (1999). *The Seven Principles for Making Marriage Work*. New York: Random House.

Gottman, J. M. (2011). *The Science of Trust: Emotional Attunement for Couples*. New York: W. W. Norton & Co.

Gartlan A; Gottman JS; Joan Declaire J (2006). *Ten Lessons to Transform Your Marriage: America's Love Lab Experts Share Their Strategies for Strengthening Your Relationship*. Random House Audio.

Gottman, J., & Silver, N. (2012). *What Makes Love Last*. New York: Simon & Schuster.

Grant, M. (1916). *The Passing of the Great Race*. New York: Charles Schriber's Sons.

Gray, D. M., & Lennertz, B. (Forthcoming). "Linguistic Disobedience." *Philosophers Imprint*.

Greene, A., & Simpson, R. M. (2017). "Tolerating Hate in the Name of Democracy." *Modern Law Review* 80, no. 4: 746–765.

Greenwald, A., McGhee, D., and Schwartz, J. (1998). "Measuring Individual Differences in Implicit Cognition: The Implicit Association Test." *Journal of Personality and Social Psychology* 74, no. 6: 1464–1480.

Grubbs, J. B., Exline, J. J., McCain, J., Campbell, W. K., & Twenge, J. M. (2019). "Emerging Adult Reactions to Labeling Regarding Age-Group Differences in Narcissism and Entitlement." *PLoS ONE* 14, no. 5: e0215637. https://doi.org/10.1371/journal.pone.0215637

Habermas, J. (1984). *The Theory of Communicative Action*, Vol. 1: *Reason and the Rationalization of Society*. Cambridge: Polity Press.

Habermas, J. (1987). *The Theory of Communicative Action*, Vol. 2: *Lifeworld and System—A Critique of Functionalist Reason*. Cambridge: Polity Press.

Habermas, J. (1990). *Moral Consciousness and Communicative Action*. Cambridge, MA: MIT Press.

Habermas, J. (1993). "Further Reflections on the Public Sphere." In C. Calhoun (ed.), *Habermas and the Public Sphere*, 2nd ed. Cambridge, MA: MIT Press, 421–461.

Habermas, J. (1998 [1992]). *Between Facts and Norms: Contributions to a Discourse Theory of Law and Democracy*. Cambridge, MA: MIT Press.

Habermas, J. (2001a). *The Postnational Constellation*. Cambridge, MA: MIT Press.

Habermas, J. (2001b). "Reflections on Communicative Pathology (1974)." In *On the Pragmatics of Social Interaction: Preliminary Studies in the Theory of Communicative Action*, trans. B. Fultner. Cambridge: Polity, 129–170.

Habermas, J. (2003 [1962]). *The Structural Transformation of the Public Sphere*. Cambridge, MA: Polity Press.

Hale, G. E. (1998). *Making Whiteness: The Culture of Segregation in the South, 1890–1940*. New York: Pantheon Books.

Hall, S. (2010). *Evil Valley*. New York: Simon & Schuster.

Hampton, J. (1988). "The Retributive Idea." In J. G. Murphy & J. Hampton, *Forgiveness and Mercy*. Cambridge: Cambridge University Press, 111–161.

Haney, C., Banks, W. C., & Zimbardo, P. G. (1973). "A Study of Prisoners and Guards in a Simulated Prison." *Naval Research Reviews* 9: 1–17.

Hare, R. D., Hart, S. D., & Harpur, T. J. (1991). "Psychopathy and the DSM–IV Criteria for Antisocial Personality Disorder." *Journal of Abnormal Psychology* 100, no. 3: 391–398.

Harman, G. (1999). "Moral Philosophy Meets Social Psychology: Virtue Ethics and the Fundamental Attribution Error." *Proceedings of the Aristotelian Society* 99: 315–331.

Harman, G. (2003). "No Character or Personality." *Business Ethics Quarterly* 13: 87–94.

Harman, G. (2009). "Skepticism about Character Traits." *Journal of Ethics* 13, nos. 2–3: 235–242.

Haslanger, S. (2012). *Resisting Reality: Social Construction and Social Critique*. New York: Oxford University Press.

Haslanger, S. (2013). "Social Meaning and Philosophical Method." Presidential address, Eastern Division of the American Philosophical Association.

Hawkins, M. (1997). *Social Darwinism in European and American Thought, 1860–1945*. Cambridge: Cambridge University Press.

Hayman, A. (1989). "What Do We Mean by 'Phantasy'?" *International Journal of Psychoanalysis* 70, pt. 1: 105–114.

Helm, B. W. (2010). *Love, Friendship, and the Self: Intimacy, Identification, and the Social Nature of Persons*. Oxford: Oxford University Press.

Helm, B. W. (2014). "Trust as a Reactive Attitude." In D. Shoemaker & N. A. Tognazzini (eds.), *Oxford Studies in Agency and Responsibility*. Oxford: Oxford University Press, 187–215.

Herpertz, S. C., Werth, U., Lukas, G., Qunaibi, M., Schuerkens, A., Kunert, H. J., ... Osterheider M. (2001). "Emotion in Criminal Offenders with Psychopathy and Borderline Personality Disorder." *Archives of General Psychiatry* 58, no. 8: 737.

Herzl, T. (1896). *Der Judenstaat*. Leipzig and Vienna: M. Breitenstein's Verlags-Buchhandlung.

Hick, D. H., & Derksen, C. (2017). "The Problem of Tragedy and the Protective Frame." *Emotion Review* 9, no. 2: 140–145.

Hieronymi, P. (2001). "Articulating an Uncompromising Forgiveness." *Philosophy and Phenomenological Research* 62, no. 3: 529–555.

Hodsden, H. L. (2018). *Women Who Hate Other Women*. Published by the author.

Hogg, M. A., & Reid, S. A. (2006). "Social Identity, Self-Categorization, and the Communication of Group Norms." *Communication Theory* 16, no. 1: 7–30.

Hogg, M. A., Turner, J. C., & Davidson, B. (1990). "Polarized Norms and Social Frames of Reference: A Test of the Self-Categorization Theory of Group Polarization." *Basic and Applied Social Psychology* 11, no. 1: 77–100.

Holroyd, J. (2010). "The Retributive Emotions: Passions and Pains of Punishment." *Philosophical Papers* 39, no. 3: 343–371.

Holton, R. (1994). "Deciding to Trust, Coming to Believe." *Australasian Journal of Philosophy* 72, no. 1: 63–76.

Hom, C. (2008). "The Semantics of Racial Epithets." *Journal of Philosophy* 105, no. 8: 416–440.

Homiak, M. (2019). "Moral Character." *The Stanford Encyclopedia of Philosophy* (Summer 2019 Edition), E. N. Zalta (ed.), https://plato.stanford.edu/archives/sum2019/entries/moral-character.

Horne, G. (2014). "Is Borderline Personality Disorder a Moral or Clinical Condition? Assessing Charland's Argument from Treatment." *Neuroethics* 7, no. 2: 215–226.

Hornsby, J. (2001). "Meaning and Uselessness: How to Think About Derogatory Words." *Midwest Studies in Philosophy* 25: 128–141.

House, T. H., & Milligan, W. L. (1976). "Autonomic Responses to Modeled Distress in Prison Psychopaths." *Journal of Personality and Social Psychology* 34, no. 4: 556–560.

Hu S., Ide, J. S., Zhang, S., & Li, C. R. (2016). "The Right Superior Frontal Gyrus and Individual Variation in Proactive Control of Impulsive Response." *Journal of Neuroscience* 36, no. 50: 12688–12696.

Hudson, S. D. (1980). "The Nature of Respect." *Social Theory and Practice* 6: 69–90.

Hume, D. A. (2000 [1739–1740]). *A Treatise of Human Nature*. Oxford: Oxford University Press, 2000.

Hursthouse, R., & Pettigrove, G. (2018). "Virtue Ethics." *The Stanford Encyclopedia of Philosophy* (Winter 2018 Edition), E. N. Zalta (ed.), https://plato.stanford.edu/archives/win2018/entries/ethics-virtue.

Isenberg, D. J. (1986). "Group Polarization: A Critical Review and Meta-Analysis." *Journal of Personal and Social Psychology* 50, no. 6: 1141–1151.

Iyengar, S., & Westwood, S. J. (2015). "Fear and Loathing across Party Lines: New Evidence on Group Polarization." *American Journal of Political Science* 59, no. 3: 690–707.

Jakobwitz, S., & Egan, V. (2006). "The Dark Triad and Normal Personality Traits." *Personality and Individual Differences* 40: 331–339.

Jaspin, E. G. (2006). *Buried in the Bitter Waters: The Hidden History of Racial Cleansing in America.* New York: Basic Books.

Jauk, E., Weigle, E., Lehmann, K., Benedek, M., & Neubauer, A. C. (2017). "The Relationship between Grandiose and Vulnerable (Hypersensitive) Narcissism." *Frontiers in Psychology* 8: 1600.

Jenkins, C. S. (2017). *What Love Is: And What It Could Be.* New York: Basic Books.

Jonason, P. K., & Webster, G. D. (2010). "The Dirty Dozen: A Concise Measure of the Dark Triad." *Psychological Assessment* 22, no. 2: 420–432.

Jones, D. N., & Figueredo, A. J. (2013). "The Core of Darkness: Uncovering the Heart of the Dark Triad." *European Journal of Personality* 27, no. 6: 521–531.

Jones, D. N., & Paulhus, D. L. (2017). "Duplicity among the Dark Triad: Three Faces of Deceit." *Journal of Personality and Social Psychology* 113, no. 2: 329–342.

Jones, K. (1996). "Trust as an Affective Attitude." *Ethics* 107, no. 1: 4–25.

Jones, K. (2012). "Trustworthiness." *Ethics* 123, no. 1: 61–85.

Jones, K. (2017). *"But I Was Counting on You!": The Philosophy of Trust.* Oxford: Oxford University Press.

Jeshion, R. (2013). "Slurs and Stereotypes." *Analytic Philosophy* 54, no. 3: 314–329.

Kahan, D. M. (2001). "Two Liberal Fallacies in the Hate Crimes Debate." *Law and Philosophy* 20: 175–193.

Kant, I. (1996 [1797]). *The Metaphysics of Morals.* Trans. M. Gregor. Cambridge: Cambridge University Press.

Kant, I. (1997 [1785]). *Groundwork of the Metaphysics of Morals.* Trans. M. Gregor. Cambridge: Cambridge University Press.

Kant, I. (2006 [1798]). *Anthropology from a Pragmatic Point of View.* Cambridge: Cambridge University Press.

Karlin, D. (1993). *Browning's Hatreds.* Oxford: Clarendon Press.

Kaye, F. W. (2000). "Little Squatter on the Osage Diminished Reserve: Reading Laura Ingalls Wilder's Kansas Indians." *Great Plains Quarterly* 20, no. 2: 123–140.

Kelly, D. (2011). *Yuck! The Nature and Moral Significance of Disgust.* Cambridge, MA: MIT Press.

Kendler, K., Aggen, S. H., Czajkowski, N., Roysamb, E., Tambs, K., Torgersen, S., Neale, M. C., & Reichborn-Kjennerud, T. (2008). "The Structure of Genetic and Environmental Risk Factors for DSM-IV Personality Disorders." *Archives of General Psychiatry* 65: 1438–1446.

Kernberg, O. (1983 [1975]). *Borderline Conditions and Pathological Narcissism*, 10th printing. New York: Jason Aronson.

Kershaw, I. (1999). *Hitler: 1889–1936 Hubris*. New York: W. W. Norton.

Kershaw, I. (1999/2000). *Hitler: A Biography*. New York: W. W. Norton.

Kim, D. H. (1999). "Contempt and Ordinary Inequality." In S. E. Babbitt & S. Campbell (eds.), *Racism and Philosophy*. Ithaca, NY: Cornell University Press, 108–123.

Kipnis, L. (2003). *Against Love*. New York: Vintage Books.

Kipnis, L. (2006). *The Female Thing: Dirt, Envy, Sex, Vulnerability*. New York: Vintage Books.

Lutz, T. (2001). *Crying: The Natural and Cultural History of Tears*. New York: W.W. Norton.

Koltonski, D (2016). "A Good Friend Will Help You Move a Body: Friendship and the Problem of Moral Disagreement." *Philosophical Review* 125, no. 4: 473–507.

Korsgaard, C. M. (1986). "The Right to Lie: Kant on Dealing with Evil." *Philosophy & Public Affairs* 15: 325–349.

Korsgaard, C. M. (2008). *The Constitution of Agency: Essays on Practical Reason and Moral Psychology*. Oxford: Oxford University Press.

Korsgaard, C. M. (2009). *Self-Constitution: Agency, Identity, and Integrity*. New York: Oxford University Press.

Korsmeyer, C. (2008). "Fear and Disgust: The Sublime and the Sublate." *Revue Internationale de Philosophie* 62, no. 246: 367–379.

Korsmeyer, C. (2011). *Savoring Disgust: The Foul and the Fair in Aesthetics*. Oxford: Oxford University Press.

Kreisman, J. J., & Straus, H. (2010). *I Hate You—Don't Leave Me: Understanding the Borderline Personality*. New York: Perigee.

Kristjánsson, K. (2008). "An Aristotelian Critique of Situationism." *Philosophy* 83, no. 323: 55–76.

Kübler-Ross, E. (1969). *On Death and Dying*. New York: Simon & Schuster.

Kübler-Ross, E. (2005). *On Grief and Grieving: Finding the Meaning of Grief through the Five Stages of Loss*. New York: Simon & Schuster.

Kukla, R. (2014). "Performative Force, Convention, and Discursive Injustice." *Hypatia* 29, no. 2: 440–457.

LaFollette, H. (1996). *Personal Relationships: Love, Identity, and Morality*. Cambridge, MA: Blackwell.

Láng, A. (2015). "Borderline Personality Organization Predicts Machiavellian Interpersonal Tactics." *Personality and Individual Differences* 80: 28–31.

Langton, R. (1993). "Speech Acts and Unspeakable Acts." *Philosophy and Public Affairs* 22, no. 4: 293–330.

Langton, R. (2012). "Beyond Belief: Pragmatics in Hate Speech and Pornography." In I. Maitra & M. K. McGowan (eds.), *Speech and Harm: Controversies over Free Speech*. New York: Oxford University Press, 72–93.

Lawson, C. A. (2000). *Understanding the Borderline Mother*. Lanham, MS: Rowman and Littlefield.

Leary, M. (2019). *Why You Are Who You Are: Investigations into Human Personality*. Chantilly, VA: Great Courses.

Leboeuf, C. (2018). "Anger as a Political Emotion: A Phenomenological Perspective." In M. Cherry and O. Flanagan (eds.), *The Moral Psychology of Anger*. Oxford: Rowman & Littlefield, 15–29.

LeBreton, J. M., Shiverdecker, L. K., & Grimaldi, E. M. (2018). "The Dark Triad and Workplace Behavior." *Annual Review of Organizational Psychology and Organizational Behavior* 5: 387–414.

Le Conte, J. (2017 [1892]). *The Race Problem in the South*, paperback ed. Whitefish, MT: Kessinger Legacy Reprints.

Lee, K., & Ashton, M. C. (2004). "Psychometric Properties of the HEXACO Personality Inventory." *Multivariate Behavioral Research* 39, no. 2: 329–358.

Leet, P. M. (1965). "Women and the Undergraduate." Student-Faculty Forum. Franklin and Marshall College.

Leonard, T. C. (2016). *Illiberal Reformers: Race, Eugenics, and American Economics in the Progressive Era*. Princeton: Princeton University Press.

Levy, K. (2014). "Why Retributivism Needs Consequentialism: The Rightful Place of Revenge in the Criminal Justice System." *Rutgers Law Review* 66: 629–684.

Levy, N. (2016). "Am I a Racist? Implicit Bias and the Ascription of Racism." *Philosophical Quarterly* 67, no. 268: 534–551.

List, C. (2014). "Three Kinds of Collective Attitudes." *Erkenntnis* 79, no. 9: 1601–1622.

Liu, E. (2019). *Become America: Civic Sermons on Love, Responsibility, and Democracy*. Seattle: Sasquatch Books.

Livingstone Smith, D. (2011). *Less Than Human: Why We Demean, Enslave and Exterminate Others*. New York: St. Martin's Press.

Livingstone Smith, D. (2016). "Paradoxes of Dehumanization." *Social Theory and Practice* 42, no. 2: 416–443.

MacDonald, K. B. (2004). *Understanding Jewish Influence: A Study in Ethnic Activism*. Occidental *Quarterly* 3, no. 2, Summer 2003: 5–38; *Occidental Quarterly* 3, no. 3, Fall 2003: 15–44; *Occidental Quarterly* 4, no. 2, Summer 2004. http://citeseerx.ist.psu.edu/viewdoc/download?doi=10.1.1.453.3815&rep=rep1&type=pdf

MacIntyre, A. (1999). *Dependent Rational Animals*. Chicago: Open Court.

MacLachlan, A. (2010). "Unreasonable Resentments." *Journal of Social Philosophy* 41, no. 4: 422–441.

Macnamara, C. (2013a). "Reactive Attitudes as Communicative Entities." *Philosophy and Phenomenological Research* 90, no. 3: 546–569.

Macnamara, C. (2013b). "'Screw You!' & 'Thank You.'" *Philosophical Studies* 163, no. 3: 893–914.

Madva, A., & Brownstein, M. (2018). "Stereotypes, Prejudice, and the Taxonomy of the Implicit Social Mind." *Noûs* 52, no. 3: 611–644.

Maibom, H. L. (2005). "Moral Unreason: The Case of Psychopathy." *Mind and Language* 20, no. 2: 237–257.

Maibom, H. L. (2008). "The Mad, the Bad, and the Psychopath." *Neuroethics* 1, no. 3: 167–184.

Maibom, H. L. (2014). "To Treat a Psychopath." *Theoretical Medicine and Bioethics* 35, no. 1: 31–42.

Maibom, H. L. (2018). "What Can Philosophers Learn from Psychopathy?" *European Journal of Analytic Philosophy* 14, no. 1: 63–78.

Main, E. C., & Walker, T. G. (1973). "Choice Shifts and Extreme Behavior: Judicial Review in the Federal Courts." *Journal of Social Psychology* 91: 215–221.

Malkin, C. (2015). *Rethinking Narcissism: The Secret to Recognizing and Coping with Narcissists*. New York: Harper Perennial.

Mandelbaum, E. (2016). "Attitude, Inference, Association: On the Propositional Structure of Implicit Bias." *Noûs* 50, no. 3: 629–658.

Manne, K. (2017). *Down Girl: The Logic of Misogyny*. New York: Oxford University Press.

Margalit, A. (2017). *On Betrayal*. Cambridge, MA: Harvard University Press.

Martin, M. G. F. (2010). "What's in a look?" In Bence Nanay (ed.), *Perceiving the World*. Oxford University Press, 160–225.

Mason, M. (2003). "Contempt as a Moral Attitude." *Ethics* 113, no. 2: 234–272.

Mason, P. T., & Kreger, R. (1998). *Stop Walking on Eggshells*. New York: MJF Books.

Mazower, M. (1992). "Military Violence and National Socialist Values: The Wehrmacht in Greece 1941–1944." *Past and Present* 134: 129–158.

McCarthy, T. (2007). "The Natural Order of Things: Social Darwinism and White Supremacy." *Contemporary Pragmatism* 4, no. 1: 7–24.

McCullough, M. E., Kurzban, R., & Tabak, B. A. (2013). "Cognitive Systems for Revenge and Forgiveness." *Behavioral and Brain Sciences* 36: 1–58.

McGeer, V. (2008). "Trust, Hope and Empowerment." *Australasian Journal of Philosophy* 86, no. 2: 237–254.

McNab, Chris. (2011). *Hitler's Masterplan: The Essential Facts and Figures for Hitler's Third Reich*. Amber Books Ltd. ISBN 978-1907446962.

McNab, Chris. (2013). *Hitler's Elite: The SS 1939–45*. Osprey.

Mele, A. R. (2001). *Autonomous Agents: From Self-Control to Autonomy*. Oxford: Oxford University Press.

Mellon, James, ed. (1988). *Bullwhip Days: The Slaves Remember*. New York: Weidenfeld & Nicolson.

Meloy, J. R. (2000). "The Nature and Dynamics of Sexual Homicide: An Integrative Review." *Aggression and Violent Behavior* 5, no. 1: 1–22.

Miceli, M., & Castelfranchi, C. (2018). "Contempt and Disgust: The Emotions of Disrespect." *Journal for the Theory of Social Behaviour* 48: 205–229.

Milgram, S. (1963). "Behavioral Study of Obedience." *The Journal of Abnormal and Social Psychology* 67, no. 4: 371–378.

Milgram, S. (1974). *Obedience to Authority: An Experimental View*. New York: Harper & Row.

Miller, J. D., Dir, A., Gentile, B., Wilson, L., Pryor, L. R., & Campbell, W. K. (2009). "Searching for a Vulnerable Dark Triad: Comparing Factor 2 Psychopathy, Vulnerable Narcissism, and Borderline Personality Disorder." *Journal of Personality* 78: 1529–1564.

Miller, J. D., Few, L. R., Wilson, L., Gentile, B., Widiger, T. A., MacKillop, J., & Campbell, W. K. (2013). "The Five-Factor Narcissism Inventory (FFNI): A Test of the Convergent, Discriminant, and Incremental Validity of FFNI Scores in Clinical and Community Samples." *Psychological Assessment* 25: 748–758.

Miller, J. D., Lynam, D. R., Hyatt, C. S., & Campbell, W. K. (2017). "Controversies in Narcissism." *Annual Review of Clinical Psychology* 13: 291–315.

Miller, R. M. (2005). "Lynching in America: Some Context and a Few Comments." *Pennsylvania History* 72, no. 3: 275–291.

Miller, S. (2001). *Social Action: A Teleological Account*. Cambridge: Cambridge University Press.

Mischel, W. (1977). "The interaction of person and situation." In D. Magnusson & N. S. Endler (eds.), *Personality at the Crossroads: Current Issues in Interactional Psychology*. Hillsdale, NJ: Lawrence Erlbaum, 333–352.

Monteiro, R., & Azevedo, I. (2010). "Chronic Inflammation in Obesity and the Metabolic Syndrome." *Mediators of Inflammation*, 289645. doi: 10.1155/2010/289645.

Moore, Wilbert Ellis. (1980). *American Negro Slavery and Abolition: A Sociological Study*. Ayer Publishing.

Mulla, L., & Trickett, L. (2018). *Misogyny Hate Crime Evaluation Report June 2018*. Nottingham's Women's Centre, http://www.nottinghamwomenscentre.com/press-release-9-07-2018-overwhelming-public-support-for-misogyny-hate-crime-policy/misogyny-hate-crime-evaluation-report-june-2018, retrieved February 8, 2019.

Mullin, Amy. (2005). "Trust, Social Norms, and Motherhood." *Journal of Social Philosophy* 36, no. 3: 316–330.

Muris, P., Merckelbach, H., Otgaar, H., & Meijer, E. (2017). "The Malevolent Side of Human Nature: A Meta-Analysis and Critical Review of the Literature on the Dark Triad (Narcissism, Machiavellianism, and Psychopathy)." *Perspectives on Psychological Science* 2, no. 2: 183–204.

Murphy, J. G. (1990a). "Mercy and Legal Justice." In J. G. Murphy & J. Hampton, *Forgiveness and Mercy*. Cambridge: Cambridge University Press, 162–186.

Murphy, J. G. (1990b). "A Qualified Defence." In J. G. Murphy & J. Hampton, *Forgiveness and Mercy*. Cambridge: Cambridge University Press, 88–110.

Murphy, J. G. (2003). *Getting Even: Forgiveness and Its Limits*. New York: Oxford University Press.

Myers, D. G., & Lamm, H. (1976). "The Group Polarization Phenomenon." *Psychological Bulletin* 83, no. 4: 602–627.

Neu, J. (2000). *A Tear Is an Intellectual Thing: The Meanings of Emotions*. New York: Oxford University Press.

Neufeld, E. (2019). "An Essentialist Theory of the Meaning of Slurs." *Philosophers' Imprint* 19, no. 35.

Niemi, J. I. (2005). "Jürgen Habermas's Theory of Communicative Rationality." *Social Theory and Practice* 31, no. 4: 513–532.

Nozick, R. (1981). *Philosophical Explanations*. Cambridge, MA: Harvard University Press.

Nussbaum, M. (2001). "Symposium on Amartya Sen's Philosophy 5: Adaptive Preferences and Women's Options." *Economics and Philosophy* 17, no. 1: 67–88.

Nussbaum, M. C. (2006). *Hiding from Humanity: Disgust, Shame, and the Law*. Princeton: Princeton University Press.

Nussbaum, M. C. (2001). *Upheavals of Thought: The Intelligence of Emotions*. Cambridge: Cambridge University Press.

Nussbaum, M. C. (2016). *Anger and Forgiveness: Resentment, Generosity, Justice*. New York: Oxford University Press.

Nussbaum, M. C. (2018). *The Monarchy of Fear: A Philosopher Looks at Our Political Crisis*. New York: Simon & Schuster.

Olin, L., & Doris, J. (2014). "Vicious Minds." *Philosophical Studies* 168, no. 3: 665–692.

Oshio, A. (2009). "Development and Validation of the Dichotomous Thinking Inventory." *Social Behavior and Personality* 37, no. 6: 729–742.

Oud, M., Arntz, A., Hermens, M. L. N., Verhoef, R., & Kendall, T. (2018). "Specialized Psychotherapies for Adults with Borderline Personality Disorder: A Systematic Review and Meta-Analysis." *Australian & New Zealand Journal of Psychiatry* 52, no. 10: 949–961.

Paternotte, C. (2014). "Minimal Cooperation." *Philosophy of the Social Sciences* 44, no. 1: 45–73.

Paulhus, D. L., & Williams, K. M. (2002). "The Dark Triad of Personality: Narcissism, Machiavellianism, and Psychopathy." *Journal of Research in Personality* 36, no. 6: 556–563.

Paulhus, D. L., Williams, K., & Harms, P. (2001). "Shedding Light on the Dark Triad of Personality: Narcissism, Machiavellianism, and Psychopathy." Presented at Society for Personality and Social Psychology Convention, San Antonio. https://www2.psych.ubc.ca/~dpaulhus/research/DARK_TRIAD/PRESENTATIONS/sheddinglight-spsp01poster.pdf, retrieved February 4, 2019.

Payne, B. K. (2001). "Prejudice and Perception: The Role of Automatic and Controlled Processes in Misperceiving a Weapon." *Journal of Personality and Social Psychology* 81: 181–192.

Payne, B. K. (2005). "Conceptualizing Control in Socil Cognition: How Executive Functioning Modulates the Expression of Automatic Stereotyping." *Journal of Personality and Social Psychology* 89: 488–503.

Payne, B. K. (2006). "Weapon Bias: Split-Second Decisions and Unintended Stereotyping." *Current Directions in Psychological Science* 15, no. 6: 287–291.

Payne, B. K., Lambert, A. J., & Jacoby, L. L. (2002). "Best Laid Plans: Effects of Goals on Accessibility Bias and Cognitive Control in Race-Based Misperceptions of Weapons." *Journal of Experimental Social Psychology* 38: 384–396.

Pereboom, D. (2014). *Free Will, Agency, and Meaning in Life*. Oxford: Oxford University Press.

Pettit, P. (2006). "Preference, Deliberation, and Satisfaction." In S. Olsaretti (ed.), *Preferences and Wellbeing*. Cambridge: Cambridge University Press, 131–153.

Pettit, P., & Schweikard, D. (2006). "Joint Actions and Group Agents." *Philosophy of the Social Sciences* 36, no. 1: 18–39.

Picciolini, C. (2017). *White American Youth*. New York: Hachette Books.

Pincus, A. L., Ansell, E. B., Pimentel, C. A., Cain, N. M., Wright, A. G. C., & Levy, K. N. (2009). "Initial Construction and Validation of the Pathological Narcissism Inventory." *Psychological Assessment* 21, no. 3: 365–379.

Pincus, A. L., & Lukowitsky M. R. (2010). "Pathological Narcissism and Narcissistic Personality Disorder." *Annual Review of Clinical Psychology* 6: 421–446.

Plutchik, R. (2001). "The Nature of Emotions." *American Scientist* 89: 344–350. https://doi.org/10.1511/2001.4.344.

Podzimek, M. (2019). "Problems of Narcissism in Education: The Culture of Narcissism as a Dangerous Global Phenomenon for the Future." *Problems of Education in the 21st Century* 77: 489–501.

Postmes, T., & Spears, R. (1998). "Deindividuation and Antinormative Behavior: A Meta-analysis." *Psychological Buttetin* 123: 238–259.

Potter, N. N. (2006). "What Is Manipulative Behavior, Anyway?" *Journal of Personality Disorders* 20, no. 2: 139–156.

Prinz, J. J. (2007). *The Emotional Construction of Morals*. New York, NY: Oxford University Press.

Prinz, J. (2004a). "Embodied Emotions." In R. Solomon (ed.), *Thinking about Feeling: Contemporary Philosophers on Emotions*. New York: Oxford University Press, 44–60.

Prinz, J. (2004b). "Which Emotions Are Basic?" In D. Evans and P. Cruse (eds.), *Emotion, Evolution, and Rationality*. Oxford: Oxford University Press, 69–88.

Prinz, J. (2009). "The Normativity Challenge: Cultural Psychology Provides the Real Threat to Virtue Ethics." *Journal of Ethics* 13: 117–144.

Protasi, S. (2016). "Varieties of Envy." *Philosophical Psychology* 29, no. 4: 535–549.

Protasi, S. (2017). "'I'm Not Envious, I'm Just Jealous!': On the Difference between Envy and Jealousy." *Journal of the American Philosophical Association* 3, no. 3: 316–333.

Railton, P. (2011). "Two Cheers for Virtue, or, Might Virtue Be Habit Forming?" *Oxford Studies in Normative Ethics* 1: 295–330.

Ramirez, E. J. (2013). "Psychopathy, Moral Reasons, and Responsibility." In A. Perry & C. D. Herrera (eds.), *Ethics and Neurodiversity*. Cambridge: Cambridge Scholars Press, 217–237.

Ramirez, E. J. (2015). "Receptivity, Reactivity and the Successful Psychopath." *Philosophical Explorations* 18, no. 3: 330–343.

Raspail, J. (1975 [1973]). *The Camp of the Saints*. New York: Scribner.

Ratcliffe, M. (2005). "The Feeling of Being." *Journal of Consciousness Studies* 12, nos. 8–10: 43–60.

Ratcliffe, M. (2008). *Feelings of Being: Phenomenology, Psychiatry and the Sense of Reality*. Oxford: Oxford University Press.

Rawls, J. (1971). *A Theory of Justice*. Cambridge, MA: Harvard University Press.

Rawls, J. (1980). "Kantian Constructivism in Moral Theory." *Journal of Philosophy* 77: 515–72.

Rawls, J. (1989). "Themes in Kant's Moral Philosophy." In E. Förster (ed.), *Kant's Transcendental Deductions*. Stanford: Stanford University Press, 81–113.

Ray, J. K. (2013). "Do Elizabeth and Darcy Really Improve 'On Acquaintance'?" *Persuasions* 35: 34–49.

Reiland, R. (2002). *Get Me Out of Here: My Recovery from Borderline Personality Disorder*. New York: Simon & Schuster.

Reiman, J. H. (1976). "Privacy, Intimacy and Personhood." *Philosophy and Public Affairs* 26: 26–44.

Reimer, M. (2010). "Moral Aspects of Psychiatric Diagnosis: The Cluster B Personality Disorders." *Neuroethics* 3, no. 2: 173–184.

Reimer, M. (2013). "Moral Disorder in the DSM-IV? The Cluster B Personality Disorders." *Philosophy, Psychiatry, & Psychology* 20, no. 3: 203–215.

Rempel, J. K., & Sutherland, S. (2016). "Hate: Theory and Implications for Intimate Relationships." In K. Aumer (ed.), *The Psychology of Love and Hate in Intimate Relationships*. Cham, Switzerland: Springer, 105–129.

Richard, M. (2008). *When Truth Gives Out*. Cambridge, MA: Harvard University Press.

Richardson-Self, L. (2018). "Woman-Hating: On Misogyny, Sexism, and Hate Speech." *Hypatia* 33, no. 2: 256–272.

Roberts, R. C. (2013). "Review of Macalester Bell, *Hard Feelings: The Moral Psychology of Contempt*." Notre Dame Philosophical Reviews, https://ndpr.nd.edu/news/hard-feelings-the-moral-psychology-of-contempt.

Rousseau, J.-J. (1978 [1762]). *On the Social Contract*, ed. Roger Masters, trans. Judith R. Masters. New York: St. Martin's Press.

Roy, O., & Schwenkenbecher, A. (2019). "Shared Intentions, Loose Groups, and Pooled Knowledge." *Synthese*, August 8. https://link.springer.com/article/10.1007/s11229-019-02355-x.

Rozin, P., & Fallon, A. E. (1987). "A Perspective on Disgust." *Psychological Review* 94, no. 1: 23–41.

Rozin, P., Lowery, L., & Ebert, R. (1994). "Varieties of Disgust Faces and the Structure of Disgust." *Journal of Personality and Social Psychology* 66, no. 5: 870–881.

Rozin, P., Millman, L., & Nemeroff, C. (1986). "Operation of the Laws of Sympathetic Magic in Disgust and Other Domains." *Journal of Personality and Social Psychology* 50, no. 4: 703–712.

Samuel, D. B., & Widiger, T. A. (2008). "A Meta-Analytic Review of the Relationships between the Five-Factor Model and DSM-IV-TR Personality Disorders: A Facet Level Analysis." *Clinical Psychology Review* 28, no. 8: 1326–1342.

Sanders, G. S., & Baron, R. S. (1977). "Is Social Comparison Irrelevant for Producing Choice Shift?" *Journal of Experimental Social Psychology* 13, no. 4: 303–314.

Scanlon, T. M. (2008). *Moral Dimensions: Permissibility, Meaning, Blame*. Cambridge, MA: Harvard University Press.

Scheel, K.R. (2000). "The Empirical Basis of Dialectical Behavior Therapy: Summary, Critique, and Implications." *Clinical Psychology, Science and Practice* 7, no. 1: 68–86.

Scheffler. (2011). "Valuing." In R. J. Wallace, R. Kumar, & S. Freeman (eds.), *Reasons and Recognition: Essays on the Philosophy of T. M. Scanlon.* Oxford: Oxford University Press.

Scheler, M. (1972 [1913]). *Ressentiment.* Trans. William W. Holdheim. Introduction by Lewis A. Coser. New York: Schocken.

Schiffrin, H. H., Liss, M., Miles-McLean, H., Geary, K. A., Erchull, M.J., & Tashner, T. (2014). "Helping or Hovering? The Effects of Helicopter Parenting on College Students' Well-Being." *Journal of Child and Family Studies* 23, no. 3: 548–557.

Schlosser, M. E. (2015). "Agency." *The Stanford Encyclopedia of Philosophy* (Fall 2015 Edition), E. N. Zalta (ed.), https://plato.stanford.edu/archives/fall2015/entries/agency.

Schopenhauer, A. (2015 [1851]). "On Women." In *The Essays of Arthur Schopenhauer; Studies in Pessimism.* Translated by T. Bailey Saunders. The Project Gutenberg eBook.

Schriber, R. A., Chung, J. M., Sorensen, K. S., & Robins, R. W. (2017). "Dispositional Contempt: A First Look at the Contemptuous Person." *Journal of Personality and Social Psychology* 113, no. 2: 280–309.

Searle, J. (1976). "A Classification of Illocutionary Acts." *Language in Society* 5, no. 1: 1–23.

Searle, J. (1990). "Collective Intentions and Actions." In P. R. Cohen, J. Morgan, & M. Pollack (eds.), *Intentions in Communication.* Cambridge, MA: MIT Press, 401–415.

Sen, A. (1977). "Rational Fools." *Philosophy and Public Affairs* 6, no. 4: 317–344.

Serano, J. (2013). *Excluded: Making Feminist and Queer Movements More Inclusive.* Berkeley, CA: Seal Press.

Serano, J. (2016 [2007]). *Whipping Girl: A Transsexual Woman on Sexism and the Scapegoating of Femininity,* 2nd ed. Berkeley, CA: Seal Press.

Serano, J. (2016). *Outspoken: A Decade of Transgender Activism and Trans Feminism.* Oakland, CA: Switch Hitter Press.

Sethi, A. S. (2018). *American Hate: Survivors Speak Out.* New York: New Press.

Shapiro, J. L. (2016). "We Hate What We Fear: Interpersonal Hate from a Clinical Perspective." In K. Aumer (ed.), *The Psychology of Love and Hate in Intimate Relationships*. Cham, Switzerland: Springer, 153–177.

Shapiro, S. (2014). "Massively Shared Agency." In M. Vargas & G. Jaffe (eds.), *Rational and Social Agency: Essays on the Philosophy of Michael Bratman*. Oxford: Oxford University Press, 257–293.

Sher, G. (2005). *In Praise of Blame*. New York: Oxford University Press.

Sherman, N. (1989). *The Fabric of Character: Aristotle's Theory of Virtue*. Oxford: Oxford University Press.

Sherman, N. (1993). "Aristotle on the Shared Life." In N. K. Badhwar (ed.), *Friendship: A Philosophical Reader*. Ithaca: Cornell University Press, 91–107.

Shoemaker, D. (2015). *Responsibility from the Margins*. Oxford: Oxford University Press.

Shoemaker, D. (2017). "Empathy and Moral Responsibility." In H. L. Maibom (ed.), *Routledge Handbook of Philosophy of Empathy*. London: Routledge, 242–252.

Siegel, S. (2017). *The Rationality of Perception*. New York: Oxford University Press.

Simpson, R. M. (2013). "Dignity, Harm and Hate Speech." *Law and Philosophy* 32, no. 6: 701–728.

Sliwa P. (2017). "Moral Understanding as Knowing Right from Wrong." *Ethics* 127, no. 3: 521–552.

Slote, M (1980). "Understanding Free Will." *Journal of Philosophy* 77: 136–151.

Slote, M. (1982). "Selective Necessity and the Free Will Problem." *Journal of Philosophy* 79: 5–24.

Slote, M. (2010). *Moral Sentimentalism*. New York: Oxford University Press.

Slote, M. (2011). *The Impossibility of Perfection: Aristotle, Feminism, and the Complexities of Ethics*. New York: Oxford University Press.

Smith, A. (2005). "Responsibility for Attitudes: Activity and Passivity in Mental Life." *Ethics* 115: 236–271.

Smith, A. (2013). "Moral Blame and Moral Protest." In D. J. Coates & N. A. Tognazzini (eds.), *Blame: Its Nature and Norms*. Oxford: Oxford University Press, 27–48.

Snyder, T. (2010). *Bloodlands: Europe between Hitler and Stalin*. New York: Basic Books.

Solomon, R. (2006). *The Passions: Philosophy and the Intelligence of Emotions*. Chantilly, VA: The Great Courses.

Sorial, S. (2015). "Hate Speech and Distorted Communication: Rethinking the Limits of Incitement." *Law and Philosophy* 34, no. 3: 299–324.

Sripada, C. (2016). "Self-Expression: A Deep Self Theory of Moral Responsibility." 173: 1203–1232.

Sripada, C. (2017). "Frankfurt's Willing and Unwilling Addicts." *Mind* 126, no. 503: 781–815.

Stangneth, B. (2011). *Eichmann before Jerusalem: The Unexamined Life of a Mass Murderer*. New York: Penguin Random House.

Stanley, J. (2015). *How Propaganda Works*. Princeton: Princeton University Press.

Stanley, J. (2018). *How Fascism Works: The Politics of Us and Them*, New York: Random House.

Steiner, L. M. (2009). *Crazy Love*. New York: St. Martin's Publishing Group.

Stepan, N. (1991). *The Hour of Eugenics*. Ithaca: Cornell University Press.

Stoffers, J. M., Rücker, G., Timmer, A., Huband, N., & Lieb K. (2012). "Psychological Therapies for People with Borderline Personality Disorder." *Cochrane Database of Systematic Reviews* 8: CD005652.

Stoner, J. A. (1968). "Risky and Cautious Shifts in Group Decisions: The Influence of Widely Held Values." *Journal of Experimental Social Psychology* 4, no. 4: 442–459.

Strawson, P. (1982 [1962]). "Freedom and Resentment." *Proceedings of the British Academy* 48, reprinted in G. Watson (ed.), *Free Will*. New York: Oxford University Press, 59–80.

Strohminger, N. (2014). "Disgust Talked About." *Philosophy Compass* 9, no. 7: 478–493.

Sunstein, C. R. (1999). *The Law of Group Polarization*. University of Chicago Law School, John M. Olin Law & Economics Working Paper No. 91.

Sunstein, C. R. (2002). "The Law of Group Polarization." *Journal of Political Philosophy* 10, no. 2: 175–195.

Sunstein, C. R. (2009a). *Going to Extremes: How Like Minds Unite and Divide*. Oxford: Oxford University Press.

Sunstein, C. R. (2009b). *On Rumors: How Falsehoods Spread, Why We Believe Them, What Can Be Done*. New York: Farrar, Straus and Giroux.

Swetnam, J. (1615). *The Arraignment of Lewd, idle, froward, and unconstant women: Of, the vanitie of them, choose you whether, with a Commendation of*

Wise, Virtuous, and Honest Women, Pleasant for Married Men, Profitable for Young Men, and Hurtful to None. London: Thomas Archer.

Szanto, T. (2018). "In Hate We Trust: The Collectivization and Habitualization of Hatred." *Phenomenology and the Cognitive Sciences*, doi.org/10.1007/s11097-018-9604-9. https://link.springer.com/article/10.1007/s11097-018-9604-9.

Tappolet, C. (2011). "Nasty Emotions and the Perception of Values." In C. Tappolet, F. Teroni, & A. Konzelmann Ziv (eds.), *Shadows of the Soul: Philosophical Perspectives on Negative Emotions*. New York: Routledge, 20–29.

Thomas, L. (1987). "Friendship." *Synthese* 72: 217–236.

Thomas, L. (1989). *Living Morally: A Psychology of Moral Character*. Philadelphia: Temple University Press.

Thomas, L. (2013). "The Character of Friendship." In D. Caluori (ed.), *Thinking about Friendship: Historical and Contemporary Perspectives*. New York: Palgrave Macmillan, 30–46.

Thompson, J. B. (1983). "Rationality and Social Rationalization: An Assessment of Habermas's Theory of Communicative Action." *Sociology* 17, no. 2: 278–294.

Tirrell, L. (2012). "Genocidal Language Games." In I. Maitra & M. K. McGowan (eds.), *Speech and Harm: Controversies over Free Speech*. New York: Oxford University Press, 174–221.

Tracy, J. L., & Robins, R. W. (2003). "'Death of a (Narcissistic) Salesman': An Integrative Model of Fragile Self-Esteem." *Psychological Inquiry* 14: 57–62.

Tracy, J. L., & Robins, R. W. (2007). "The Psychological Structure of Pride: A Tale of Two Facets." *Journal of Personality and Social Psychology* 92: 506–525.

Tschalaer, M. H. (2017). *Muslim Women's Quest for Justice: Gender, Law and Activism in India*. Cambridge, UK: Cambridge University Press.

Twain, M. (1986 [1884]). *The Adventures of Huckleberry Finn*. New York: Penguin.

Twenge, J. M. (2013). "The Evidence for Generation Me and against Generation We." *Emerging Adulthood* 1: 11–16.

Twenge, J. M., & Campbell, W. K. (2009). *The Narcissism Epidemic: Living in the Age of Entitlement*. New York: Simon & Schuster.

Twenge, J. M., and Foster, J. D. (2010). "Birth Cohort Increases in Narcissistic Personality Traits among American College Students, 1982–2009." *Social Psychological and Personality Science* 1, no. 1: 99–106.

Twenge, J. M., Konrath, S., Foster, J. D., Campbell, W. K., & Bushman, B. J. (2008). "Egos Inflating over Time: A Cross-Temporal Meta-Analysis of the Narcissistic Personality Inventory." *Journal of Personality* 76: 875–902.

Twenge, J. M., Martin, G. N., & Spitzberg, B. H. (2019). "Trends in U.S. Adolescents' Media Use, 1976–2016: The Rise of Digital Media, the Decline of TV, and the (Near) Demise of Print." *Psychology of Popular Media Culture* 8, no. 4: 329–345.

Vargas, M. (2004). "Responsibility and the Aims of Theory: Strawson and Revisionism." *Pacific Philosophical Quarterly* 85: 218–241.

Vargas, M. (2006). "On the Importance of History for Responsible Agency." *Philosophical Studies* 127: 351–382.

Vargas, M. (2008). "Moral Influence, Moral Responsibility." In N. Trakakis and D. Cohen (eds.), *Essays on Free Will and Moral Responsibility*. Cambridge: Cambridge Scholars Press, 90–122.

Vargas, M. (2013a). *Building Better Beings: A Theory of Moral Responsibility*. Oxford: Oxford University Press.

Vargas, M. (2013b). "Situationism and Moral Responsibility: Free Will in Fragments." In A. Clark, J. Kiversein, and T. Vierkant (eds.), *Decomposing the Will*. Oxford: Oxford University Press, 325–349.

Velleman, D. (1992). "What Happens When Someone Acts?" *Mind* 101, no. 403: 461–481.

Venker, S. (2017). *The Alpha Female's Guide to Men and Marriage: How Love Works*. Brentwood, TN: Post Hill Press.

Volkan, V. (1988). *Six Steps in the Treatment of Borderline Personality Organization*. Northvale, NJ: Jason Aronson.

Von Leers, J. (1933). "Das Ende der jüdischen Wanderung." *Nationalsozialistische Monatshefte* 38: 229–231.

Waldinger, R. J. (1993). "The Role of Psychodynamic Concepts in the Diagnosis of Borderline Personality Disorder." *Harvard Review of Psychiatry* 1, no. 3: 158–167.

Waldron, J. (2012). *The Harm in Hate Speech*. Cambridge, MA: Harvard University Press.

Walen, A. (2016). "Retributive Justice." *The Stanford Encyclopedia of Philosophy* (Winter 2016 Edition), E. N. Zalta (ed.), https://plato.stanford.edu/archives/win2016/entries/justice-retributive.

Walker, M. U. (2006). *Moral Repair: Reconstructing Moral Relations after Wrongdoing*. Cambridge: Cambridge University Press.

Wallace, R. J. (2011). "Dispassionate Opprobrium: On Blame and the Reactive Sentiments." In R. J. Wallace, R. Kumar, & S. Freeman (eds.), *Reasons and Recognition: Essays on the Philosophy of T. M. Scanlon*. Oxford: Oxford University Press, 348–369.

Watson, G. (1975). "Free Agency." *Journal of Philosophy* 72: 205–220.

Watson, G. (1993). "Responsibility and the Limits of Evil: Variations on a Strawsonian Theme." In J. M. Fischer & M. Ravizza (eds.), *Perspectives on Moral Responsibility*. Ithaca: Cornell University Press, 119–150.

Watson, G. (1996). "Two Faces of Responsibility." *Philosophical Topics* 24: 227–224.

Watson, G. (2004). *Agency and Answerability: Selected Essays*. Oxford: Oxford University Press.

Weld, Theodore. (1839). *American Slavery As It Is; Testimony of a Thousand Witnesses*. New York: American Anti-Slavery Society.

Wells-Barnett, I. B. (1895). *The Red Record: Tabulated Statistics and Alleged Causes of Lynching in the United States*, http://www.gutenberg.org/files/14977/14977-h/14977-h.htm, retrieved November 29, 2019.

Wilder, L. I. (1935). *Little House on the Prairie*. New York: HarperCollins.

Williams, Y. R. (2001). "Permission to Hate: Delaware, Lynching, and the Culture of Violence in America." *Journal of Black Studies* 32, no. 1: 3–29.

Wilson, B. A., & Wilson, L. L. (1999). "Offense Mechanisms in Couples." *Journal of Family Psychotherapy* 10, no. 2: 31–48.

Wu, E. D. (2013). *The Color of Success: Asian Americans and the Origins of the Model Minority*. Princeton: Princeton University Press.

Yahil, L. (1991). *The Holocaust: The Fate of European Jewry 1932–1945*. Oxford: Oxford University Press.

Yancy, G. (2008). "Elevators, Social Spaces and Racism: A Philosophical Analysis." *Philosophy and Social Criticism* 34, no. 8: 847–848.

Yardi, S., & Boyd, D. (2010). "Dynamic Debates: An Analysis of Group Polarization over Time on Twitter." *Bulletin of Science, Technology & Society* 30, no. 5: 316–327.

Zachar, P., & Potter, N. N. (2010). "Personality Disorders: Moral or Medical Kinds—or Both?" *Philosophy, Psychiatry, & Psychology* 17, no. 2: 107–117.

Zeigler-Hill, V., & Wallace, M. T. (2011). "Racial Differences in Narcissistic Tendencies." *Journal of Research in Personality* 45: 456–467.

Zeki, S., & Romaya. J. P. (2008). "Neural Correlates of Hate." *PLOS One* 3: e3556.

Zimbardo, P. (2007). *The Lucifer Effect: Understanding How Good People Turn Evil*. New York: Random House.

INDEX

For the benefit of digital users, indexed terms that span two pages (e.g., 52–53) may, on occasion, appear on only one of those pages.